The Harlequin Years

The Harlequin Years

MUSIC IN PARIS 1917–1929

ROGER NICHOLS

With 69 illustrations

Thames & Hudson

For Sarah

Every sober-sided history is at least half sleight-of-hand:
the right hand waving its poor snippets of fact, out in the
open for all to verify, while the left hand busies itself with
its own devious agendas, deep in its hidden pockets.

Margaret Atwood, *The Robber Bride*

First published in the United Kingdom in 2002 by
Thames and Hudson Ltd
181A High Holborn
London WC1V 7QX

www.thamesandhudson.com

British Library Cataloguing-in-Publication Data
A catalogue record for this book is available from the British Library

ISBN 0-500-51095-4

Printed and bound in Singapore by Star Standard Industries (Pte) Limited

Contents

Map: Paris in the 1920s 6

Introduction 9

Acknowledgments 11

Chronology 12

1. The legacy of peace and war 18

2. Orchestras, conductors, chamber ensembles 41

3. The Opéra 59

4. The Opéra-Comique and other musical theatres 78

5. Opérettes, music hall, revues, chansons 106

6. Ballet 134

7. The Establishment: the teaching institutions; 176
   the churches; the salons; the press

8. Composers old and new 209

9. Paris, the past and elsewhere 250

Select bibliography 279

List of photographs 282

Index 283

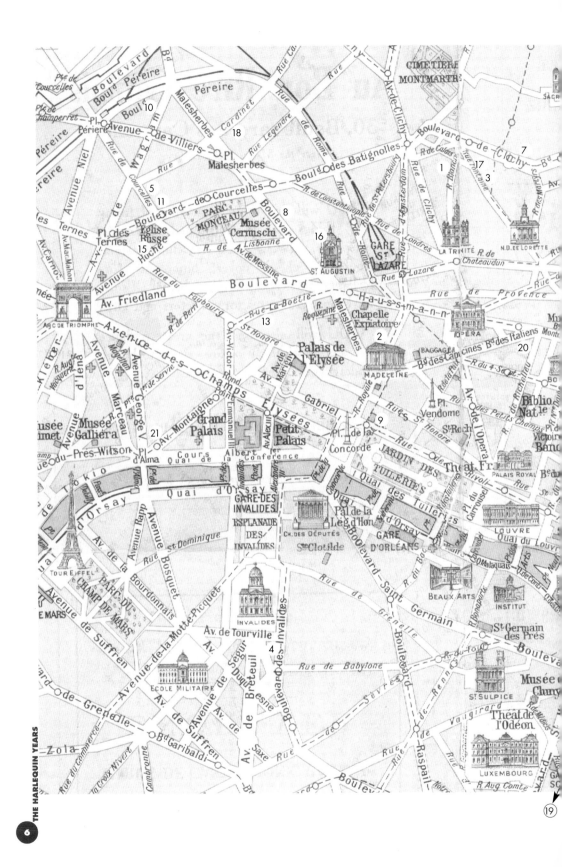

Paris in the 1920s

1. Nadia Boulanger, 36 rue Ballu, 9e
2. Reynaldo Hahn, 7 rue Greffulhe, 8e
3. Arthur Honegger, 21 rue Duperré, 9e
4. Vincent d'Indy, 7 avenue de Villars, 7e
5. André Messager, 103 rue Jouffroy-d'Abbans, 17e
6. Olivier Messiaen, 65 rue Rambuteau, 4e
7. Darius Milhaud, 10 boulevard de Clichy, 18e
8. Francis Poulenc, 83 rue de Monceau, 8e
9. Maurice Ravel, Hôtel d'Athènes, rue St. Florentin, 1er
10. Albert Roussel, 157 avenue de Wagram, 17e
11. Camille Saint-Saëns, 83bis rue de Courcelles, 17e
12. Salle Erard, 13 rue du Mail, 2e
13. Salle Gaveau, 45 rue La Boétie, 8e
14. Salle Pleyel, 22 rue de Rochechouart, 9e (until 1927; Stravinsky had a studio here)
15. Salle Pleyel, 252 rue du Faubourg St. Honoré, 8e (from 1927)
16. Conservatoire national de musique, 14 rue de Madrid, 8e
17. Ecole Niedermeyer, 10 rue Neuve-Fontaine St. Georges, 9e
18. Ecole normale de musique, 78 rue Cardinet, 17e
19. Schola Cantorum, 269 rue St. Jacques, 5e
20. Opéra-Comique, place Boïeldieu, 2e
21. Théâtre des Champs-Elysées, 13 avenue Montaigne, 8e
22. Théâtre de la Gaîté-Lyrique, 3–5 rue Papin, 3e

For much of this information I am indebted to Nigel Simeone, *Paris: a Musical Gazetteer*, Yale University Press, 2000.

A view looking west along the boulevard St-Germain in 1917

Introduction

MUSIC ASIDE, the Twenties were a crucially important decade for France. They saw a questioning, in a number of uncomfortable ways, of the old assumptions of what it was to be French and of France's place in the world order. Some of this questioning arose directly from the war. The heavy loss of life among the soldiery (1,400,000 killed, including 300,000 in the first five months) led in some quarters to a refusal to subscribe to the ancient notion of 'la gloire'. The presence of tens of thousands of *mutilés de guerre* made forgetting difficult, not to mention the difficulties of their own lives and those of their womenfolk. The war and its aftermath also added to the strain on the country's less than stable financial situation. It had led to women taking on more responsibility and to abandoning corsets and long hair as they increasingly ceased to be defined by male admiration or rejection, and these changes were not going to be reversed. The advent of American troops, bringing money and jazz, also sharpened the split between traditional and new values.

At the same time the French, whether through taste or financial constraints, were among the most homebound of European nations. In 1929 twice as many Britons as French visited Switzerland and the following year three times as many Germans as French visited Italy. Meanwhile numbers of French living abroad actually fell between 1911 and 1931.[1] The French were in fact 'net receivers' of tourism, and as such were torn between regarding it on the one hand as only natural that the greatest nation on earth should be the subject of such interest, and fearing on the other for the integrity of their culture. Of the 2,906,472 people resident in Paris in 1921, according to the census of that year, no fewer than 400,000 were foreigners. Jean Cocteau's 1918 pamphlet, *Le coq et l'arlequin*, in which the cock, the national symbol of France, is set amid the many-coloured splendour of foreign influences (and from which the title of the present volume is taken), thus found a sympathetic audience.

Travel to Paris was made quicker, if not easier, by the opening of the air route from London on 27 August 1919, when Britons could, for the considerable outlay of £6 6s (£12 return), reach Paris in under two and a half hours: although Baedeker advised that 'delicate persons will have to grow used to the slight dip or oscillation.... Luncheon baskets may be obtained at the aerodrome (Croydon/Le Bourget) restaurant, but for an initial trip it is wiser to depend upon a few dry biscuits and a little fruit.' From the same source we learn that the suburb of Passy is 'now mostly composed of handsome villas and apartment houses, with a large Anglo-American element among the residents'.

Among the most numerous and noticeable incomers were the émigrés from the 1917 Russian Revolution, who brought a certain relishable colour to the Parisian scene (the many who took to driving taxis had their own magazine, *Le chauffeur russe*; situations in which French aristocrats found themselves being driven by a man whom they had last talked to across a dinner table made interesting demands on etiquette). Not that these Russian émigrés had a monopoly on French sympathy. In France 'the Communists could always employ the emotional appeal to the tradition of revolution, and there was an ample supply of social grievances and injustices in French society to provide motivation for a revolutionary party'.[2] These grievances were probably exacerbated by the overwhelming victory of the Right in the elections of 1919, and in 1924 the situation was reversed with the Cartel des Gauches taking over the government.

Some of the questioning of French values came from concerns common to all nations after the war: the increase in the speed, volume and noise of motor traffic, the arrival of radio to back up the gramophone, the newfangled crazes for dancing and sport, the value that now seemed to be set on youth, vibrancy and novelty. In the eyes of some in France, all this technological and emotional uproar spelt danger for that considered grace which had for long been one of the inalienable characteristics of French culture and which was now being threatened by all that was hard, sharp, glossy, bright and loud: much of it looked ephemeral, but one had to take account of the fearful possibility that it was not. France shared too in the financial instability of postwar Europe. Inflation was, as always, hard on those with fixed incomes, and in the early summer of 1926 financial catastrophe seemed near when the pound, for many years prewar steady at around 25 francs, stood at 243. The dollar likewise spiralled up from around 5 francs to 50. Even though there was a good recovery between then and 1928, we should still bear in mind that, although pay rose between 1913 and 1929 (on average a domestic servant's pay increased in these years from 1,075 to 6,400 francs), it still lagged some 20 per cent behind inflation. The number of domestic servants also fell markedly over this period, which we could to some extent interpret as showing that the upper and middle classes were no longer as well off as they had been.[3]

It was against this background of anxiety, anger, remorse, instability and defensiveness, combining somewhat uneasily with traditional French qualities of pride, intellectual energy and sense of superiority, that the musical events chronicled in the following pages were played out.

Notes

1. These and further statistics in Theodore Zeldin, *France 1848–1945*, III, *Intellect and Pride* (Oxford, 1980), pp. 87–89.
2. Alfred Cobban, *A History of Modern France*, III, 1871–1962 (London, 1965), p. 130.
3. Alfred Sauvy, *Histoire économique de la France entre les deux guerres* (Paris, 1972), pp. 324, 332.

Acknowledgments

THE GROUNDWORK FOR THIS BOOK was laid by researches in Paris in the early 1980s and later for a series of twelve programmes broadcast by BBC Radio 3 in 1986, also entitled *The Harlequin Years*. I am grateful to the then Controller of Radio 3, Ian McIntyre, and to the then Head of Music, Christine Hardwick, for making this series possible and for providing funds towards an extended stay in the French capital. I am also grateful to my producer, Arthur Johnson, not only for his meticulous editing but also for his habit of asking sensible and searching questions.

In Paris, Gerald and Priscilla Pointon were generous with hospitality. My gratitude also goes to the musicians I interviewed for their memories of the twenties. Some have died in the meantime, including Georges Auric, Henri Barraud, Lennox Berkeley, Gaby Casadesus, William Chappell, Doda Conrad, Yvonne Gouverné, Arthur Hoérée, Mme Jacques Ibert, Yehudi Menuhin, Olivier Messiaen, Henri Sauguet and Alexandre Tansman. I am happy to say that, at the time of writing, three others, Madeleine Milhaud, Vlado Perlemuter and Manuel Rosenthal, are still alive. All of them received me with great kindness and have provided invaluable material.

My researches have, of course, depended heavily on the cooperation of libraries and of other scholars. The willing efficiency of the staff of the Département de la Musique in the Bibliothèque nationale de France, under the direction first of François Lesure and now of Catherine Massip, continues to be a model for all other libraries, and I was able to do much useful work in the equally helpful surroundings of the Bibliothèque de l'Opéra and of the Bibliothèque de l'Arsenal. Among other friends and those with an interest in this period of history, I owe a debt of gratitude to Jutta Avaly, Edward Blakeman, Pierre Boulez, Sidney Buckland, Myriam Chimènes, the late Michael de Cossart, Jeremy Drake, Marc-Olivier Dupin, Henri Dutilleux, Roy Howat, Richard Langham Smith, Patrick O'Connor, Arbie Orenstein, Jann Parry, Mme Yvette Poiré-Gaubert, Jean Roy, Mme Jean Seringe, Nigel Simeone, Andrew Thomson, Ornella Volta, Stephen Walsh and the late John C. G. Waterhouse. Two scholars have shown a particularly durable interest in the book and deserve my warmest thanks. Jean-Michel Nectoux has provided innumerable useful leads as well as continual encouragement, while Robert Orledge has found the time to read the whole book in draft and to give it the benefit of his wide and expert knowledge. Any errors that remain can be attributed to the author's obduracy.

My final thanks go to my publishers, Thames & Hudson, who have never faltered in their commitment to the book through its long and sometimes wayward development, and to my copy editor Ingrid Grimes who, apart from introducing a welcome order into my punctuation, has made many useful clarifications and suggestions.

Roger Nichols, Kington, September 2001

Chronology

1917 April 16   Nivelle offensive

May 18   Mutinies in French army

                Châtelet: Satie, *Parade*

September 26 Death of Degas

October 15   Mata Hari executed

November 10 Société nationale de musique (SNM): Fauré, Second Violin Sonata

November 17 Death of Rodin

November 23 Opéra-Comique: Messager, *Béatrice*

December 11 Théâtre du Vieux-Colombier: Poulenc, *Rapsodie nègre*

1918 January 15   Théâtre du Vieux-Colombier: Honegger, *Six poèmes d'Apollinaire*

January 19   SNM: Fauré, First Cello Sonata; Caplet, *Le vieux coffret*

February 1   German bombers kill 45 people in Paris

March 21   Opéra: revival of Rameau, *Castor et Pollux*

March 25   Death of Debussy

April 3   57 avenue Henri-Martin (Polignac salon) private premiere

                of Satie, *Socrate*:

November 3   Opéra: reopens with Massenet, *Thaïs*

November 9   Death of Apollinaire

November 11 Armistice

November 13 Bouffes-Parisiens: Christiné, *Phi-Phi*

December 2   Théâtre du Vieux-Colombier: Honegger, *Le dit des jeux du monde*

1919 February 9   Salle Huyghens: Poulenc, *Trois mouvements perpétuels*

March 15   Death of Lili Boulanger

April 5   Concerts Delgrange: Milhaud, Fourth String Quartet; Poulenc, Sonata

                for two clarinets

April 11   Société musicale indépendante (SMI): Ravel, *Le tombeau de Couperin* (piano)

May   Salle Gaveau: Stravinsky, *Pribaoutki*

May 1   80 policemen injured in May Day riots

May 14   SNM: first Paris performance of Fauré, *Fantaisie* for piano and orchestra

May 17   Concerts Pasdeloup: Ravel, *Alborada del gracioso*

June 6   SMI: first French performance of Delius, Cello Sonata

June 15   Concerts Delgrange: Milhaud, *Les choéphores*

June 20   SMI: Honegger, First String Quartet

June 28   Signature of Treaty of Versailles

October 15   Opéra-Comique: Henry Février, *Gismonda*

	December 3	Death of Renoir
	December 7	Concerts Lamoureux: Debussy, *Fantaisie* for piano and orchestra
	December 10	Théâtre Lyrique du Vaudeville: first staging of Debussy, *La boîte à joujoux*
	December 22	Théâtre-Lyrique: Boito, *Mefistofele*
	December 24	Opéra (Ballets russes): Rossini, *La boutique fantasque*
	December 27	SNM: Fauré, *Mirages*
1920	January 3	Last US forces leave France
		Cirque d'hiver: first public performance of Honegger, *Le chant de Nigamon*
	January 10	SNM: Milhaud, *Poèmes juifs*
	January 23	Opéra (Ballets russes): Falla, *El sombrero de tres picos*
	January 23	Salle du Conservatoire: Dupré begins series of ten recitals of complete Bach organ works
	February 2	Opéra (Ballets russes): Stravinsky, *Le chant du rossignol*
	February 21	Comédie des Champs-Elysées: Milhaud, *Le boeuf sur le toit*
	February 23	Comédie des Champs-Elysées: Satie, *Trois petites pièces montées*
	February 28	Pasdeloup: Ravel, *Le tombeau de Couperin* (orchestral version)
	March 4	Opéra-Comique: Fauré, *Masques et bergamasques*
	March 8	Galerie Barbazanges: Satie, *Musique d'ameublement*
	April 1	SMI: Durey, *Le bestiaire*
	May 15	Opéra (Ballets russes): Stravinsky, *Pulcinella*
	June 3	SMI: Milhaud, *Soirées de Pétrograd*
	June 4	Treaty of Trianon signed
	June 6	Opéra: d'Indy, *La légende de Saint-Christophe*
	June 14	Opéra (Ida Rubinstein): Schmitt, *Antoine et Cléopâtre*
	July 10	Opéra: Malipiero, *Sette canzoni*
	July 20	Rabaud appointed to succeed Fauré as director of the Conservatoire
	October 25	Théâtre des Champs-Elysées: Ballets suédois, opening night
	October 26	Concerts Colonne: Milhaud, *Deuxième suite symphonique* (*Protée*)
	November 11	Unknown French soldier buried under Arc de Triomphe
	December 2	SMI: Honegger, Viola Sonata
	December 12	Concerts Lamoureux: Ravel, *La valse*
1921	January 5	Opéra: Wagner, *Die Walküre* (first postwar revival)
	January 6	SMI: Milhaud, Fourth String Quartet
	February 17	Salle Gaveau: Honegger, *Pastorale d'été*
	March 23	Death of de Séverac
	April 3	Théâtre des Champs-Elysées: Wagner, *Tristan und Isolde* (in Italian)
	April 23	Salle du Conservatoire: Honegger, Cello Sonata
	April 29	Concerts Koussevitzky: first Paris performance of Rakhmaninov, *Isle of the Dead*
	May 17	Gaîté-Lyrique (Ballets russes): Prokofiev, *Chout*

	May 21	SNM: Fauré, Second Piano Quintet
	May 24	Théâtre Michel: Poulenc, *Le gendarme incompris*; Satie, *Le piège de Méduse*; Milhaud, *Caramel mou*; Auric, *Les pélicans* (incid. mus.)
	June 6	Théâtre des Champs-Elysées (Ballets suédois): *L'homme et son désir*
	June 10	Opéra: Berlioz, *Les troyens* (first complete performance)
	June 18	Théâtre des Champs-Elysées (Ballets suédois): *Les mariés de la tour Eiffel*
	October 7	Opéra: Wagner, *Das Rheingold* (first postwar revival)
	October 29	Concerts Colonne: Roussel, *Pour une fête de printemps*
	November 26	First radio broadcast of a concert, from the transmitter at Melun
	December 1	Concerts Koussevitzky: Honegger, *Horace victorieux*
	December 16	Death of Saint-Saëns
1922	January 16	Salle Gaveau: first Paris performance of Schoenberg, *Pierrot lunaire*
	January 20	Théâtre des Champs-Elysées: Honegger, *Skating Rink*
	February 7	Marie Curie elected to Académie des Sciences
	February 25	Opéra: Saint-Saëns, *Samson et Dalila*, 500th performance
	February 26	Concerts Colonne: Saint-Saëns, *Le carnaval des animaux*; d'Indy, *Le poème des rivages*
	March 4	Concerts Pasdeloup: Roussel, Second Symphony
	April 6	SMI:Ravel, Sonata for violin and cello; Milhaud, Fifth String Quartet
	April 22	Concerts Pasdeloup: first French performance of Schoenberg, Five Orchestral Pieces op. 16
	May 13	SNM (50th anniversary concert): Fauré, Second Cello Sonata, *L'horizon chimérique*
	May 15	Concerts Koussevitzky: Prokofiev, Third Piano Concerto
	May 18	Opéra (Ballets russes): Stravinsky, *Renard*
	June 3	Opéra (Ballets russes): Stravinsky, *Mavra*
	October 19	Opéra (Concerts Koussevitzky): Mussorgsky/Ravel, *Tableaux d'une exposition*
	November 18	Death of Proust
	December 7	SMI: first French performances of Szymanowski, *Masques*; Falla, *Fantasia bética*
	December 14	Théâtre des Champs-Elysées (Concerts Wiéner): first French performance of Webern, Five Movements for string quartet op. 5
1923	January 4	Théâtre des Champs-Elysées (Concerts Wiéner): Poulenc, Sonata for clarinet and bassoon, Sonata for horn, trumpet and trombone
	January 15	Opéra: Pierné, *Cydalise et le chèvre-pied*
	January 25	100,000 French troops sent to the Ruhr to collect war reparations
	March 2	50th anniversary of Concerts Colonne
	March 25	Concerts Colonne: Caplet, *Le miroir de Jésus*
	March 26	Death of Sarah Bernhardt

April 7	Théâtre des Variétés: Hahn, *Ciboulette*
April 28	SNM: Fauré, Thirteenth Barcarolle, Thirteenth Nocturne
May 12	SNM: Fauré, Piano Trio
May 21	The International Congress of Dancing Masters condemns the foxtrot and the tango
May 25	Théâtre des Champs-Elysées (Ballets suédois): Tailleferre, *Le marchand d'oiseaux*
May 30	Death of Chevillard
June 1	Opéra: Roussel, *Padmâvatî*
June 5	Salle Pleyel (Concerts Wiéner): Honegger, Sonatina for clarinet and piano
June 13	Gaîté-Lyrique (Ballets russes): Stravinsky, *Les noces*
June 25	Polignac salon: Falla, *El retablo de maese Pedro*
October 18	Opéra (Concerts Koussevitzky): Stravinsky, Octet
October 25	Théâtre des Champs-Elysées (Ballets suédois): Milhaud, *La création du monde*; Cole Porter, *Within the Quota*
December 10	Opéra-Comique: Milhaud, *La brebis égarée*
December 21	Salle des Agriculteurs: Satie, *Ludions*

1924

January 2	Seine floods lead to closing of main railway stations
January 6	Concerts Lamoureux: Ibert, *Escales*
January 30	SMI: Honegger, *Le cahier romand*
March 14	Salle Gaveau: Honegger, *Le roi David* (third version)
March 22	SNM: first French performance of Vaughan Williams, String Quartet in G minor
April 24	Théâtre des Champs-Elysées: first Paris performance of Stravinsky, *Histoire du soldat*
May 7	SMI: Ravel, *Ronsard à son âme*
May 8	Opéra (Concerts Koussevitzky): Honegger, *Pacific 231*
May 17	Théâtre de la Cigale (Soirées de Paris): Milhaud, *Salade*
May 22	Opéra (Concerts Koussevitzky): Stravinsky, Concerto for piano and wind
May 26	Théâtre des Champs-Elysées (Ballets russes): Poulenc, *Les biches*
June 4	Théâtre des Champs-Elysées (Ballets russes): Auric, *Les fâcheux*
June 15	Théâtre de la Cigale (Soirées de Paris): Satie, *Mercure*
June 20	Théâtre des Champs-Elysées (Ballets russes): Milhaud, *Le train bleu*
July 5	Olympic Games open
October 15	Salle Gaveau: Ravel, *Tzigane* (violin and piano luthéal)
October 28	France recognizes USSR
November 4	Death of Fauré
November 17	Salle Pleyel: Honegger, *Six poésies de Jean Cocteau*
December 4	Théâtre des Champs-Elysées (Ballets suédois): Satie, *Relâche*
December 24	Death of Bakst

1925
February 16	SMI: Delage, *Sept Haï-Kaï*; Koechlin, Third String Quartet; Ibert, *Le jardinier de Samos*
March 3	50th anniversary of premiere of *Carmen*
April 22	Death of Caplet
April 30	Exposition des Arts Décoratifs opens
May 2	SNM: d'Indy, Piano Quintet
May 23	Opéra (Concerts Koussevitzky): Honegger, Concertino for piano and orchestra
June 12	SNM: Fauré, String Quartet
June 17	Gaîté-Lyrique (Ballets russes): Auric, *Les matelots*
June 30	Opéra: Roussel, *La naissance de la lyre*
July 1	Death of Satie
July 14	French troops begin evacuation of Ruhr
October 15	Opéra: film of Schmitt, *Salammbô*
	SMI: Roussel, Second Violin Sonata; Falla, *Psyché*
November 14	First Surrealist exhibition opens
December 9	Death of Gigout

1926
February 1	Opéra-Comique: Paris premiere of Ravel, *L'enfant et les sortilèges*
May 2	Salle des Agriculteurs: Poulenc, *Chansons gaillardes*, Napoli, Trio for oboe, bassoon and piano.
May 5	SMI: Piston, Piano Sonata
June 13	Salle Erard: Ravel, *Chansons madécasses*
July 23	Poincaré government elected
October 28	SMI: Debussy, *Lindaraja*
October 30	Concerts Pasdeloup: Debussy, *Musique pour Le roi Lear* (orch. Roger-Ducasse)
November 26	Opéra: Chabrier, *Gwendoline* (revival)
December 5	Société des concerts: d'Indy, *Diptyque méditerranéan*
	Death of Monet

1927
January 20	Théâtre Bériza: Ibert, *Angélique*
February 6	Yehudi Menuhin debut in Lalo, *Symphonie espagnole*
February 8	Opéra: Strauss, *Der Rosenkavalier*
February 18	Opéra (Ballets Ida Rubinstein): Honegger, *L'impératrice aux rochers*
February 21	Opéra-Comique: Delannoy, *Le poirier de misère*
February 26	Théâtre Bériza: Milhaud, *Les malheurs d'Orphée*
April	Concerts Straram: Milhaud, *Agamemnon*
April 7	Opéra: Gance's film *Napoléon* shown
May 5	Concerts Straram: Roussel, *Concert pour petit orchestre*
May 21	Théâtre des Champs-Elysées (Concerts Koussevitzky): Roussel, *Suite in F*
May 27	Théâtre Sarah-Bernhardt (Ballets russes): Sauguet, *La chatte*
May 30	Théâtre Sarah-Bernhardt (Ballets russes): Stravinsky, *Oedipus rex*

May 30	Salle Erard (Concerts Durand): Ravel, Second Violin Sonata
June 1	Théâtre Sarah-Bernhardt (Ballets russes): Satie, *Mercure*
June 7	Théâtre Sarah-Bernhardt (Ballets russes): Prokofiev, *Le pas d'acier*
	Salle Pleyel: Roussel, Piano Concerto
June 13	Opéra (Ballets Ida Rubinstein): Roger-Ducasse, *Orphée*
June 16	*chez* Dubost: *L'éventail de Jeanne*
October 22	Salle Pleyel opened
December 8	Concerts Colonne: Schoenberg conducts his works
December 15	SMI: first French performances of Schoenberg, Suite op. 25, Five Piano Pieces op. 23
December 16	Opéra-Comique: Milhaud, *Le pauvre matelot*

1928 February 2	Concerts Straram: Berg, Chamber Concerto
February 25	Concerts Colonne: Prokofiev, *Classical* Symphony
March 12	Opéra-Comique: Falla, *El retablo de maese Pedro*, *La vida breve*, *El amor brujo*
March 29	Opéra: Puccini, *Turandot*
May	Opéra: season of Vienna Opera
June 12	Théâtre Sarah-Bernhardt (Ballets russes): European premiere of Stravinsky, *Apollon musagète*
July 19	Salle Pleyel gutted by fire
October 19	Théâtre des Champs-Elysées (Orchestre symphonique de Paris, inaugural concert): Honegger, *Rugby*
October 26	Opéra-Comique: Smetana, *The Bartered Bride*
November 22	Opéra (Ballets Ida Rubinstein): Honegger, *Les noces de Psyché et de l'Amour*; Milhaud, *La bien-aimée*; Ravel, *Boléro*
November 27	Opéra (Ballets Ida Rubinstein): Stravinsky, *Le baiser de la fée*
December 3	Gaîté-Lyrique: Tchaikovsky, *The Queen of Spades*
December 4	Opéra (Ballets Ida Rubinstein): Sauguet, *David*

1929 January 26	SNM: d'Indy, String Sextet
February 24	Death of Messager
March 4	Opéra: *L'éventail de Jeanne*
March 15	Orchestre symphonique de Paris: Malipiero, *Saint-François d'Assise*
April 25	Opéra: Roussel, *Psalm LXXX*
May 3	Salle Pleyel: Poulenc, *Concert champêtre*
May 15	Opéra: Ibert, *Persée et Andromède*
May 21	Opéra (Ballets Ida Rubinstein): Auric, *Les enchantements d'Alcine* Théâtre Sarah-Bernhardt (Ballets russes): Prokofiev, *Le fils prodigue*
May 23	Opéra (Ballets Ida Rubinstein): Ravel, *La valse*
June 19	*chez* le vicomte de Noailles: Poulenc, *Aubade*
August 19	Death of Diaghilev
October 24	Wall Street crash

1. The legacy of peace and war

ON SUNDAY, 4 JANUARY 1914, the Paris Opéra mounted the first production in France of Wagner's *Parsifal*. Productions of the opera had been given in North and South America from 1903 onwards, even though the work was not supposed to be performed outside Bayreuth until midnight on 31 December 1913, thirty years after its premiere, and was indeed given its Spanish premiere on that date and hour in Barcelona. But the French (rather unusually, we may think) had stuck to the rules. And they had still got in one day ahead of Berlin and, what was probably more important to them, of the Théâtre de la Monnaie in Brussels.

With this production, the Opéra (as I shall call the Paris house from now on) closed the cycle of mature Wagner operas which, effectively, it had begun with *Lohengrin* in 1891 – effectively, because the three isolated performances of *Tannhäuser* in 1861, in setting light to the straw of French chauvinism, produced more in the way of smoke than further performances. Elsewhere in Paris, the tally before 1891 had run to thirty-eight performances of a heavily cut *Rienzi* at the Théâtre-Lyrique in 1869 and a single performance of *Lohengrin* at the Théâtre Eden in 1887.

Much has been written about the impact of Wagner's music on that of France before the First World War and certainly no picture of postwar developments in Paris would be complete without examining how far they were driven by a desire to react against Wagner, and of the way that reaction manifested itself. But it cannot be stressed strongly enough that the 'Wagnermania' which engulfed Paris in the 1880s was, to some degree at least, a bastard phenomenon. There were of course the real enthusiasts, like d'Indy, Chabrier, Chausson, Duparc and Debussy, who took the trouble to go to Bayreuth and undergo the Complete Wagner Experience. But mostly the rage was fed by concert performances of what Ernest Newman later called 'bleeding chunks' and by those *littérateurs* (never in short supply in the French capital) who were as much interested in Wagner's ideas as in his music.

We could say then that, before 1891, Wagner's operas tended to belong in the French mind to a kind of museum of

PAS DE WAGNER A L'HORIZON?

the imagination. Music-lovers were forced to invent their own ideal Wagnerian theatre and their own ideal performances (no doubt in French, as the Opéra's real performances were to be), as they had to again when Wagner's music was proscribed in France during the First World War and for a brief period after it. This led in many cases to a mental appropriation of and even identification with Wagner's music, both highly resistant to criticism of the composer/idol and intolerant of any alternative musical philosophies and languages. Nor was the intolerance all one way: after the 1891 *Lohengrin* performances, the Opéra directors found themselves accused of accepting bribes from German financiers and publishers.[1]

By 1914, both kinds of intolerance had become less marked. The premiere of Debussy's *Pelléas et Mélisande* in 1902 and its subsequent success had proved to all but the most intransigently cloth-eared that Wagner's way with music drama was not the only one; and if there were still operagoers in 1911 who resented the lowering of the house lights for the first complete French production of *Der Ring* (and after all, part of Charles Garnier's brief in designing the Opéra had been to ensure that the audience could *be seen*), three years later we are told that the audience for *Parsifal* listened 'with true fervour to the three acts of the sacred drama'. The fact that the premiere was given on a Sunday, outside the traditional *abonnement* series that covered Mondays, Wednesdays and Fridays, and that the prices were raised, naturally gave this performance snob appeal. But later performances at reduced prices were equally well attended, with the Wagner connoisseurs being identified as belonging to two classes: the regular attenders at Sunday concerts, and the bourgeoisie 'who also like to say that they have "seen that"'.[2]

As far as French composers were concerned, Wagner was at once a saviour and a demon – an Elsa and a Kundry. Some, like Ravel and Satie, managed to keep clear of his influence and so spare themselves the pains of detoxification. Others, among whom were many now forgotten, succumbed. The third, and for us perhaps the most interesting group, given the way French music was to go in the 1920s, consisted of those like Chabrier and Debussy who were ambivalent towards Wagner, sometimes tapping into the chromaticism of *Tristan* and especially of *Parsifal*, sometimes hurrying back to the safety of plainsong, folksong or the eighteenth century. It is at least arguable that renouncing Wagner totally, as Ravel and Satie did, led to their music being impoverished: this is a question I shall return to in my final chapter.

Saint-Saëns during the First World War, listening out for any unwelcome strains of Wagner

Whatever the relationships with Wagner of French composers in the years between 1871 and 1914, there can be no doubt that it was one of the most brilliant and fertile periods in French music. But, as always with such periods, towards the end there were signs of revolt, even of disillusion. We may take the two leading figures, Debussy and Ravel, as exemplars, and 1911 as a convenient date. After the publication of his first book of *Préludes* in 1910, Debussy embarked on a second which was in general to be more extreme in its musical language and which showed signs of the new spikiness of Stravinsky's ballet *Petrushka*, premiered in Paris in June of 1911. Four weeks earlier, the first performance took place of Ravel's *Valses nobles et sentimentales* for piano in which, the composer later said, was to be found, 'after the virtuosity which formed the background to *Gaspard de la nuit*, a style of writing which is decidedly more clarified, which toughens up the harmony and emphasizes the outlines of the music'.[3]

If we subscribe to the idea of a Zeitgeist, then we may like to note that 1911 was also the year of Schoenberg's Six Little Piano Pieces op. 19, and of Sibelius's Fourth Symphony, both of which turn their back on comfortable Romantic luxuriance. But even if we do not so believe, it is obvious that both Debussy and Ravel felt they had come to the end of what has loosely and inaccurately been called an 'Impressionist' style – what has been more accurately defined by Edward Lockspeiser as 'the technique of illusion'.[4] Although Lockspeiser is referring specifically to piano music, the idea of 'illusion', inherited from works such as Berlioz's *Symphonie fantastique*, runs through much of French music before the First World War: the illusion that the whole can be more than the sum of its parts, that some of those parts are not meant to be heard so much as felt or 'intuited', that the essence of music is a magic and a mystery that should not be subjected to analysis. Debussy described this position in a newspaper article in 1913 in a wonderful sentence which is not only virtually untranslatable, but shows also to what extent he still remained a divided soul after the realistic epiphany of *Petrushka* two years earlier:

> seuls, les musiciens ont le privilège de capter toute la poésie de la nuit et du jour, de la terre et du ciel, d'en reconstituer l'atmosphère et d'en rythmer l'immense palpitation.[5]

> ['Composers alone have the privilege of capturing all the poetry of night and day, of earth and sky, of re-creating their atmosphere and of setting their mighty pulsations within a rhythmic framework.']

In the light of such ambivalence, what would have been the path, we may wonder, for Debussy himself, or indeed for French music as a whole, if war had not supervened?

Some readers at this point will reject such a question as being, like all 'if' questions, essentially unhistorical. It is nonetheless pertinent to try and separate those developments that would clearly have continued even in peacetime from those that became entangled in the net of Franco-German hostilities, by which they were either emphasized, curtailed or merely postponed.

Among those that would surely have continued, we may uncontentiously include the music of Saint-Saëns and Fauré, at the outbreak of war aged seventy-eight and sixty-nine respectively – since even through the First World War and the short balance of their lives afterwards both composers continued on their road pretty well undisturbed. True, Saint-Saëns wrote a song called *Vive la France* in 1915, but then he had already written another called *Vive Paris, vive la France* in 1893. Fauré's wartime production meanwhile consisted of finishing his song cycle *Le jardin clos* and writing the Twelfth Nocturne and Barcarolle, the Second Violin Sonata and the First Cello Sonata, with not a patriotic sentiment in sight.

Other composers, however, used the war as an opportunity to focus on just such patriotic sentiments which, maybe, they had long held but for which, in peacetime, they could find no acceptable musical expression. Debussy, for example, had been campaigning in his newspaper articles for some years against the pernicious influence of Wagner on French music: the first hint appearing in only his third article, in which he mentions listeners who, on coming out of the concert hall, can be heard whistling the 'Spring Song' or the opening of *Die Meistersinger*. 'I'm well aware,' he writes, 'that for many people this is what the future glory of music consists of. One may nonetheless hold the opposite opinion without drawing too much attention to oneself.'[6] Perhaps more importantly he, unlike Saint-Saëns or Fauré, was in wartime prepared to make musical capital out of his dislike of things German, which he did in both a negative and a positive sense.

The two 'negative' works are of very differing quality. The *Noël des enfants qui n'ont plus de maisons* is a mediocre little song to his own maudlin, sentimental text. But the two-piano suite *En blanc et noir* is a masterpiece, with an especially powerful central movement in which the Germans, symbolized by the chorale 'Ein' feste Burg', fight it out with the French and the *Marseillaise*. The 'positive' works from Debussy's wartime years, such as the three chamber sonatas, rather than decrying the enemy or his musical products, emphasize the strength of the French tradition; and here again, Debussy was building on beliefs already expressed in his articles, that France had turned its back on the music of Couperin and Rameau and followed false gods – not only Wagner, but Gluck.

Wonderful piece though *En blanc et noir* is, its very individuality offered little or nothing to those who would try and copy it (and here we may recall Ravel's refusal to give Debussy's orchestration as a model to his pupils because it is inimitable).[7] The easier path was to turn instead to the three chamber sonatas of 1915–17 because behind these, on Debussy's own admission, lay his admired eighteenth-century models. Even for lesser composers than Debussy, these models might be expected to yield some palatable fruit. The phenomenon generally known as 'Neoclassicism' is a more complex one than might at first appear, containing as many variations as composers subscribing to it, or being taxed as subscribing to it; we shall be making regular attempts to untangle it in the pages that follow.

Of developments that were curtailed by the First World War, two in particular merit attention. First those promising composers *morts pour la France*. Surprisingly, considering the huge losses sustained by the French army, these can be reckoned as

The legacy of peace and war

just two: André Caplet and Albéric Magnard. Caplet, who died in 1925 from the delayed effects of poison gas, had been a fellow pupil of Ravel's at the Conservatoire at the turn of the century and then Debussy's friend and amanuensis – a sufficient indication of his musical abilities. Between 1918 and 1922 he took on a number of major posts, including the conductorship of the Opéra, the Concerts Lamoureux and the Concerts Pasdeloup, but had to give them all up because of poor health. Although he brought to his music a spirituality born of his profound Roman Catholic beliefs and did introduce innovations in the solo harp writing of *Le masque de la mort rouge*, a 1919 instrumental work based on Poe's tale *The Mask of the Red Death*, his musical language clearly derives from Debussy and it is hard to believe that he would have brought about any revolutions in this area. The loss of his talents as a conductor was perhaps even more serious, since he seems to have had all the gifts and especially a genius for training and conducting singers. As it was, his health reduced him to taking choral classes for ladies of the *haute bourgeoisie* in order to make ends meet, a task that understandably was often a strain on his patience.[8]

Albéric Magnard died in the very early days of the war, defending his country house against the invaders – since he fired the first shots, killing two German cavalrymen, there was initially some dispute as to whether he could be classified as *mort pour la France* for copyright reasons, but the case was eventually decided in his favour (or rather, that of his heirs). Magnard's father had been the editor of *Le Figaro*, but Magnard refused to become any kind of establishment figure and, bypassing musical publishers, confided his works to a printers' union. If he used his father's influence, it was only to place in his paper in 1894 a plea for the publication of the complete works of Rameau. In 1902, his *Hymne à la justice* was inspired by his support for Alfred Dreyfus. This intransigent individuality extended to his music which, just before the war, had a passionate admirer in the twenty-year-old Milhaud, 'because I found in it unpolished, rural qualities and a harmonic austerity which were a refuge from the tendencies of Impressionism. At the Opéra-Comique I had heard [his opera] *Bérénice* which, despite the lack of refinement in its orchestration, or perhaps because of it, had moved me.... I liked his four symphonies too for their openness; their solid scherzos smell of the French countryside.'[9]

As we have seen, Debussy too was taking refuge from Impressionism; the danger came rather from his imitators, the 'debussystes' who, he admitted to a friend in 1915, were 'killing' him.[10] His revenge on them could be unkind, too: the composer Louis Aubert who, as a boy, had sung the 'Pie Jesu' in the first performance of Fauré's *Requiem* and had then followed a *debussyste* path in writing songs like *Crépuscules d'automne*, was referred to in the Debussy household as 'Louizaubert', casting doubt on his manhood in both those activities.[11] As for Ravel, his progress after the newly astringent *Valses nobles* of 1911 was, in the public's eyes at least, confused by the Ballets russes production of *Daphnis et Chloé* in the summer of 1912. In fact, most of *Daphnis* had been written before Ravel started on the *Valses nobles* and the works that truly date from 1911 to 1914 – the *Trois poèmes de Stéphane Mallarmé*, the *Deux mélodies hébraïques*, the Piano Trio, possibly even a little of *Le tombeau de Couperin* – all give a new slant to Impressionism, insofar as they subscribe to it at all.

Ravel had written the *Trois poèmes* in Clarens in the spring of 1913, while working with Stravinsky on a new version of Mussorgsky's *Khovanshchina* for the Ballets russes. Stravinsky had been bowled over by a performance of Schoenberg's *Pierrot lunaire* in Berlin the previous December and, even though he had already composed the piano version of the first of his *Trois poésies de la lyrique japonaise*, in composing the other two and scoring all three for an ensemble of two flutes, two clarinets, piano and string quartet he clearly had *Pierrot*'s sound world in his head. Ravel's songs use the same forces. In a half-serious, half-joking letter of 2 April 1913 to Mme Alfredo Casella, Ravel suggested that the Société musicale indépendante (SMI – which Ravel had helped to found) might like to put on a 'concert scandaleux' consisting of (a) *Pierrot*, (b) Stravinsky's *Poésies* and (c) his own Mallarmé songs:

> (a) and (b) will provoke shouting; (c) will calm things down and
> the audience will depart humming tunes. N.B. I must point out to my
> revered colleagues that I only know (a) from hearsay [Stravinsky]. But
> we ought to play this work which, in Germany and Austria, is giving
> rise to bloodshed.[12]

Pierrot, however, was not to be heard in Paris for another nine years, after bloodshed of a more real and terrible kind. But the Stravinsky and Ravel songs were both given their first performance at the SMI in their chamber ensemble versions on 14 January 1914, and some listeners may have heard, in the string harmonics of the first Ravel song, a relapse into the comfortable Impressionist sonorities of yore. If so, Ravel, not for the first or last time, was playing tricks on them: the arpeggiated gesture may have reminded them of the Dawn Scene in *Daphnis*, but the harmonic edge is borrowed from the *Valses nobles*. Likewise, critics who detect echoes of *Pierrot* in the actual notes are probably fooling themselves.

As far as we know, knowledge of Schoenberg's music among French composers before the war was limited to a tiny group, to Ravel, Debussy and Koechlin, and perhaps Milhaud. The critic M.-D. Calvocoressi later recalled 'the publication, in 1911 [in fact, 1909] of his [Schoenberg's] famous piano pieces op. 11 – I remember Ravel and Stravinsky looking at them at my house; Stravinsky was particularly excited about certain things in them, and Ravel, although colder, was greatly interested.'[13] In 1947, Schoenberg himself wrote, in discussing his Six Little Piano Pieces op. 19: 'Of course, a new style had to be created, differing from Schumann's and Liszt's and – perhaps Debussy's. Of the latter I did not know anything before the First World War, though Stravinsky had played my piano pieces for him.'[14] It is not clear from this whether Schoenberg is referring just to the Six Little Pieces or to op. 11 as well.

But certainly Ravel did not know *Pierrot* when he wrote his Mallarmé songs, and it is probably nearer to the truth to say that 'the atonality we can detect in [them] consists of a pulverization of contradictory tonalities, a desire for ambivalence and a deliberate rethinking of tonal "data", all procedures which could be regarded as mirroring Mallarmé's unexpected syntax'.[15]

With these Ravel settings and those for voice and piano by Debussy, also of 1913, French musical interest in Mallarmé came to an abrupt end, not to be revived until Boulez's two *Improvisations sur Mallarmé* of 1957. What Ravel referred to as Mallarmé's 'visions unbounded, yet precise in design, enclosed in a mystery of sombre abstractions'[16] did not fit in with the emerging ethos of French culture. If Ravel and Debussy were to some extent turning away of their own accord from all that was sumptuous or decadent, perhaps the decisive curtailment brought about by the war was in the matter of sheer size. Obviously the general mobilization on 2 August 1914 hit the Parisian opera houses and orchestras hard. Although the musical press after the war was at pains to stress how much music still went on despite the lack of manpower, and, in the later years, air raids and blackouts, the scale of operations was greatly reduced. As Richard Buckle has written of the Ballets russes, 'the 1914 season was indeed the end of a period; and the *ne plus ultra* of the Ballet's first phase coincided with the end of *la belle époque*, the end of *art nouveau*, the end of the *World of Art* movement, the end of empires'. The highlight of the season at the Opéra was *La légende de Joseph*, with music by Richard Strauss. This ballet, 'for which two German intellectuals had provided the libretto (for Count Harry Kessler had joined forces with Hugo von Hofmannsthal)...was planned to be more stupendous a spectacle even than *Schéhérazade* or *Le dieu bleu*'.[17] As an advance on performance rights, Diaghilev had borrowed from Thomas Beecham to pay Strauss and von Hofmannsthal the staggering sum of 100,000 francs, over 12 per cent of the Opéra's annual state subsidy, and, since *La légende* disappeared for ever from Diaghilev's repertory after the six performances of May and June 1914, Lynn Garafola suspects 'that the debt remained unpaid and that the production became the property of the Beecham organization'.[18]

The details are perhaps less important than the general picture of an organization suffering from advanced elephantiasis. If we add to this the fact that, with the Opéra premiere of *Parsifal*, French duty to Wagner had now been seen to be done, it begins to look as though Paris may have been ripe for a revolution in musical taste, war or no war.

The truth of this can only be tested by looking further at those trends which, like Ravel's volte-face in the *Valses nobles*, continued to flourish through the hostilities and afterwards. To some extent this testing can be done negatively: that is to say, ideas stood a better chance of survival from 1914 onwards if they did not require large forces, if they were not expensive to put on, if they did not subscribe to a Symbolist aesthetic that was now increasingly seen as old-fashioned, and certainly if they were not German.

Some of the strongest anti-German sentiments are to be found, not surprisingly, in Debussy's letters written between 1914 and 1917, but he was not in a position to turn these feelings into any kind of actions except, as we have seen, the writing of *En blanc et noir*. Saint-Saëns on the other hand, together with various of the great and good including d'Indy, Charpentier and the one-time director of the Conservatoire, Théodore Dubois, in March 1916 formed the committee of a *Ligue nationale pour la défense de la musique française*. It would have been more honest to call it a league *pour la proscription de la musique allemande moderne*. The League aimed

> by every means to expel and then hunt down the enemy; to prevent in future the recurrence of baneful infiltration.
>
> Even if there can be no question, for us and our young successors, of repudiating the 'classics', which constitute one of the immortal monuments of humanity, it is our task to condemn *modern* PanGermanism to silence.[...]
>
> First, we must banish from our land, for many years to come, the public performance of *contemporary* Austro-German works which are *still in copyright*, as well as their interpreters, Kapellmeisters and virtuosos, their Viennese operettas, their ever multiplying cinematographic films, their more or less faked phonographic discs, and unmask their manoeuvring, the pseudonyms of those popular song composers who, even as we write, are escaping the censor; we must see to it that the enemy 'does not pass'.[19]

Only then does the document go on to consider measures to defend and propagate French music.

Sad to say, the League had some measure of success, at least for the duration of the war: 'sometimes', wrote Proust, 'the siren would sound like the harrowing call of a Valkyrie – the only German music that had been heard since the beginning of the war'.[20] The insistence that the ban should concern only German works still in copyright could be interpreted as a patriotic desire not to bring comfort to the enemy through the generation of royalties, but in fact it is unlikely whether in wartime these would have been paid. More to the point, it proscribed the music of Wagner which strictly was still in the private domain. The thinking behind this comes close to Debussy's: that in the years up to the war, Wagner's music had usurped the place of truly French music (whatever that might be) and had in some way actually weakened the moral fibre not only of French music but of the whole French nation. German wartime propaganda certainly put it about that the French race was in physical and intellectual decline, though understandably not blaming Wagner for this, and in July 1918 Koechlin was one of seven French intellectuals led by Théodore Reinach on a visit to the USA to provide visible proof that these claims were untrue.[21]

The Wagner issue raises sharply the question of what the role of music was seen to be at this point in French society. A copy of the League's manifesto reached Ravel in June 1916 in the area round Verdun, where he had been for three months driving his lorry Adélaïde. In his reply, from the 'Zone des Armées', he explained that in general he could not agree less with the document: 'where I cannot follow you is when you put forward the principle that "the role of the Art of Music is economic and social". I had never considered music or the other arts in this light.' And he went on to say that

> it would even be dangerous for French composers systematically to ignore the works of their foreign colleagues and so to form a sort of national coterie: our music, which is so rich at the present time, would soon degenerate and become enclosed in self-reproducing formulae.[22]

Ravel could with justice make the point about the economic and social role of music, since the epigraph to the *Valses nobles*, from Henri de Régnier, reads 'Le plaisir délicieux et toujours nouveau d'une occupation inutile' ('The delightful and ever novel pleasure of a pointless pastime'). He also unwittingly confirmed what Proust would later write of the marquis de Saint-Loup, who quoted Romain Rolland and Nietzsche 'with that independence of fighting men who do not have the same fear of mentioning a German name as those behind the lines'.[23]

Before we leave Wagner, it may be as well to attempt briefly to understand the

A woman wearing a tricolour sings a patriotic song to celebrate the Armistice

awe and indeed fear he excited in the French. Perhaps the answer lies in words of Joseph de Maistre (1754–1821) who wrote that 'an idea is never adopted by the world until a writer of genius takes hold of it and expresses it well.... Perhaps nothing is properly understood in Europe until the French have explained it.'[24]

Although de Maistre was discussing writers rather than composers, the same desire to 'explain', or at least to make one's products open to explanation, runs continually through the succession of French composers. Berlioz, as usual, is something of an exception, but even Messiaen, so often wrongly described in the English-speaking press as a mystic, was always anxious to explain not only his technical procedures but, through his music, the theological texts on which much of it is based.

Taking a long view of French musical history, it is hard then for us not to regard Wagner and his influence in the Debussyan manner, as an aberration, an excrescence. De Maistre, who never heard a note of Wagner, believed that 'what is called the art of speaking is eminently the talent of the French, and it is by the art of speaking that one rules over men'. And yet orchestral fragments from Wagner's operas did indeed take over much of French music in the 1880s, without recourse to words and, perhaps worse still, resisting attempts to analyse them verbally – though, Heaven knows, the French critics did try.

By 1914 some Frenchmen were identifying the eminence in French life not only of Wagner but also of Diaghilev's Ballets russes with some kind of moral sickness. One reason for this, regrettable but undeniable, was that Diaghilev, through his Paris agent Gabriel Astruc, had turned for much-needed financial support to the city's rich. In the words of Lynn Garafola:

> Mostly German-Jewish in origin, families like Bischoffsheim, Gunzburg, Oppenheim, Natanson, Lippmann, Schiff, Fould, Lazard, Reinach, Erlanger, Hirsch, Stern, Gugenheim, Pelletier, Haas, Ulmann, Bernheim, and Pourtalès, had risen to social and financial prominence in the tolerant religious climate of the Second Empire and early years of the Third Republic. They had intermarried, formed business and family alliances with the Rothschilds and other financial clans, and by the closing decades of the century had begun to marry into le gratin, the upper crust of French society. From the 1880s onward this group played a key role in French cultural life as patrons, collectors, salonnières, artistic dilettantes, and supporters of innovative artistic trends. Here, in a nutshell, was le tout Paris mined by Astruc for Diaghilev's audience.[25]

The polarization of Parisian society by the Dreyfus case clearly did not help, and the resentment it left behind could readily be projected on to such targets as the above.

In this climate, there were some artists who actually welcomed the war as

The legacy of peace and war

something that would cleanse the soul of France. By the end of 1914, d'Indy was writing:

> I consider this war extremely beneficial since it has forced from the depths of our hearts our old qualities of clarity, logic, integrity, and uprightness.... All these qualities have now come to the surface again, breaking through the crust, and I believe that artistic progress will take the road of simplicity and beauty instead of seeking the small and the rare as in recent years, at least I hope so with all my heart.[26]

Such an attack on 'the small and the rare' marked d'Indy out as a reactionary, as did the completion the following year of his third music drama *La légende de Saint-Christophe*, 'a work of monumental stature' but one in which,

> for all its passages of inspired invention, it is hard to deny the sense of a closing of the circle, the construction of a bulwark against the advancing tide of modernism and progressivism, with traditional Catholicism and regionalism pitted against the forces of social and cultural disintegration.[27]

– or at least social and cultural disintegration as d'Indy himself saw them.

But there were those who did not see the old French qualities of clarity, logic, integrity and uprightness as being the real issue. In 1911, Degas's friend Daniel Halévy noted in his diary:

> I do not wish to deny the moral and social disorder which is ours. But in fact it is not order which has ever been the French characteristic. The nation has survived through the vitality of its people, the warmth of their characters, the abundance of individual talents. It is menaced today, not by disorder, which is always with us, but by the diminution of its physiological vitality, its impoverishment in men.[28]

In fact the makers of the new, their physiological vitality not noticeably diminished, were already at work in that cardinal year of 1911 before the old had fully run its course. Two of them deserve our notice here: one was a poet and art critic; the other, rather curiously, had been a pupil at the Schola Cantorum, the institution effectively run by d'Indy since its inception in 1894.

In 1911 the Polish writer Wilhelm Apollinaris de Kostrowitzky, alias Guillaume Apollinaire, recently acquitted of stealing the Mona Lisa from the Louvre, was still under attack as a supporter of the Cubist painters, and indeed as a foreigner. To cheer him up, a friend invited him to contribute articles to a new art review, and 'in February 1912, the *Soirées de Paris* appeared in a dignified chocolate-brown cover and led off with a near manifesto by Apollinaire justifying the abandonment of "resemblance" and "subject matter" in modern painting'.[29] In 1911 he had published his first collection of poems, *Le bestiaire ou Cortège d'Orphée* with illustrations by Dufy, and in 1913 attracted attention with his second collection, *Alcools*, the first poem of which ('Zone') begins with the lines:

A la fin tu es las de ce monde ancien
Bergère ô tour Eiffel le troupeau des ponts bêle ce matin
Tu en as assez de vivre dans l'antiquité grecque et romaine

['Finally you are weary of that ancient world/ O Eiffel tower shepherdess the flock of bridges is bleating this morning/ You have had enough of living in Greek and Roman antiquity']

Without our delving too deeply into lit. crit., three points at least spring off the page here. The lack of punctuation forces us into a closer study of the text (in this case, of line 2). Similarly, the apparently irrelevant irruption of that line into the sense of lines 1 and 3 arouses curiosity, tempered to a greater or lesser extent by irritation. And thirdly, even if we ignore line 2, we are faced with a declaration of war, not on Wagner or groups of German-Jewish bankers, but more shockingly on that Graeco-Roman world which had

Guillaume Apollinaire with his head wound bandaged; a drawing by Irène Lagut

for centuries been the touchstone of respectability and value in French art: again in 1911, the classical aura round Debussy's *Le martyre de Saint Sébastien* had helped validate that mystery play, despite the Archbishop of Paris's objections to d'Annunzio's text and Ida Rubinstein's all too feminine legs. As a final twist, we may note, Apollinaire writes not 'je suis las', but 'tu es las' – in modern parlance, 'go on, admit it! You're sick to death of that ancient world!' This appeal to honesty, to an end of illusions, sets up an even stronger frisson when juxtaposed with the apparently fanciful second line; but when one actually climbs up through the skirts of the Eiffel shepherdess and looks down on the flocking bridges over the Seine....

Apollinaire, excited by the new life that war offered, joined the French army and was wounded in the head in 1916. His last volume of poetry, *Calligrammes*, apart from indulging in wonderfully imaginative typography, contains, in its final poem 'La jolie rousse', couched in the simplest of language, a moving appeal that was to be too often ignored by critics of the arts in the years that followed:

Et sans m'inquiéter aujourd'hui de cette guerre
Entre nous et pour nous mes amis
Je juge cette longue querelle de la tradition et de l'invention
De l'Ordre et de l'Aventure

Vous dont la bouche est faite à l'image de celle de Dieu
Bouche qui est l'ordre même
Soyez indulgents quand vous nous comparez
A ceux qui furent la perfection de l'ordre
Nous qui quêtons partout l'aventure

['And without concerning myself today with this war/ Between ourselves
and for ourselves my friends/ I judge this long quarrel between tradition
and invention/Between Order and Adventure/ You whose mouth is made
in the image of God's/ Mouth which is order itself/ Be indulgent when you
compare us/ To those who were the perfection of order/ Us who seek
adventure on every hand']

Like Wordsworth a century earlier, Apollinaire was telling his readers that
important thoughts did not need 'important' language and that it was time for
poetry, and all the arts, to use this 'non-important' language in order to come to
terms with the real contemporary world in all its surprising complexity.

Apollinaire's most direct influence on the French music of the 1920s came
through his involvement with *Parade* and through the setting Poulenc made of *Le
bestiaire* in 1918–19. But meanwhile a largely parallel, or at least complementary
influence was being exerted on French music by Apollinaire's friend Erik Satie. It is
not without interest that, according to Satie, 'It was painters who taught me the
most about music.'[30] Given that Satie, like Apollinaire, was greatly interested in
the Cubists, we may take this as indicating that Satie in his music was likewise
concerned with the presentation of familiar objects in unfamiliar perspectives and
with the nature of the relationships between those objects. The point of the
unfamiliar perspectives was not, though, to allow the artist to indulge in any self-
regarding quirkiness; it was to try and get as close as possible to the ultimate truth
of an object, its essence. I shall have more to say on this in the last chapter.

Apollinaire, impatient with the world of Greek and Roman gods, was not alone in
feeling that he was living through a crucial change in sensibility. The war could be
seen both as cause and effect of this. Satie's teacher, Albert Roussel, who at forty-six
had joined up as a lieutenant in the transport division of the French army, in a letter
home to his wife tried to see past the end of the war to the artistic life beyond it,
with an eye on the future production of his as yet unfinished opera-ballet *Padmâvatî*.
Of his ballet *Le festin de l'araignée*, produced by Jacques Rouché at the Théâtre des
Arts in 1913, he said:

All that will now belong to 'prewar things', that's to say things which will be separated from us by a wall, a veritable wall.... We are going to have to start living all over again, with a new conception of life, which is not to say that everything made before the war will be forgotten, but that everything made after it will have to be made differently. I was thinking about this yesterday and wondering whether, with *Padmâvatî* in mind, I did not have cause to fear this new state of mind [*état d'esprit*] which will result from the present crisis, given that *Padmâvatî* was entirely conceived and composed before the war. On careful reflection, I don't think so. I don't see in my work any trace of morbid or deliquescent influences. On the contrary, I feel its general tone is rather virile and strong and that it will be capable of surviving the test of a two- or three-year delay (and what years!) before it is offered to the public....[31]

Even if Roussel was unduly optimistic about the length of the delay – *Padmâvatî* would not be produced at the Opéra until 1 June 1923 – his equation of prewar French music with morbidity and deliquescence and his sense that virility and strength were the qualities needed for a work's survival show that d'Indy's view of the war as a purifying agent could be shared even by someone who saw the horrors of warfare at close quarters.

The prewar/postwar dichotomy bears a somewhat different interpretation, though, in the works and philosophy of two men who were to be key figures on the French musical scene in the 1920s: Igor Stravinsky and Jean Cocteau. It is in the nature of geniuses of Stravinsky's calibre to be well ahead of the game – indeed, very often to set the rules of a quite new game.

If *L'oiseau de feu* was essentially a successful bid for a *permis de conduire* on the musical/theatrical road, *Petrushka* and *Le sacre* opened up and described new tracts of scenery, both seductive and challenging, to which French composers would be drawn again and again over the succeeding two decades. But, as many of them discovered, giving a fresh slant on known scenery can be no less difficult than discovering the unknown. Like Wagner, Stravinsky was a hard act to follow, the more so since he remained vigorously alive and also inclined to indulge in Protean changes of appearance.

To simplify rather drastically, the message of *Petrushka* for French composers was twofold. Firstly, it undermined the notion of high art as necessarily treating of the noble, the sublime or the grandiose – and this a little ahead of Apollinaire's dismissal of classical culture. True, there had been earlier, isolated attempts to 'proletariatize': in Charpentier's opera *Louise*, produced at the Opéra-Comique in 1900, which tried to go one better than Puccini's *La bohème* and, in so doing, drew Debussy's scorn as evincing 'the sentimentality of a gentleman returning home around four in the morning and being moved to tears by the sight of the roadsweepers and rag-and-bone men',[32] and in Ravel's song-cycle *Histoires naturelles* with its imitation of populist, *café-concert* diction which, though provoking initial outrage among the audience, led to no lasting movement. One of the strengths of Stravinsky's extraordinary score is that it is *not* a bourgeois outsider's patronizing view of the lower classes at play but, in a way that is perhaps impossible to analyse, an experience seen from the inside and shared by both composer and listener: from the first squeeze-box sounds of the milling crowd we are 'in there'. For French composers trying to get away from the stranglehold of polite society music-making, *Petrushka* was to remain a touchstone.

The work's second message was a technical one, in its proof of the poetic possibilities inherent in writing music in two keys simultaneously (bitonality). Not everyone was convinced of these (Milhaud was later delighted to find Saint-Saëns's judgment of his Second Symphonic Suite as a collection of 'aberrations charentonnesques' – Charenton being a lunatic asylum – and framed the review to hang on the wall of his study),[33] but at the very least Stravinsky's use of dissonant trumpet calls to evoke Petrushka's alienation gave composers a model in their response to a newly uncertain and fragmented world. It was left to Milhaud, as we shall see, to codify and expand on Stravinsky's usage.

The legacy of *Le sacre* was also both general and particular. On the general front, it set new standards in Paris of dissonance and volume beyond even those of Strauss's *Salome*, first heard at the Châtelet in 1907 (*Elektra* did not reach the city until 1932), and it has been suggested that no Parisian had ever before been subjected to this level of noise except on a battlefield. The nine-year-old Doda Conrad, taken by Mme Casella to Monteux's concert performance of *Le sacre* at the Casino de Paris in April 1914, grumbled at one point in the performance: 'Je n'aime pas ça, ce n'est pas joli.' To which Mme Casella responded sharply: 'Ce n'est pas joli, c'est beau.'[34] This distinction between the pretty and the beautiful was crucially important since, whatever musical miracles had been performed by mainstream French composers like Saint-Saëns, Fauré, Debussy and Ravel, they had very rarely stepped beyond the boundaries of the 'joli': exceptions such as Debussy's 'Ce qu'a vu le vent d'ouest' or the near-hysterical ending to the 'Feria' in Ravel's *Rapsodie espagnole* merely prove the rule. Even in 1915, two years after the *Sacre* premiere, Debussy could still articulate the traditionally French point of view in writing to his publisher Jacques Durand of his *Etudes* that 'one does not catch flies with vinegar'.[35]

The smart answer to this might be: 'Who wants to catch flies anyway?' Stravinsky, it could be argued, was after bigger game. *Le sacre* gave notice that the French charm offensive, while not over, now no longer had things all its own way and echoes of the ballet's *chic brutal* ('primitive music with all modern conveniences' as Debussy rather unkindly dubbed it)[36] continued to make themselves heard in French music through the 1920s and beyond. One danger was that the reversal of taste might be complete, that ugliness might become an end rather than a means. In this respect maybe *Le sacre* does have something to answer for, although ultimately Stravinsky was no more responsible for consequent manifestations of the new ugliness than Debussy was for the 'debussystes'. The most important general point, though, made by *Le sacre* was that, despite Apollinaire, there did still exist a 'monde ancien' that was relevant to contemporary artistic needs: not that of the classical world, but of a timeless, primordial world incorporating Stravinsky's dream of 'a scene of pagan ritual in which a chosen sacrificial virgin danced herself to death'.[37]

The more detailed influence of *Le sacre* on French music lay in its orchestration, in its rhythmic insistence and in the circling nature of much of its melodic material. Stravinsky spent many fruitless hours over the rest of his long life trying to reorganize the scoring so that the strings would not be drowned by the wind and brass, especially in the final 'Danse sacrale'. The truth is that *Le sacre* is at heart a windy, brassy piece, and the demotion of the strings after their long preeminence in the Western European orchestra (a process begun less blatantly a few years earlier in Debussy's *La mer*) is not the least of the work's revolutionary features. Since woodwind playing, in particular, was a skill the French prided themselves upon, it is no surprise that this new order of things began to show up in French scores, even if they often took pains to distance themselves from the primitive, ritual element in Stravinsky's ballet.

However, this element also manifests itself on the rhythmic front in the obsessive ostinatos that tick, throb and pound their way through the score. Here, the French were to find distancing themselves an altogether more difficult business. One reason was that the eighteenth- and nineteenth-century sonata structures taken over from the Germans had never sat altogether easily with the French cast of mind. Whereas in Haydn, Mozart, Beethoven, Schumann and Brahms development seems in general to flow naturally from the inherent qualities of the musical material, with Gounod and Saint-Saëns the development tends to sound imposed from without – Berlioz, as always, does his own inimitable thing – and even in Bizet's youthful C major symphony, one of the best French symphonies of all time, there is in the first movement, as Winton Dean notes, 'the tendency in the development section to repeat the material in contrasted keys instead of treating it organically'.[38] In our own day, Pierre Boulez has chastised the French propensity for composing in what he calls 'blocks' as 'dilettantism; sometimes at a very high level, but still dilettantism'.[39] Whether that is true or not, it cannot be gainsaid that the lessons of *Le sacre* in what could be done with ostinatos, together with the examples found in Debussy, Satie and Ravel, fell on fertile French soil.

The third influence of *Le sacre*, that of its circling melodic material, is more debatable, partly because this essentially Russian habit had already reached French music through Mussorgsky's *Boris Godunov* and his song-cycles *The Nursery* and *Sunless* and hence through Debussy's *Pelléas* and subsequent songs. Perhaps the safest conclusion is that the revolving themes in *Le sacre*, even if Stravinsky borrowed many of them from Russian folksong, had the effect of renewing the validity of the *Pelléas* style of wordsetting, which otherwise might have been abandoned together with its outworn Symbolist aesthetic.

On the outbreak of war, Stravinsky and his family moved to Switzerland. The two last works of his to be premiered in Paris before hostilities began – the *Trois poésies de la lyrique japonaïse* in January 1914 and the ballet *Le rossignol* by the Ballets russes in May – can have done little to affect the impact of *Le sacre*. The *Trois poésies* had, as we have seen, already done their work on Ravel, and exposure in the restricted milieu of the SMI can barely have added to this, while *Le rossignol* 'provoked no scandal or incident; but neither did it make any great impression on the public'.[40] Stravinsky's position after *Le sacre* is well summarized by Stephen Walsh:

> Not surprisingly, instrumental sonority, the search for the right sound,
> played an increasing part in Stravinsky's music of the next few years.
> These works would inherit the energy and vitality, but not the violence
> or barbarism of *The Rite of Spring*. They would separate its radical elements
> of sound, form and rhythm from its expressionist elements, which, for all
> the shock waves they sent through the Théâtre des Champs-Elysées on
> 29 May 1913, now seem comparable in their late-romantic extravagance
> to anything in Mahler or Strauss. Looked at in this way, *The Rite of Spring*
> seems like the collision of two epochs. When the smoke and dust cleared,
> very little was left of the older one.[41]

With Stravinsky's move to Switzerland, much disapproved of by Diaghilev, Paris saw very little of him or his music during the war. On 29 December 1915 he appeared for the first time in the capital as a conductor, in a performance by the Ballets russes of *L'oiseau de feu* at a Red Cross charity matinée at the Opéra, but Paris heard none of the post-smoke-and-dust Stravinsky until the first performance of *Pribaoutki* at the Salle Gaveau in May 1919. So any clearing away of Expressionist elements that occurred in French music did so without Stravinsky's immediate assistance. There is even the possibility that Stravinsky's new, simpler, non-Expressionist language was indebted to that of Satie: although little work has been done on this, the two men had been close friends since meeting *chez* Debussy in 1911, and Stravinsky later remembered that around that time Satie 'played many of his compositions for me at the piano'.[42] In 1915, Stravinsky wrote 'the ice-cream wagon Valse' in the Three Easy Pieces for piano duet

> in homage to Erik Satie, a souvenir of a visit to him in Paris. Satie, a very
> touching and attractive personality, suddenly had become old and white,
> though not less witty and gay. I tried to portray something of his esprit
> in the Valse.[43]

Another, more fragile, prewar liaison came about between Stravinsky and the fashion-conscious Parisian aesthete Jean Cocteau over their projected collaboration on a ballet called *David*. Their letters on the subject[44] set the tone of their relationship over the next half century: on Cocteau's side, an absolute awareness of Stravinsky's genius, leading at times to overfulsome flattery; on Stravinsky's, a suspicion that Cocteau might at heart be no more than a talented *arriviste* together with a conviction that he was no musician, leading at times to a distinct guardedness. What, for example, was he as a composer to make of Cocteau's thesis that 'the [dancer's] body must arouse itself in a burst, becoming another instrument of the orchestra. The anatomy must comprise a visual curve among the sonorous curves, and serve the ensemble'? After the initial flurry of missives between February and May 1914, Stravinsky clearly goes off the whole idea, and the correspondence closes with two letters from Cocteau of 1915 and 1916, the latter declaring that

> I am not going to discuss *David*: a youthful excess, a fogginess [of vision] brought on by city life and a series of inopportune circumstances, all culminating in the bungling of my first attempt at a work of which, undoubtedly, I was not yet worthy.[45]

Since both Stravinsky and Cocteau figure largely in the history of postwar Paris music-making, it is worth looking briefly at the projected *David* in more detail to try and discover what Cocteau hoped to get out of it and what prompted Stravinsky's ultimate coolness.

The scenario, as relayed by Cocteau, was as follows:

> An acrobat was to announce to the public the grand spectacle of *David* which was supposedly being given inside; a clown who then turned into a box, in a theatrical pastiche of the fairground phonograph and a modern version of the antique mask, was to chant through a loudspeaker the exploits of David and beg the public to come in and see the show.
> It was, after a fashion, the first sketch for *Parade*, but needlessly complicated by scriptural quotations and a text.[46]

For us, looking back on Cocteau's career, it is possible to see this as an early manifestation of his interest in the ambiguities of theatrical production and in the games that can be played with reality. More prosaically, we could also see it as an attempt to rescue his reputation from the memories of *Le dieu bleu*, a ballet with a scenario by him and music by Reynaldo Hahn which Diaghilev had staged in 1912 and which had then sunk with all hands (or possibly feet); Cocteau's biographer Frederick Brown was not being unduly severe when he gave his opinion that Cocteau's argument for *David* 'reads as if written by a haberdasher', and that, after playing happily with a mock theatre as a child, 'at twenty-three, without childhood to excuse him, he was a dilettante puttering about a real theatre'.[47] By holding on to the coat tails of the undisputed new genius of the ballet world, he hoped no doubt to be propelled towards the stardom he felt he deserved.

Cocteau's view that Stravinsky lost interest in the project because he found 'the querulous atmosphere of the Ballets russes' repugnant, is hard to take seriously. The composer's genius was matched by his toughness. A far more likely reason was that he distrusted Cocteau's motives. Like any major artist of limited financial means, Stravinsky had to engage in a continual balancing act between what he wanted to write and what impresarios and the public would pay him to write – what he did not need was interference from another, lesser artist. Another reason was that the project was too similar to *Petrushka*. One of the many artistic attitudes Stravinsky shared with Debussy was a determination never to repeat himself: the three great prewar ballets, for example, had already proved what a variety of form and substance Stravinsky could embrace within the unchanging context of the Ballets russes. Now, in a series of little songs to Russian words, in *Les noces*, begun at Clarens in 1914, and in *Renard*, begun at Château d'Oex the following year, he embarked on an exploration of his Russian heritage that was focused less on stories or local colour and more on the language, or rather on the 'succession of words and syllables, as well as the cadences they give rise to, which produce on our sensibility an effect very closely akin to music'.[48] With hindsight we can see that he was therefore unlikely to be seduced by a ballet on an Old Testament subject which Cocteau himself came to regard as being '*needlessly* complicated by scriptural quotations and a text' (my italics).

This particular instance well illustrates the general problems that Stravinsky was to pose for the French in the years that followed. Although both parties were on the side of change, their reasons were rather different. For the French, as always, the dictates of fashion were important; for Stravinsky, only his own work mattered. Also, there were problems of timing and patriotism. Stravinsky and French fashion did not always move at the same speed, nor was there general agreement over the extent to which the foreigner Stravinsky should be allowed to set the French musical agenda. But the only real way to prevent a genius like him from doing so was for French composers to come up with music that was not only different but as good or better. Unsurprisingly, such music proved to be in short supply.

Picasso and his assistants sitting on the drop-curtain for *Parade*

Two Fridays in the year 1917 saw decisive events for French culture. Firstly, on the afternoon of 6 April, President Woodrow Wilson signed the declaration of war passed that week by Congress. Whether or not this tipped the balance of power can still be argued; what is unarguable is the powerful presence in 1920s Paris of Americans who had discovered the city's delights while in uniform.

Secondly, on the afternoon of 18 May, Diaghilev's Ballets russes gave the fourth of the eight performances making up their rather brief tenth season, this fourth performance concluding with the premiere of Satie's *Parade*. Or Cocteau's, or Picasso's, or Massine's *Parade*, depending on whom you believe....

Cocteau always claimed, with some justice, that he was the ballet's prime mover.

He was less eager to point out that its success was vital to his career as a serious artist. After the failure of *Le dieu bleu* and the abandonment of *David*, Cocteau had considerable ground to make up. With his usual flair, he approached Satie and Picasso, both men whose stock in 1916 seemed likely to rise.

For Picasso, the project came at a good time. He was already moving away from analytical Cubism, from its petty jealousies and its refusal to see a world beyond geometrical patterns and Spanish guitars. Working for the theatre also gave him an opportunity to experiment with forms and colours in three-dimensional space. For Massine, *Parade* was simply his first opportunity as a choreographer, and one he seized with relish. As for Satie, the ballet spelt a modicum of fame at last after so many years in Debussy's shadow, and more than a modicum of money (he promptly splashed out on buying umbrellas).

There was therefore a determination on all fronts that the new ballet should be different, surprising and even shocking. Cocteau, for one, had not forgotten Diaghilev's injunction 'Etonne-moi', and one of his ways of obeying it was to cast aside Impressionism and exotic, picturesque paraphernalia. Even the Chinese conjuror has less to do with the voluptuous Orient of Ravel's *Shéhérazade* than with the spare athleticism of contemporary circus. There was not even to be a hint of the

supernatural, as in *Petrushka*. Instead, in this 'ballet réaliste', as he called it, simplicity was to be the keynote.

It would, nonetheless, be a grave mistake to take *Parade* entirely at face value, like the woman in the audience whom Picasso overheard to say 'If I'd known it was going to be so silly, I'd have brought the children.' On the day of the first performance, it is true, Cocteau published an article in the press saying: 'Laughter is natural to Frenchmen: it is important to keep this in mind and not be afraid to laugh even at this most difficult time.' But the sentence previous to this reads: 'Our wish is that the public may consider *Parade* as a work which conceals poetry beneath the coarse outer skin of slapstick.' Exactly what that poetry might consist of, he does not say.

The programme printed for the first performance announced that the scene represents a Sunday Fair in Paris. There is a travelling theatre, and to publicize the show a 'parade' (or 'trailer') is held, in the form of three turns: by a Chinese conjuror, an American girl and a pair of acrobats. Three Managers try to persuade the public to come inside the theatre, insisting they must not take the 'parade' to be the real thing. They are unsuccessful. The four artists then make an appeal on their own account. But it is too late.

Parade may be seen as being about the real emotions, especially of sadness and unfulfilment, lying behind the manufactured emotions called for by the performers' brave public personae, and perhaps it is in the pull between the two that the poetry resides. But there is at least one further level in the work that forces itself on our attention. Cocteau later called *Parade* 'the greatest battle of the war'. This may strike us as an example of flippancy verging on the heartless, given that in early May 1917 French soldiers were being slaughtered in their thousands, leading in some quarters to mutiny. But Cocteau took a longer view. 'I was able to see', he wrote later, almost in the manner of d'Indy, 'how the war rid us in Paris of foolishness, which found enough to do elsewhere.' More than that, there would be life beyond the war. As Picasso remarked, 'Won't it be awful when Braque and Derain and all the rest of them put their wooden legs up on a chair and tell about the fighting?' *Parade* was indeed a great battle: to preserve the French spirit and to proclaim that art is greater than war, and a sense of humour more valuable to humanity than hate.

Paradoxically, some critics chastised *Parade* as being the work of 'sales Boches'. A few months later, the princesse de Polignac took Satie's side in the lawsuit brought against him by the critic Jean Poueigh, who had objected to being called a 'cul' on an open postcard. An official of the Ministry of the Interior, learning of her support, commented:

> What a mistake the princesse de Polignac is making in concerning herself with those Boches. *Parade* and the Ballets russes are 'Boches' and poorly regarded at the front, where their noisy manifestations have had an extremely bad effect.[49]

Apollinaire's programme note prophesied that the audience would, through the ballet, 'come to know all the grace of modern movement, which they have never dreamt of'. If this was unduly hopeful, there was no scandal on the scale of *Le sacre*. The diplomat Paul Morand felt that 'Cocteau's idea of replacing the stereotyped movements of ballet with fragments of everyday behaviour, and his stylized modern actions – starting up a motor-car, taking a photograph, etc. – did not seem quite worked out. Much applause and a few whistles.'[50]

Diaghilev's opinion of *Parade* is perhaps best indicated by how often it appeared on his Paris programmes. In this first run in 1917 there were five performances, between 18 and 26 May. After that, Diaghilev brought it out just nine times in Paris in the following seven years, with three performances in 1920 and three pairs in 1921, 1922 and 1924. We could not therefore claim that Diaghilev in any way disowned it, but this total of fourteen performances does compare unfavourably with thirty-two for *Petrushka* during the same period.

On the positive side, the aesthetic lessons of *Parade* were such as could be learnt in a single evening. Many of them found their way into Cocteau's famous literary manifesto *Le coq et l'arlequin*, published in 1918, in which the Cock represents French culture and Harlequin the multifarious foreign influences which were beginning to make themselves felt: 'the composer must cure music of its intertwinings, its tricks, its gambits, he must make it remain as far as possible directly opposite the listener'; 'the beautiful looks easy. That's what the public mistrust'; 'enough of clouds, waves, aquariums, water-nymphs and nocturnal scents – we need a music with its feet on the ground, an everyday music'. But even before *Le coq*, as its dedicatee and co-compiler Georges Auric remembered sixty years later,

> increasingly we were convinced of the value of *Parade*, of the lesson Satie was teaching us through it. We used to discuss it every time we met, and a new admirer, Francis Poulenc, appeared to our great delight. A current of fresh air had just begun to blow over our little world.[51]

...and with the appearance of Poulenc, the stage is set for the founding of Les Six and the 1920s.

Notes

1. Frédérique Patureau: *Le palais Garnier dans la société parisienne, 1875–1914* (Liège, 1991), p. 247.
2. Ibid., pp. 425, 418.
3. Maurice Ravel, 'Esquisse autobiographique', in *La revue musicale*, no. spécial, December 1938, p. 21 (dictated in 1928).
4. Edward Lockspeiser, *Debussy: His Life and Mind*, II (Cassell, 1965; 2nd edn 1978), pp. 33–51 (heading to Ch. 2).
5. *S.I.M.*, 1 November 1913, in *Monsieur Croche et autres écrits*, ed. François Lesure (Paris, 1987), p. 246.
6. *La revue blanche*, 1 May 1901, in Lesure (ed.), *Monsieur Croche.*, p. 35.

The legacy of peace and war

7. Manuel Rosenthal, in conversation with the author.

8. Yvonne Gouverné, in conversation with the author.

9. Darius Milhaud, *Ma vie heureuse* (Paris, 1973), p. 46.

10. René Peter, 'Du temps d'Achille', in *La revue musicale*, 2, 1 December 1920, p. 164; trans. in Roger Nichols, *Debussy Remembered* (London, 1992), p. 128.

11. Paul Bertrand, *Le monde de la musique* (Geneva, 1947), p. 240.

12. *Maurice Ravel. Lettres, écrits, entretiens*, ed. Arbie Orenstein (Paris, 1989), p. 128.

13. M.-D. Calvocoressi, *Musicians Gallery* (London, 1933), pp. 227–28.

14. Letter to George MacManus, 7 April 1947, Catalogue of Sotheby's sale, London, 28 May 1993, lot 174.

15. Marcel Marnat, *Maurice Ravel* (Paris, 1986), p. 373.

16. Maurice Ravel, 'La musique contemporaine', 7 April 1928; see Bertrand, *Le monde*, p. 53.

17. Richard Buckle, *Diaghilev* (London, 1979; repr. 1984), p. 274.

18. Lynn Garafola, *Diaghilev's Ballets Russes* (Oxford, 1992), p. 285.

19. For full text see Orenstein (ed.), *Ravel. Lettres*, pp. 527–28.

20. Marcel Proust, *A la recherche du temps perdu*, III (Paris, 1954), p. 777.

21. Robert Orledge, *Charles Koechlin (1867–1950): His Life and Works* (Luxemburg, 1989), p. 12.

22. See Orenstein (ed.), *Ravel. Lettres*, p. 157.

23. See Proust, *A la recherche*, p. 754.

24. 'Trois fragments sur la France', in *Oeuvres inédites du comte J. de Maistre* (1870), pp. 7–9; excerpts in Eng. trans. in Theodore Zeldin, *France 1848–1945*, III, *Intellect and Pride* (Oxford, 1980), p. 18.

25. Garafola, *Diaghilev's Ballets Russes*, p. 281.

26. Andrew Thomson, *Vincent d'Indy and his World* (Oxford, 1996), pp. 182–83.

27. Ibid., p. 188.

28. Daniel Halévy, *Degas parle* (Paris, 1995), p. 184. (Diary entry of 29 February 1911.)

29. Roger Shattuck, *The Banquet Years* (London, 1959), p. 214.

30. Ornella Volta, 'Satie sur la butte', *Erik Satie à Montmartre* (Paris, 1982), p. 8.

31. Robert Bernard, *Albert Roussel* (Paris, 1948), p. 31.

32. Letter to Pierre Louÿs of 6 February 1900, in *Debussy Letters*, ed. François Lesure and Roger Nichols (London, 1987), p. 110.

33. Milhaud, *Ma vie heureuse*, p. 92.

34. Doda Conrad, in conversation with the author.

35. Letter of 12 August 1915, in *Lettres de Claude Debussy à son éditeur*, ed. Jacques Durand (Paris, 1927), p. 145.

36. Letter to André Caplet of 29 May 1913. See Milhaud, *Ma vie heureuse*, p. 270.

37. Igor Stravinsky and Robert Craft, *Expositions and Developments* (London, 1962), p. 140.

38. Winton Dean, *Bizet* (London, 1948; 3rd edn 1975), p. 134.

39. Pierre Boulez, in conversation with the author.

40. Eric Walter White, *Stravinsky: The Composer and his Works* (London, 1966; 2nd edn 1979), p. 49.

41. Stephen Walsh, *The Music of Stravinsky* (London, 1988; 2nd edn 1993), pp. 51–52.

42. *Stravinsky in Conversation with Robert Craft* (London, 1962), p. 82.

43. Igor Stravinsky and Robert Craft, *Dialogues and a Diary* (London, 1968), p. 41.

44. Stravinsky, *Selected Correspondence*, ed. and with commentaries by Robert Craft, I (London, 1982), pp. 74–85

45. Ibid., p. 85.

46. Jean Cocteau, *Le rappel à l'ordre* (Paris, 1926), p. 53.

47. Frederick Brown, *An Impersonation of Angels* (London, 1969), pp. 89–90.

48. Igor Stravinsky, *Chroniques de ma vie* (Paris, 1962), p. 63.

49. Letter of Erik Satie to Jean Cocteau of 16 August 1917, *Erik Satie. Correspondance presque complète*, réunie et présentée par Ornella Volta (Paris, 2000), p. 297.

50. Buckle, *Diaghilev*, p. 331.

51. Jean Cocteau, *Le coq et l'arlequin* (Paris, 1978), pp. 17–18.

2. Orchestras, conductors, chamber ensembles

THE NEW MUSICAL WINE trodden by Satie and Cocteau in *Parade* contained, for all its novelty, a number of traditional elements. Much attention has been paid to the typewriter tappings, Morse code bleeps, sirens and lottery wheel noises, all of which Cocteau envisaged as essential to his score. Picasso had never been keen on these and initially carried Satie with him. But eventually the composer accepted some of them, because 'we are dealing with a lovable maniac',[1] and, as a result, the percussion section is augmented.

But all these noise-making instruments are grafted on to what was, for 1917, a conventional orchestra, a slightly reduced version in fact of the one used twelve years earlier by Debussy in *La mer*. The score of *Parade* can therefore stand fittingly as a symbol for the continuous tension between old and new which is one of the most fascinating aspects of the period. In this chapter I shall be looking at the orchestral forces as constituted after the war and at the interplay between composers and these large, not always well regulated bodies.

The main Paris orchestras after the war were four in number – three of whom had been operating in 1914, while one was a revival from thirty years before that. The fact that they continued to hold the premier positions in the city's musical life until 1939 speaks perhaps for their musical standards but more certainly for the loyalty of a large number of the concert-going public to institutions and conductors they knew and trusted.

The oldest of the four orchestras was the one belonging to the Société des Concerts du Conservatoire. Under the baton of François Habeneck they had given their first concert on 9 March 1828. The orchestra was composed, as it continued to be, of Conservatoire professors as well as their pupils, both current and those who had left the institution, and initially it was Habeneck's intention to play all Beethoven's symphonies, and 'to play them as they should be played, as Beethoven had never heard them except in his head'.[2] With time, this pioneering spirit faded somewhat and, by the early twentieth century, the Conservatoire Concerts (to give them a more convenient title) were not predisposed to break any lances for modern music. The flautist Philippe Gaubert, who rose from assistant conductor to chief conductor in 1919, continued the high standards inculcated by the martinet Messager but, as his own modally inspired music suggests, found much to admire in recent traditional French music: in the 1920/21 season we find works by Ropartz, Grovlez, Jongen, Gedalge, Rabaud, Roger-Ducasse, Pierné, Fauré and Ravel (*Ma mère l'oye*).

The general attitude is put succinctly in a review, written presumably by a Conservatoire functionary, that appeared under the prospectus for these concerts in the *Annuaire des artistes* covering this season:

> In its first concert, on 7 November [1920], the Society...included a novelty: Mme Croiza sang three curious songs by M. A. Caplet.... They are, as has been said, 'declamations enveloped in a very rich and suggestive orchestration'.

But the old Society, wishing to preserve its educative role, prefers to lend itself to hallowed works, by Bach, Haydn, Mozart, Beethoven, Schumann. Symphonies by César Franck, Saint-Saëns and Théodore Dubois have been heard together with some of Schumann's.

From this it seems that 'suggestive' orchestration was not appreciated by the committee – perhaps not by the players? – and that André Caplet was likely to remain unperformed from here on, together with Schubert, Brahms and any number of others whose profile did not fit. On the positive front, the continued existence of such an orchestra, nourished by a long tradition and as a forum where the Conservatoire's values and playing styles were proudly and publicly displayed, acted as a vital counterweight to the influx of foreign music and foreign executants in the postwar years. Nor was there any financial incentive for the organizers to change policy since the 1924 Paris Baedeker informs us that 'the seats are all taken by subscribers and tickets are not easily obtained'.

The next oldest orchestra was the Concerts Colonne, which had given its first performance in 1873. Its founder, Edouard Colonne, who conducted it until his death in 1910, was famous as a Berlioz interpreter and also championed the music of Franck, Bizet, Lalo, Saint-Saëns and Chausson. Debussy entrusted to the orchestra the first performances of 'Gigues' and 'Ibéria' as well as the first concert performance of *Jeux* in 1914. His one-time fellow student, Gabriel Pierné, took over from Colonne in 1910 and remained in situ until 1934, making him one of the most powerful men on the postwar Paris scene. He also remained open to most of the new music (the Colonne programme for the 1923/24 season contained twenty-two new works or parts thereof, including pieces by Aubert, Canteloube, Fairchild, Schmitt, Tcherepnin, Caplet's *Epiphanie* for cello and orchestra, and excerpts from Enesco's opera *Oedipe*), and it was Pierné who ventured to give the first performance of the symphonic suite from Milhaud's *Protée* on Sunday, 24 October 1920. When it was met with whistles and jeers, he decided to play it again the following Sunday: this time, according to the *Annuaire des artistes*, 'it was heard with astonishment, but without provoking any shouting'. Milhaud treasured an extract from a letter (already quoted in part in Chapter 1) addressed to Pierné after this event by the 85-year-old Saint-Saëns: 'I see with sadness that you are opening the door to lunatic aberrations and that you impose them on the public when it protests. Several instruments playing in different keys do not make music but a mish-mash (un charivari).'[3]

In 1881, eight years after the Concerts Colonne, Charles Lamoureux had founded the Concerts Lamoureux and he played a crucial role in the dissemination of Wagner's music through lengthy concert extracts. His son-in-law, Camille Chevillard, succeeded him in 1897 and, while continuing to perform Wagner, also specialized in the symphonic poems of Liszt and Richard Strauss and in the works of the Russian school. Schumann too was popular, even if at the hands of D.-E. Inghelbrecht, standing in for Chevillard at the end of 1919, the quick movements of the First Symphony were, according to René Brancour in *Le ménestrel*, 'pitilessly metamorphosed into *pas redoublés* and quadrille-like galops'[4] – from which we may deduce that Chevillard's Schumann was a more stately affair.

But in the Concerts Lamoureux's 1920/21 season this wide outreach shrank considerably: Beethoven and Wagner appear in the last concert on 10 April, but all of the music in the preceding twenty concerts was French, by men like Ropartz, Aubert, Caplet, Gaubert and d'Indy. On Chevillard's death in 1923, the 37-year-old Paul Paray was unanimously elected to succeed him and, if the programming remained angled towards French music, first performances did include those of Ibert's *Escales* and Canteloube's *Chants d'Auvergne*.

The one revival in the orchestral world was of the Concerts Pasdeloup. Jules Pasdeloup founded his Concerts populaires in 1861 in order to bring orchestral music within the financial means of the average Parisian. His first concert at the Cirque d'Hiver on 27 October, including Beethoven's Pastoral Symphony and the Mendelssohn Violin Concerto, was attended by 4,000 people, with the cheapest seats at 75 centimes.[5] Although Pasdeloup had retired in financial disarray in 1884, the memory of these 'popular concerts' was still alive in Paris in 1918, and it prompted a M. Serge Sandberg, who had interests in the cinema business, to underwrite a new orchestra under the Pasdeloup name.

As its conductor, Sandberg chose René Baton, known as Rhené-Baton, whose interpretations, according to a contemporary critic, 'conquered by their velvety suppleness and breadth rather than by their precision, clarity of outline or rhythmic tautness'.[6] Henri Barraud later confirmed that Rhené-Baton was nothing very special as a conductor,[7] and in 1926 Milhaud wrote to his friend Paul Collaer to complain of the 'Orchestre Pasdeloup, le plus mauvais de Paris'.[8] Before vilifying Rhené-Baton too thoroughly, one should be aware of two factors which arguably placed him at a disadvantage compared with his competitors.

Orchestras, conductors, chamber ensembles

Firstly, the Pasdeloup orchestra never knew from one season to the next where its home base would be. Whereas the Colonne orchestra was firmly entrenched in the Châtelet and the Lamoureux in the Salle Gaveau, the Pasdeloup orchestra, like its predecessor starting out in January 1918 at the Cirque d'Hiver, moved to the Opéra from 1920 to 1923, to the Trocadéro in 1923 and 1924, to the Théâtre Mogador from 1925 to 1928, and then to the Théâtre des Champs-Elysées from 1928 to 1934. Since the acoustics of a hall are something any orchestra only slowly comes to terms with, it is hardly surprising that Milhaud should have been able to find fault.

A programme cover for the Conservatoire Concerts

The second factor was that in January 1921 the orchestra became the Association des Concerts Pasdeloup, with the players assuming a large measure of control. No doubt this was connected with the militancy shown by the French unions around the end of 1920, and perhaps the players took advantage of Rhené-Baton's velvety suppleness. Someone at least, perhaps André Caplet who conducted, was brave enough to programme Schoenberg's Five Orchestral Pieces op. 16 on 22 April 1922, a performance greeted by animal noises and one woman shouting: 'It's a disgrace to subject war widows to stuff like this!' (The next Paris performance of these pieces took place in 1957). The Pasdeloup administration was also the first among the major orchestras to press for Wagner's reinstatement on the concert platform, putting the matter to an audience vote at three concerts in the autumn of 1919: the result was 'oui' 4,983, 'non' 213, and the *Meistersinger* overture was duly played that November. Even so, it was programmed as a final supplement to the concert proper, 'to allow members of the audience who might feel unable to stand this performance to leave the hall'.[9] A further blow for German music was struck by the Pasdeloup organization in performances of music by the almost unknown Gustav Mahler: of *Lieder eines fahrenden Gesellen* in 1928 and of *Das Lied von der Erde* the following year. But this initiative was not followed up in the 1930s, and it is significant that the name Mahler does not appear in the index to Dumesnil's history of the interwar period.[10]

By 1924 Sandberg, though remaining as honorary president, had withdrawn his financial support, and the orchestra had to survive on receipts and whatever tiny subventions it and the other three main orchestras could squeeze out of the government. In 1927, for instance, it was granted a subsidy of 2,000 francs, some two months' wages for the average Parisian grocer and barely enough for one rehearsal at union rates. And if the story of music in Paris has one lesson to teach, it is that for any French organization to succeed, someone, somewhere, had to be in absolute control. As late as 1938, the conductor Roger Desormière wrote of the Conservatoire Concerts:

> there are two rehearsals a week, the Tuesday one being considered by
> these gentlemen as a little meeting where you can recount the interesting

TROISIÈME CONCERT, 21 NOVEMBRE 1920

things you did on Monday (fishing, pinocle or other amusements); the rehearsal should start at 9.30, but I've never been able to begin before 10.00, and at 11.00 these gentlemen leave; what's more, there are always three or four soloists missing who easily get permission not to turn up that day. There remains the Thursday rehearsal at which one can work, but it's not enough.[11]

The schedules of these four main Paris orchestras hardly changed between the wars. In the early 1920s, Pasdeloup were offering a concert at 3 p.m. and Colonne at 5 p.m. on a Saturday (these were the days before football took over) and Pasdeloup also played at 3 p.m. on a Thursday, taking advantage of the regular school half-holiday. Otherwise, concert-going was a Sunday affair, as Prokofiev later noted:

the functioning of the symphony orchestras [is] completely abnormal. They are numerous in Paris, even too numerous, but their work is done without any overall plan. They are all private enterprises which run simultaneously and prevent each other from surviving. Certain orchestras are founded thanks to money donated by individuals, others function at their own risk and split the proceeds among the players. The latter have to struggle against the large orchestras organized by individuals with large amounts of money at their disposal.

Sometimes, one independent orchestra is set against another in the same category. On Sundays, for instance, around six orchestral concerts are fighting for audiences at the same time and for that reason halls are never full. Poor receipts affect the orchestras' budget and prevent them having a sufficient number of rehearsals...not to mention the 'starvation' salary most orchestral musicians have to survive on. And in Paris these musicians are often of the highest calibre and can get round any modern score you care to give them.[12]

Prokofiev's was an unduly gloomy view, perhaps, since all four main orchestras did survive until the Second World War, but his basic criticisms cannot be faulted. The *Annuaire des artistes* for 1920/21 lists fifty-five 'grands concerts' and, even if the epithet 'grands' has in some cases to be taken with a pinch of salt, it nevertheless represented a good deal of music-making to spread over a total population of greater Paris amounting to some three million, of whom perhaps ten thousand were serious music-lovers.[13] Concerts could not generally be given on Monday, Wednesday or Friday evenings, because these were subscribers' nights at the Opéra, but orchestras may seem to us to have been unimaginative in not making more use of Tuesdays and Thursdays. Even when, on 18 January 1923, the Conservatoire Concerts did venture to perform on a Thursday evening, successfully and to a large audience, for some reason the experiment was not repeated.

Lack of rehearsal time too often meant not only shoddy performances but a choice of conventional or untaxing repertoire. A look at the first performances given by these orchestras during the decade reveals little that is now remembered and much, like Marguerite Canal's *La flûte de jade* (Pasdeloup, 16 January 1926) or Adolphe Borchard's *Sept estampes amoureuses* (Colonne, 23 January 1927) that would seem to hark back to prewar days. By and large, the interesting new music was being performed elsewhere.

The performing body most adversely affected by the First World War was the Société nationale de musique (SNM). This had been founded in 1871 by Saint-Saëns and others under the motto 'Ars Gallica' as a shopwindow for the best in French music. Indeed, before 1914 many of the most famous works of the period were performed under its auspices – Debussy's *Prélude à l'après-midi d'un faune* and Ravel's song-cycle *Shéhérazade*, to name but two. But after the war, increased union rates meant that the SNM had to cut back to being a chamber music organization and never regained anything like its former prestige, when Chausson had claimed that having a first performance there was like going in for an examination. Even so, its claims, as printed in the *Annuaire des artistes*, remained lofty enough, being to

> give a hearing to works, whether published or not, by French composers
> belonging to the Society; to support the performance and diffusion of
> all serious musical works; and to encourage and expose, as far as it can,
> all musical enterprises in whatever form, providing they give evidence
> of their composers' elevated and truly artistic aspirations.

On the chamber music front, the real success story belonged to the Société musicale indépendante (SMI). This had been founded in 1910 by a number of Fauré's Conservatoire composition students, with Ravel very much to the fore. Like many such bodies, it was brought into being in response to a perceived need, in this case to counter the stranglehold over the SNM exerted by d'Indy to the exclusion, it was felt, of works by young composers who did not toe the d'Indy line of Beethovenian/Franckian symphonic rectitude. Ravel set the tone by using the opening concert to introduce his piano duet suite *Ma mère l'oye* (elevated aspirations?), and the range of the SMI's activities can be gauged by looking at its second and fourteenth concerts, which included Wanda Landowska playing harpsichord music by Purcell and Bull (4 May 1910) and a performance of the first movement of Bruckner's Ninth (7 June 1911).

In 1915 the SMI and the SNM merged – reasonably enough, one might think, since their aims were to some extent similar, and in the difficult conditions, with lack of manpower and blackouts at night, one joint body could easily cover the available musical ground. But all did not go as smoothly as might have been hoped. On 18 December 1916 d'Indy wrote to his friend and colleague Auguste Sérieyx:

Orchestras, conductors, chamber ensembles

Yesterday Fauré and I tried for an *honest* rapprochement between the Société nationale and the SMI. I was aiming wholeheartedly and with no ulterior motive for a union of *all* French composers.... It didn't work at all. Ravel, Koechlin, Grovlez, Casadesus and Co. refused, in the name of their 'Aesthetic'???...'which cannot be the same as ours' – I admit to finding that so funny, I'm still chuckling about it.... The only person who finds it sad is poor Fauré, who would like to escape from that SMI set-up.[14]

D'Indy might chuckle, but it was no secret in French musical circles that his enormous energy and administrative abilities, together with a penchant for having things his own way, made him a difficult *confrère*. Michel Duchesneau suggests that the antipathy may have stemmed from positions taken at the turn of the century in the Dreyfus case, with principal members of the SN (d'Indy, Bréville and Sérieyx) being Catholic, right-wing anti-Dreyfusards and the SMI including several socialist Dreyfusards (Koechlin and Ravel).[15] In any case, a look at the works the two separate organizations espoused over the next dozen years or so suggests that Ravel and his friends were right in standing firm over their 'aesthetic'.

Serge Koussevitzky with his Amati double bass in the early 1920s

The premieres given by the SNM cannot be said to have been very inspiring – at least, with the wisdom of hindsight. Violin sonatas by Pierre de Bréville and the young Claude Delvincourt (later to be an outstanding director of the Conservatoire), d'Indy's Piano Quintet and Gustave Samazeuilh's *Chant d'Espagne* were the standard fare, and the only two works that can be said to have risen above this level, in that they are still in the general repertoire today, were Fauré's Second Piano Quintet (22 May 1921), whose inclusion in this milieu suggested that he at least was concerned not to score points in the societal battle, and Roussel's *Joueurs de flûte* (7 February 1925).

By contrast, the SMI's list of first performances is extraordinarily impressive. In 1918 the fifteen-man committee included Caplet, Casella, Falla, Koechlin, Florent Schmitt, Turina and, of course, Ravel, and they were clearly intent on following the line proposed by Ravel two years earlier in his letter attacking the National League for the Defence of French Music: that stimulation from foreign music was vital if music in France were not to 'degenerate and become enclosed in self-reproducing formulae' (see p. 26). Between Lord Berners's *Trois petites marches funèbres* in 1918 and the 25-year-old Lennox Berkeley's Violin Sonatina in 1929, audiences could have heard, apart from Poulenc's Sonata for two clarinets and Ravel's Duo for violin and cello, three songs by Sorabji, Szymanowski's piano suite *Masques*, Hindemith's First String Quartet played by the Roth Quartet, Falla's *Psyché*, and a programme of American music given under the patronage of the American Ambassador, Myron T. Herrick, including chamber works by Virgil Thomson, Copland and Piston. Then, on 15 December 1927, a Schoenberg concert consisting of the Suite op. 29, piano pieces played by Emmanuel Steuermann, the Four Songs op. 6 and finally *Pierrot lunaire* conducted by the composer. Ravel, however, missed this last concert, pleading problems with fatigue and blood pressure....[16]

Finally, the SMI was unusual in that it allowed the level of its concert-giving activities to depend to some degree on their contents. To turn once again to the *Annuaire des artistes* for 1920/21, we find that

> concerts are given on the first Thursday of each month, from December to May inclusive. The repertoire consists of musical works, mostly modern, being given their first performance. Extra concerts and even orchestral ones are given according to the number of works which have been accepted by the committee.

The 'committee' seems often to have consisted just of Ravel,[17] who took over as president on Fauré's death in 1924, and it is noteworthy that the SMI's last concert on 3 May 1935 followed fairly closely on the serious deterioration in Ravel's health that led to his death two and a half years later. But the above list of first performances knocks on the head any idea that Ravel may have been minded to exercise a d'Indy-esque authority: on 6 April 1922, the SMI hosted the first performance of Milhaud's Fifth String Quartet just six months after Milhaud had condemned *La valse* in print for its harmonic progressions which at times tended to turn its charming Viennese atmosphere into 'Saint-Saëns for the Ballets russes'.[18] Ravel, it is true, was a great admirer of Saint-Saëns but, coming from Milhaud, the connotations of the phrase were without doubt condemnatory.

The only organization to match the SMI's innovative programming was that headed by Serge Koussevitzky. The Russian double-bass-player-turned-conductor had founded an orchestra in Moscow in 1909 in order to play a predominantly contemporary repertoire, and in 1913 he was the instigator of Debussy's Russian tour. As Harold C. Schönberg has noted: 'In a way, Koussevitzky and Beecham were similar. Both were, at the beginning, inspired dilettantes; both had the money to buy orchestras upon which to learn; both took a long time to develop.'[19] Debussy wrote admiringly of Koussevitzky's 'devotion to music' and, crucially, of the 'exact discipline' he exerted over his orchestra.[20]

Orchestras, conductors, chamber ensembles

Having survived the 1917 revolution, the conductor took over the State Symphony Orchestra until 1920. Then, like many of his compatriots, he left Russia for Paris, and on 22 April 1921 the Concerts symphoniques Koussevitzky gave the first of two concerts, including Prokofiev's *Scythian Suite* and the first performance in France of Rakhmaninov's *Isle of the Dead*. Encouraged by the success of these, he set up a longer series at the Opéra the following winter, on Thursday evenings. Again, recent and contemporary Russian music was a feature, but he also gave the French a lesson in how to conduct both their own music and the classics. Milhaud, reviewing the concerts in *Le courrier musical*, echoed Debussy's remarks of eight years earlier:

> Monsieur Koussevitzky has formed an orchestra from the best
> instrumentalists in Paris and has engaged the most celebrated soloists....
> The first concert was marvellous. We are not used to performances in
> which everything is so meticulously in place, with such minute attention
> to detail, as in Debussy's Nocturnes, in which, even so, I could have
> wished for more abandon.[21]

No doubt Koussevitzky's access to money caused jealousy in some quarters, but Milhaud, as always, rose above such petty sentiments and put his finger squarely on the truth: that there was no substitute for good players (mainly from the Colonne and Lamoureux orchestras), enough rehearsal time and a conductor possessed of authority and taste. He applauded also Koussevitzky's performance of Beethoven's Fifth for its adherence to the markings in the score, turning what was in general a hackneyed piece in the Paris of the time into one that became 'what it was on the day Beethoven finished it, a work of a seething, tormented Romantic youthfulness'.[22] In the context of this praise, Milhaud's reservations over the lack of abandon in the Debussy *Nocturnes* appear rather marginal: his comments about Koussevitzky's 'mise en place méticuleuse', together with Roger Desormière's testimony quoted earlier (p. 44), suggest that abandon was a quality all too prevalent in the main Paris orchestras, and one not always distinguishable from rank indiscipline.

Koussevitzky's financial independence also meant that he felt no need to temper the winds of modernity or unfamiliarity. His programme of 1 December 1921 showed a determination to forgo anything light-hearted, such as *The Flight of the Bumblebee* which had graced his concert of 10 November. After Beethoven's *Egmont* overture, he conducted the first performance of one of Honegger's grittiest scores, *Horace victorieux*, and, to Milhaud's chagrin, Rakhmaninov's Third Piano Concerto with Cortot as soloist. Milhaud did not stay for two further first performances in Paris, of Brahms's *Schicksalslied* and Hugo Wolf's *Der Feuerreiter*, but again Koussevitzky's funding made possible such choral works, which, because of rising union rates, lay increasingly beyond the resources of the mainstream orchestras.

On 15 May 1922, Koussevitzky conducted the first performance of Prokofiev's Third Piano Concerto with the composer as soloist, and on 20 October the first performance of Ravel's orchestration of Mussorgsky's *Tableaux d'une exposition*. In 1923, still at the Opéra, he made room in his programme of 18 October for Stravinsky to conduct the first performance of the Octet for wind instruments, finished five months earlier. The venue may well strike us as unlikely for such a witty piece of chamber music, and Eric Walter White may be right in supposing that

> to some of those who were present, the sight of Stravinsky's insect-
> like gesticulations in front of an intimate group of eight players set
> off by screens must have given the impression they were viewing
> the performance through the wrong end of a telescope.[23]

But here again, Koussevitzky's imagination paid off. Jean Cocteau was reminded by Stravinsky's back view of 'an astronomer working out a magnificent calculation in figures made of silver':[24] Stravinsky himself, more prosaically, remembered that, thanks to the screens, 'the sound was well balanced',[25] while Milhaud in his review of the concert remarked that 'the audience gave the work a warm reception, even though they sometimes smiled during the performance. I've often noticed (without ever knowing why) that audiences always feel like laughing when they hear wind instruments.'[26] If this continued to be so, then Paris must have heard plenty of laughter over the next five years, as Stravinsky continued to subvert nineteenth-century habits, demoting the strings from their traditional dominance over woodwind and brass.

By the autumn of 1923, it had become known that Koussevitzky was to leave Paris to take over the Boston Symphony Orchestra, a post he held for the next twenty-five years. Milhaud was not alone in regretting his departure, but in fact Koussevitzky continued to make at least a little time in his schedule to visit Paris. On Thursday, 8 May 1924, he introduced Honegger's *Pacific 231* with such success that it had to be repeated a week later, followed the Thursday after that by Stravinsky's Concerto for piano and wind with the composer as soloist, and the Monday after that by Prokofiev's 'incantation' *Sept, ils sont sept*.

From here to 1928, Koussevitzky's contributions were fewer in number, but no less interesting, and included Honegger's Piano Concertino (30 May 1925), Alexandre Tansman's First Piano Concerto (27 May 1926), Hindemith's Viola Concerto (bravely programmed on 12 June 1928 against Stravinsky conducting the first performance of *Apollon musagète* at the Théâtre Sarah-Bernhardt) and, two days later, the second act of Prokofiev's opera *L'ange de feu*. After 1928 his commitments in Boston and elsewhere in the world put an end even to these more limited appearances.

If no other concert-giving body matched Koussevitzky's in range, flair and impact, two deserve more than a passing mention. Walter Straram came late to conducting. His first appearance on the Paris musical scene was conducting the staged premiere of Honegger's *Le dit des jeux du monde* at the Théâtre du Vieux-Colombier on 2 December 1918, which was a lively occasion. The composer, writing on Christmas Eve, recorded that

Orchestras, conductors, chamber ensembles

apart from the dress rehearsal in front of the artistic elite of Paris, the performances all gave rise to frightful uproar. There was such a hubbub in the hall of shouting, yelling, whistling and applause that on some evenings you couldn't hear a word of the text or a note of the music. People even came to blows and exchanged cards.[27]

Thereafter Straram took a leaf out of Koussevitzky's book by forming an orchestra from the best players in the four Paris orchestras 'and even from the Paris Opéra orchestra'.[28] From 1923 until his death ten years later, he gave an annual series of ten concerts in the early spring, generally on Thursday evenings. For his venue he chose first the Salle Gaveau, and then the Théâtre des Champs-Elysées, still recognized as offering some of the best acoustics in Paris, but in the 1920s vitiated by uncertain management. Being funded by a rich American lady, Straram, like Koussevitzky, was able to branch out from the traditional repertoire, arrange a lavish number of rehearsals and give a fair number of first Paris performances, including the Prelude to Honegger's incidental music for *The Tempest* (1 May 1923), Berg's Chamber Concerto (6 February 1928) and Marcel Dupré's Symphony in G minor for organ and orchestra (9 May 1929). The programme on 6 February 1928 was typical of Straram's determination not to follow the herd. After Haydn's Symphony no. 97 and Rameau's Second Concert for strings came a suite from *Le marchand des lunettes* by the 29-year-old Marcel Delannoy, and then the Berg Chamber Symphony. This was the cue for another splendid rumpus. Charles Tournemire, reviewing the concert for *Le courrier musical*, regretted that the noise from the audience prevented him drawing any considered conclusions. At one point between movements Straram, with arms folded, shouted 'I shall play Berg's piece to the last bar!' – to no avail. Roussel's *Le festin de l'araignée* brought the concert to a peaceful conclusion at midnight.[29]

In the early 1930s Straram also gave first performances of two works by the young Olivier Messiaen, *Offrandes oubliées* (19 February 1931) and *Hymne au Saint Sacrement* (23 March 1933), while the ultimate seal of approval was set on his orchestra by Toscanini, who used it for his Paris concerts from 1932 onwards. With good reason did the historian René Dumesnil refer on the first page of the preface to his account of these years to the 'jeudis inoubliables de l'orchestre Straram'.[30]

The second orchestra deserving a mention was the Orchestre symphonique de Paris (OSP) which gave its first concert on 19 October 1928; this was to have been in the newly built Salle Pleyel, but a fire that July put the hall out of commission for some months so the OSP used the Théâtre des Champs-Elysées instead. The director of the firm of Pleyel, Gustave Lyon, had the backing of two bankers, the brothers Ménard, and their sister Mme Dubost to form an orchestra based on the Salle Pleyel – and it is possible that the ending of Koussevitzky's Paris concerts in 1928 provided further incentive. Three years earlier, the writer Georges Gromort was lamenting that 'a capital city which, despite everything, has remained one of the refuges of taste and which contains a score of music halls, does not possess a single hall truly dedicated to music': the Salles Gaveau, Pleyel and Erard were all private institutions, with their own agendas to pursue, and both the last two and the beautiful old Salle du Conservatoire were on the small side. The Trocadéro, built for the 1878 Exhibition was, on the other hand, too large with wildly resonant acoustics.[31] It seems that those of the shortly-to-be-incinerated Salle Pleyel were on the generous side too. Monsieur Lyon was always trying to improve them by the latest scientific methods, but he failed to remove the impress of the hall's nicknames: 'le garage Pleyel' and 'la gare de Lyon'!

The directors of these concerts included Ernest Ansermet, Louis Fourestier (fresh from his first prize in the 1925 Prix de Rome) and Alfred Cortot. The opening concert focused rather on Cortot's pianistic skills than on innovative programming – he played the solo part in Franck's *Variations symphoniques* and harpsichord continuo in Bach's Second Brandenburg Concerto – but by the end of the decade the OSP had given first Paris performances of Casella's Partita (3 November 1928), Francesco Malipiero's *Saint-François d'Assise* (15 March 1929), Poulenc's *Concert champêtre* (3 May 1929) and Hindemith's Concerto for Orchestra op. 38 (13 October 1929). Unfortunately, hope to some extent triumphed over experience: with five rehearsals scheduled for each concert, the money began to run out by the spring of 1929 and, although the OSP survived until the Second World War, the initial high standards of performance were not always maintained. But, as always, performances to a large extent depended on conductors: Milhaud wrote to his friend Paul Collaer on 9 May 1929, after hearing Wanda Landowska in Poulenc's *Concert champêtre* conducted by Monteux, 'the orchestra absolutely on the button. This orchestra is unrecognizable since Ansermet has been sent back to his Swiss pastures.'[32]

Some idea of the total picture of concerts and recitals can be gained from statistics for the 1927/28 season published in *Le courrier musical* on 15 July 1928 (still today, 14 July marks the end of summer activity in Paris until the *rentrée* in September). In descending order, the breakdown of concerts included the following:

Orchestral concerts with soloists	267
Piano recitals	223
Chamber concerts	193
Song recitals	115
Orchestral concerts with choir	102
Violin recitals	49
Organ recitals	25
Recitals of old music	25
Unaccompanied choral concerts	24
Dance recitals	21
Cello recitals	17
Mechanical music concerts	9
Guitar recitals	2

Jazz concerts		2	
Cymbalom recital		1	

The total number of concerts that season, incorporating some not listed above, came to 1,419. This compared with only some seven hundred concerts in 1913. After 1929 the number again fell somewhat, standing at 1,009 in 1938/39.[33]

The orchestral concerts in 1927/28 included 133 first Paris performances of works by 105 composers. Those given by the six main orchestras were apportioned as follows:

ORCHESTRA	CHIEF CONDUCTOR(S)	CONCERTS	FIRST PERFS
Conservatoire	Gaubert	41	1
			(Bach's
			Wedding
			Cantata!)
Colonne	Pierné	44	22
Lamoureux	Paray	49	11
Pasdeloup	R-Baton/Wolff	54	28
Straram	Straram	16	13
Koussevitzky	Koussevitzky	4	12

Albert Wolff, associate conductor of the Pasdeloup Orchestra

On these figures, the Conservatoire Concerts would seem to have been well named, at the opposite extreme from those of Koussevitzky, who went out with a bang.

Perhaps the last thing to mention about the Paris orchestral scene is that the seat prices were not exorbitant. In 1922 you could attend a Pasdeloup concert for as little as 2 francs 50 centimes, and the cheapest subscription for the series of twelve concerts, in one of the better seats, was only 54 francs. And in this particular year you also had the added entertainment of the Schoenberg Five Orchestral Pieces scandal.... But the other side of the equation was, as Prokofiev noted, the very low wages paid to orchestral players. Although the unions were active in the early 1920s, their militancy was not long-lived, and in any case players' wages, traditionally low, had not kept pace with inflation: in studying this decade we should continually be aware, as those on fixed incomes certainly were, that food prices, for example, over the whole of France rose from a base of 100 in 1913 to 364 in 1920. After falling in 1921/23, they rose back to 366 in 1924 and then went on up, reaching 568 in 1929.[34]

In 1927 the Concerts Colonne were temporarily under threat because their lease on the Châtelet was running out. The orchestra's conductor, Gabriel Pierné, thought it judicious to publish the facts: in the 1928/29 season, the 48 concerts and 72 rehearsals brought a section leader between 2,000 and 3,600 francs, which was below the union rate (this could be done because the Colonne Orchestra was 'en association'), to be topped up with whatever he (or less often, she) could earn from teaching.[35] (That this was a crowded profession is clear from the list of some five hundred double bass teachers printed in the *Annuaire des artistes* for 1920/21). As points of financial comparison, a 'Stentor' phonograph bought on credit cost at this time 179 francs, a gas-heated bath 400 francs, a moderately priced fur cloak 450 francs and a Maurice Bommer piano (not one of the great names, though guaranteed for fifteen years) 2,800 francs. The July numbers of musical journals were full of what composers, conductors and eminent soloists were plan-ning to take in the way of summer holidays, as were the October numbers of what they had in fact done, but naturally not a word was written of what happened to the rank and file who were deprived by the annual exodus from Paris of any teaching whatever. Both Debussy and Satie at various times complained of the financial desert the capital became in these months.

Philippe Gaubert conducting the Conservatoire Orchestra

As mentioned above, the majority of orchestral players were male, with women figuring in two departments only. In 1924, an amateur orchestra called 'La Pastorale' contained eight women in its string section, while in the professional orchestras the situation was similar: the Pasdeloup in 1927/28 also included eight women (two first violins, three violas, two cellos and

the second harp) out of a total complement of 82, and the Colonne the following year six women (two first violins, one second violin, one viola and both harps) out of 91. Detailed research remains to be done on the role of women in the Paris orchestras, but on this showing it would appear that it was still regarded as unseemly for the fair sex to blow things in public – an embargo harking back possibly to the ancient Greeks, among whom the fashion-conscious Alcibiades condemned flute-playing as 'an activity fit only for the lower classes and slaves'.[36]

The overall picture of concert life is, then, one of various dualities. Against the standard fare offered by the Conservatoire Concerts and, to some degree, the other three main concert-giving bodies and the SNM, were set the more adventurous policies of Koussevitzky and Straram who relied on private money; while both these men together with the SMI catered for music from abroad. For all the complaints of people like Prokofiev, it was relatively easy for general music-lovers to find a niche where they would not be subject to unpleasant surprises (the Pasdeloup Schoenberg scandal must certainly have been exacerbated by those members of the audience who considered it an unpardonable breach of good form to insert such cacophony into a normally reliable milieu). There was also a large number of lower-profile concerts such as the Concerts Rouge and the Concerts Touche, which guaranteed not to offend, because they could not afford to, even though they were pleased to claim on their publicity that they, like the *grands concerts*, were 'subventionnés par l'Etat et la Ville de Paris'. Two programmes for the Concerts Touche, for 3 p.m. and 8.45 p.m. on Sunday 1 February 1925 at 25 boulevard de Strasbourg in the unfashionable 10th arrondissement, illustrate the flavour, and the length, of many others of the type:

3 p.m.	Mozart	Overture, *Die Zauberflöte*
	Franck	*Offertoire* for cello and organ
	Glazunov	Second Serenade
	Beethoven	Pastoral Symphony
	Chausson	*Poème* for violin and orchestra
	Kreisler	*Caprice viennois*
	Schubert	*L'abeille*
	Roussel	*Le festin de l'araignée*
	Saint-Saëns	*Ouverture de fête*
8.45 p.m.	Grieg	March from *Sigurd Jorsalfar*
	Bruneau	Entracte from opera *Messidor*
	Haydn	Symphony no. 85
	Handel	Largo (with violin, organ and orchestra)
	Debussy	*Suite bergamasque*
	Wagner	Overture, *Die Meistersinger*

Beethoven	Romance in F
Chabrier	*Bourrée fantasque*
Saint-Saëns	*Une nuit à Lisbonne*
Rimsky-Korsakov	*Capriccio espagnol*

The violin soloist at the matinée was a Mlle Odette Gogry, who had won a first prize at the Conservatoire the previous summer, and she too was typical of many such prizewinners who, perhaps, preferred to launch their solo careers in the relatively undemanding surroundings of the Concerts Touche and similar bodies, before risking a high-profile appearance with one of the four front-line orchestras.

Nothing in either of the two programmes would have raised eyebrows among the audience. The only two points of interest are the Haydn symphony, in a culture which in general regarded Haydn as 'le musicien aux yeux bleus', lacking either the power of Beethoven or the spirituality of Mozart, and Roussel's ballet score *Le festin de l'araignée*, which allowed listeners to enjoy Impressionistic textures and yet feel that, in experiencing the gruesome events of the scenario (in the course of which the Spider takes mouthfuls out of the Butterfly), they were being modern and unshockable.

As I have already said, Prokofiev's strictures over the amount of music performed in concerts in the 1920s seem, on the surface, to carry considerable weight. But against these strictures are ranged the facts that, on average, the concerts continued through the 1920s and 1930s at well above the prewar frequency; that audiences did go to them; that money was found to run them; and that new works by both traditional and avant-garde composers continued to find at least some place in them. It is possible, therefore, to argue that Parisian concert life was, at some level, a responsive, even a self-regulating mechanism. Did a Zeitgeist develop after the First World War that imperiously demanded feeding in despite of all prudent financial calculations? Had the privations of the war sharpened the Parisians' appetite, for pleasure, for scandal, for novelty, to the point where these were the only things that mattered? And (perhaps the most important question for us today) did more mean, not worse, but better?

Notes

1. Boris Kochno, *Diaghilev and the Ballets Russes*, trans. Adrienne Foulke (New York, 1970), p. 120.
2. Elisabeth Delafon-Bernard, 'Habeneck et la Société des Concerts du Conservatoire: un destin exemplaire', in *Le Conservatoire de Paris, 1795–1995* (Paris, 1996), pp. 97–116.
3. BnF (Bibliothèque nationale de France, Département de la musique), LA (Lettres autographes) Milhaud 4, n.d. (undated).
4. René Brancour, in *Le ménestrel*, 2 January 1920.
5. *Cinquante ans de musique française, 1874–1925*, II, ed. L. Rohozinski (Paris, 1925), p. 274.
6. Dominique Sordet, *Douze chefs d'orchestre* (Paris, 1924), p. 42.
7. Henri Barraud, in conversation with the author.
8. Letter of 31 May 1926, in Paul Collaer, *Correspondance avec des amis musiciens* (Liège, 1996), p. 225.
9. *Le courrier musical*, 15 November 1919.
10. René Dumesnil, *La musique en France entre les deux guerres, 1919–1939* (Geneva, 1946).
11. See Collaer, *Correspondance*, p. 349. Pinocle is a card game for between two and four players.
12. Serge Prokofiev, *Profil de la vie musicale parisienne* (1931–32), pub. in French trans. in Claude Samuel, *Prokofiev* (Paris, 1960), p. 167.
13. Figures from *Le courrier musical*, 15 February 1921.
14. Vincent d'Indy, Henri Duparc, Albert Roussel, *Lettres à Auguste Sérieyx*, ed. M.-L. Sérieyx (Lausanne, 1961), pp. 24–25.
15. Michel Duchesneau, *L'avant-garde musicale et ses sociétés à Paris de 1871 à 1939* (Brussels, 1997), p. 212.
16. Letter to Henry Prunières of 6 December 1927, in *Maurice Ravel. Lettres, écrits, entretiens*, ed. Arbie Orenstein (Paris, 1989), pp. 253–54.
17. Manuel Rosenthal, in conversation with the author.
18. Darius Milhaud, review in *Le courrier musical*, 24 November 1921, p. 345; repr. in *Darius Milhaud. Notes sur la musique*, ed. Jeremy Drake (Paris, 1982), p. 67.
19. Harold C. Schönberg, *The Great Conductors* (London, 1968), p. 305
20. 'Concerts Colonne', *S.I.M.*, 1 January 1914, repr. in *Monsieur Croche et autres écrits*, ed. François Lesure, p. 256.
21. Review of concert of 10 November 1921, in Drake (ed.), *Darius Milhaud*, p. 63.
22. Ibid., p. 64.
23. Eric Walter White, *Stravinsky: The Composer and his Works* (London, 1966; 2nd edn 1979), p. 313.
24. Jean Cocteau, *Le coq et l'arlequin* (Paris, 1979), pp. 110–11.
25. Igor Stravinsky and Robert Craft, *Dialogues and a Diary* (London, 1968), p. 40.
26. See Schönberg, *The Great Conductors*, p. 79.
27. Harry Halbreich, *Arthur Honegger* (Paris, 1992), p. 65.
28. Piero Coppola, *Dix-sept ans de musique à Paris* (Paris/Geneva, 2nd edn 1982), p. 85.
29. *Le courrier musical*, 1 March 1928.
30. See Dumesnil, *La musique en France*, p. 9.
31. See Rohozinski (ed.), *Cinquante ans*, p. vi.
32. Collaer, *Correspondance*, p. 261
33. Theodore Zeldin, *France 1848–1945*, IV, *Taste and Corruption* (Oxford, 1980), p. 140.
34. Alfred Sauvy, *Histoire économique de la France entre les deux guerres* (Paris, 1972), p. 340, table 17.
35. André Coeuroy, *Association artistique des Concerts Colonne* (Paris, 1929), p. 10.
36. Plutarch, *Alcibiades II*, pp. 2–3.

3. The Opéra

THE VEXED QUESTION of how much music-making in Paris was a 'good thing' barely touched the two opera houses, since their schedule was bound by rules that even the iconoclastic spirit of the 1920s fought shy of breaking. To a large extent the relative inflexibility of the operatic scene was born of the buildings in which Parisian opera was given; and since the Opéra and Opéra-Comique were buildings and institutions with quite distinct characters and purposes, it makes sense to look at them separately, at least in the first instance.

The façade of the Opéra with the Métro entrance

If today you come out of the Palais Royal métro station and head north-west, you at once find yourself at the southern end of the avenue de l'Opéra and your eye is inescapably drawn to Charles Garnier's opera house at the northern end of the 1,000-metre-long avenue. Alone of the *grands boulevards*, the avenue de l'Opéra is bereft of trees, so as not to spoil the view. For all the changes – in shop fronts, vehicles and pedestrian costumes – the impact is still surely much the same as when it was opened on 5 January 1875. Quite apart from the building's architecture, the siting itself determines the Opéra as a focus of 1,000 metres of activity in the heart of Paris and as a landmark that is impossible to ignore.

Historically, opera and ballet had always tended towards an elitism funded initially by the court and then by the state. When in 1861 Napoleon III's Minister of State, the comte de Walewski, announced a competition for a new opera house, it was in large part to promote 'the emperor's desire to present himself as a socially liberal ruler with a strong interest in the arts'. At the same time, the brief programme set out for the competitors included the provision of 'an imperial box with its own entrance from a carriage vestibule away from the street'.[1] To these requirements we may add Garnier's own retrospective description of the principles underlying his winning entry:

> if a great dramatic work can be produced on any old stage whatever, on the other hand this work will be in particular demand once large, fine-looking theatres have been erected. To an extent which we should take seriously, the architecture of theatres will stimulate the creation and development of dramatic literature at the same time as directing public taste towards art that is elevated, powerful and of moral influence.[2]

Just as an imperial box was redundant in the 1920s, so the promotion of 'l'art élevé, puissant et moralisateur', matched in concert life by the aims of the increasingly marginalized Société nationale de musique, pulled in a diametrically opposite direction to those of a large majority of postwar artists and, in general, of audiences. French governments of the 1920s might well have had pretensions to being 'socially liberal', but these pretensions extended only sporadically to what could have been termed 'a strong interest in the arts'. Governments, of course, usually have more pressing concerns than the condition of musical life, but the perception of music's status in Paris was not helped by an exchange that travelled at high speed along the musical grapevine in November 1924. Fauré had just died. His friends asked the Arts Minister, François Albert, for the composer to be given a state funeral. The request was eventually granted, but not before Albert had initially responded with the words 'Fauré? Who's he?'[3]

Like any opera house, the Palais Garnier (or the Académie nationale de musique, to give it the longest of its three names) had had its share of problems since 1875. In general terms, these could be diagnosed as repertorial, socio-political and financial.

The ideal, as always, was to find new operas and ballets that were instant hits. On the ballet front this ideal had been realized with some success, as will be recounted in Chapter 6. But on the operatic front it happened no more often at the Opéra than elsewhere. Between 1875 and 1914 the only new French operas that had drawn the crowds and stayed the course were Reyer's *Sigurd* and Massenet's *Le cid* in 1885 and Massenet's *Thaïs* in 1894. Otherwise the 'new' consisted either of flops (numerous), operas taken over from the Opéra-Comique or other Paris theatres (Gounod's *Roméo et Juliette* in 1888, Saint-Saëns's *Samson et Dalila* in 1892) or of operas from foreign composers (the French premiere of *Aida* in 1880).

There were therefore grounds in the postwar period for saying that the Opéra in the forty years up to 1914 had failed to live up to its socio-political role, which might be described as combining that of Notre-Dame, the Elysée Palace and the Eiffel Tower. In those forty years, the state had supported the Opéra to the tune of 800,000 francs a year, expecting in return some addition to French *gloire*. Understandably, there were arguments as to whether the above tally, together with the canon of Wagner's mature operas, had constituted a fair exchange, particularly since directors of the Opéra, while having to make good any deficit in running costs, also got to keep any profits (which were of course more easily made by a repertoire that played safe with old chestnuts like *La juive* or with operas that had proved themselves abroad). Insofar as French ideas of *la gloire* had contributed to the horrors and losses of the First World War, we might expect the Opéra of the 1920s to be functioning on a different mandate. But before we consider this, we must look at a single personality who, as director, dominated the Opéra from 1914 to 1945.

Jacques Rouché (1862–1957) may not these days be a name to conjure with, but the history of the Opéra in the first half of the twentieth century would have been utterly different without him. For a start, he was rich, belonging to a family of high-class *parfumeurs*. While this may present problems to a modern historian of the Opéra, in that Rouché's secret subsidizing of the house (to an extent that did not please his family)[4] makes financial analysis of the institution difficult, it only serves to underline the point made in the previous chapter, that musical success in Paris thrived on a compound of firm direction and plentiful funding.

Had Rouché merely been rich, his directorship might soon have foundered. But he was also highly intelligent and, on leaving the family business before the First World War, had toured Germany and Russia to learn at first hand of their theatrical innovations: he visited Georg Fuchs in Berlin, the Künstler Theater in Munich, and absorbed the theories of Meyerhold and Stanislavsky in Moscow. In 1910 he published his *L'art théâtral moderne*, urging, among other things, that modern theatrical design should catch up with modern art and that stage directors should 'work to reduce the contrast, often so shocking in our theatres, between the rhythmic objects which are alive on stage and the fictions immovably represented on the backcloths of the decor'. Tellingly, he claimed that 'the greatest effects can be obtained through the smallest *means*', and that 'all art lives by suggestion, and I do not see for a moment why dramatic art should partake of it less than the others'.[5] If this sounds like the manifesto of a turn-of-the-century Symbolist, that is probably what it was: Rouché was an exact contemporary of Debussy. But it boded well for a director of the Opéra in the 1920s, when money for the institution was in even shorter supply than in the previous decades. His interest in lighting may also be seen as particularly relevant at the Opéra whose raked stage, *à l'italienne*, meant that scenery had to be anchored in position. On the other hand, even by the end of the 1920s he had not been able to bring patrons to accept the lowering of the auditorium lights during performances –

in this respect the productions of *Der Ring* and *Parsifal* in 1911 and 1914 remained isolated occasions.

This confluence of intelligence, experience and money gave Rouché the authority he needed in dealing with the politicians who held the purse strings, as well as with conductors, singers, players and (not least in this house) stagehands who had become a byword for militant individualism. He served a three-year apprenticeship from 1911 to 1914 in the Théâtre des Arts in the Batignolles district. Here, in 1912, he staged Roussel's ballet *Le festin de l'araignée* and the ballet version of Ravel's *Ma mère l'oye* and, in 1913, such 'unknown' works as Chabrier's *L'éducation manquée*, Rameau's *Pygmalion* and Monteverdi's *L'incoronazione di Poppea* in the version by d'Indy.

In 1914, just after the outbreak of war, he was appointed to the Opéra on a provisional basis, being confirmed in his post only at the end of hostilities. The house closed on 31 July 1914, the imminent conflict even causing the cancellation that evening of Gounod's *Faust*, and did not reopen until December 1915. For the next three years it operated at less than full capacity, with re-creations of eighteenth-century spectacles and concerts in aid of the war effort. But even in wartime Rouché showed that he was not going to be hamstrung by tradition: the 1916/17 season opened with the one completed act of Chabrier's opera *Briséis*, conducted by Chevillard, and on 10 January 1917 a ballet called *Les abeilles* was given, based on Stravinsky's *Scherzo fantastique*.

Rouché waited until after the war and the confirmation of his appointment before committing his first truly revolutionary act. Diaghilev's right-hand woman Misia Sert remembered it some thirty years later in her autobiography:

In those days [the turn of the century] I had one of those lovely boxes at the Opera that were situated on the stage itself. They were removed after the 1914–18 war, when there was some vague idea of modernising the stage, and they are a great loss, for nothing could have been lovelier or more decorative than those small balconies of red velvet, overhanging the stage to right and left, with women in evening dress leaning gracefully over the performance. Each box had a kind of little boudoir at the back, with a few velvet chairs and some mirrors. Here actors and friends would

come in the intervals to drink champagne. It was also a refuge from
boredom: if the performance was poor, one could retire there for a
quiet talk.[6]

Rouché was still alive when Misia's autobiography was published in 1950 and must
have been amused to find his innovations of thirty years earlier dismissed as 'some
vague idea of modernising the stage'. But Misia's comment shows how hard social
habits died in hierarchical, style-conscious Paris society, and that Garnier had been
all too successful in meeting that part of his brief demanding that the audience
should be able not only to see but to be seen: it is worth noting that the space taken
up in the Opéra by landings, staircases, vestibules and foyers is equal to that of the
auditorium itself. It was, too, the same Misia who, when the Ballets russes were
forced to emigrate from the central Parisian theatres to the unfashionable Gaîté-
Lyrique in 1921, looked round the packed auditorium and exclaimed: 'But there's
nobody here!'[7]

Another problem Rouché inherited was the privileged status of the abonnés des trois
soirs, the subscribers to both Monday, Wednesday and Friday performances, perhaps
most vividly recorded as the gentlemen in top hats and tails we see in Degas's paintings. It was possible to buy tickets by letter or phone for most of the house, while all
seats on the fourth level and the boxes on the fifth were sold only at the ticket office;
but the baignoires (side-stalls) and premières loges (lowest boxes all around) were almost
all taken by the abonnés. In 1920, boxes on the fourth and fifth levels cost 6 francs,
while any of the baignoires and premières loges not taken by abonnés cost 30 francs (by
1927 these had risen to between 51 and 61 francs respectively).

The abonnés paid handsomely for their privileges, but since these included the
right to come backstage actually during performances it is not surprising to find
Rouché in 1928, a full ten years after the confirmation of his directorship, still trying
to remedy what he regarded as an abuse of their status, and noting 'that the large
number of spectators standing onstage during performances...has always surprised
directors and artists from abroad, as well as music-lovers'.[8] Not that love of music was
the prime motive for the peregrinations of many abonnés, who were more interested
in the charms of young chanteuses and danseuses. In fact, Rouché never succeeded in
ousting them, so strong and so rich was the network of abonnés, composed mainly of
bankers and businessmen, with a smaller proportion from the liberal professions
such as doctors and lawyers, and a much smaller one of professors and teachers.
There was also a highly influential minority of aristocrats whose abonnements had been
handed down within the family for generations: they remained at the top of the heap
while the regulator appointed by the committee of abonnés, the marqueur de places, disposed of seats among the lower orders. As Rouché noted, the marqueur 'prided himself
on knowing how to apply certain laws of hierarchy or long standing membership.
The abonné began by being placed at the side of the house and ended up in the
centre.' It may have been in an attempt to outflank this group that in 1922 Rouché

instituted a new *abonnement de quinzaine*. This offered the possessors seats in the orchestra stalls and balcony, not the boxes, and ran for eight months between October and June, operating every other week on just one of the three *abonnement* evenings. By some virtuosic scheduling, Rouché was able to present these *abonnés de quinzaine* with sixteen different operas on the maximum of sixteen evenings.

Given that Rouché had to please not only the powerful and inflexible clique of the *abonnés des trois soirs* but also the government and his own financial backers (even he was not rich enough to supply what was lacking from the first two sources), we may well wonder that he made any sort of mark at all. All directors since 1875 had suffered from the mixed funding of the house, and in particular from governments who refused to increase the annual subvention but felt they had a right nonetheless to complain when the repertoire was not to their liking or when a production was thought to be below an acceptable standard. Directors had in any case to obey the rulings prescribed by the *cahier des charges* which governed, among other things, the seat prices and the requirement to stage operas by composers who had won the Prix de Rome (although in the event this last clause was largely circumvented, leaving a number of disappointed middle-aged also-rans).

In addition, Rouché was faced with strikes of the Opéra personnel over wages in the autumn of 1918 and again in those of 1919 and 1920. In October 1920 a group of theatres, not including the Opéra or the Opéra-Comique, gave into the union demands, putting pressure on those two theatres to follow suit. The sums agreed are

worth recording and should be viewed in the light of the inflationary indices mentioned in the Introduction (see p. 10). An article in *Le ménestrel* of 8 October 1920 states that, as a result of the successful claims,

artists engaged for specific productions will get 30 francs per performance for both evenings and matinées; artists engaged annually will get 650 francs a month, with an extra 20 francs for each matinée on Sundays and holidays and 15 francs for matinées on Thursdays and other days.... The directors did not accept clause no. 1 which demands that they should employ only union members. Agitation persists at the Opéra among the chorus and the dance troupe. But a new conflict seems likely to break out with the dressers, both male and female. It seems these are still required even and especially when, as in our music-halls, the women are practically naked.

Rouché duly put pressure on the government and the subvention was almost doubled that November from 800,000 to 1,550,000 francs. This might seem generous, but Rouché's application contained detailed figures to show that even this increase would not keep pace with inflation: dancers' shoes, which in 1914 cost 929 francs per month, now cost 6,770; while the cost of heating the Opéra had risen from 49,000 francs per month to 249,000. As a result, during the period from 1 January to 30 September 1920, despite gross receipts of 5,024,316 francs 55 centimes, the deficit amounted to 1,358,211 francs.[9] The average cost of each production was 33,000 francs, with average receipts of 27–28,000 francs.[10] The general secretary of the Opéra, Louis Laloy, made the further points that out of the 9,000,000 francs annual gross receipts, the house had to find 1,440,000 francs (16 per cent) in tax, including 10 per cent for the *droits des pauvres* (charitable but mandatory donations to the poor) and 6 per cent for a new tax imposed since 1918; and that, because orchestra and chorus were paid so badly, they were forced to play in concerts and sing in churches, so that opera matinées were not possible.[11] The Palais Garnier added further to its own expenditure by continuing to employ not one but two understudies for every role. Cancellation of an opera, on the other hand, was not only costly but bad for the image of the city's premier musical theatre.

The increase in government subsidy meant that Rouché could at least now settle the strike. The settlement gave orchestral leaders 12,500 francs a year and rank and file 10,500, with an additional 15 francs for each rehearsal, in return for which they were expected to play for 260 performances per annum. They were also given the right to put the magic phrase 'de l'Opéra' after their name. Salary for chorus members rose to 10,000 francs a year and for dancers to anything from 6,500 to 11,000 francs. At the same time, pay for professors at the Conservatoire rose to only 6,000 francs a year, allowing *Le courrier musical* to make the point that 'even the least elastic dancer gets more than MM. Widor, Vidal, Gedalge, Cortot and other Conservatoire professors'.[12] Whatever one thinks of the comparison, there were to be no more strikes at the Opéra until 1949.

Despite all the forces tending to preserve the Opéra as a bastion of conservatism, the standard repertoire in the 1920s differed quite markedly from that of forty years earlier when Debussy had been finishing his Conservatoire studies. In the 1880s, it had consisted of some eleven operas: *Robert le diable*, *Les huguenots*, *Le prophète* and *L'africaine* by Meyerbeer, Halévy's *La juive*, Donizetti's *La favorite*, Mozart's *Don Giovanni*, Weber's *Der Freischütz*, Rossini's *Guillaume Tell*, Gounod's *Faust* and Ambroise Thomas's *Hamlet*. Three of the four Meyerbeer operas vanished before the war, with just *Les huguenots*

An *abonné* of the Opéra

having a run of fourteen performances in 1920. *La juive*, still being produced in 1893, then underwent a forty-year silence until 1933, when it was revived with Paul Franz as Eléazar, and *La favorite* reached its two hundred and fiftieth performance at the Opéra in 1918. But only the last five on the above list remained in the repertoire in the 1920s, boosted by four 'newcomers': Saint-Saëns's *Samson et Dalila* reached its five hundredth performance at the Opéra on 25 February 1922; Berlioz's *La damnation de Faust* its hundredth on 21 March 1924; Massenet's *Hérodiade* its hundredth on 22 February 1926; and his *Thaïs* its four hundredth on 10 October 1927 (*Manon* and *Werther* continued to remain the prerogative of the Opéra-Comique).

This renewal might have seemed a healthier sign if only the most recent of the newcomers, *Thaïs*, written by a composer who died in 1912, had not been premiered as long ago as 1894. Where was the new operatic blood that the Conservatoire, through the Prix de Rome, was supposed to be encouraging? The critics of the time could not know that this dearth was a worldwide problem and that the line of large 'Romantic' operas was soon to come to an end with Puccini's *Turandot*: they blamed more local circumstances, and the caustic tone of many articles makes us realize the extent to which the Opéra stood as a symbol of France's musical and even spiritual health.

One of the more outspoken articles came from André Messager who, as co-director of the house from 1908 to 1914, knew whereof he spoke.[13] He stated baldly that the Opéra was too large and expensive for the financial conditions in which it now found itself: the backcloth, for instance, required 400 square metres of painting (a square with a cricket pitch as each side), and it was impossible to put on a new production of any large work in under six months. (The auditorium held 2,200 people, and when Rouché took over in 1915 he was handed a total of 7,593 keys). Messager also attacked the whole principle of *abonnement*, which he called 'the death of new works'. After the premiere of a new opera, it would regularly be placed for its next eight performances among those offered to the *abonnés*. This may seem an enlightened policy, intended to stimulate interest in new music. The problem, Messager complains, is that when, at the tenth performance, the work is finally offered to an audience paying to see it on its own and not as part of a series, the receipts are seen to drop sharply, everyone grumbles and the work is promptly taken off. Messager goes on to make the crucial point that 'in subsidized theatres, we should do well not to lose sight of the fact that the subsidies are not meant to increase the theatre's profits, but to put on and to *give continuing support to* new works'.

The vetting of the Opéra's use of its subsidy lay in the hands of the Arts Minister, who was occasionally prodded by the more chauvinistic elements in the Chamber of Deputies to be more active on behalf of French composers. Nor was this a recent development. Fifty years earlier, the Opéra had been described in a humorous dictionary as an 'imposing French theatre dedicated by French contributors to the glory of foreign composers'.[14] But since Rouché was putting so much of his own money into the Opéra, clearly any Minister had to tread carefully. However, at the root of the problem lay the undisputed fact (or rather, a fact disputed in the twentieth century only by totalitarian governments) that geniuses are not automatically produced by financial investment, and that, even if they do appear, they may well not be inducible to write the operas that the money men think they ought to write. In the 1920s, Satie and Ravel were cases in point. For one reason and another, Satie chose to channel his energies into writing for ballet, while Ravel's opera *L'enfant et les sortilèges*, with its peculiar brand of intimate lyricism, was clearly destined for the Opéra-Comique rather than the Opéra after its Monte Carlo premiere. When it did finally reach the Opéra, in 1939, in a production by Rouché himself, this was not regarded as a successful move.

On the positive side, though, Rouché probably did as much as was feasible in the way of putting on new French operas. Between the end of the war and the close of the 1928/29 season, the Opéra saw the following twenty world premieres of French operatic works (numbers in brackets indicate numbers of performances before 1962; an asterisk indicates that the opera went on being performed after 1929):

1918/19	Max d'Ollone: *Le retour* (3)
1919/20	d'Indy: *La légende de Saint-Christophe* (19)
1920/21	Gabriel Dupont: *Antar* (40)*
1921/22	Charles Silver: *La mégère apprivoisée* (13)
1922/23	Roussel: *Padmâvatî* (39)*
1923/24	Alfred Bruneau: *Le jardin du paradis* (27)
	Charles Tournemire: *Les dieux sont morts* (5)
1924/25	Widor: *Nerto* (7)
	d'Ollone: *L'arlequin* (14)
	Alexandre Georges: *Miarka* (7)
	Antoine Mariotte: *Esther* (9)
1925/26	André Bloch: *Brocéliande* (11)
	Henri Février: *L'île désenchantée* (7)
1926/27	Léo Sachs: *Les burgraves* (2)
	Philippe Gaubert: *Naïla* (5)
1927/28	Jules Mazellier: *Les matines d'amour* (6)
	Sylvio Lazzari: *La tour de feu* (36)*
1928/29	Canteloube: *Le mas* (8)
	Ibert: *Persée et Andromède* (11)
	Maurice Emmanuel: *Salamine* (8)

A proportion for those operas surviving beyond 1929 of three out of twenty may not seem to show Rouché as overly successful in his choices, let alone the one out of twenty (*Padmâvatî*) that has retained the interest of today's opera-lovers (it was recorded by French EMI in 1988 with Marilyn Horne in the title role). But as I have said, in the 1920s opera was going through a difficult transitional period worldwide.

Most of the successful new operas were by established composers such as Puccini, Busoni and Richard Strauss, or by composers such as Stravinsky, Janáček, Weill and Krenek who, tapping into popular culture, produced works that turned their back on the ceremonious *monde ancien* of grand opera and hence on the Palais Garnier. The production at the Opéra in 1922 of Stravinsky's *Renard* and *Mavra* may be seen as an exception, on the same lines as the performance there of his Octet.

But three of the operas in the above list deserve a closer look: *Padmâvatî*, first of all. Roussel wrote this two-act opera-ballet, inspired by a visit to India in 1909, between 1914 and 1918. Writing to his fellow composer Jean Cras from Brittany on 24 August 1918, Roussel said, 'While I've been here I've finished the orchestration of *Padmâvatî*, the two-act opera-ballet which Rouché asked me for before the war and it will, I hope, be produced once victory has led to peace.'[15]

We can only guess as to Rouché's feelings about the opera he had commissioned, now that the *monde ancien* had been so decisively swept away. Roussel certainly made several requests – unsuccessfully – for a production over the next five years. But in the Opéra prospectus in October 1922 *Padmâvatî* was at last announced for the coming season and Roland-Manuel wrote a laudatory article about the composer in *La revue musicale*, complete with photograph and an extract from the work, to encourage Rouché to stick to his promise – a showing in the prospectus being far from a guarantee of performance.[16]

The very notion of an opera-ballet played on French ideas of pomp and *gloire*. That Roussel was thinking on a large scale can be seen, not only from the score, but from his detailed production notes for the work.[17] In Act I, for example, he demands that 'the part of the stage left free should be *vast* enough [my italics] to allow for the movement of the procession and the action of the ballet, with the escort being strung around the outside of the palace and the houses'.

Rouché's hesitation in staging the work may have been due to worries over the expense as well as the ethos of the work, but equally, to judge from the press notices after the premiere on 1 June 1923, it may have been prompted by the music. 'Monsieur Roussel's new score will no doubt shock our most entrenched traditionalists,' wrote Henry Malherbe in *Le temps* on 6 June 1923, and he was right.[18] The 65-year-old Camille Bellaigue, who twenty years earlier had found in Debussy's *Pelléas et Mélisande* 'germs of decadence and death', now accused *Padmâvatî* of being

> inextricable. The harmonic conflict is part of a series: there is conflict
> between keys, between the words and the notes, as there is between the
> notes themselves. To which we may add the abuse of Indian local colour,
> which is perhaps authentic and certainly monotonous.[19]

The problem was that any composer talented and experienced enough to manipulate such large forces was likely, possibly by 1914 and certainly by 1923, to have evolved a musical language that left the Bellaigues of this world some way behind.

In this sense, Roussel did not so much hark back to the heady, aristocratic days of seventeenth- and eighteenth-century opera-ballet, as attempt to refashion the form in a modern idiom and to prove that *la gloire*, even with an Indian scenario, was not beyond the scope of the age. It may be worth noting that, after the thirty performances achieved by this initial production, the next nine were given in the season 1946/47, when French morale again needed boosting.

One of the most surprising operas in the list on p. 67, though giving an interesting clue as to the temper of the times, is Ibert's short two-act opera *Persée et Andromède*. Such a return to Apollinaire's scorned *monde ancien* may seem curious from a composer perhaps best known for his riotous *Divertissement*, but this is far from being a conventional retelling of the legend, taken as it is from Jules Laforgue's *Moralités légendaires*. Although these had originally been published as long ago as 1887, their mordant, satirical tone chimed well with the 1920s attitude to classical culture. In *Persée et Andromède*, Andromeda is in danger not so much from starvation or exposure to the elements as from sheer boredom. She asks the Dragon (who is by far the most sympathetic character): 'Can't you take me on your back and transport me to countries where there's some society?' In the Opéra performance, this was given extra edge not only by Ibert's sparkling and witty music and by a matching libretto from his brother-in-law (signing himself Nino), but by the fact that the role of Andromeda was taken by the young and beautiful Belgian soprano Fanny Heldy, who was much feted and ended up marrying a millionaire. The overall effect is of such mid-nineteenth-century *opéras comiques* as Victor Massé's *Galathée* and Gounod's *Philémon et Baucis*, or even of Offenbach's *La belle Hélène* and *Orphée aux enfers*.

The programming of *Persée et Andromède* suggests that ten years in the job had not blunted Rouché's sense of humour or his determination to keep trying new things. Nor, for that matter, had they changed the views of diehards among the *abonnés*: when Rouché in this same year (1929) asked them to send in a list of their ten favourite operas, one reply ran: 'I'd rather hear *Faust* a hundred times than any modern work twice. You must realize, we come to the opera to amuse ourselves and see our friends.'[20]

In the face of such intransigence, Rouché no doubt shrugged his shoulders and reminded himself that the subscriber in question still seemed prepared to pay for his *abonnement*, and that as long as this was the case, the treatment of the Opéra as a social centre left him freer to experiment than he might otherwise have been. (He was, incidentally, left freer still by those gentlemen whose only involvement with productions was to enter the foyer to buy a programme to take home to their wives, thus providing a clear evening to enjoy themselves elsewhere).

In the years of Rouché's directorship until 1929, few innovations aroused as much interest as his plans for Sylvio Lazzari's opera *La tour de feu* in January 1928. This was the first time that film effects were used on the operatic stage. The hero of the story, Yves, is a lighthouse keeper and in the final act he sets fire to the lighthouse and perishes in the flames. For Rouché, this was a splendid opportunity to extend his interest

in lighting effects. The Opéra dossier on the production records that the cinematog-
rapher, Germaine Dulac, had to go to Biarritz, Dieppe and St Malo, before she finally
found some suitably stormy water off Cherbourg. She delivered her film
in December 1927, only a month or so before the production, and
Rouché admitted that balancing the film, projected on to the
lower part of the backcloth, with the live action was not easy.[21]
Obviously he was not prepared to say in an official record that
Georges Thill, who sang the role of Yves, was one of those
tenors who preferred just to stand and sing.... Critics differed as
to whether the cinematic projection appeared more or less real
than the decor that surrounded it, but in general the idea was
thought to be ingenious.

Having spent over 10,000 francs on the filming, and having been unable
to persuade Gaumont, who owned the rights, to make a commercial film of the
piece, Rouché revived the opera in 1933 and again in 1939. By the 1930s, film was
recognized as being around for good. But it is worth mentioning that in 1925 Rouché
had had to ask permission of the Arts Minister to show film at all in a subsidized
opera house, such was the fear of this new medium and its capacity to draw audiences
away from concerts and operas. The Minister allowed him a 'super-production ciné-
matographique' once a year for a period of five years, 'on condition that it be
accompanied by an important, unpublished score'.[22] The first of these, *Salammbô*,
with music by Florent Schmitt, was shown at the Opéra on 15 October 1925.

Apart from the standard operas and the new French works described above, the
remainder of the Palais Garnier's repertoire in the 1920s was made up of operas
imported either from the Opéra-Comique or from abroad. The Opéra-Comique
yielded the following (dates of Opéra-Comique premieres in brackets, followed by
principal singers in the Opéra productions):

1918/19   Saint-Saëns: *Hélène* (1905) – Franz
1921/22   Ravel: *L'heure espagnole* (1911) – Heldy
1922/23   Rabaud: *La fille de Roland* (1904) – Lubin, Franz
           Massenet: *Grisélidis* (1901)
1923/24   Massenet: *Esclarmonde* (1889) – Heldy
1927/28   Rabaud: *Mârouf* (1914) – Thill, Journet

Three points can be deduced from this. Firstly, Rouché made no attempt to 'poach'
the Opéra-Comique's standbys, *Manon*, *Werther*, and *Carmen* (which did not enter the
Opéra repertoire until 1959). Secondly, after 1924 he seems more or less to have
exhausted the stock of transferable works. And thirdly, he was mostly careful to give
his casts strong leads: the sopranos Fanny Heldy and Germaine Lubin, the tenors
Paul Franz and Georges Thill, and the bass-baritone Marcel Journet.

In any case, this transference was far from being universally welcomed. As we shall

see in Chapter 4, there was considerable anxiety among the critics of
the time over the state of French singing, with the Opéra-Comique being
regarded as a vital home for a particular kind of intimate French opera.
The fears were that, with the Opéra
abstracting large parts of the smaller
house's staple fare, audiences would
come to prefer these operas in their
'inflated' versions and the Opéra-
Comique would be driven into an
even more restricted repertoire.
Transference of works in the other
direction during the 1920s was
limited in number to three, including
Tristan und Isolde (see below, p. 76).
Rouché's reason for supplying the
transferrals with star leads may just
have been a matter of suiting voices
to roles, but he must also certainly
have seen this as covering his back
by helping to validate these operas'
appearances on a larger stage.

No such problems, of course, attached to importing operas from abroad. The
Palais Garnier had a long history of putting on the world's best operas, always in
French, though it could never have been accused of doing so with unseemly haste: as
well as the Wagner operas already mentioned, *Rigoletto* was produced in 1885, *Otello*
in 1894, *I pagliacci* in 1902, Strauss's *Salome* in 1910 – all at least five years after their
world premieres and, in the case of *Rigoletto*, thirty-four years.

Rouché, like any Opéra director, had to balance the claims of cosmopolitan with
those of chauvinist opera-lovers. In the period 1918–29, he introduced the following
eight foreign works:

1919/20	Malipiero: *Sette canzoni*
1921/22	Verdi: *Falstaff*
1922/23	Mozart: *Die Zauberflöte*
	Mussorgsky: *Khovanshchina*
1925/26	Puccini: *Tosca* (one gala performance)
1926/27	Verdi: *La traviata*
	Strauss: *Der Rosenkavalier*
1927/28	Puccini: *Turandot*

Of these, some again were borrowed from the Opéra-Comique. *Falstaff* had first been given at the smaller house in 1894, *Die Zauberflöte* in 1879 (though 128 performances had previously been given at the Opéra up until 1827 of a four-act version called *Les mystères d'Isis*, including music by Haydn), *Tosca* in 1903 and *La traviata* in 1886. Only the remaining four (*Sette canzoni*, *Khovanshchina*, *Der Rosenkavalier* and *Turandot*) therefore really qualified as novelties.

Rouché's boldest choice by some way was Gian Francesco Malipiero's *Sette canzoni*, the central panel of a triptych *L'Orfeide* first produced in its entirety in Düsseldorf in 1925. It had its Opéra premiere on 10 July 1920 and proceeded to stir up an extraordinary hubbub among the critics, mostly asking why Rouché had chosen this foreign work rather than one by a French composer (conveniently forgetting that he had done precisely that with d'Indy's *La légende de Saint-Christophe*, premiered a month earlier). Nor could Rouché claim that he had not been warned: the 1 April number of *Le courrier musical* had cited the example of the Théâtre de la Monnaie in Brussels 'which, during the last four months of this season, has not programmed a single Italian work by those well-known *verismo* practitioners but only French ones. [Rabaud's] *Mârouf* has now passed its fiftieth performance'.

In the magazine *Comoedia* of 14 July, a dignified letter from Malipiero to Rouché was printed, saying: 'I expected my work to be discussed, but I see that objections to my nationality have entered into the debate. In these conditions, I feel the production of *Sette canzoni* is inopportune at the present moment.'[23] But as so often with the Paris press, this was far from being the whole story. The composer's letter was in fact written by Rouché himself. A letter of 18 July, really written by Malipiero to G. M. Gatti, spells out in detail the true train of events, starting with the first night:

> The Paris public listened religiously from the first to the last note. When, following the usual custom, it was announced that the opera that had just had the honour of being performed was by the Italian composer Gian Francesco Malipiero, a certain Lalou, who has in his drawer sixteen unperformed operas, began to shout out 'Vive la France! Et les compositeurs français?' The reaction was whistles and then seven curtain calls for the artists....
> On Monday I went to see [Rouché] to fix the rehearsals for the chorus who had sung so badly.... Then Rouché told me that Bruneau, Lalou and le Borne had organized a scandal for the second performance on the Friday and that no fewer than two hundred people were to whistle, preventing my opera from being performed. The whole demonstration was directed against Rouché, who was blamed for favouring foreigners: I was the fifth foreigner favoured by him.... The scandal compromised the availability of the subsidy, which was being secretly discussed at that time, not to mention Rouché's position as director. He proposed that I should withdraw the work.[24]

It was indeed taken off immediately (an indisposition of one of the leading singers was diplomatically announced) and, although Rouché gave a verbal undertaking that he would mount it later in the season, it has never been staged at the Palais Garnier since. Instead, Parisians had a chance to see it at the Théâtre des Mathurins, conducted by Robert Siohan, in May 1925, nearly six months before the premiere of the whole trilogy in Düsseldorf. If, as Malipiero says, he was the 'fifth foreigner' favoured by Rouché, it must remain a matter of guesswork to identify the other four. But the whole of May and the first few days of June had been given up to the twelfth season of the Ballets russes, including the premieres of *Pulcinella* and of Respighi's orchestrations of Cimarosa entitled *Astuzie femminili*, so perhaps 'four' was a notional figure to indicate general chauvinist discontent. Let us hope this did not extend to the performance of *Aida* on 5 May with Claudia Muzio in the title role....

The Paris musical press responded with a resounding silence about the whole affair. But if Malipiero is to be believed, seven curtain calls for the artists sound suspiciously like enthusiasm on the part of the audience. Certainly there was nothing in the music to confound them, beyond a few fleeting moments of bitonality. But the storyline was a quite different matter – the link between the seven short sections of the opera (it lasts only three-quarters of an hour) is highly symbolic and, one might have thought, not to be readily grasped by any audience which, like that of the Opéra, had been brought up on good, meaty plots; nor had Rouché improved matters by scheduling *Sette canzoni* at the end of an evening otherwise devoted to *Rigoletto*. We might have expected the audience to be mystified by a scene like the sixth, 'Le sonneur de cloches', in which 'a bellringer, ringing a peal of bells, sings a cheerful song and does not seem to worry about the terrible fire that is raging in the city. When he stops ringing and his song is finished, the fire too has been quelled'; or to object to words like those in which the bellringer's song describes an amorous old woman: 'She smells of tanned leather or of dead dog or of the vulture's nest...she's always got a drop hanging from her nose, she smells of mash and suet.'[25] The press and a pressure group combined can now be seen to have overpowered any true appreciation there might have been of the opera's qualities.

It is understandable that after this embarrassing and expensive débâcle, Rouché should have drawn in his horns somewhat. Neither *Khovanshchina*, for which Diaghilev's production of *Boris Godunov* paved the way, nor *Der Rosenkavalier* nor *Turandot* was in any sense a brave

The soprano Germaine Lubin as the Marschallin in *Der Rosenkavalier* (1927)

choice: by the time *Der Rosenkavalier* reached the Opéra stage in February 1927, it had already been given in twenty-eight other European centres (including Birmingham) since its premiere in 1911, while *Turandot*, just in the two years between its Milan premiere in April 1926 and the Opéra production of April 1928, had already been given in fifteen centres.

The greatest loss to the Opéra, and to French musical life, brought about by the influence of the chauvinists, was perhaps Rouché's failure to put on Berg's *Wozzeck*. By 1932, seven years after its Berlin premiere, this seminal twentieth-century opera had reached Leningrad, Vienna, Brussels, Amsterdam and Philadelphia; patrons of the Palais Garnier were not to see it until 1963. Pierre Boulez conducted, and it says everything about the reactionary forces Rouché had to battle against that, on this occasion, 'Boulez was the first to demand, and indeed to get his way in demanding that the players present at rehearsals should be the same ones who played for the performances.'[26] It is perhaps to Rouché's credit that he did not attempt a performance of such a complex opera with irregularly floating personnel.

The only other category of performance given at the Palais Garnier was that by two touring opera companies. In February and March 1926 the Opera of The Hague brought three operas, *Fidelio, Beatrice* by Guillaume Landré (recently premiered in The Hague) and *Tristan und Isolde*. The rehabilitation of Wagner in postwar Paris had been slow. In the summer of 1920, Rouché had asked the Ministre de l'Instruction Publique, Monsieur Honnorat, whether Wagner might be allowed back on to the Opéra stage, and was refused permission.[27] But Wagner's return was clearly only a matter of time, since Paul le Flem, reviewing a Pasdeloup concert on 23 November 1919, had been able to write that 'Wagner makes a new appearance with the Prelude to *Parsifal*, not heard since the war.... Not a concert takes place that does not make a point of restoring him to his place of honour.'[28]

Honnorat was duly persuaded in the autumn of 1920 that Wagner was not a serious threat to the moral health of France, and on 5 January 1921 the Opéra staged *Die Walküre*, conducted by the veteran Camille Chevillard, with Germaine Lubin as Sieglinde and Paul Franz as Siegmund. The house was packed, the average receipts of 27–28,000 francs rising to 36,000.[29] *Siegfried* followed in March, providing support for Milhaud who, on 15 June 1921, was moved to review a Pasdeloup concert in an article notoriously entitled 'A bas Wagner' because 'it was Wagner every Sunday. Apart from some of his overtures, Wagner's music should never be played in the concert hall.' The article 'provoked a regular scandal. I received letters of remonstrance and insult, even anonymous ones.'[30] It also had no effect whatever on the number of Wagner extracts played at concerts: in the 1922/23 concert season Wagner appeared 334 times, Beethoven trailing in second place with 139.[31]

The Wagner revival at the Opéra continued on 17 May 1922 in the form of *Lohengrin*, with Franz in the title role, Heldy as Elsa and with Chevillard appearing for the

last-but-one time in the Opéra pit: his final appearance was to be in *Die Meistersinger* in March 1923, a couple of months before his death. Interestingly, though, the first postwar production of *Tristan und Isolde* in Paris was given, not at the Opéra, but at the Opéra-Comique in a run of eleven performances beginning on 26 May 1925, conducted by D.-E. Inghelbrecht with Suzanne Balguerie as Isolde. This production was then revived in May 1926, a couple of months after the one by The Hague Opera at the Palais Garnier, but there was still no sign of Rouché mounting the work.

Then, in the week of 6–13 May 1928, Rouché pulled off the coup of getting the Vienna Opera to come to the Palais Garnier to perform a series of six operas: *Fidelio*, *Don Giovanni*, *Le nozze di Figaro*, *La serva padrona*, *Die Entführung*…and *Tristan und Isolde*. It was not until 28 February 1930 that he organized the first home-grown *Tristan* at the Opéra since the war, with Franz as Tristan and Lubin as Isolde. Did Rouché perhaps regard *Tristan* as the most dangerous and subversive of Wagner operas, one liable to cause fits among the more patriotic *abonnés*? More realistically, Lubin may not have felt ready until 1930, when she was rising forty, to take on this most arduous of soprano roles. And, as with *Wozzeck*, Rouché may have been prepared to wait rather than risk endangering a masterpiece. If we can indeed add patience to his other gifts of imagination, experience and a ready purse, then he must surely come high on anyone's list of the best twentieth-century opera house directors.

Notes

1. Christopher Curtis Mead, *Charles Garnier's Paris Opéra* (New York, 1991), pp. 59, 60.

2. Charles Garnier, *Le théâtre* (Paris, 1871; repr. Arles, 1990), pp. 53–54.

3. Jean-Michel Nectoux, *Gabriel Fauré. A Musical Life*, trans. Roger Nichols (Cambridge, 1991), p. 467.

4. Mme Poiré-Gaubert, in conversation with the author.

5. Jacques Rouché, *L'art théâtral moderne* (Paris, 1910), pp. 5, 7, 10.

6. *Misia* (Paris, 1950); trans. Moura Budberg, as *Two or Three Muses* (London, 1953), pp. 79–80.

7. Richard Buckle, *Diaghilev* (London, 1979; repr. 1984), p. 381.

8. Article in *Comoedia* of 30 January 1928, quoted in Frédérique Patureau, *Le palais Garnier dans la société parisienne, 1875–1914* (Liège, 1991), p. 364.

9. *Le ménestrel*, 3 December 1920.

10. *Le courrier musical*, 1 January 1921.

11. Ibid., 1 March 1921.

12. Ibid., 15 November 1920.

13. Ibid., 1 January 1921.

14. Aldo, *Dictionnaire musico-humoristique* (Paris, 1870), p. 5.

15. *Albert Roussel. Lettres et écrits*, ed. Nicole Labelle (Paris, 1987), p. 77.

16. Roland-Manuel, in *La revue musicale*, November 1922, pp. 11–23.

17. Labelle (ed.), *Albert Roussel*, pp. 219–24.

18. For selections from eight notices in the Paris press, see Louis Vuillemin, *Albert Roussel et son oeuvre* (Paris, 1924), pp. 96–98.

19. Camille Bellaigue, in *Revue des deux mondes*, 1 July 1923.

20. Information supplied by Arthur Hoérée.

21. For an explanation of the technical procedure, see *L'illustration*, 21 January 1928, pp. 73–74.

22. *Le courrier musical*, 15 July/1 August 1925.

23. Malipiero to Rouché, in *Comoedia*, 14 July 1920.

24. *Gian Francesco Malipiero: il carteggio con Guido M. Gatti 1914–1972*, ed. Cecilia Palandri (Florence, 1997), pp. 63–64. The Lalou referred to cannot be Louis Laloy, since he was the secretary-general of the Opéra and wrote a favourable article about *Sette canzoni* in *Comoedia* on 12 July.

25. Details from booklet accompanying the recording conducted by Hermann Scherchen (Tahra TAH 190/191). I am grateful to the late Dr John C. G. Waterhouse for bringing this recording and the previous article to my notice.

26. Charles Dupêchez, *Histoire de l'Opéra de Paris* (Paris, 1984), p. 261.

27. *Le ménestrel*, 6 August 1920.

28. Ibid., 15 December 1919.

29. Louis Laloy, *La musique retrouvée* (Geneva, 1946), p. 16.

30. Darius Milhaud, *Ma vie heureuse* (Paris, 1973), p. 97.

31. René Dumesnil, *La musique en France entre les deux guerres, 1919–1939* (Geneva, 1946), p. 18.

4. The Opéra-Comique and other musical theatres

IF IT IS TRUE THAT COMPOSERS like Meyerbeer and Halévy left their imprint on French 'grand' opera, dealing, as Wagner unkindly said, in 'effects without causes', it was nevertheless possible for an outsider like Verdi to write two operas, *Les vêpres siciliennes* and *Don Carlos*, specifically for the Opéra – or three, if we count *Jérusalem*, a revised version of *I lombardi* with the extra ballet music obligatory in this environment.

On the other hand, it never occurred to any director of the Opéra-Comique, officially founded in Year IX of the Revolutionary era (1801) and otherwise known as the Salle Favart, to commission compositional talent from outside France. Not only was there a rich stock of French operas already in the repertoire at that time (such as Monsigny's *Le déserteur*, Grétry's *Zémire et Azor* and *Richard Coeur-de-lion*, and Devienne's *Les visitandines*), but the *opéra comique* genre had, after absorbing Italian influences through men like Duni and Grétry in the late eighteenth century, become essentially national, whereas 'grand' opera remained essentially international. The tone at the Salle Favart was natural and intimate, with dialogue and recitative spoken instead of sung and, in the best examples, with nuances of characterization replacing extravagant scenic effects. It was not until the mid-1890s that the director Léon Carvalho was able to persuade the Société des auteurs to relax their contract with the Opéra-Comique stipulating spoken dialogue and recitative.

Saint-Saëns called operetta 'a daughter of the *opéra comique*, a daughter who went to the bad'. Conversely, we could regard *opéra comique* as the respectable mother of operetta and one who, like respectable mothers throughout the ages, came eventually to seem out of touch with the world around her. As Martin Cooper has written:

> The comedy of Chaucer and Molière draws its strength from the fact that both writers worked within the solid framework – or against the solid background – of a universally accepted moral code; and it was only natural that the Revolution of 1789, which dealt the first serious, overt blow at that moral code, should have brought about also an almost immediate deterioration in the opéra comique...the Second Empire brought to the surface much that had hitherto remained hidden, and the War of 1870 and the Commune destroyed at least in Paris – and the opéra comique has been a specifically Parisian form from its beginnings – the last traces of a universally accepted moral code.[1]

But as with many deep imbalances in human society, the problems with *opéra comique* took some time to work to the surface. An habitué of the 1880s would probably have taken great umbrage at any suggestion that his favourite evening's entertainment was on the slide, and a chronological list of the Opéra-Comique repertoire of the time would have given him reasonable cause (dates in brackets are of entry into the repertoire, followed where relevant by those of the hundredth or further productions):

LIST A

Méhul: *Joseph* (1807; 100/1883)

Nicolo: *Les rendez-vous bourgeois* (1807; 692/1900)

Boïeldieu: *Le nouveau seigneur du village* (1813; 379/1892)

Paer: *Le maître de chapelle* (1821; 437/1900)

Boïeldieu: *La dame blanche* (1825; 1500/1886)

Devienne: *Les visitandines* (1825; 110/1900)

Auber: *Fra diavolo* (1830; 878/1900)

Hérold: *Zampa* (1831; 686/1913)

Hérold: *Le pré aux clercs* (1832; 1500/1891)

Adam: *Le chalet* (1834; 1407/1900)

Auber: *Le domino noir* (1837; 1000/1882)

Donizetti: *La fille du régiment* (1840; 935/1900)

Grétry: *Richard Coeur-de-lion* (1841; 500/1887)

Monsigny: *Le déserteur* (1843; 333/1893)

Thomas: *Le caïd* (1849; 401/1900)

Massé: *Galathée* (1852; 448/1908)

Les noces de Jeannette (1853; 1105/1900)

Meyerbeer: *Le pardon de Ploërmel* (1859; 180/1886)

Pergolesi: *La serva padrona* (1862; 128/1900)

Thomas: *Mignon* (1866; 1000/1894)

Louis-Aimé Maillart: *Les dragons de Villars* (1868; 331/1900)

Mozart: *Le nozze di Figaro* (1872; 174/1886)

Gounod: *Roméo et Juliette* (1873; 391/1887)

Mireille (1874; 333/1901)

Bizet: *Carmen* (1875; 500/1891)

Gounod: *Philémon et Baucis* (1876; 203/1900)

Mozart: *Die Zauberflöte* (1879; 118/1892)

Offenbach: *Les contes d'Hoffmann* (1881; 100/1881)

Delibes: *Lakmé* (1883; 100/1891)

Massenet: *Manon* (1884; 285/1898)

Rossini: *Il barbiere di Siviglia* (1884; 100/1887)

Verdi: *La traviata* (1886; 100/1893)

The Opéra-Comique and other musical theatres

The only six foreign works in this list of thirty-two need little explaining away. Donizetti wrote *La fille du régiment* for the Opéra-Comique and, in the words of one authority, 'it is a tribute to the composer's grasp of the Gallic spirit that this opera became a staple of the French repertoire and that Marie's *cabaletta* in Act II, "Salut à la France!", attained the status of a patriotic song'.[2] Pergolesi's *La serva padrona*, perhaps the most famous of all eighteenth-century *opere buffe*, had done much to influence the development of *opéra comique* in the years after its premiere in 1733, having been staged at the Théâtre-Italien in 1746 and at the Foire St-Germain, one of the Opéra-Comique's predecessors, in 1754. As for Mozart, by the late nineteenth century he was becoming adopted almost as an honorary Frenchman. And just as *Le nozze di Figaro* naturally brought *Il barbiere di Siviglia* in its train, so an audience that was charmed and moved by *Manon* might be expected to react in the same way to *La traviata*.

For anyone trying to analyse the Opéra-Comique's position after the First World War, comparison is again instructive between the above repertoire list (List A) and those for the 1920s (operas in List B are those still current from List A, operas in List C are newly introduced):

LIST B

Adam: *Le chalet* (1,500/1922)

Pergolesi: *La serva padrona* (136/1929)

Thomas: *Mignon* (1,759/1943)

Mozart: *Le nozze di Figaro* (346/1933)

Gounod: *Mireille* (500/1920)

Bizet: *Carmen* (2,000/1930)

Offenbach: *Les contes d'Hoffmann* (500/1927)

Delibes: *Lakmé* (1,000/1931)

Massenet: *Manon* (1,500/1931)

Rossini: *Il barbiere di Siviglia* (379/1924)

Verdi: *La traviata* (265/1938)

LIST C

Lalo: *Le roi d'Ys* (1888; 490/1940)

Messager: *La basoche* (1890; 181/1929)

Mascagni: *Cavalleria rusticana* (1892; 500/1922)

Massenet: *Werther* (1893; 1,000/1928)

   La navarraise (1895; 165/1928)

Gluck: *Orphée* (1896; 221/1929)

Puccini: *La bohème* (1898; 500/1926)

Charpentier: *Louise* (1900; 500/1921)

Debussy: *Pelléas et Mélisande* (1902; 206/1930)

Puccini: *Tosca* (1903; 500/1926)

Massenet: *Le jongleur de Notre-Dame* (1904; 246/1933)

Erlanger: *Aphrodite* (1906; 174/1926)

Puccini: *Madama Butterfly* (1906; 500/1929)

Dukas: *Ariane et Barbe-bleue* (1907; 56/1927)

Leoncavallo: *I pagliacci* (1910; 100/1922)

Rabaud: *Mârouf* (1914; 100/1923)

Fauré: *Pénélope* (1919; 63/1931)

List B shows that, of the eighteen operas in List A premiered before 1860, only one (*Le chalet*) was still in the repertoire in the 1920s, and rather precariously, with forty-seven performances in 1922 and none beyond then. This may surprise some people, since the Opéra-Comique is generally presumed to have been highly conservative, catering as it did for the *petits bourgeois* music-lovers of Paris who knew what they liked and liked what they knew. Clearly, though, the tastes of this audience moved at least partly with the times – it was never a function of Opéra-Comique directors in the nineteenth century to mould public taste, rather to reach an accommodation with it. *Le chalet* aside, the remaining ten operas in List B continue in the world repertoire seventy years later, so we can hardly criticize this accommodating spirit, any more than we

An Opéra-Comique poster of 1920

can the contents of List C, which again boasts a fair proportion of survivors and certainly a more impressive one than the Opéra generated during the same period.

Even so, Martin Cooper's remarks about the destruction of a universally accepted moral code have to be taken seriously, together with Roussel's comments to his wife (see p. 31) about the great gulf that would separate prewar from postwar French music: if what Yeats called 'the ceremony of innocence' had had to fight hard against the tide of the Franco-Prussian War and the Commune, it was finally drowned by the horrors of the First World War. Given that the last work in List C, Fauré's *Pénélope*, despite its Opéra-Comique premiere in 1919, had been finished well before the war in 1912, we can see that this admittedly rich crop was not perpetuated in the years that followed. It remains arguable whether this famine was due merely to a fortuitous lack of good composers in the genre, or whether, as I tend to believe, it marked some crucial shift in French popular perception of what now constituted good or acceptable theatre.

The above lists contain at least four other points of interest. Firstly, we can hardly be amazed to find that operas offering an idealized, glamorized view of military life (*La fille du régiment, Le déserteur, Les dragons de Villars*) went to the wall. Secondly, the Opéra-Comique was surprisingly prompt in taking on works of *verismo*, among which we can class not only four of the five Italian works (excepting *La bohème*), but also *La navarraise* and *Louise*. Thirdly, and in a spirit of complementarity, it still favoured legendary scenarios such as *Le roi d'Ys, Orphée, Le jongleur de Notre-Dame, Aphrodite, Ariane et Barbe-bleue* and *Pénélope*, or those set in a pseudo-historical milieu like *La basoche* and *Mârouf*. And fourthly, it continued the tradition of stories dealing with the love life of ordinary people (*Werther, La bohème*).

All of which leaves the perennially unclassifiable *Pelléas et Mélisande* in isolation. The credit for introducing this opera to the Salle Favart in 1902 must go fairly equally to André Messager, who was impressed by a private performance with Debussy at the piano and who was to conduct the premiere, and to the administrator Albert Carré.

After a disastrous fire that destroyed the second Salle Favart in 1887, with considerable loss of life, the Opéra-Comique played in the old Théâtre-Lyrique and then briefly in the Théâtre du Château d'Eau until a third theatre, still happily standing, was completed on the site of the previous one and inaugurated on 7 December 1898. Carré had been appointed to succeed Carvalho the previous January and soon made it clear that he intended to break with tradition and mount contentious, even experimental operas, instead of aiming for the accommodation previously mentioned: he had already begun with *La bohème* while the troupe was still at the Théâtre-Lyrique. Carré's first directorship lasted until the end of 1913 when he was succeeded by P.-B. Gheusi and the brothers Emile and Vincent Isola. Then in October 1918, Carré replaced Gheusi, with the Isola brothers still looking after the financial side. In 1925 they in turn were replaced by Louis Masson, a Fauré pupil and a conductor, and by Georges Ricou, who had already served in the house under Carré before the war for a seven-year term, with Carré retained as honorary director and 'technical counsellor'. Ricou retired early, in 1931, leaving Masson on his own, but by the end of his term in 1932 Masson had had enough and Gheusi was reappointed.

Immediately after the First World War, the Salle Favart seemed to have survived in fairly good health. In 1920, Carré decided, 'in view of the large and regular attendance...not to suspend performances during July and August. The operas will come from the repertoire'.[3] But as the decade progressed, even the most superficial browse through the musical periodicals brings the reader face to face with 'the crisis at the Opéra-Comique', as relayed by different journalists. Many of their complaints are summed up by René Dumesnil, writing with the benefit of hindsight just after the Second World War:

it has to be said that never had the repertoire been in such need of renewal; however durable and persistent the success of works like *Carmen, Manon, Werther, Il barbiere di Siviglia, Le nozze di Figaro...*, an opera house cannot live by exploiting them alone. Renewing and varying the programme is the only way of attracting music-lovers every evening and of keeping the custom of the *abonnés* whose annual subscription is an important item in the receipts, and clearly one does not do this by putting on the same works every week....

    Everyone agrees that every opera that starts well still has to be supported. There should be no hurry to take it off as soon as receipts start to fall. A national opera house should not live 'by the week'. The directors did have some excuses: the subsidy at that time was ridiculously inadequate and, in the political milieu on which it depended, the national opera houses were regarded as commercial enterprises which should cover their costs – while they are in a sense museums of the sonorous arts, just as the Louvre and the Luxembourg are museums of the plastic ones.[4]

Such complaints were easier to make than to address; and the blunt facts were that in the 1926/27 season, for example, the Opéra-Comique gave 28 performances of *Louise*, 32 of *Madama Butterfly*, 38 of *Manon* and 43 of *Carmen*. It was all very well to plead for a 'renewal' but, as I have already said, this could not be guaranteed just by wishing nor even by spending money, though, as Dumesnil rightly states, the subsidies for the national opera houses were not large enough to encourage directors to take many risks. In any case we may question Dumesnil's claim that *abonnés* hankered after variety, given the answer to Rouché's 1929 Opéra questionnaire (see p. 69). The complaint about the Opéra-Comique living 'by the week' echoes what Messager had to say about new works (see p. 66), but more contentious by some way is Dumesnil's reference to the opera houses as 'museums' (conflicting, too, with his plea for renewal). His citing of the Louvre and the Luxembourg as models suggests that he, at least, wanted the Opéra and the Opéra-Comique to act partly as repositories of a central French repertoire, with the occasional side gallery provided for works by foreigners.

Such chauvinism shows up even more strongly in the chronicles of the 1920s. This is altogether understandable. After the losses of the war, not to mention the mutinies of French troops in 1917, the nation needed to re-establish its identity and in this the arts fulfilled a role barely lower than that of French fashion. The Opéra represented France's public face and it was, as always, to the Palais Garnier that foreign royalty and dignitaries continued to be invited. But for France's validation in her own eyes, the Opéra-Comique was crucial, and the difficulties the house experienced between the wars mirrored to a large degree the difficulties the French now had in deciding what sort of people they were. Touching on this problem of identity, Dumesnil again provides some interesting comments:

Le Petit 🐓 Journal

ADMINISTRATION   15 CENT.   SUPPLÉMENT ILLUSTRÉ   15 CENT.   ABONNEMENTS
6r. RUE LAFAYETTE, 6r.
Les manuscrits ne sont pas rendus   31me Année   —:—   Numéro 1,515   France et Colonies .... 5 fr. ▮ ▮
On s'abonne sans frais
dans tous les bureaux de poste   DIMANCHE 4 JANVIER 1920   Etranger .... 9 fr. 10 fr.

AU TRAVAIL !

« *Point de relâche, point de vaines querelles. La France à refaire. Hâtons-nous !...* »
(Conclusion du discours de M. Clemenceau le jour de rentrée de la Chambre)

While *La dame blanche*, *Le domino noir* and *La fille du régiment* disappeared
from the repertoire, the stage on which, once upon a time, 'everything
used to end up in marriages' turned into one where, every evening round
midnight, there were played out the gloomiest tales, and long gone were
the days of cheerful couplets and wild embracing.[5]

    Dumesnil may have had a point in lamenting that many talented composers delib-
erately turned their back on lightheartedness in pursuit of fame through operas that
were 'heavy and ambitious',[6] and that they would have done better to follow the
'back to Chabrier' movement which also took place in the 1920s and 1930s. But this
was to ignore two vital facts. Firstly, 'not everyone is a Chabrier'.[7] And secondly, by
going 'back' to any style whatever or to any olde-worlde subject matter, a composer,
unless his name was Stravinsky, would almost certainly be contributing to the
museum culture and not forging that link between the opera and real life which had

traditionally enabled the Opéra-Comique audience to identify with events onstage, in a way that the Opéra audience only rarely had.

Martin Cooper's 'universally accepted moral code' no longer existed. Men who had lived through trench warfare may have found sentimental stories in which 'tout finissait par des mariages' all very charming, but can hardly have regarded them as representing the culture they had been fighting for. For all its superficial frivolity and increased speed, life was for many French people a more serious, and expensive, business than before the war, as witness the rise in drug-taking and the fourfold increase in consumption of alcohol over the decade.

Any composer in the 1920s thinking of writing a work for the Opéra-Comique might very reasonably have pondered for just for a few minutes before going on to something else – an operetta, a *chanson* or some music for the silent screen. We have already seen that Fauré's *Pénélope*, completed in 1912 and produced at the Opéra-Comique in 1919, was the last opera to find a secure place in the repertoire during the 1920s: it was given three further runs in the decade, in 1922, 1924 and 1927. A more melancholy statistic is the one for the number of operas premiered at the Opéra-Comique during the decade which failed to reach twenty performances by 1950 – a total of thirty works, ranging in time from Sylvio Lazzari's *Le saute-riot*, premiered on 8 April 1920, to Henri Busser's *La pie borgne*, premiered on 13 November 1929. Carré and his successors certainly tried, whatever the critics and historians have said, but history proved too strong for them, a fact confirmed by a second wave of disappearances, in the wake of the Second World War, of operas which had been strong enough to survive the first, such as Messager's *Fortunio*, given its seventy-seventh and last performance in 1948 – a victim of the Cold War, twelve-note music and American films.

'To work!' Georges Clemenceau's call on the return of the French parliament in January 1920

Two letters from Carré to the Breton composer Guy Ropartz indicate the kind of problems the director felt he had to mention. In 1913 the Opéra-Comique had put on Ropartz's opera *Le pays*, in a run of only eight performances. Carré's letter to Ropartz of 23 March 1923 was presumably written in reply to a grumble from the composer that *Le pays* had still not been revived and that Raoul Laparra's *La habanéra* had been preferred to it. Carré tactfully does not point out that, when *La habanéra* was first produced in 1908, it ran to twenty-four performances instead of a mere eight, contenting himself with the unspecific statement that it had a 'prior claim'; nor did he rub it in that *La habanéra* was currently continuing to draw the crowds. 'Your turn will come,' he wrote to Ropartz, 'and it is certain that we shall be able to revive *Le pays* next season...'.[8] And indeed they did, when it ran for another six performances before disappearing from the repertoire for ever – the only positive factor one can identify being that it was given with exactly the same cast as eleven years earlier, proving that the war had not been the total watershed historians have so often claimed.

Carré's second letter to Ropartz, of 10 May 1925, looks forward to a possible new work from him and puts in a nutshell what the director needed from such a work. Suggesting a libretto based on René Bazin's novel *Donatienne*, Carré went on:

> Would you like to take the opportunity of reaching the wider public, the public that makes for lasting successes? That doesn't prevent one from writing good music, not that you would be able to write anything else – but, as Scribe used to say, it's the libretto that leads to the first performance and the music that leads to the hundredth.[9]

Nothing came of the project.

In theory the Opéra-Comique had the option to renew its repertoire by upgrading successful works from the fields of operetta and elsewhere, by borrowing from the Opéra and by importing works from abroad. Its directors did so, but to a very limited degree. The only instance I know of when they attempted to fill out an 'incomplete' score was in asking Reynaldo Hahn to expand his music for Sacha Guitry's 'comédie musicale' *Mozart*, which had been performed with enormous success in 1925; Guitry and his then wife Yvonne Printemps were to repeat their roles as Mozart and Constanze.[10] But no more was heard of this idea.

On 18 March 1925 the directors put on Jules Mazellier's *Graziella*, of which the second act only had been performed at the Opéra in 1916; and a year later, on 20 May 1926, they produced Alfred Bachelet's *Scèmo*, previously given six performances at the Opéra in the summer of 1914. Lasting for nine and seven performances respectively, before they were then definitively dropped, neither work did wonders for the Opéra-Comique's finances. The only significant borrowing from the Opéra, and the only one the Opéra continued to mount after the Opéra-Comique's acquisition of it, was *Tristan und Isolde*, which was revived regularly at the Palais Garnier after the Opéra-Comique's performances in 1925 and 1926 with Suzanne Balguerie as Isolde. Writing of the first night on 26 May 1925, Paul Bertrand justified the work's appearance in this theatre by pointing out that the lack of exterior action fitted the opera well for intimate performance. His regrets were over a few cuts in the music and over the scenery, 'aiming at that kind of anachronistic realism' so much favoured by this particular house.[11] Photographs of Opéra-Comique sets of the 1920s in general confirm this view, suggesting that Carré's taste never really moved on beyond the Jusseaume and Ronsin sets he commissioned for *Pelléas*, which Debussy was already finding old-fashioned before the First World War. Carré's successors Masson and Ricou seem to have been no more imaginative and possibly less competent.

In 1927 Henri Rabaud penned a series of angry letters over the treatment of his opera *Mârouf* which, he complained, had not been staged for a year (not an altogether unreasonable complaint, given that it had reached its hundredth performance at the Opéra-Comique in 1923). Rabaud had lost confidence in the management after that last run, in which 'walk-on characters and woebegone chorus members glumly threw themselves around the stage in a production that was...missing!' He withdrew the work; Masson and Ricou billed it; he refused to reconsider; they took him to court; and, in March 1929, he won his case.[12] Quite apart from the rights of the matter, it says little for the plaintiffs' common sense that they should so thoroughly alienate such an influential person as the director of the Conservatoire. The five imports from abroad during the decade were also much what one would have expected. The only surprise might be *La tisseuse d'orties* by the Swiss composer Gustave Doret (though, having conducted the first performance of *Prélude à l'après-midi d'un faune* in 1894, he presumably counted as an honorary Frenchman). This too lasted for only ten performances. The other four made more telling bids for permanence. On 26 June 1920 André Messager conducted *Così fan tutte*. This opera, which caused such heart-searching to well-meaning opera directors in the nineteenth century, had been through the usual trials, including its first performance in Paris in 1807 under the title of *Le laboureur chinois*! Messager's version, produced by Albert Carré, stayed somewhat closer to Mozart's original and starred the capital's leading coloratura soprano, Gabrielle Ritter-Ciampi, as Fleurdelyse (Fiordiligi), a role she continued to take for the next two revivals in 1924 and 1926.

The next foreign import was of more recent vintage, but hardly more daring: Puccini's *Gianni Schicchi*, first given on 6 November 1922, less than four years after the New York Metropolitan premiere of *Il trittico*, with the great Vanni Marcoux in the title role. It was presented as part of a double bill with the premiere of Alfred Bachelet's *Quand la cloche sonnera*, one of the more successful native scores which was to reach its fifty-sixth performance by 1936. Two newspaper notices of *Gianni Schicchi* may be taken as representing the opposing sides over the Puccini question. Charles Tenroc, although finding the ensemble 'hesitant, without warmth or conviction', liked the work a lot and had nothing but praise for Marcoux in the title role.[13] Gustave Samazeuilh, on the other hand, took the opportunity to deliver himself of a more general swipe at Puccini's music, animadverting on

> the fluttering void of the musical mishmash with which, in this instance, Monsieur Puccini's undeniable stage talents content themselves...better, when all's said and done, this minimum of music than *Tosca's* extravagant swoonings or *Madama Butterfly's* tear-jerking sentimentality.[14]

The two final imports both reached the Opéra-Comique stage in 1928. Falla's *El retablo de maese Pedro* (Master Peter's Puppet Show) had been commissioned by the princesse de Polignac and was first performed in her salon on 25 June 1923. The Don Quichotte of that performance, Hector Dufranne (the original Golaud in Debussy's *Pelléas et Mélisande*), again sang the role in the Opéra-Comique premiere. At the 1923 salon performance the elite audience, including Picasso, Stravinsky, Poulenc, Milhaud, Henri de Régnier and Paul Valéry, had been deprived of an immediate encore of this half-hour piece only because the princesse had failed to invite the performers to the elegant dinner beforehand. This sent them into a concerted fit of pique and they declined to perform again.

Falla had worried then that the intimacy of the opera would be lost, even in the small-scale environment of the Opéra-Comique.[15] In the event, Tenroc agreed with him, feeling that the work would come over better in concert performance. He was also 'afraid that the composer's temperament and talent suit him rather for emotion than for musical entertainment', which suggests that he radically misunderstood the work.[16] Another critic, Jean Chantavoine, also decried Falla for having no sense of humour.[17] Truly, foreign composers had a hard row to hoe.

This production of *El retablo* by Georges Ricou ran for fifteen performances, so it cannot be written off as an outright failure. Indeed, if any Paris theatre was a suitable venue, that theatre was the Salle Favart; although, as the critic Henry Malherbe wrote in 1925, it had weaknesses as well as one important strength:

> To tell the truth, the third Salle Favart, which ought to have been the most modern and best set up of our theatres, offers none of the advantages we might have expected from it. Its façade does not face the boulevards. Its decoration, inside and out, is of a pretentious banality and an embellished ugliness to astonish any artist.... More regrettable still, the stage is very narrow and has no depth. No space is set aside for the scenery which has to be moved to and fro for every performance and every rehearsal. What is more, although the acoustics are excellent in the upper storeys, they are not good in the lower boxes and in certain parts of the orchestra stalls. The orchestra pit itself is neither deep nor large enough.
>
> But all these problems and faults aside, the third Salle Favart is pleasingly proportioned. The public is attracted to the Opéra-Comique both by the highly popular repertoire and by the new, compact setting in which it is possible to stage productions that are more intimately and truly human than in other opera houses.[18]

The lack of space backstage, which was remedied only in the late 1990s, obviously provided some reason at least for the unadventurous realism noted above in productions of the 1920s. But if Malherbe was right, and the house's strength was its provision of 'une humanité plus intime et plus vraie', then we would do well to ask what exactly that phrase meant to him.

For one thing, we have already noted the criticisms levelled against reality when it was presented as gloomy or sordid. The success of *Carmen* must take some of the

blame for this. In 1873 Bizet was held up in his composition of the opera because the management jibbed at the story's promiscuity and violent ending, which they deemed unsuitable for an audience containing a fair number of well-brought-up young girls in search of husbands. But, as we know, the management duly relented. It must be asked whether in the 1920s, after the war experiences of many of the men in the audience (who in those days were the sex paying for the tickets), they still regarded *Carmen* as an exhibition of 'intimate, truthful humanity' or merely of an exotic and hence irrelevant violence redeemed by sublime music.

Even if any answer to this question must of necessity be largely guesswork, the question is still worth asking. One small piece of evidence comes from the reaction to Milhaud's opera *La brebis égarée*, written between 1910 and 1914, but not produced at the Opéra-Comique until December 1923. Henry Malherbe later congratulated the directors, claiming that in mounting *La brebis égarée* they 'gave a fine example of courage and generosity' at a time when 'most new works offered us no more than safe, self-seeking imitations of old scores'.[19] Although the receipts for the run of five performances (above 18,000 francs each after the first night) were well in line with those for *Werther* or *Louise*, the work was not played again in Paris until a recording session in 1960. The reason, it seems, lay not in the music but in the libretto, based on a text by Francis Jammes, which included the reading of a railway timetable ('Page 48...Puyoo 4.53...Puyoo...Puyoo...from Audaux to Puyoo it's a two-hour journey...'), as well as a request to put an umbrella into the umbrella stand, 'otherwise you'll make wet marks on the parquet'. As one reviewer remarked, 'we saw the other evening how hilarity took the place of criticism';[20] and the awful suspicion raises itself that the full houses may have been made up by people coming to the Salle Favart for a good laugh. At any rate, this was clearly not the kind of 'intimate, truthful humanity' the public was looking for.

Another candidate for this role was the last of the foreign operas to be heard at the Opéra-Comique in the 1920s, Smetana's *The Bartered Bride*, as *La fiancée vendue*. We may find it surprising that this opera, 'so full of spontaneous charm',[21] should have taken as long as this to reach a Parisian stage – after its premiere in Prague in 1866, it had been produced in fourteen other centres before the turn of the century, including Vienna, Berlin, Chicago and London. But this 62-year delay only confirms the blind spot in the French musical soul for things Czech: performances of Dvořák's orchestral music were almost unknown in Paris during this decade.

Some of the press articles on the production make amusing reading. From the social point of view, reviewers felt bound to mention that it marked, or at least coincided with, the tenth anniversary of the Czech Republic and that therefore the opening night was attended by the Czech Ambassador and his retinue as well as by *le tout Paris*. But there was no way they could then scotch the impression that, but for this anniversary, *The Bartered Bride* might have had to wait another sixty-two years for a Paris airing. No one was prepared to speculate in print as to why the opera had been neglected; all in all, the best that could be done was to hint (something at which French critics have always been past masters) that really the opera was not quite the earth-shattering masterpiece certain Czech enthusiasts would have everyone believe.

Jean Chantavoine chimed with the general tone in saying that, while Smetana could not be held responsible for the Opéra-Comique chorus singing consistently off the note, he did indulge in formulae and repetition to a considerable extent, and that in bulk these became wearing on the ear. In making this judgment, Chantavoine betrayed his German training and his predilection for Mozart and Beethoven, composers who tended to work their 'formules et redites' cunningly into a symphonic whole. On the other hand he appreciated the work's colour and comic verve, while managing to indicate that its naivety placed it beyond the consideration of serious music-lovers. The opera ran for a highly respectable thirty-three performances, but was not seen again at the Opéra-Comique until after the Second World War.

But out of all the new operas performed there between 1917 and 1929, one now stands head and shoulders above the others and therefore merits not only individual treatment but a look at how it interpreted and developed the Opéra-Comique tradition: Ravel's *fantaisie lyrique*, *L'enfant et les sortilèges*. This project had begun with the librettist, Colette, taking her outline to Jacques Rouché, clearly with the Opéra in mind. Nor was Ravel their first thought as the composer, whatever may have been said with hindsight, since on 14 April 1916 Rouché wrote to Paul Dukas:

> Cher Maître et ami, Colette de Jouvenel has brought me a delightful
> libretto for a ballet-opera. Her wish is to read it to you and you can
> understand what she has in mind; you can also understand how happy
> I am to be the intermediary.[22]

But presumably Dukas was not taken with the idea.

In the event, *L'enfant* was rare in being an opera by a French composer which was premiered outside France, in Monte Carlo in March 1925. Ravel here was following the example of Massenet who, beginning with *Le jongleur de Notre-Dame* in 1902, arranged premieres of five of the operas produced in the last decade of his life to take place in the Monegasque capital, removing them for his peace of mind from the gossip and intrigue of Paris. By the mid-Twenties Ravel was living in the little village of Montfort-l'Amaury, some fifty kilometres south-west of the city, so it seems unlikely that peace of mind played a part in his choice of Monaco for the premiere. But whatever the reason, the production was a success, helped by the conducting of Victor de Sabata and by one of the earliest of Georges Balanchine's choreographies. Not many Paris critics bothered to travel down to it, but one who did and responded to the work enthusiastically was Henry Prunières, the influential editor of *La revue musicale*. His review no doubt helped to prompt Messrs Masson and Ricou, who were to take over the direction of the Opéra-Comique that autumn, to include the work for their first season. It had its Opéra-Comique premiere on 1 February 1926.

In an autobiographical sketch, dictated in 1928, Ravel stated that

> the predominant concern with melody derives naturally from the story,
> which I took the liberty of treating in the spirit of an American operetta.
> Madame Colette's fairy-tale libretto justifies this liberty. The vocal line
> must dominate. The orchestra, though not renouncing virtuosity, is
> nevertheless of secondary importance.[23]

Prunières's review of the Monte Carlo premiere drew attention to this emphasis on the vocal lines, finding them 'much more melodious than in *L'heure espagnole*'. He also noted how much that sounded spontaneous was in fact most carefully crafted: 'to obtain certain special effects, Ravel sometimes uses unexpected scholastic procedures. The Armchair and the Shepherdess sing an inexorably inflexible canon, and at the end the animals intone a celestially suave fugal chorus.'[24]

Ravel's insistence that the orchestra was secondary to the voices was no doubt triggered by André Messager's unsympathetic review of the Paris premiere, in which he claimed that Ravel, turning his back on sensitivity and emotion, seemed intent only

> on bringing to our notice that virtuosity in the orchestra which appears to
> be the main object of his researches. As a virtuoso he is incomparable. No
> one can touch him when it comes to the mixing of timbres, the blending
> of unaccustomed sonorities, the use of instrumental extremes and the
> most paradoxical combinations of harmonies. But don't ask him for
> emotion, still less for tenderness. He refuses to lend himself to what
> he sees as a concession to bourgeois sentimentality.[25]

Admittedly, Messager had a reputation for speaking his mind, but he was certainly no old fogey: in the summer of 1924 he had possibly even imperilled his Légion d'Honneur rosette by agreeing to conduct three distinctly 'modern' ballets: Poulenc's *Les biches*, Auric's *Les fâcheux* and Milhaud's *Le train bleu*. But it would seem that the orchestral virtuosity, which Ravel could not deny, blinded Messager to the emotion and tenderness that the opera undoubtedly contains – and it could well be that the Opéra-Comique orchestra, especially if it had its usual quota of deputies, failed to absorb the technical difficulties into what Messager's hypercritical ear deemed a seamless and stylish performance.

An autograph excerpt from the duet between the Child and the Princess in Act I of Ravel's opera *L'enfant et les sortilèges*

The young Georges Auric had written, in his review of the Monte Carlo premiere, that 'an undeniable poetry rises from the orchestra pit and envelops the characters of the story',[26] which suggests that for him emotion and tenderness did find a place in the work. But as interesting for us as Messager's failure to find these qualities in the Paris performance is his assumption that they were virtues to be expected of any work given at the Opéra-Comique. Of course, they are highly subjective entities. But it is instructive that their absence should have been regretted by the highly intelligent but 72-year-old Messager, whose own career as an Opéra-

Comique composer had begun with *La basoche* as long ago as 1890, whereas the 26-year-old Auric detected the opera's 'poésie' with such force that he now came round to Ravel's side after denigrating him for some years. More than that, Auric detected one of the truly modern elements in Ravel's opera:

> for anyone who has seriously considered the problem of musical theatre, reading a score like this (and especially the first scene) is a highly important event. Its contrasting scenes catch the attention and the ear of the spectator.

This emphasis on the use of contrast was picked up, if negatively, by the critic Emile Vuillermoz in his review of the Paris premiere, when he complained of the unsatisfactory staging, admitting at the same time that it was as ingenious as it could be 'in the present state of theatrical technique, which is several years behind that of the music hall and the cinema'.[27] Shortly after Ravel's death in 1937, his brother Edouard, on seeing Walt Disney's *Snow White*, said: 'This is the way *L'enfant* should be presented.'[28]

Ravel's opera, then, may be seen as a classic example of the mixing of old and new to take the genre forward. The old elements include not only the canon and fugue already mentioned, but the little aria 'Toi, le coeur de la rose', modelled on 'Adieu, notre petite table' in Massenet's *Manon*, and the coloratura showpiece for the Fire 'Arrière! Je rechauffe les bons' which, though brief, is in the tradition of Delibes's *Lakmé*: Fire portrayed as the exotic, dangerous Other.

Among the new elements in the score we find the cinematic use of contrasts, the inclusion of ragtime and *café-concert* music, the virtuoso orchestral writing Messager objected to, birdsong (with a magical role for the swanee whistle) and, of course, the cat duet, going far beyond the discretion of the nineteenth-century example by Berthold (often attributed to Rossini); throughout the run of twenty-one performances in 1926 this never failed to rouse the audience to whistles and catcalls of their own.[29]

But perhaps Ravel's, and the librettist Colette's, most revolutionary act was to change the audience's point of identification. By making the Child the central character, with his love for his mother taking the place of boy-meets-girl interplay, the authors bypassed the traditional template according to which 'tout finissait par des mariages'. They also hinted, through the Child's senseless violence, at a critical position vis-à-vis the recent World War and, providentially, France's current military involvement in Morocco.

Set for Ibert's one-act opera *Angélique*

Here, then, was an *opéra comique* for the times. Its designation as a *fantaisie lyrique* further hinted that a future for the genre might lie in the realm of fantasy and in getting away from the 'anachronistic realism' lamented by Paul Bertrand. Unfortunately, no one during the Salle Favart's troubled times in the late 1920s and 1930s followed up this lead – perhaps, in any case, it needed a Ravel to make it work.

Unfortunately, the true history of the Salle Favart from this point was less elevating. Whatever the real reasons – the motor-car, weekend sport, the radio, the world economic crisis, the salaries demanded by the unions, the insufficient grant from government were all blamed – in the early Thirties the house went into free fall. The nadir was reached at the end of June 1936 when, for a broadcast performance of the *Contes d'Hoffmann*, the curtain rose to reveal the whole company on stage. The orchestra played the Marseillaise, the audience stood up, and a spokesman stepped forward to explain to the whole of France what was going on and demand Gheusi's resignation; after which the company then organized a sit-in for a fortnight until Gheusi obliged.[30] A fourteen-man committee was appointed to manage the house until, at the beginning of 1940, Jacques Rouché took control of both Opéra and Opéra-Comique under the title of the *Réunion des théâtres lyriques nationaux*.

Although the Opéra and the Opéra-Comique together attracted most of the critical interest in musical theatre, no survey would be complete without a look at other operatic venues in Paris. And finally, as a coda to Chapters 3 and 4, I shall note some of the most popular singers in all three areas and attempt a brief description of the character of their art.

I have already said that, as the twentieth century progressed, the Opéra-Comique shed its older repertoire – roughly the first twenty or so operas printed as List A on p. 79. Luckily for those diehard opera buffs who still hankered after such fare, it was taken up, together with a number of operettas, by two minor theatres, the Gaîté-Lyrique, with a capacity of 2,000 seats, and the Trianon-Lyrique with half that number. Their programmes for 1920 and 1921 give a good idea of what they would be providing over the whole decade.

In March 1920 at the Gaîté-Lyrique, Messager added a waltz specially for a new production of *Véronique*, with Jean Périer, in his original role of Florestan; Carré's wife Marguerite sang in Sidney Janes's *The Geisha* and in Lecocq's *La fille de Mme Angot*; and that autumn you could have heard two other old favourites, Offenbach's *La fille du tambour-major* and Planquette's *Les cloches de Corneville*. This repertoire helps explain the surprise of locals in the 10th arrondissement when, as related above, Diaghilev brought Prokofiev's ballet *Chout* to the theatre in May 1921. Indeed, in January of that year even the conservative Messager complained that the Gaîté was only doing seven operetta repeats and had introduced nothing new since October 1919.[31]

The Trianon-Lyrique in Montmartre was, like the Opéra and the Opéra-Comique, a subsidized theatre and as in their case its subsidy brought with it a *cahier des charges* regulating its repertoire, preventing it on the one hand from descending too far in the direction of operetta and on the other from leaning dangerously towards modernism. In the six months between October 1920 and the end of March 1921, its director Louis Masson programmed nine operas, identifiably from the same sources as many of those on List A, even if not identical (the order is that of performance during the 1920/21 season; dates in brackets are of first performance in Paris):

Planquette	*Les cloches de Corneville* (1877)
Pergolesi	*La serva padrona* (1746)
Philidor	*Le maréchal ferrant* (1761)
Boïeldieu	*Ma tante Aurore* (1803)
Dalayrac	*Une heure de mariage* (1804)
Gounod	*Philémon et Baucis* (1860)
Offenbach	*La chanson de Fortunio* (1861)
Audran	*Le grand mogol* (1884)
Cimarosa	*Il matrimonio segreto* (1801)

By the 1927/28 season, the Trianon had moved on to some of the Gaîté's staples, including the two 'daughters' (of Mme Angot and the Drum Major), but had also edged into Opéra-Comique territory with two works by Delibes, *Lakmé* and *La cour du roi Pétaud*. But for those who felt inclined to complain at this restricted repertoire, one signal fact did a certain amount to disarm their complaints, even if they were unaware of it at the time. In Stravinsky's *Chroniques de ma vie*, the composer recalled:

During the winter of 1922/23, I often went to the little theatre called the Trianon-Lyrique, that modest and attractive venue with a long history. Its director, Louis Masson, was a serious musician and an excellent conductor, with a good technique and excellent taste. There he used to present evening entertainments that were unpretentious yet perfectly put together. We should be grateful to him for having the courage to revive works of great musical quality which, alas, have been abandoned by the official theatres as being out-of-date and not attracting mainstream audiences. This attitude of the major theatres is even more distressing because not only do they deny the discriminating musician a source of certain enjoyment, but they let slip the opportunity to educate the masses and direct their taste in a fruitful direction. Personally, I enjoyed those evenings a good deal, especially Cimarosa's *Il matrimonio segreto* and Gounod's *Philémon et Baucis*. Listening to this last opera, I again felt the charm exercised by that very personal aroma given off by Gounod's music. Diaghilev was every bit as much in love with it as I was and it gave us the idea of researching in his output with the hope of finding works that had been forgotten.[32]

They found, as well as *Philémon* itself, *La colombe* and *Le médecin malgré lui*, to which Diaghilev added Chabrier's *L'éducation manquée*, commissioning Auric, Poulenc, Satie and Milhaud respectively to turn the spoken dialogue of these four operas into recitative. All four were given in Monte Carlo over the New Year of 1923/24 (*Philémon* without Auric's recitatives, rejected by Gounod's heirs), but only *L'éducation manquée* came to Paris, for three performances in June, after which Diaghilev dropped it from his repertoire.

It is tempting to think that Stravinsky's exposure to the Trianon-Lyrique's offerings may have been more important than Diaghilev's for 1920s music-making – though here one is dealing with slippery supposition rather than hard evidence. When Stravinsky blames the larger theatres for missing the opportunity to direct their audiences' taste 'in a fruitful direction' ('dans une direction utile'), we have to ask 'utile' for whom? I feel the answer might well be 'for Stravinsky'. It is at least possible to detect in works like the Serenade in A for piano of 1925 and the ballet *Apollon musagète* of 1927/28 the same kind of gently seductive charm and underheated emotion we find in *La colombe* and *Le médecin* – not to mention the wonderfully sly, economical humour of the latter, comparable with Stravinsky's in the Capriccio for piano and wind and the ballet *Jeu de cartes*. But however convincing or otherwise we may find these comparisons, there can be no doubting that the 'direction utile' Stravinsky had in mind was, as with *Pulcinella*, governed by the precept that one way of going forward was to go back; what Constant Lambert a little later was memorably to refer to as Time Travelling[33] (on which, see further on p. 274). I submit that on this front alone the impact of the Trianon-Lyrique may have been disproportionate to the size of its state subsidy or of its audience.

Like other opera houses the world over in those days before jet travel, the lyric theatres of Paris operated on the basis of a strong, permanent staff of singers, some of whom would remain with the house for a quarter of a century or more. The family atmosphere, which in Paris lasted until the early 1960s, allowed for very occasional visits by outside 'stars', as well as for visiting troupes, like the Vienna Opera at the Palais Garnier in 1928, but the great majority of productions were 'home grown'.

All the same, the traditionally individualistic slant of Parisian culture, taking corporate effort for granted and laying emphasis on those who shone, allied with the increasing popularity in those years of the gramophone, led effectively to a star system within the repertory one. Charles Tenroc's criticism of the sloppy ensemble work in the Opéra-Comique's production of *Gianni Schicchi* was one of many such in the 1920s press, none of which seem to have had any startling effect. At the same time, it is not perhaps too late to congratulate the stalwarts, largely unsung by the critics: Marguerite Julliot, for example, who sang 41 roles at the Opéra-Comique between 1902 and 1929; or Madeleine Lalande, who sang 53 at the Opéra between 1921 and 1943; or Emile Rousseau who, in his twenty-eight years at the Opéra-Comique, sang no fewer than 78, beginning with Schaunard in *La bohème* in 1923 and ending with Homais in Emmanuel Bondeville's *Madame Bovary* in 1951, by way of sundry policemen, equerries, pilots, bailiffs, monks, doctors, sculptors and night-watchmen. It was against the background of such workaday, reliable efforts that the stars could shine.

As with opera generally, the basses and mezzos of the time were less *en vue* than the baritones, tenors and sopranos. Only two basses and two mezzos rose to anything like celebrity. Of these, Vanni Marcoux possessed a range that encompassed both bass and baritone roles – Sparafucile in *Rigoletto* and Golaud in *Pelléas et Mélisande*. Wisely, he took his time, remaining in the provinces until he was thirty, when he made his Opéra debut as Méphistophélès in *Faust*. In the 1920s he confined himself to two roles there, Boris Godunov and Méphisto in *La damna-tion de Faust*, as well as Don Giovanni and Gianni Schicchi at the Opéra-Comique. His dark, incisive tone and fine acting regularly drew praise.

The other notable bass, Marcel Journet, was a more interna-tional figure. How much the Opéra allowed its 'stars' to travel depended on how much it needed them. It was a compliment to Journet that he was allowed unusual freedom, but then he had sung for eight seasons at the Metropolitan even before his Opéra debut in 1908 and went on to record *Faust* with Caruso and Geraldine Farrar. In the 1920s he sang Wotan at the Opéra in both *Rheingold* and *Siegfried* and in 1924 he sang the title role in Boito's *Nerone* at La Scala under Toscanini. As with Marcoux, the voice

The bass-baritone Vanni-Marcoux in the title role of Massenet's *Don Quichotte* (1924)

was large but rounded, without any of the barking that basses and bass-baritones have sometimes indulged in, and his diction was exemplary.

The two outstanding mezzos of the period, Claire Croiza and the younger Germaine Cernay, had lower profiles, Croiza excelling in recital and oratorio rather than opera, and Cernay travelling only as far as the Théâtre de la Monnaie in Brussels. The judgment that Cernay had 'the nobility and simplicity of the great mezzos, which gave her singing intensity and classicism'[34] can also be applied to Croiza: both sound utterly natural and unforced, to the point of vulnerability.

With the baritones of the time, one begins to find more variety. André Baugé and Roger Bourdin, who sang in both Paris houses in the 1920s, represent the middle of the range, with lightish, lyrical voices incorporating, though not obtrusively, a typically French fast beat. Charles Panzéra, the prince of baritones when it came to *mélodies*, also sang regularly at the Opéra-Comique, beginning with the role of Albert in *Werther* in 1919. His smooth, slightly plangent tone was much admired in the role of Pelléas.

The extremes of baritone timbre were exemplified by two men of very different ages. Hector Dufranne, born in 1871, had sung Golaud in the original 1902 production of *Pelléas*. Maggie Teyte remembered how, in the 1908 production: 'The characters were so *strong*. It was very misty, and dark, and sombre and all that, but the *men*... Golaud (Dufranne), he sings and uses his voice like Klingsor.'[35] Dufranne's 1925 recording of an extract from the opera confirms Teyte's view – the voice has an edge and an intensity that flirt with ugliness. At the turn of the century he had been an Opéra-Comique regular in tough roles, as Escamillo, Scarpia, and Ourrias in *Mireille*. Like Journet, by the 1920s he was regularly allowed time off from the two Paris houses to sing elsewhere, including the United States, and his

appearance in *El retablo* at the Opéra-Comique in 1928 was one of only a few in the decade.

The other extreme is represented by the extraordinary Lucien Fugère. Born in 1848, this eighth child of a zinc engraver received a minimum of vocal tuition, but through hard work and his own ability managed to join the Opéra-Comique in 1877. In 1927 he celebrated his fiftieth anniversary with the house, and the following year began to make records. With due allowance made for his eighty years, these show a quite astonishing command of diction and timing, allied to a timbre that is as friendly as Dufranne's is sinister. He was still making occasional appearances on stage up to 1932. Here we reach the crossover point between *opéra comique* and operetta (already officially touched in December 1918 when the music hall star Dranem played the role of Buteux in the house's first postwar production of *La fille de Madame Angot*), in which delivery and tone of voice unmistakably lord it over musical accuracy.

In the tenor realm, we find not only a fairly sharp split between two styles of singing, but the nearest there was to a split between the two Paris houses. David Devriès, born in 1881, made his debut at the Opéra-Comique in 1904 and sang Belmondo in *Die Entführung* at the Opéra the same year. But there his Opéra career ended. Apart from a single season at the Metropolitan Opera in 1910/11, he remained at the Opéra-Comique until the end of his singing life. He sang major roles too: Don José, Ottavio, Pinkerton, des Grieux, Werther, Pelléas, and the Rodolfos in both *La traviata* and *La bohème*.

No documentary evidence is known as to why his Opéra career ended so abruptly, but the evidence of his recorded voice strongly suggests that his was a style of voice production that was already seeming outmoded for the Palais Garnier before the First World War – pure, white, rather thin, with a very pronounced beat (what the French less kindly term 'chevrotement'), and with none of the baritonal colour that Caruso exemplified both on disc and in his first appearance at the Palais Garnier in 1908, as the Duke in *Rigoletto*. Devriès's well-known recording of the aria 'Vainement, ma bien-aimée' from Lalo's *Le roi d'Ys* conjures up a lover who is poetic rather than ardent, willowy rather than heroic.

This interpretation is supported by the career of the slightly younger Charles Friant, born in Paris in 1890, who was a much admired principal tenor at the Opéra-Comique from his debut as Werther in 1920 until a few months after the outbreak of war in 1939, but who never once sang at the Opéra. Even if his voice has slightly more body to it than Devries's (a review in 1919 of his singing in Massenet's *Cléopâtre* actually referred to it as 'powerful'), it is still thin by modern standards, and again with a rapid beat and some tightness at the top. In his recording of 'Salut, demeure chaste et pure' from Gounod's *Faust*, he follows the dictates both of his vocal attributes and of his training by taking the high C in head voice.

The split between the two main houses on the tenor front becomes unambiguous in the case of three of the Opéra's tenors, Paul Franz, Fernand Ansseau and René Verdière (born in 1876, 1890 and 1899 respectively). The first two of these never set foot on the Opéra-Comique stage, while the third did so only in 1930, after four years of taking major roles at the Opéra. Franz sang in London, Milan and Buenos Aires as well as Paris, while Ansseau spent some time in the mid-1920s in the United States. Both were tenors in the heroic mould and, to put it bluntly, they did not need the Opéra-Comique, nor indeed was the Opéra-Comique a suitable venue for their style of singing. As for Verdière, in the Salle Favart's desperate days of the early 1930s the directors could not afford to turn down a tenor of his quality who, for whatever reason, travelled very little outside France, and he was given the heavier roles such as Canio in I pagliacci, Don José in Carmen and Cavaradossi in Tosca.

The split, however, was not total. Two fine tenors at least were happy to make parallel careers during the 1920s in both opera houses. Miguel Villabella, born in 1892 and beginning his pro-fessional life as a champion roller-skater, studied after the war with the celebrated teacher Jacques Isnardon before joining the Opéra-Comique in 1920 and the Opéra in 1928. Both houses used him for major roles such as Pinkerton in Madama Butterfly and Rodolphe in La traviata. One of his most famous roles, though, was as Georges Brown [sic] in Boïeldieu's La dame blanche, one of the Opéra-Comique standbys which the Opéra never annexed. He starred in the 1926 revival, and his recording four years later of the aria 'Viens, gentille dame' proves that, for all the nasality of his production, he was not lacking in either brilliance or power on high A flats and B flats, and was comfortable taking the two high Cs in chest voice. But still Caruso's baritonal quality is lacking.

Miguel Villabella, Spanish tenor and French rollerskating champion

We cannot say that that quality had been entirely absent from the Paris Opéra, since Paul Franz, who had been singing the Wagnerian roles there since 1909, pos-sessed a voice as robust as any Wagner fan could have wished for. But there seemed to be no successor in sight until, in January 1924, the part of Nicias in Massenet's Thaïs was taken by the 26-year-old Georges Thill. It would be fair to say that Thill's arrival on the scene was greeted with a mixture of admiration and relief, tainted with concern: admiration and relief because here was a tenor who seemed capable of con-quering both the French and Italian repertoire (his Duke in Rigoletto that September was a triumph); concern because the most superficial research revealed that Thill had attended the Paris Conservatoire for two years from 1918 without success, and that his tone and technique, even his wonderfully clear diction, were the fruit of subsequent lessons in Naples from Fernando de Lucia. What hope was there for French singing, the critics muttered, if a pupil of Thill's promise could slip through the net?

It is interesting to note that the specific lacuna in his Paris training had been its inability to give him a solid tone for his medium and lower register. From de Lucia he had acquired a baritonal resonance at least up to the central D; it was altogether a voice that was 'warm, flexible, with a solid core and, finally, moving because of its vigour'.[36] A crude but sufficient indicator of his value to the Opéra is that by 1939 he was being paid 10,000 francs a performance.

In the 1930s, though, Thill was to take the gilt off his marvellous voice by singing too many heavy roles and by burning the candle at both ends. Rouché too must take some responsibility: it is really not sensible to schedule your leading tenor for *five* rehearsals of *Die Meistersinger* on the same day. But Thill's vocal problems gave ammunition to those who had never trusted de Lucia's technique, and left the future of tenor singing in France open.

There were, inevitably, similar dire prognostications about the condition of French singers of all kinds. 'Where', asked Charles Tenroc in 1921, 'are the tenors, the *falcons*, the deep basses, the authentic contraltos, the light-voiced prime donne, the *trials*? Mixed up in all-purpose tessituras. What are they taught at the Conservatoire or in the theatres?'[37] Not that such complaints were anything new. Villabella's teacher, Jacques Isnardon, recalled in 1911 how, 'when I was a pupil at the Conservatoire, I use to hear old music lovers deploring the way singing had declined. Each year, at the summer competitions, the newspapers were full of these lamentations. There was talk of those heroic epochs when so many great masters had graced the stages of France and Italy.'[38]

Where their sopranos were concerned, it does not seem in retrospect that the French in the 1920s had great cause for alarm. At least nine come to mind (Suzanne Balguerie, Germaine Féraldy, Yvonne Gall, Fanny Heldy, Emma Luart, Germaine Lubin, Gabrielle Ritter-Ciampi, Ninon Vallin and Geneviève Vix) whose recordings continue to give pleasure. If none burst on to the Paris stage with quite Georges Thill's éclat, this was partly because five of them had made their debuts before the war: Gall in 1908 at the Opéra, Heldy in 1912 at La Monnaie, Lubin and Vallin both in 1912 at the Opéra-Comique, and Vix as long ago as 1906 in the same house, where she went on to create the role of Concepcion in Ravel's *L'heure espagnole* in 1911.

There was therefore none of that feeling that France's honour was at stake, so evident in the case of its tenors. Space does not allow a detailed survey of the characteristics of all these nine. But between them they more than sufficiently covered the current repertoire of the two major houses. The lightest voice was that of Ritter-Ciampi, a coloratura specialist of stunning sparkle and accuracy, while Gall, a superb *Thaïs*, commanded a warmer tone. The Belgians Luart and Heldy exemplified the slightly acid, oboe-like tone which marks off those French-language singers from sopranos of today, while Vallin, 'la princesse du chant', as a woman's magazine dubbed her in 1927, with her pure yet powerful production remains a unique artist. Finally, the larger voices of Balguerie and Lubin prove that, size notwithstanding, the French training of the time was able to produce full, high notes that lacked any sense of strain. Balguerie, singing 'Divinités du Styx' from Gluck's *Alceste* in 1932, floats effortlessly above the stave, yet chills the blood with the low-lying phrase 'ministres de la mort', while Lubin banishes all memories of French acidity in her radiant, sheerly beautiful rendering of 'Salut à toi, noble demeure' ('Dich teure Halle') from *Lohengrin*.

Lubin was the first French singer after the war to be invited to the Vienna Staatsoper, and the Viennese loved her. Korngold in the *Neue Freie Presse* described her voice as 'a silvery soprano of clear timbre. At the top it sounds like a high oboe, with the pure and striking colour of a young boy's voice.' She sang Elsa in *Lohengrin* and the name part in Richard Strauss's *Ariadne auf Naxos*. The critic of the *Neues Wiener Journal* noted that 'her Elsa is not a Gretchen or Kätchen, but a princess full of spirit who takes her destiny and shapes it with a royal force and superiority'.[39] Lubin's 'spirit', allied to the praise she received from Strauss and to her experience of German-speaking opera houses, led her to be impatient with some of Paris's habitual ways of doing things. Back home at the Opéra as a different Ariadne, in Dukas's *Ariane et Barbe-bleue*, she was furious to hear the stage-hands talking behind the scenery. Came the scene where Ariane breaks the windows of the prison holding Bluebeard's wives, and Lubin put her head through and issued an ultimatum – either they stopped talking straight away or she would stop singing and would march up to the footlights and explain to the audience why. She sang on undisturbed.

What comes across from recordings of all these singers, male and female, is the importance they attach to the French language. Very rarely indeed does the listener have to strain to hear what is being said – and I use the word 'said' deliberately, since the underlying philosophy is clearly that singing is merely heightened speech and that the verbal message should never be obscured by a search for more volume or a captivating sound. This 'tone-before-everything' approach was ridiculed by Reynaldo Hahn in a series of nine lectures he gave in Paris in 1913/14 which were later collected into a book. He conjures up the scene of a salon singer who introduces the songs he is about to sing 'in the most natural way in the world'. Then he starts to sing and

> suddenly, you hear a sound and wonder where it's coming from; you don't recognize the voice that has just been speaking. Instinctively, you look under the furniture.... It seems as though the voice comes from elsewhere, far away, and that you are hearing it through something interposed between it and you.[40]

There had always been the odd renegade like Saint-Saëns, who thought fine-tuning a libretto was a waste of time since audiences at best heard only the occasional word. But critics in the 1920s largely disagreed. When, as noted above, Charles Friant was a success in 1919 in Massenet's *Cléopâtre* at the Théâtre-Lyrique, one notice declared that 'here is a young tenor of whom it is possible to expect much, especially if he improves his enunciation'.[41]

From this, it is possible to deduce that the French had little time for 'opera as mystery' or 'opera as hot bath' – or even 'opera to be listened to head in hands', to quote Jean Cocteau on Wagner.[42] The same requirements were made of opera singers as of actors at the Comédie-Française or of performers in the music halls. Isnardon in his lively volume *L'art théâtral* even proposes street vendors as models of production and articulation and as what he calls 'virtuosos without being aware of it', being able to intone 'fresh mussels' for hours at a time.

Recordings of French opera singers from the 1920s reveal only the very rarest occasion when a voice becomes blowsy or uncontrolled at the top; in general, high notes are placed with no more apparent effort than low ones, and, again, the words are audible. Isnardon begins his chapter on 'La phonation' by saying that 'the quality of the voice resides only in its timbre, not in its volume.... The art consists of making your voice carry and not in singing loudly.... Every singer who gets tired is tiring.'[43]

All these factors point to the singing of the time as being an act of communication and not merely one of making an impression or going through a routine. We may think on the other hand of the British who, if we are to believe Sir Thomas Beecham, 'don't like music but love the noise it makes'. Although the French played up to the star quality of their stars (Georges Thill fans would even let down the tyres of his Hispano-Suiza in order to get a longer, closer look at him), this emphasis on communication meant that there was a very direct rapport across the footlights. This was particularly the case at the Opéra-Comique; and it was one of the greatest tragedies of the decade that the musical institution which, as I have said, offered the French one of the clearest reflections of their own character and mores should, by the end of the 1920s, be falling victim to musical and historical forces beyond its control. With the 1929 financial crash, confusion on both sides of the footlights became patent and increasingly intolerable.

Notes

1. Martin Cooper, *Opéra Comique* (London, 1949), pp. 70–71.
2. William Ashbrook, article on Donizetti, in *The Viking Opera Guide*, ed. Amanda Holden with Nicholas Kenyon and Stephen Walsh (London, 1993), p. 285.
3. *Le ménestrel*, 2 July 1920.
4. René Dumesnil, *La musique en France entre les deux guerres, 1919–1939* (Geneva, 1946), p. 63.
5. Ibid., p. 64.
6. Ibid., p. 65.
7. Henri Dutilleux, in conversation with the author.
8. BnF, LA Carré 16.
9. BnF, LA Carré 18.
10. *Le courrier musical*, 1 January 1926.
11. Paul Bertrand, in *Le ménestrel*, 29 May 1925.
12. BnF, LA Rabaud 45–49, 53.
13. Charles Tenroc, in *Le courrier musical*, 15 November 1922.
14. Gustave Samazeuilh, in *Le ménestrel*, 10 November 1922.
15. Michael de Cossart, *Une américaine à Paris* (Paris, 1979), pp. 166–67.
16. Charles Tenroc, in *Le courrier musical*, 1 April 1928.
17. Jean Chantavoine, in Le ménestrel, 16 March 1928.
18. *Cinquante ans de musique française*, ed. L. Rohozinski, I, (Paris, 1925), p. 145.
19. Ibid., p. 193.
20. Gabriel Marcel, in *L'Europe nouvelle*, 22 December 1923, quoted in *Association Francis Jammes*, Bulletin no. 2 (December 1983), p. 43.
21. John Tyrrell, article on Smetana; see Holden, Kenyon and Walsh (eds), *Viking Guide*, p. 990.
22. BnF, Lettres à Paul Dukas, 495.
23. Roland-Manuel, 'Une esquisse autobiographique de Maurice Ravel', in *La revue musicale*, December 1938.
24. Henry Prunières, 'L'Enfant et les sortilèges', in *La revue musicale*, 1 April 1925; repr. in *L'enfant et les sortilèges/L'heure espagnole*, *L'avant-scène* no. 127 (Paris, 1990), pp. 68–69.
25. André Messager, in *Le Figaro*, 4 February 1926.
26. Georges Auric, in *Les nouvelles littéraires*, 11 April 1925.
27. Emile Vuillermoz, in *Excelsior*, 3 February 1926.
28. Madeleine Goss, *Bolero: The Life of Maurice Ravel* (New York, 1940), p. 197.
29. Manuel Rosenthal, in conversation with the author.
30. Jean Gourret, *Histoire de l'Opéra-Comique* (Paris, 1978), p. 197.
31. André Messager, in *Le courrier musical*, 1 January 1921.
32. Igor Stravinsky, *Chroniques de ma vie* (Paris, 1935; repr. 1962), pp. 120–21.
33. Constant Lambert, *Music Ho!* (London, 1934; repr. 1948), pp. 47–53.
34. Elizabeth Giuliani, booklet accompanying two discs of *Le chant français retrouvé* (Paris, n.d.), p. 57.
35. BBC interview with John Amis, 27 September 1966.
36. Claude Bagnières, writing in unidentified magazine, 4 March 1953, BnF Fonds Montpensier, file Georges Thill.
37. Charles Tenroc, in *Le courrier musical*, 15 March 1921.
38. Jacques Isnardon, *Le chant théâtral* (Paris, 1911), p. 4.
39. Quoted in *Comoedia*, 19 March 1924.
40. Reynaldo Hahn, *Du chant* (Paris, 1957), pp. 75–76; repr. as *On Singers and Singing*, trans. Léopold Simoneau (Portland, 1990).
41. Quoted, without source, in sleeve note by Michael Scott to Rubini GV 524.
42. Jean Cocteau, *Le coq et l'arlequin* (Paris, 1918; repr. 1979), p. 79.
43. Isnardon, *Le chant théâtral*, p. 66.

5. Opérettes, music hall, revues, chansons

IN HIS DETAILED OVERVIEW of French operetta from 1855 to 1924, Jacques Brandejont-Offenbach, out of understandable loyalty to the family name, barely veiled his opinion that the genre had been on a downhill slope since the composer of *Orphée aux enfers* died in 1880. He divided its history into three phases:

> *Opéra bouffe* – or *opérette bouffe* – a parody of grand opera, which flourished
> from 1855 to 1870.
> Operetta, enjoyable, light and with elements of fantasy, a daughter
> of *opéra comique*, which was all the rage after the [Franco-Prussian] war.
> The vogue for it lasted, with decreasing vigour, until 1914.
> Finally, what I shall call musical comedy or musical vaudeville: products
> inspired by English and Viennese operettas, with verses set to dance tunes
> – dancing is now the thing![1]

The author is far from approving this invasion of the grossly physical into what had been a typically French vehicle of verbal subtlety and charm. After the 'exuberant joy' of *opéra bouffe* and the 'frank, fresh and healthy communicative gaiety' of operetta, had come what he supposed he must call 'modern operetta'. Its characteristics were that it had

> diminished and simplified the importance of the music, the libretto and
> the production. The size of the orchestra has been reduced, there are no
> choruses, actors who can sing a bit have replaced singers, since these have
> now lost the secret of 'la fantaisie'. Scenery made up of modern elements
> can be used for anything: every theatre always has in its storerooms at
> least a drawing-room, a restaurant, a dance hall, a garden, a beach – all
> places, in short, where you can dance, since these days dancing alone has
> taken the place of processions, finales, quartets, trios and even ballets![2]

What Monsieur Brandejont-Offenbach meant by 'la fantaisie' is not wholly clear, but he goes on to mention that several of the operettas produced during the First World War were on military subjects (and this even as late as December 1917, when most French citizens had long ceased to regard the war as an idealistic adventure). It is worth noting too that, by the side of *Le poilu* and *La fiancée du lieutenant*, appeared a number of operettas with an Anglo-Saxon tinge: *Miss Flirt, Mam'zelle Boy-Scout* (pronounced, of course, Scoot) and *White and Black*. There was also a pre-echo of the typewriter in *Parade* in *La petite dactylo* (The little typist), produced at the Gymnase in October 1916.

Inevitably, the number of operetta productions in Paris had dwindled during the early years of the war, from twenty-three in 1913 to six in 1914 and five in 1915. There was then a slight revival to eight in 1916 and thirteen in 1917, before the number fell again to seven in 1918. But those seven contained one which outshone all others for years on either side, Henri Christiné's three-act operetta *Phi-Phi*. Certainly its success owed something to the timing of the premiere at the Bouffes-Parisiens, on 13 November 1918, two days after the Armistice. But its verve and tunefulness still come across eighty years later, even though Brandejont-Offenbach saw fit to absorb its success into his general lament:

> This music clearly had rhythm, if of a fairly uniform kind. It gave the
> public hearing it for the first time the impression that they already knew
> it. Built on dance rhythms like shimmies and foxtrots, it rapidly became
> the prey of all the delirious negro orchestras and jazz bands. It arrived at
> the right moment, when everyone was dancing madly; it was the signal
> for that great pulsating ball which, for two years, sucked old and young
> into its swirling mêlée.[3]

Christiné began as a schoolmaster in Switzerland but then fell in love with a *café-concert* singer, went to Nice, where he started writing songs for music hall artists, and thence to Paris. He capitalized on his classical education by setting to music a story located in Athens in the fifth century BC, involving the Greek sculptor Phidias (the Phi-Phi of the title), whose mistress also attracts the attentions of Pericles. But true to the temper of the times, these classical allusions are either brought up to date, as James Harding has pointed out, by further references to people meeting in various Parisian locations such as the rue du Panthéon, the Odéon and the rue d'Athènes, or directly juxtaposed with the names of 'silent screen heroes of the time, Pearl White and Mabel Normand and even *"le fameux* Douglas Fairbank" [sic]'.[4] Needless to say, the listener is not required to possess any historical knowledge as a background to the plot which consists of the usual merry-go-round of attachments, enlivened by the natural propensity of Phidias's models to display a large portion of their charms.

As Brandejont-Offenbach said, the costumiers and decorators who accepted a percentage of the profits in lieu of cash in advance had no cause to grumble. After a slow start it became the thing to do; 'everyone went to see *Phi-Phi*, no one talked of anything but *Phi-Phi*, no one sang anything but *Phi-Phi* and orchestras played nothing but *Phi-Phi*'.[5] By January 1921 it reached its thousandth performance at the Bouffes-Parisiens, about the time Charpentier's *Louise* reached its five hundredth round the corner at the Opéra-Comique. By November 1926, publicists for a revival of the operetta could plaster Paris with unflattering posters, à la Bateman, of 'the man who hasn't seen *Phi-Phi*'.[6] In short, whatever Brindejont-Offenbach might say, the operetta genre now saw a spirited upturn in its fortunes.

A 1980s revival of Christiné's piece at the Bouffes-Parisiens, together with discs of numbers from it, indicate that 'seeing' *Phi-Phi* was as important as hearing it. Christiné's musical language, as was the case with almost all popular music of the time, went back to the 1890s or earlier and his tunes now seem no more memorable than those of other popular composers of the time. But the productions were slick, the storyline entertaining enough, pretty girls well to the fore, and Christiné continued to supply this lucrative market even if only one of his later operettas quite matched *Phi-Phi*'s success. With *Dédé*, produced at the Bouffes-Parisiens in November 1921 and starring Maurice Chevalier, Christiné not only confirmed the rage for such titles based on the traditional nicknames of the *faubourgs* – spawning *Clo-Clo*, *Zozo*, *Lulu* and *You-You* among others – but attracted an altogether higher class of customer than usual. During *Dédé*'s 1924 revival, again starring Chevalier, Diaghilev's secretary Boris Kochno went to see it and

> came away not only enchanted by the songs but raving about the talents of Maurice Chevalier (then thirty-six years old). Diaghilev jumped to the conclusion that Boris was attracted by Chevalier and went secretly to see *Dédé* out of curiosity about the type his friend found irresistible. 'But he's an old man!' he later exclaimed incredulously. Nevertheless, the music fascinated him....[7]

Perhaps through jealousy, the 52-year-old Diaghilev was being unkind in describing the 36-year-old Chevalier as old, and in not giving him credit for putting over his songs in his first operetta role. It was the Chevalier numbers – solos with and without chorus and duets – that were hummed and whistled all over Paris, and recordings show the wonderful vocal control that was to be the singer's hallmark for another forty years.[8] Christiné's tunes, like many popular hits before and since, are built around oft-repeated refrains of six or seven notes (what nowadays is known as a 'hook', for catching the ear), and Chevalier had the knack of throwing these off nine or ten times with exactly the same intonation and the same little flourishes and slides, so that the 'hook' latches on well and truly.

In *Dédé*, the librettist, the ubiquitous Albert Willemetz, one-time secretary to Georges Clemenceau who was to collaborate at the end of the decade with Honegger on the frothy *Les aventures du roi Pausole*, set the scene as far from Ancient Greece as one could be, in a contemporary Parisian shoe shop. Chevalier, as the ruined playboy, gets the heroine in the end, and the mood throughout is one of civilized charm and gaiety, as one can tell from the titles of the songs – 'Elle porte un nom charmant', 'Dans la vie faut pas s'en faire' ('In life one mustn't take things to heart') and finally 'Tous les chemins mènent à l'amour' ('All roads lead to love'). Whether or not Diaghilev would later die singing extracts from *La bohème*, as Stravinsky believed, he must surely have responded to Christiné's clever Puccini pastiche in the heroine's 'C'est un plaisir si grand', which harks back to an age when operetta lived by guying the 'mother' medium. The only other number that would not have found a place in an operetta of 1890 is 'Tango, lorsque tu nous tiens', celebrating fairly discreetly the dance which had been banned as immoral by the Archbishop of Paris in 1913, but now almost regarded as respectable – perhaps helped by Queen Mary's request to see it danced at the English court in 1914.

The vogue for dancing, so loudly deplored by Monsieur Brindejont-Offenbach, surfaced far more obviously in the next great operetta hit, *Ta bouche*, premiered in April 1922, with Willemetz again writing the song texts and with music by the 31-year-old Maurice Yvain. The unlikely plot was merely an excuse to ridicule the snobs of the postwar era for whom money and position were paramount, but the quality of the music indicated that Christiné now had a rival and one who was at home with the modern American dance number: 'during the 1922/23 season the whole of Paris was dancing the "one-step" and the "foxtrot and shimmy" which made *Ta bouche* such a success'. As in *Dédé*, 'tout finit par des mariages', but not before the leading lady and female chorus have had a chance to declare 'Non, non, jamais les hommes' over a catchily rhythmical accompaniment. Yvain's ear for rhythm is also nicely put over in the song 'Pour toi' in which the two words of the title are accentuated differently in different lines, 'POUR toi' on a downward phrase leading finally to 'pour TOI' on an upward one. Willemetz's later collaborator, Arthur Honegger,

A 1925 exhibition of modern dancing in the presence of the authorities and of representatives of the Church, to demonstrate that modern dances do not offend against morality

was to make a habit of just this kind of reversed accentuation, though for more serious purposes.

Ta bouche was the first of three operettas for which Yvain was contracted in 1921. The third, *La dame en décolleté*, sharing the sauciness of its title with Raoul Moretti's *Trois jeunes filles nues* of 1925 and René Mercier's *Déshabillez-vous* of 1928 (with the young Jean Sablon in a minor role), was a disappointment, but the second of the three, *Là-haut*, went down well. Even though Monsieur Brindejont-Offenbach lamented yet again the intrusion of the dance, in this case the foxtrot, such that for all Yvain's attempts at variety in other areas, 'he keeps on coming back relentlessly to the same rhythm which grabs hold of us when the curtain rises and does not let us go until it falls',[9] success was assured by having Yvain's friend Chevalier as the father-to-be. As the result of a too generous toast to the impending arrival, he imagines himself in heaven – cue a small bevy of decorous girl-angels, an authoritarian St Peter and the favourite comic singer Dranem (alias of Albert Menard) as a guardian angel, complete with halo and cigar. Dranem's 'C'est la vie' is matched by Chevalier's 'C'est Paris', and elsewhere Chevalier begins a set of couplets with the line 'Anges purs, anges radieux', lifted from Marguerite's final aria in Gounod's *Faust*, though to quite different music over an oompah bass. If it is the mark of a good composer to be able to reuse similar materials to new effect, then Yvain qualifies through giving the title phrase, 'là-haut', essentially the same descending 'hook' as 'pour toi' in *Ta bouche*.

These operettas, like their forebears, were not about complication, except occasionally in their lyrics (though the title of Chevalier's song 'Ose Anna!' perhaps merits groans rather than plaudits). Rather, they were expressions of relief that the war was over, that Paris had survived it as *the* centre of Western European entertainment and, not least, that all these rich Americans were bringing their dollars over the Atlantic. Dancing their foxtrots and one-steps was not only fun and *chic*, but also an easy way of incorporating such visitors into the Parisian harlequinade and making them feel at home. As for the dancing craze, most Parisians were as willing to ignore the new Archbishop of Paris's ritual condemnation of the latest dances like the shimmy and the java as immoral as they were to risk the dangers resulting from this activity, set out in some detail by a gynaecologist, Dr Pagès: 'insomnia,...dizziness, migraines...more or less generalized spasmodic neuroses...speech difficulties, anomalies of salivation, indeed even sphincteral accidents, etc.'.[10]

Side by side with works like *Dédé*, *Ta bouche* and *Là-haut*, which purists insisted were 'comédies musicales' rather than 'opérettes', Paris also welcomed examples of traditional operetta. One of the most successful of these was *Ciboulette*, produced at the Théâtre des Variétés on 7 April 1923 with a text by the marquis Robert de Flers and Francis de Croisset and music by Reynaldo Hahn. In his ballet for Diaghilev *Le dieu bleu* of 1912, Hahn had pleased few people. He was destined, it seemed, to remain a salon composer and singer, or, as Messager described him after their falling-out, 'a singing-teacher for old ladies in fashionable drawing-rooms'.[11] But this was altogether to underrate Hahn's musical talents: as a conductor, he was responsible for some of the most spirited and accurate performances of Mozart operas to be heard in the decade – he had after all been invited to conduct *Don Giovanni* at Salzburg in 1906 when he was only thirty-one, with a cast including Lili Lehmann as Donna Anna and Geraldine Farrar as Zerlina.

Understandably, this Mozartean experience grafted on to his training at the hands of Massenet did not incline Hahn to the writing of one-steps, shimmies and black bottoms. Their absence in this case was not remarked on, as *Ciboulette* was set in the time of the Second Empire and told the tale of a young vegetable seller, the Ciboulette (or 'chive') of the title, whose future, as predicted by an old market-woman, comes true in three distinct instances. Both story and music lie fair and square in the tradition of Lecocq's *La fille de Madame Angot*, and *Ciboulette* was one of the last attempts by a composer approaching fifty to recapture something of prewar innocence. It succeeded, I feel, partly because of Hahn's delightful and subtle music (to listen to *Ciboulette* after Yvain's *Là-haut* is to be aware of a great gulf in technique, especially of harmony and orchestration) and partly because of the cast. Edmée Favart, the Ciboulette, was an Opéra-Comique regular (just a couple of months before the premiere of *Ciboulette* she had been singing the part of Cherubino there), as was Jean Périer, the creator of Pelléas twenty-one years earlier. Even the tenor lead, Henri Defreyn, though never a member of the Opéra-Comique, had far more of a voice than a Dranem or a Chevalier. In short, *Ciboulette* briefly turned the clock back by substituting purely musical values for those of dancing, patter, energy, noise and up-to-dateness. After a revival at the Théâtre Marigny in 1926 with many of the original cast, the work finally reached the stage of the Opéra-Comique in 1953 – an accolade never granted to *Là-haut*, *Phi-Phi* or *Dédé*. Americanization passes; Frenchness lives on.

Possibly a third reason for *Ciboulette*'s success in certain quarters was that it celebrated traditional values of femininity. It is true that French women never emulated the strenuous methods of British suffragettes in pursuit of the vote, but in 1919 'the chamber voted for full female suffrage by 344 to 97. The senate rejected it by 156 to 134 and renewed its opposition for the next twenty years on successive occasions.'[12] Finally, General de Gaulle imposed the female vote by decree in 1944. In 1923, then, the dispute between chamber and senate was still in Parisians' minds. So was the scandal of Victor Margueritte's novel *La garçonne* in 1922, provoked by the author's portrayal of the 'new woman', with Eton crop, flat chest, no corset and ideas about liberating herself from her traditionally secondary role in French society, including sexual passivity. Margueritte was duly stripped of his Légion d'Honneur rosette.

Ciboulette has no such notions. In her air 'Moi, je m'appelle Ciboulette' she makes fun, in true operetta fashion, of the grand names of the bourgeoisie – Camille, Charlotte, Victoire, Yolande – and gives as her reason for preferring Ciboulette the simple fact that 'ça plaît aux garçons'.

Nostalgia also ruled in *Mozart*, billed in 1925 as a 'comédie musicale' with words by Sacha Guitry and music by Hahn, after Messager had turned the project down. Still

today, the discs of Yvonne Printemps as the boy composer exude charm, and in the 1940s the critic James Agate remembered how

> people were seen to cry, and by 'cry' I mean shed tears, when Music's heavenly child appeared at the top of the gilt staircase and descended it to kneel at the feet of Madame d'Epinay.[13]

As I have already said, Mozart had achieved iconic status in Paris, and Hahn's infiltration of his score with Mozartean moments is expertly done, as we might expect. But Agate's mention of the 'gilt staircase' suggests that musical values were enhanced for the audience by touches of eighteenth-century visual splendour. On a more realistic level, when Printemps came to London in Guitry's plays with music, Agate noted how easily she moved from speech to song and back again, but also that occasionally her long notes outstayed their welcome. One has to counter Agate's objection by saying that this latter practice had good eighteenth-century provenance, even if Printemps merely felt the wish every now and then to display her superior vocal talent in the same way as Mistinguett displayed her legs.

Overall, one of the most notable differences between Hahn's operettas and 'comédies musicales' and those of his modern rivals is that in his the pace is more gentle. It seems sometimes as though the French music of the 1920s, even in the second half of the decade, is still running full tilt to escape the memory of war and afraid to indulge in introspection for fear of what may be found. With Hahn, the only other composer to hark back to more restful times was Messager. After his *Fortunio*, premiered at the Opéra-Comique in 1907 and, interestingly, already described as a 'comédie musicale', Messager's time was taken up with directing the Opéra and he returned to composing for the stage only in 1917, with the 'légende lyrique' *Béatrice*. After the operettas *Monsieur Beaucaire* and *Passionnément*, his swansong in the genre was *Coups de roulis*, produced at the Théâtre Marigny in 1928, the year before his death. The action takes place on a battleship in the present and includes many swipes at the notoriously corrupt and unstable French government of the Third Republic – 'coups de roulis' strictly decribes the rolling motion of the ship, but also by inference the in-and-out motion of the plot and of ministerial appointments.

Messager's achievement is to take this plot, in which nostalgia is replaced by satire, and articulate it with masterly skill through music that he could easily have written for *Véronique* thirty years earlier. Like his great enemy Reynaldo Hahn, Messager is not afraid to slow things down. Certainly, where required, he can (as *Véronique* had proved) get as excited as anybody, and the song 'Avec la danse', in which the vice-admiral extols the virtues of dancing as a way of attracting the opposite sex, is a delicious combination of new and old in which Messager pays passing homage to the shimmy without for a moment being seduced by it. But the song 'Ce n'est pas la première fois', the young hero's apology for a stolen kiss, moves from its introductory violin solo into a truly moving, *andante sostenuto* avowal of love, based on the sort of pulsating chords that Fauré made popular in his *mélodies*.

Yvonne Printemps

For all the beauties and subtleties of *Ciboulette* and *Coups de roulis*, a direct, even raw energy was the distinguishing mark of the times, realized most openly in revues, in music hall, in popular songs and, of course, in the newly imported jazz.

Various claimants have been put forward for the honour of introducing jazz to Paris. Syncopated music first reached the city around the turn of the century with Sousa marches. These were followed by Satie's Le Piccadilly in 1904 and by Debussy in his two attempts at a cakewalk, 'Golliwogg's Cake Walk' of 1908 and *Le petit nègre*, published the following year. No doubt the Parisians, like the rest of humanity, got to know Irving Berlin's *Alexander's Ragtime Band* at the time of its composition in 1911, but jazz seems not to have been incorporated into Parisian music-making until the 'Steamboat Ragtime' forming part of the section called 'La petite fille américaine' in Satie's *Parade*. The painter Gabriel Fournier later recalled that Satie used to amuse his friends by playing ragtime pieces, particularly those of Jelly Roll Morton. According to Fournier's account, he played not from the sheet music, but by imitating records of Morton brought back from America in 1916 by the conductor Ernest Ansermet.[14] But Morton did not in fact make any records until 1923 (the first records of syncopated music would seem to have been those by the Original Dixieland Jazz Band, issued in 1917). However, Morton did visit Paris during a trip to Europe in 1914, and Satie may have met or at least heard him then.[15] Ragtime appeared again in Stravinsky's *Histoire du soldat* in 1918, when René Dumesnil confirms the dance was still 'in its earliest days',[16] although the work did not reach Paris until a staged performance was given at the Théâtre des Champs-Elysées in April 1924. Stravinsky himself later wrote, incidentally differentiating his involvement from Satie's:

Gaby Deslys 'in a dramatic flurry of feathers and sequins'

> My knowledge of jazz was derived exclusively from copies of sheet music, and as I had never actually heard any of the music performed, I borrowed its rhythmic style not as played, but as written. I *could* imagine jazz sound, however, or so I liked to think. Jazz meant, in any case, a wholly new sound in my music, and *Histoire* marks my final break with the Russian orchestral school.[17]

Eric Walter White notes the close resemblance between the orchestra for *Histoire*, consisting of clarinet, bassoon, cornet, trombone, violin, double bass and percussion, and the line-up of the 1916 Original Dixieland Jazz Band, of clarinet, trumpet, trombone, piano and drums.[18]

Ragtime for eleven players and *Piano-Rag-Music* were also first performed before 1920 in Switzerland, where the composer was living at the time, and it has proved impossible to discover a certain date for the first Paris performance of either. But the performance of *Piano-Rag-Music* given at the SMI by Alberta Heskia on 2 June 1921 was not billed as a first performance in Paris, although it might have been the last if concert organizers had listened to André Schaeffner, who rated it as 'a probably ephemeral form of a Far Western fashion'.[19] It is hard, therefore, to calculate the respective influence of these three pieces on French composers. Although *Ragtime* was published in Paris in 1919, by Editions de La Sirène, the other two were published in London by J. and W. Chester, *Piano-Rag-Music* in 1920 and *Histoire* not until 1924. On the other hand again, Chester's links with the young French composers were very close at this time.

A third contender as the earliest proponent of jazz in Paris was the music hall star Gaby Deslys, whom Noël Coward remembered seeing in London 'enjoying a

tremendous vogue and much adoration...drenched in pink ostrich feathers'.[20] In 1923 Darius Milhaud recalled how, not long returned to Paris from Brazil, he was bowled over by the show with the apparently provocative title *Laissez-les tomber*, in which Deslys and her partner Harry Pilcer starred at the Casino de Paris in 1918 (although the pure-minded could reasonably ignore the title's provocation and assume it referred to the shells that Big Bertha was raining on Paris, as Debussy lay dying). In the words of James Gardiner,

the awe-inspiring sets, the towering headdresses, the vast – sometimes nude – chorus; the jazz music; the whole thing being built around a glamorous female star, or *meneuse*, clad in a dramatic flurry of feathers and sequins; all this set the style for subsequent revues at the Casino de Paris, which were universally copied for decades to come.[21]

It says a good deal for Milhaud's sang-froid that out of all this it was the jazz music that chiefly caught his attention. His 1923 memoir gives such a detailed description that it is worth quoting at length and may stand as the template for the jazz elements which 'serious' composers of the decade found so attractive:

> There is the importance of syncopation in the rhythms and melodies, heard against an inexorably regular background that is as basic as the circulation of the blood, the heartbeat or the pulse; the organization of the percussion, all the instruments of that family which figure in our orchestration treatises, now simplified and grouped together, turning into a single complex instrument so complete that when Monsieur Buddy, the drummer of the Syncopated Orchestra, plays a percussion solo, we find ourselves in the presence of a piece rhythmically constructed and balanced and with an incredible variety of expression deriving from the timbres of the different percussion instruments he is playing at the same time. Then there are the new instrumental techniques: the piano with the dryness and precision of a drum and a banjo, the resurrection of the saxophone, the trombone whose *glissandi* become one of the most popular means of expression and to whom are entrusted the gentlest tunes, as they are to the trumpet, the frequent use by both instruments of the mute, the swoop, vibratos with both slide and valve, flutter-tonguing high up on the clarinet, with a violence of attack, a volume of sound and a technique of slides and oscillations which puts a strain on our finest players; the introduction of the banjo, drier, more nervy and with more body than the harp or string quartet; the very special technique of the violin, thin and harsh, using the widest vibrato and the slowest *portamenti*.[22]

Because Milhaud had visited Harlem, the black district of New York, in 1922, where the jazz he heard was 'absolutely different from what I knew', we cannot be sure exactly how many of the above elements were to be heard in *Laissez-les tomber*. But as Jeremy Drake has pointed out, Milhaud's shimmy of 1920 entitled *Caramel mou* is as different from *La création du monde* of 1923 as what he called 'Broadway' jazz (that is, the Deslys variety) is from 'Harlem' jazz.[23] In any case, we should beware of making assumptions about what the French of this period meant by the word 'jazz'. As Marc Robine points out,

> at the beginning of the Twenties, the word 'jazz' was still a fairly fluid term: a blanket word that designated orchestras with a percussion section

rather than any precise musical genre. Also, when mention is made of 'un jazz', the formula applies more often to an instrumental combination than to a style or a rhythm, which may be very far removed from what we mean by the term nowadays.[24]

The Parisian enthusiasm for jazz, however constituted, was no short-lived craze. On 12 May 1921, Ravel wrote to his friend Georgette Marnold: 'Have you been to see the negroes? Their virtuosity is sometimes alarming.'[25] This alarm was to have fruitful results in both *L'enfant et les sortilèges*, which he was already working on, and the second Violin Sonata. Later that year, the composer and pianist Jean Wiéner organized his 'concerts salade', mixing serious and popular pieces, new and old, the first of which consisted of three sections: jazz from the Billy Arnold Orchestra, fragments from *Le sacre du printemps* (with Stravinsky pedalling and twiddling the knobs of a pianola) and Milhaud's ten-minute Sonata for flute, oboe, clarinet and piano which he had begun in Rio de Janeiro in 1918. Wiéner also formed, with the Belgian Clément Doucet, a superb two-piano team which was one of the major attractions at the night club Le Boeuf sur le Toit in the rue Boissy d'Anglas. Their discs are some of the most life-affirming yet sophisticated products to come out of Twenties Paris (their jazzed-up 'Chopinata' was even approved by Alfred Cortot), and in their collaborations with Maurice Chevalier their sharp rhythmic sense provided a wonderful backing for his superficially more leisurely style – as in their superb *La leçon du Charleston* of 1926, where the pianists' riff before the third verse puts most other white imitations of jazz piano utterly in the shade.

But to begin with, there was resistance to this musical invasion, and in 1919 not everyone was happy with these and other American imports, as presented in Gaby Deslys's next show. On 8 April she opened at the Théâtre Fémina in *La marche à l'étoile*, with designs by Erté. Some of her wealthier fans paid up to 9,000 francs for the few available boxes but, in the words of her biographer,

> Paris was still full of American troops, and many reviewers felt that the whole revue was aimed at them – with its jazz score, English songs, and even some dialogue in English. Many French people were unhappy about this. Critics voiced the opinion that Gaby had spent too many years away from France to know what French audiences wanted; she had performed for too long in countries where eccentricity was a prerequisite of success.[26]

This last charge may seem a bit rich coming from a culture which, in the 1890s, had presented the world with the exploits of *le pétomane* who played tunes by expelling air, though not through his upper orifices. But even if the first large influx of American troops into Paris in the summer of 1917 had been welcomed with songs like 'Les Sammies à Paris', 'Le drapeau américain' and 'Vive l'oncle Sam', it was not

P. 104: MISS HARRYET.
CONCERT MAYOL. 1927.

long before the French became alarmed about the swamping of native songs by the likes of foxtrots and shimmies, and French impresarios and songwriters felt obliged to confirm that Paris was primarily for the Parisians, and that visitors should after all be prepared to take the city on its own terms. This comes across plainly from the titles of the revues of the decade. The Casino de Paris put on *Paris qui jazze* in 1920, *Bonjour Paris* in 1924, *Paris en fleurs* and *Paris* in 1926, *Tout Paris* in 1928 and *Paris-Miss* in 1929, while at the Moulin Rouge you could have seen *Paris en l'air* in 1921, *Ça c'est Paris* in 1927, and *Paris qui tourne* and *Paris aux étoiles* in 1928 – with an ambiguous attempt in *New York–Montmartre* in 1924. To us today this may seem as though promoters were protesting too much. But it must have paid off, or they would not have done it.

As with the French operettas of the period, we are now chiefly dependent for any feeling of the world of revues, music halls, *café-concerts*, cabarets and 'dancings' on memoirs and photographs, and on gramophone records, many of which, especially in acoustic examples from before 1925, make for difficult listening even when transferred to CD.

Among the larger venues offering popular musical entertainment were the Casino de Paris, the Moulin Rouge, the Alhambra (burnt down by 1927), the Bouffes du Nord-Concert, the Folies-Bergère and the Olympia, the last two each with an audience capacity of 2,000. The 1920/21 *Annuaire des artistes* gives a huge price differential for the Olympia of ninety to three francs, ranging from boxes close to the stage to the 'promenoir' behind the stalls, a distinction underlining that the acts were intended primarily to be seen, with audibility a less important feature.

The theatre's publicity stated roundly that 'acrobats exercising harmoniously, jugglers of astonishing dexterity and ingenuity...tirelessly whirling dancers...wonderful trainers of clever dogs, parrots and sea-lions are artists, just like operatic tenors or leading actors in tragedy and comedy, and sometimes great artists'; and in company with the Weldons, acrobats in evening dress, the clown Boby and his menagerie of cocks, hens and pigs, and Fred Curtiss, 'the man who triples his weight', we find Lucie Caffaret 'the piano virtuoso, playing Chopin and Saint-Saëns' – perhaps not what she had had in mind when she won her Premier Prix, but at least she was reaching a wide audience. Debussy, too, had he still been alive, might have been surprised to see billed, on 2 July 1920, *L'antre des gnômes* (The Gnomes' Grotto). Accompanying the tale of a witch, ruling over the gnomes and turning a visitor into another of them, were pieces by Debussy, orchestrated by Gabriel Grovlez: four of the piano *Préludes* in fact, 'Ondine', 'Général Lavine', 'M. Pickwick' and 'Minstrels'. 'This music', ran the blurb, 'accompanies and articulates these disturbing and fantastic visions like a shudder.'

The number of music halls and *café-concerts* in Paris stayed more or less steady throughout the 1920s, with 42 in 1920, 49 in 1923 and 47 in 1927 (although the Olympia was almost immediately turned into a cinema following the Wall Street crash of 1929); likewise the slightly more up-market 'cabarets artistiques' (23, 25 and 27 in the same years) which congregated around Montmartre – these included the Cabaret Aristide Bruant, who made a very brief return just before his death in 1924 and, still popular, Le Chat Noir, both on the boulevard de Clichy. Many artists worked in all three types of venue, making appropriate changes in repertoire, dress and gesture.

The *grande dame* of the circuit was undoubtedly Yvette Guilbert. Already by the 1890s she had become a legend, her gaunt features and black gloves immortalized by Toulouse-Lautrec. Charles Gounod, in the last year of his life, had asked her to come and sing to him. At the 'cabaret artistique' called *Le divan japonais* in Montmartre she had smuggled *doubles entendres* on to the stage by the simple expedient of bribing the censors' office boy with a five-franc tip to help herself to the official stamp, and in 1896 she added to these saucy numbers a 'Negro song, "I want you, mah honey"', she

had brought back from her American tour. By the turn of the century she was becoming fascinated by the French *chansons* of the Renaissance, and further back as far as the eleventh century. Her repertoire, then, was idiosyncratic by the standards of that first decade of the twentieth century. How would it be received when, after seven years in America, she returned to Paris in 1922, to 'an era of giant dislocations, a present at odds with the past', in which 'to create a new world had become the categorical imperative – and who cared how raw, if only different!'?[27] In the event, her medieval songs now attracted only an elite audience at the Salle Gaveau, but in 1924, at the new Empire music hall, only a year short of her sixtieth birthday, she once again triumphed with her old favourites, 'Le petit cochon', 'L'hôtel du numéro 3' and, of course, 'Le fiacre'.

Mistinguett and Maurice Chevalier, though younger than Yvette (they were born in 1875 and 1888 respectively), had also both made their names before the war. It cannot be said that Mistinguett's musical gifts were her main assets – her voice was thin and acidulous even by French standards and lacked the variety of a Guilbert or an Yvonne George. Those assets consisted rather in her devotion to her work, her elegant legs and dancing skills, and her ability to 'walk down a staircase carrying fifteen pounds of plumes on her head and dragging seven yards of feathers behind her'.[28] She was also shrewd enough to capitalize on her fame by letting it be known that at any one time on stage she might be wearing 150,000 francs' worth of clothes, feathers and jewelry, and that her legs were insured for half a million francs – for which you could buy a house on the Champs-Elysées. But it would be churlish to deny the vitality of her singing in Yvain's song 'Mon homme', with its remorseless three-note 'hook', which was the hit of the revue *Paris qui jazze* in 1920 and made the composer's reputation. As with much of what she sang, there was a fascination in the contrast between her gorgeous appearance and her singing style, which was deliberately 'peuple', or 'common', reassuring French audiences that, beneath all the flummery, she was a good-hearted Parisian girl and one who would even, as in 'Mon

Yvette Guilbert,
drawn by
Toulouse-Lautrec
in 1894

Rue du faubourg
St-Denis in 1920 with
a sign for the
Concert Mayol

Opérettes, music hall, revues, chansons

homme', 'stand by her man' when he ignored or beat her. All in all, it is safe to say that one would have had to see her on stage to appreciate the magic.

As for Chevalier, Jacques Damase spoke no more than the truth when he said that he 'doesn't sing particularly well' and 'can't dance particularly well, either'. And he was surely right too when he claimed that in the case of both artists, 'the conscientiousness, the firm, inventive authority, the touches of elegance and taste, the polish...derived from their knowledge of the life of the streets and of the common people [and] made them into supreme international entertainers'.[29] Chevalier had the advantage of having fought in the war and been taken prisoner – it was in prison that he learnt English from captured British soldiers and so was able to pursue his career after the war in Britain and America. Coming from an ex-squaddy his cheerful approach to life was taken to heart by the Parisian public: it was respected as being the attitude of the *débrouillard* (the resourceful coper with difficulties),[30] which had finally won France the war, rather than any striking abilities shown by their generals.

Before 1914 Chevalier had been a gawky comic, basing himself on Dranem and using a full repertoire of funny faces and curious postures. After the war he took to the cane and boater that became his trademark and adopted the persona of an *insouciant*, always smiling and looking on the bright side of things, as in the two 1921 hit songs 'Avec le sourire' from the revue of the same name, and 'Dans la vie faut pas s'en faire' ('In life one mustn't take things to heart') from *Dédé*. Less positively, this insouciance extended in real life to his treatment of women: he claimed that, as a result

Mistinguett and Maurice Chevalier in prewar guise

...in a more sophisticated postwar incarnation

of the war, 'we have learned the vanity of words and fine pretexts'. Despite his great success in *Dédé*, he did not take kindly to competition in it from his erstwhile hero Dranem, and never again appeared in operetta. He was careful even in revues to see that his star was not in danger of being outshone, and preferred the strains of solo work for the undivided limelight it afforded him, as well as the chance to cultivate his insouciant persona. Whether through his influence or not, it is certainly true that in the Twenties French men sang songs predominantly of humour and fantasy, and it was left to the women to chart the turbid world of the emotions.

A third artist who, like Chevalier, became a supreme international entertainer, and without whom no picture of Paris in the Twenties would be complete, arrived at the Gare St-Lazare on 22 September 1925. André Daven, the producer of the forthcoming show at the Théâtre des Champs-Elysées met the train and recalled:

> Out spilled a little world, rocking, boisterous, multicolored, carrying
> bizarre musical instruments, all talking loudly, some roaring with laughter.
> Red, green, yellow shirts, strawberry denims, dresses in polka dots and
> checks. Incredible hats – derbies – cream colored, orange and poppy,
> surmounted thirty ebony faces, wild and joyous eyes.[31]

Josephine Baker and *La revue nègre* had arrived.

As with Mistinguett, Josephine's voice was certainly not the most startling part of her, but this did not prevent her launching several long-running songs, like 'La petite Tonkinoise' and 'J'ai deux amours, mon pays et Paris', both by Vincent Scotto (who produced more than four thousand songs in his career and was to be one of the leading songwriters after Yvain). An article in the magazine *Candide* summed up Josephine's curious blend of high glamour and low humour:

> The revue begins at ten fifteen.... Paris Society crowds the darkened
> auditorium.... The negro musicians file past the pearl-grey curtains with
> their instruments.... The curtain rises: the scene is a port by night. Away in
> the distance, you can see cargo-boats lit up, the moon, bales on wharves,

> and women in shirts and dresses, some wearing turbans, come on stage and sing a short song.... They dance a Charleston.... Then a curious figure dashes on stage, sagging at the knees, wearing a pair of tattered shorts and looking like a cross between a boxing kangaroo, a piece of chewing-gum and a racing cyclist – it's Josephine Baker![32]

Josephine's extraordinary magnetism prolonged 'the jazz age' in Paris perhaps beyond its natural life span; but it is interesting that many of the songs she was regularly asked to sing over the next fifty years were little indebted to jazz. During her funeral at

Opérettes, music hall, revues, chansons

the Madeleine on 15 April 1975, after performances of 'Sonny Boy' on the harp and of Mozart's *Requiem* with full forces, the three-manual Cavaillé-Coll rounded off the ceremony with a rendering of the decidedly non-jazzy 'J'ai deux amours'.[33]

For the moment, though, 'she was like a revolution or a tidal wave. Not since 1909, when Diaghilev presented the Ballets russes starring Nijinsky and Pavlova, had Paris been witness to such a sweeping conquest.'[34] From the Théâtre des Champs-Elysées she moved to the Folies-Bergère and from there to the Casino de Paris. She made films, appeared in Offenbach's operetta *La créole*, and in 1928 embarked on her first world tour. Throughout the decade, Paris audiences relished the contradictions in her character: she was sexy, she was a clown; she was savage, she was knowing; she was good-hearted, she was cruel. But Paris left its mark on her nonetheless. As Petrine Archer-Straw relates:

Josephine Baker with jewelry

> After her 1930 performances at the Folies-Bergère and the Casino de Paris, a special catalogue of more than one hundred reviews was produced to commemorate the highlights of her career. A significant feature of the catalogue is its before-and-after approach. Images of and articles about Josephine before 1925 are compared with those made in 1930. The early reviews are selected to reflect her savage nature, while the later ones praise her sense of poise and polished performance. This 'packaging'…provided an identity for Baker that was better suited to refined bourgeois taste. Advertisements for her performances at the Folies-Bergère and the Casino de Paris show her as a picture of refinement – bejewelled, coiffured and dressed in designer clothes.
>
> France warmed to Baker because they felt she loved their country and the new life and status it had brought her. Josephine's adoption by the mainstream suited the needs of colonialism. It reinforced notions of civilization that were constantly being questioned by the avant-garde. French audiences witnessed what they believed was her successful transformation from an African 'savage' to an urbane, sophisticated lady. In the ambivalent years after the war, her life was a public affirmation of France's colonial success abroad, and of its promise for the future.[35]

Or, to put it more crudely, 'we may have needed help to overcome the Boches, but at least we can still teach the non-Caucasians a thing or two'.

We have already seen (p. 70) the apprehension caused in serious musical circles by the popularity of the cinema. In 1923, the critic Charles Tenroc could even claim that 'the music hall in its turn is ailing, gravely undermined by the silent screen'.[36] This turned out to be untrue. As noted above, the number of music halls remained more or less constant throughout the decade, while the number of cinemas

LA REVUE DES
FOLIES-BERGERE
1926-1927

JOSÉPHINE BAKER

Photo Waléry, Hélischroma Vanzelai.

decreased sharply, from some 300 in 1920 to 200 in 1923 and 180 in 1927. Admittedly the threat then became more real with the advent of the talkies and, in the mid-Thirties, the film with singing. And not only on the popular front, of which the instigator was Chevalier's Hollywood-produced *La chanson de Paris*, first shown in the capital in July 1929 – Georges Thill, for example, made two films, *Chansons de Paris* and *Aux portes de Paris* in 1934 and one of Charpentier's *Louise* in 1938 with Grace

Moore and André Pernet. More threatening from the music hall's point of view was the slight increase during the Twenties in dance halls ('bals-dancings') from 90 in 1920 to 110 in 1927.

Although Yvette Guilbert found the music hall dull and tired when she returned to Paris in 1922, clearly force of habit among the audience was strong. This habit was supported increasingly by the fact that the stars in all fields – operetta, revue, music hall, *café-concert* and cabaret – were putting their songs on record. In some cases, as with *Dédé* and *Ciboulette*, these recordings were made before the first night so as to be sure of hitting the market at the most propitious moment. As a body, these recordings provide one of our best insights into the temper of the times, both through their content and through the different styles they espoused.

It had long been a feature of Parisian popular song, as of urban entertainment everywhere, that it cast a sardonic light on the events of the day. As we have seen with the operettas *Sur la bouche* and *Coups de roulis*, the *nouveaux riches* and the politicians were both reckoned to be fair game. In one remarkable instance in May 1920, life followed art, when the President of the Republic, Paul Deschanel, 'an amiable nonentity'[37] who had been appointed to keep Clemenceau from power, fell out of a train in the middle of the night and was found next morning wandering along the track in his pyjamas in a state of mental disarray ('I knew he was someone important', said the railway worker's wife who found him, 'because his feet were so clean'). The songwriter Lucien Boyer was quick to come up with what he called a 'chanson express' entitled 'Le pyjama présidentiel', but altogether more extraordinary was the fact that four years earlier Charles Borel-Clerc had written a song called 'Le train fatal', which was sung by the popular male singer Bérard. Happily for them, though, it had never been recorded and now they could hardly believe their luck. They did not even need to change the words to accommodate this latest event – the title was enough.

Another political talking-point had been the decision by MM. Deschanel and Millerand earlier in 1920 to put a tax on musical instruments (whether Deschanel's insanity took hold before or after he made this decision was debated). Although the levy was intended to be on all musical instruments, it was interpreted and referred to as a piano tax because every middle-class household had one. The pages of *Le courrier musical* and *Le ménestrel* tell something of the extended battle that ensued. In March 1920 the Conseil municipal de Paris announced that the annual tax would be 30 francs on upright pianos and 60 francs on grands. The following month, the publisher Jacques Durand wrote complaining that no other working tool or implement of trade was taxed in this way. But in January 1921 the tax was voted in, at the above rates and applicable retrospectively to 1 January 1920; nor were professional pianists exempt. By February 1921 the opposition was beginning to mount, with the critic Louis Vuillemin advocating non-payment. In March it was decided by sixty-five votes to three to delay a final decision until June, perhaps under the influence of the new director of the Conservatoire, Henri Rabaud, who came out strongly against the tax. At the end of July the tax was finally accepted at the suggested rate, but with professionals now exempt. By January 1927, of the 147,000 pianos registered, 132,000 were subject to the tax, with only 15,000 exempt.

On the face of it, it looked like a victory for the government over its critics. But what they could not legislate over were Parisians' feelings or their sense of humour. Within weeks of the initial announcement in March 1920, the Casino de Paris had commissioned a revue from Maurice Yvain called *Cach' ton piano*, whose title song became a hit, the lyrics of the ubiquitous Albert Willemetz urging Parisians to hide anything that might be construed as a musical instrument, including sticks and wooden clappers. For the price of the tax, admittedly not small, the government had to pay through being the butt of longstanding resentment – one more nail, possibly, in the coffin that was finally wheeled out with the victory of the Popular Front in 1936.

But the satire was more telling for being apparently good-humoured. The unknown author of the words of the 1921 song 'Il était syndiqué' struck at the unionization of everybody – post-office workers, road-sweepers, the lot – so that you couldn't afford to offend anyone any more, but the very exaggeration of the lyrics takes the song into the realms of fantasy. The song's evident good nature seems all the more remarkable since it was written in the shadow of strikes by railway workers in February 1920 which paralysed large parts of the country. The miners soon followed, and the social unrest led directly to the formation, that December, of the French Communist Party. Another, less political vein occasionally exploited was to take a well-known operatic heroine and reinterpret her situation in a contemporary musical style: hence the 'Tango de Manon' of 1920 and the *Faust* parody 'J'ai vendu mon âme au diable' of 1922, although neither made use of the original music.

But the two most popular topics, as ever in Paris, were love and fashion. Among the female singers about love, it is almost possible to distinguish two kinds according to the pitch of their voices. The high, thin sound of Mistinguett, Josephine Baker, Judic or Gaby Montbreuse is, to the male ear at least, sexually unthreatening, even though the words may have more than a little edge. On the other hand, there is an unmistakably sexual, even erotic charge in the contralto tones of the 57-year-old Eugénie Buffet, singing in 'Ma chanson' of 1923 of the poor and down-and-outs whose cause she championed with such fervour; or of Damia, who had made her name in Paris during the war singing to troops on leave; or especially of Yvonne George.

George was hailed by many as the successor to Yvette Guilbert, but unlike Guilbert she chose to live the life of which she sang:

> Each season she became more frail, the prey of both excessive drug
> addiction and harsh antidotes to drunkenness...and she developed a
> passion for Montparnasse cabarets and their new exotic atmosphere.
> She loved ports: Antwerp, Marseilles and Villefranche, American

sailors coming ashore, their athletic bodies and lithe hips in tight jerseys and bell-bottom trousers.[38]

But before her early suicide in Genoa she put on to disc some of the decade's most disturbing sounds, a world away from Mistinguett's or Chevalier's nonchalant bonhomie. Her 1925 recording of 'C'est pour ça qu'on s'aime' is a terrifying portrait of a masochistic mistress, half-obsessed and half-revolted by her lover's brutal ways. Her singing, quite apart from its high technical ability, is a valuable reminder that, behind all the glitter of the *années folles*, for the great majority of the French population it was a time of poverty and anxiety, and, for many, a time of grieving over those killed in the war.

For some years after 1917, the song 'La Madelon' had been one of the most popular of all. It told of a simple, innocent barmaid, and caught on at home and in the army, reminding those on both fronts of the values they were fighting for, while steering clear of any uncomfortable realism. With variations, this song remained a favourite for some five years, but by 1923 the patriotic song in whatever guise was starting to disappear, and with it the prewar figure of the comic 'squaddy'. Instead, the preferred subjects of love and fashion were increasingly shot through with nostalgia for the Paris of old, before the war and before the invasion of Americans and Americana.

Two artists perhaps above all expressed the mood of the city, and in doing so conformed to the convention by which the male role was largely to mock and to fantasize, the female role to assume the burden of life's sorrows. Damia had begun her career in 1911, when still in her late teens. After singing for the troops at the front, she developed her gifts as a dancer and actress as well as a singer, and Marc Robine may well be right in suggesting that she was slow to put her songs on disc (which she did not begin to do until 1926) because she could not imagine them shorn of their scenic trappings.[39] Another explanation, though, may simply be that she did not trust the earlier stages of the acoustic recording process to reproduce faithfully the individual timbre of her voice. In the years 1920–26 this process had improved considerably, before electrical recording became the norm in 1927.

In the 1970s, Christopher Isherwood, looking back to the prewar Berlin he had known, wrote that 'Paris had long since cornered the straight-girl market',[40] provoking those of Berlin to cater for more recherché tastes. This was true to the extent that the female entertainers of Paris were grounded in the city's mythology: life was hard, but love conquered all; men could be brutes, but one would not be without them; and as a counterpart to the men's gaiety and bravado, women should cultivate style and charm or, failing those, a heroic stoicism. Damia epitomized the stoic female. In 'Le portrait', one of the first songs she recorded in 1926, it is easy to see how she became a model for Edith Piaf. Gazing at the portrait of her faithless lover, Damia sings of the love that will never leave her heart. The hard, lived-in quality of her tone and the clarity of her diction ensure that not a nuance is lost, and the unusual backing of a piano quintet lends its own peculiar emotional support – the ever-present trumpets and cymbals of the conventional male *chanson* belong to another world. Finally, like most of the dramatic female singers of the time, Damia is a true contralto, happier below the treble stave than on it. While never for a moment crossing the gender divide, she seems to use this low register to minimize the distance between the sexes – 'vive la différence', she seems to say, 'but we're human too, why don't you treat us as such?'

For some tastes Damia laid the drama on a touch strongly. The same realism she sought was achieved by means of irony and parody in the songs of Georgius, one of the suprisingly few performers who wrote his own words. If Georgius's work has always been little known outside France, that is because his style of very fast patter incorporating multiple puns does not translate (even Chevalier, for somewhat different reasons, had difficulty in America with 'Valentine', which became his signature tune, the 'petits tétons' (little tits) he liked to squeeze having to be curiously bowdlerized for any prudish French-speaking Americans in the audience into a 'petit python'). Georgius was the epitome of the perky, witty, unputdownable Parisian. He

> skilfully exploited so much that was perceived to be distinctly French that
> his songs were hailed by critics throughout the 1920s as a sign that the
> traditional French popular song was not dying. Assuming the role of
> defender of the French song, he played to his audiences' critical sense
> of what was French and what was the Other offstage, too. In the early
> Twenties he organized and led a 'Union indépendante' of *café-concert*
> singers in a campaign of opposition to German performers (and indeed
> to all foreign acts, except Belgian ones). This 'counter-offensive of the
> caf' conc' ', as reviewer Fréjaville termed it, was a struggle to stem the tide
> of exoticism and cosmopolitanism engulfing the music halls and even
> threatening the more distinctively French venue of songs, the caf'-conc'.[41]

This defensive spirit lasted throughout the decade, and in 1928 we find the singer Perchicot scoring a hit with a number simply entitled 'La chanson française', looking back to the happy days of the 'Madelon' and, through a blessedly unhistorical mist, to those of the 'Marseillaise'.

It says much for Georgius's standing that even André Breton, the famously non-musical leader of the Surrealists, was a devotee of his work. Certainly Georgius exemplified both possible definitions of the word 'surréalisme', either as 'super-realism' or as something that goes beyond realism – 'ultra-realism'.

A popular example of the former was his 1927 song 'Qu'est-ce qu'il faut fair' pour gagner son bifteck?', a super-realistic litany of the jobs people have to do to earn a living: showmen at fairs have to swallow swords, a prostitute has to please a seventy-year-old customer who is taking his time, a surgeon has to spend the day with his hands covered in intestines, and the wet-nurse pulls out her breast with no more thought than you or I would give to shaking hands. The realism is increased if anything by Georgius's upbeat delivery and the song's resolute grounding in the major mode: no lamenting *à la Damia*. As Charles Rearick says, 'the song envelops resignation in levity'.[42]

Levity could also be used, though, to protest about those details of life which, with a little thought, could be changed, or which smacked of pretension and thus demanded to be satirized. In his 1929 song 'Le piéton' (The pedestrian), Georgius inveighs against the traffic which is gradually making Paris intolerable. Crossing the road has now become a major enterprise, and his tip for pedestrians is to arm themselves with a doll in a pram and launch themselves behind it into the unending stream. Whatever marks we give Georgius for 'surrealistic' inge-nuity, the deeper message is not hard to detect: that in modern, high-speed Paris, humanity has been so degraded that only babies command respect any more. For able-bodied Parisians, the motto is 'sauve qui peut'. As for satirical songs, they acted, as always, as a vehicle through which die-hards could let off steam about the modern fads – as in the 1927 *chanson* 'Elle sait conduire une automobile...Cécile', where the young lady in question, apparently mistress of her car (and her fate?), rather spoils things by being overheard asking the mechanic to 'grease my tyres and blow up my back-axle'.

Cabaret l'Enfer on
the boulevard de Clichy
in 1920

All in all, as in the world of the Opéra-Comique, the popular songwriters, singers and audiences were torn between postwar and prewar attitudes. The Paris of the revue titles – *Paris qui jazze, Paris-voyeur, Paris qui tourne* – generated not only interna-tional status, but large amounts of money for a nation which was trying to rebuild the wreckage of 812,000 houses, 54,000 km of roads and 5,500 km of railway track, and to bring back into production some seven million acres of agricultural land. If the internationalization and exotification of French culture made some people uneasy about what now defined the French identity, market forces ensured there could be no going back to a time when Paris was 'mon village', except in the memory. Tradition-alists, though, had the consolation that they could now hear the old songs not just in *caf'-conc's* and music halls, or on the streets, but in the privacy of their own homes, without venturing out into the dangers of the city. Much as you might resent the tax on your piano, it would at least have made you feel you ought to get your money's worth out of it, and family singsongs were as much a feature of 1920s Paris as of Vic-torian England. With the improvement of record technology, collectors amassed enough discs to make every night nostalgia night if they so wished, and with the first music broadcast from the Eiffel Tower on 22 June 1921 a further avenue for private listening was opened up. Needless to say, the combination of records and radio pro-vided an enormous fillip for the popular music publishers, who until now had relied for their income solely on public performances and the sale of sheet music. One of the largest of these publishers, Francis Salabert, with *Phi-Phi, Dédé* and many of the

revues in his catalogue, was able to use the profits to underwrite music by serious composers, including Auric, Poulenc, Milhaud and Sauguet.

The tensions in popular culture between old and new and between French and foreign were maintained throughout the 1930s. There were those, like the critic Eugène Dabit, who even denied that these tensions should be allowed to coexist, insisting that the time had come to face reality:

> The illusion must end – people must know that we are in 1933, with Montparnasse and *boîtes de nuit* nearby, and war and revolution or fascism before us. Life is not easy, sure, slow, and men are ever more beastly to each other, and more sick in their joys or their hatreds.[43]

To some extent this complaint was out of date by 1933, when the effects of the Depression were belatedly being felt in France – for one thing, the number of foreign tourists dropped from 1,910,000 in 1929 to a mere 390,000 in 1935. No one, not even the most besotted devotee of nostalgia, could avoid experiencing these new hard times; and it seems a little unkind of Monsieur Dabit to try and deny Parisians the hopes embodied in so many of the old songs: that life was tough but might, just possibly, get better; and that, whatever incursions the city had to suffer, the essence of the old Paris would always survive. In the event it was to survive even the German Occupation.

Notes

1. *Cinquante ans de musique française*, ed. L. Rohozinski, I (Paris, 1925), pp. 199–322.
2. Ibid., p. 200.
3. Ibid., p. 310.
4. James Harding, *Folies de Paris: The Rise and Fall of French Operetta* (London, 1979), p. 167.
5. Rohozinski (ed.), *Cinquante ans*, I, p. 310.
6. *Le courrier musical*, 1 December 1926.
7. Richard Buckle, *Diaghilev* (London, 1979; repr. 1984), p. 425.
8. 'L'opérette française par ses créateurs, 1921–1934', 2 CD box, EPM 982482 ADE 684, with accompanying leaflet, from which some of my information comes.
9. See Rohozinsky (ed.), *Cinquante ans*, I, p. 320.
10. Charles Rearick, *The French in Love and War* (New Haven, 1997), p. 91.
11. Harding, *Folies de Paris*, p. 160.
12. Theodore Zeldin, *France 1848–1945*: I, *Ambition and Love* (Oxford, 1973; enlarged edn 1979, repr. 1988), p. 360.
13. Quoted, see Harding, *Folies de Paris*, p. 161.
14. Gabriel Fournier, 'Erik Satie et son époque', in *La revue musicale*, 214 (1952), p. 130.
15. Robert Orledge, *Satie the Composer* (Cambridge, 1990), p. 357 n. 15.
16. René Dumesnil, *La musique en France entre les deux guerres, 1919–1939* (Geneva, 1946), p. 34.
17. Igor Stravinsky and Robert Craft, *Expositions and Developments* (London, 1962), p. 92.
18. Eric Walter White, *Stravinsky: The Composer and his Works* (London, 1966; 2nd edn 1979), p. 271.
19. *Le ménestrel*, 10 June 1921.
20. Foreword to Jacques Damase, *Les folies du music-hall* (London, 1970).
21. James Gardiner, *Gaby Deslys: A Fatal Attraction* (London, 1986), p. 152.
22. Darius Milhaud, 'L'évolution du jazz-band et la musique des nègres d'Amérique du Nord', in *Le courrier musical*, 1 May 1923; repr. in *Darius Milhaud. Notes sur la musique*, ed. Jeremy Drake (Paris, 1982), pp. 99–100.
23. Ibid., pp. 30–31.
24. Booklet accompanying *Anthologie de la chanson française*, vol. 20/30, EPM, Paris, pp. 13–14.
25. *Ravel au miroir de ses lettres*, ed. René Chalupt, (Paris, 1956), p. 177.
26. Gardiner, *Gaby Deslys*, p. 171.
27. Bettina Knapp and Myra Chipman, *That was Yvette* (London, 1966), pp. 67, 98–99, 141, 245.
28. Damase, *Les folies*, p. 26.
29. Ibid., p. 28.
30. Charles Rearick, *The French in Love and War* (New Haven, 1997), p. 8.
31. Lynn Haney, *Naked at the Feast* (London, 1986), pp. 49–50.
32. Damase, *Les folies*, p. 28.
33. Josephine Baker and Jo Bouillon, *Josephine*, trans. Mariana Fitzpatrick (New York, 1977), p. 293.
34. Haney, *Naked*, p. 61
35. Petrine Archer-Straw, *Negrophilia, Avant-garde Paris and Black Culture in the 1920s* (London, 2000), p. 133.
36. Charles Tenroc, in *Le courrier musical*, 15 April 1923.
37. Alfred Cobban, *A History of Modern France*, III (London, 1965; repr. 1975), p. 123.
38. Damase, *Les folies*, p. 10.
39. *Anthologie de la chanson française*, p. 33.
40. Christopher Isherwood, *Christopher and his Kind* (London, 1977), p. 29. I am grateful to Patrick O'Connor for this reference.
41. Rearick, *The French*, p. 115.
42. Ibid., p. 113.
43. Ibid., p. 124.

6. Ballet

The Palais Garnier

NOWHERE WAS THE INVASION of foreign talent more prevalent than in the world of the ballet. We have perhaps to force ourselves to remember that the Paris Opéra, officially called the Académie nationale de musique, regularly programmed ballet music in addition to that found in operas themselves, and that in pre-Diaghilev days this ballet music had had a high profile, especially for the male members of the Opéra's audience. Two dancers especially, Carlotta Zambelli and Albert Aveline, held popular favour for some years before the First World War and through the 1920s: Zambelli, for instance, danced the role of the Snow Fairy in Paul Vidal's *La maladetta* in its second run in 1900 and was still dancing it in 1927. It would be idle to pretend that, musically, the Opéra's home-grown ballets during the 1920s offered the novelty and excitement of the troupes led by Diaghilev, Rolf de Maré and Ida Rubinstein (to which I shall turn in due course), but in view of the neglect into which these indigenous offerings have fallen, it will be as well to give a menu of the staple diet at the Palais Garnier during the period 1917–29, as well as of new productions. Only those ballets that achieved ten performances in this period are included. Since, interestingly, the documentation of ballet at the Palais Garnier for these years is less complete than that for opera, in some cases we have to be content with approximate figures (*p* stands for Opéra, but not necessarily world, premiere, *r* for revival):

> Delibes: *Sylvia*, r1919/1929 (Zambelli, Aveline)(46 perfs)
> Delibes: *Coppélia*, r400th perf 1920/ 500th 1927
> Auber, Boïeldieu, Meyerbeer, Weekerlin, arr. Busser: *Taglioni chez Musette*,
>   p1920/r1926 (Zambelli, Aveline) (55 perfs)
> Dukas: *La péri*, p1921 (Pavlova)/r1929 (Spessivtseva) (c.50 perfs)
> Grovlez: *Maimouna*, p1921 (22 perfs)
> Hahn: *La fête chez Thérèse*, r1921 (10 perfs)
> Ravel: *Daphnis et Chloé*, p1921 (Fokina, Fokine)/r1927 (Zambelli, Aveline)
>   (18 perfs)
> Chopin arr. Messager, Vidal: *Suite de danses*, r1922/192 (c.80 perfs)
> Debussy arr. Busser: *Petite suite*, p1922 (26 perfs)
> Schmitt: *La tragédie de Salomé*, r1922/1928 (Spessivtseva) (47 perfs)
> Vidal: *La maladetta*, r1922 (Zambelli, Ricaux)/1927 (Zambelli, Aveline)
>   (11 perfs)

Chopin arr. Aubert: *La nuit ensorcelée*, p1923 (Zambelli, Staats)/r1927
   (Johnsson, Aveline) (93 perfs)

Pierné: *Cydalise et le chèvre-pied*, p1923 (26 perfs)

Adam: *Giselle*, r1924 (18 perfs)

Hüe: *Siang Sin*, p1924/r1927 (74 perfs)

Delibes arr. Busser: *Soir de fête*, p1925 (Spessivtseva) (c.80 perfs: taken from
   La source)

Delmas: *Cyrca*, p1927 (10 perfs)

Inghelbrecht: *Le diable dans le beffroi*, p1927 (Aveline) (14 perfs)

Pierné: *Impressions de music-hall*, p1927 (41 perfs) (Zambelli, Aveline)

Roland-Manuel: *L'écran des jeunes filles*, p1929 (17 perfs)

Ravel, Ferroud, Ibert, Roland-Manuel, Delannoy, Roussel, Milhaud, Poulenc,
   Auric, Schmitt: *L'éventail de Jeanne*, p1929 (16 perfs)

Messager: *Les deux pigeons*, r100th perf 1935

Of these twenty-two ballets, five (*Sylvia, Coppélia, Giselle, La source* and *Les deux pigeons*) were old favourites, although *Sylvia* was now performed with a new choreography by the Opéra's ballet master Léo Staats. Both *La péri* and *La tragédie de Salomé* had formed part of Trouhanova's 1912 season at the Châtelet, while *Daphnis et Chloé* had been given that same year by the Ballets russes. Three further works, *Taglioni chez Musette, Suite de danses* and *La nuit ensorcelée*, belonged to the old class of potpourri, continuing the dominance of music and dance over the storyline. While Rouché could not be taxed with carrying on the historically backward-looking programming he had espoused during the war, when he had provided distraction from the hostilities by reproducing 'the fantastic ballets in which Louis XIV danced in his youth and the so-called "musical suppers" which diverted him in his old age',[1] nonetheless all the composers represented in the above list were French (or, in the case of Chopin, French by residence). Only eight of these ballets (*Maimouna, Cydalise et le chèvre-pied, Siang Sin, Cyrca, Le diable dans le beffroi, Impressions de music-hall, L'écran des jeunes filles* and *L'éventail de Jeanne*) can be classed as wholly original products, and of these *L'éventail* reached the Opéra via Mme René Dubost's salon, while both *Maimouna* and *Siang Sin* tapped somewhat tired Oriental sources.

Two of the twenty-two merit further attention. On 15 January 1923, Chevillard conducted the premiere of Gabriel Pierné's *Cydalise et le chèvre-pied*. As Lynn Garafola suggests, this 'may well have been Rouché's answer to *The Sleeping Princess*', Diaghilev's production of Tchaikovsky's *The Sleeping Beauty* which had been seen in Paris twelve times in the previous eight months. She pertinently quotes the ballet historian André Levinson, who wrote in 1924 of this

charming thing in the manner of Sèvres porcelain [which] juggles
with anachronisms and delights in historical paradox. What matters...
is the grace of faded things, their naughty and melancholic smile;

not the vase, but the perfume; not the austere truth, but the
imaginary splendor.[2]

It was the higher-class counterpart of those popular songs that harked back to a time
when Paris had not yet become a large city, and all was right with France.

An attempt may be seen to counterbalance this nostalgia in the same composer's
one-act ballet *Impressions de music-hall*, premiered at the Palais Garnier on 6 April 1927.
The more elderly habitués were not amused by the sight of their adored Carlotta
Zambelli dancing a cakewalk, nor by a troupe of chorus girls and three families
of 'musical clowns'. Even if one feels that Pierné was, at the age of sixty-three and
as a member of the Institut, not a first choice to produce this kind of music, he did at
least come close to embodying Ravel's passionate wish, when embarking on *L'enfant
et les sortilèges*, 'to have two negroes singing a ragtime at the Académie nationale
de musique'.[3]

But overall it seems clear from the Opéra's ballet repertoire in the 1920s that
Rouché was not intent on taking the art into uncharted waters. As we have seen from
his problems with the operatic side of the Palais Garnier, and with Malipiero's *Sette
canzoni* in particular, a policy of chauvinism was enjoined on him both by the *abonnés*
and by those responsible for delivering the government's subsidy. The Opéra's Festival of French ballet in 1922 accorded absolutely with these demands. Also, perhaps,
he realized his luck in having Zambelli and Aveline as popular, respected leading
dancers and Léo Staats as a reliable choreographer. In the other four ballet enterprises I shall now examine, popularity and respect were not universal constants,
either within the companies themselves or in their views of each other.

Diaghilev and the Ballets russes

Parade in May 1917 had already signalled that Diaghilev was moving away from the
Russian and Oriental spectacle which had dominated his prewar productions. This
change coincided with, and was possibly reinforced by, Nijinsky's defection and subsequent descent into insanity: he danced with the Ballets russes for the last time in
Buenos Aires on 26 September of that same year. But when Diaghilev's company
made its postwar return to Paris for the 'eleventh Russian season', at the Opéra, on
Christmas Eve 1919, it would have been difficult for any member of the audience to
guess what new direction the impresario was going to take.

Nor would the programme of sixteen evenings, lasting until 16 February 1920,
have provided much illumination. The one world premiere, Stravinsky's *Le chant du
rossignol*, with designs by Matisse and choreography by Massine, drew heavily for its
music on the 'conte lyrique' Diaghilev had produced five years earlier (Eric Walter
White describes it as 'a pleasant orchestral reminder of some of the lyrical delights
that are to be found in the opera').[4] Of the other ballets in that season, nine had been
seen in Paris before, and the only newcomers to the city were *La boutique fantasque*

(Respighi's orchestration of Rossini piano pieces) and Falla's *El sombrero de tres picos*. It is hard to avoid the impression that Diaghilev was marking time, getting the smell of the postwar Paris, before launching out on some *nouvelle vague*.

In her thorough and penetrating study of the Ballets russes, Lynn Garafola identifies three trends which in her opinion seem to unify the period:

> The first, which I have baptized 'lifestyle modernism', was associated with Jean Cocteau's art of the sophisticated commonplace. The second, 'retrospective classicism', mirrored the French elite's fascination with the aristocratic culture of the *grand siècle*. The third, 'choreographic neoclassicism', was the offspring of Bronislava Nijinska and George Balanchine, émigré representatives of the Soviet dance vanguard. Overlapping, sometimes even in the same work, these trends coexisted uneasily in the Diaghilev repertory – and in ballet at large – during most of the 1920s.[5]

The third of these trends is for the most part too narrowly focused on the dance to have had much impact on the music of the period (*Les noces* and *Apollon musagète*,

choreographed by Nijinska and Balanchine respectively, might constitute exceptions only if we could be sure that in each case Stravinsky's music was a concomitant rather than a determining factor). But the conflict between 'lifestyle modernism' and 'retrospective classicism' lies at the heart of the music of the time, both serious and popular, forming a vital element in the search by the French, and most ostensibly by the Parisians, for a postwar identity, as we saw in the case of the Opéra-Comique.

Stravinsky, Diaghilev, Cocteau and Satie, drawn by Larionov

Jean Cocteau was a key figure in the fashioning and publicizing of 'lifestyle modernism' and 'in the ballet *Parade* and in *Le coq et l'arlequin*, a treatise he published in 1918, he absorbed, transformed, and tamed key futurist precepts, laying the foundation'[6] for the trend. As Garafola goes on to point out, the 'turns' in *Parade* 'likened the ballet to a music-hall show – that jumble of animal, dance, magic, tumbling and "bioscope" numbers that so appealed to the futurists'. Pierné's *Impressions de music-hall* may therefore be seen as a belated and rather tame attempt on the same goal, and both ballets as a complete volte-face from the unified whole which contemporary critics had been so impressed to find in *L'oiseau de feu* and its two successors and on which Fokine was so determined in choreographing *Daphnis et Chloé*; long before the collaboration with Ravel was envisaged, he had written that 'the ballet must be uninterrupted – a complete artistic creation and not a series of separate numbers'.[7] We may therefore ask why there should have been this turning away from a continuous whole and a reversion to diversity. Was there something in the Paris air of the 1920s that militated against what Fokine called 'a complete artistic creation'?

The answer might well be 'yes' to the extent that 'a complete artistic creation' suggests music one listens to 'with one's head in one's hands', as Cocteau puts it in *Le coq et l'arlequin*. In all the arts, there were moves away from a linear, cumulative narrative leading to an ecstatic or cathartic climax. Diaghilev, though, for all his general willingness to embrace the future, remained a Wagner lover, with at least some of what that implied; and in 1923 Nijinska had a battle with him over the scenario of *Les noces*:

> He could not readily discard the idea of a literary libretto for the ballet.
> Yet in spite of this, with great efforts, I was able to carry my ideas of
> the form of the ballet as I conceived them into my productions with
> Diaghilev. These ballets of mine ...carried out the negation of the literary
> libretto, having a pure dance form for their foundation and moulding
> this into a new species of composition. *Noces* was the first work where
> the libretto was a hidden theme for a pure choreography; it was a
> choreographic concerto.[8]

Balanchine followed the same line, declaring that 'in ballet it is possible for a character to explain that he is the ballerina's lover, but not that he is her brother-in-law'.[9] It seems that Nijinska's success in this area quickly reconciled Diaghilev to the dethroning of narrative, since he told the American composer John Alden Carpenter in 1924 to write a ballet about the modern city without regard to story or action.[10]

Both Cubism and Surrealism disrupted linear narrative, relying instead on elements of perspective and contrast. Linked with these was the whole 1920s notion of speed: not only speed of movement, but speed of perception and especially speed of movement between perceptions. Beneath Diaghilev's famous challenge to Cocteau, 'Etonne-moi!' lay the subtext 'A tout prix ne m'ennuie pas!' – 'Whatever you do, don't bore me!'

One of the characteristics of what Garafola calls 'lifestyle modernism' was naturally that it moved at a modern speed. This could be realized not only by fast tempi but also by abrupt intercutting of ideas, as in the circus, the music hall or the cinema. Another, equally important characteristic was that the modern ballet should *look* modern: the tutu was to be replaced by up-to-date Parisian chic. It has been pointed out often enough that this eschewing of the exotic or the historical, both of which had been mainstays of Parisian spectacle for centuries, was in itself a novelty. But surely of equal importance was the implied notion that Parisian high life was now itself validated as a theatrical spectacle. At smart parties you no longer saw, as it were, the scions of the upper middle class disporting themselves, but the characters of *Les biches* and *Le train bleu*. This stage personification therefore served the purposes not only of novelty, ever one of Diaghilev's goals, but of confirming to the bourgeoisie that in the increasingly populist era of the 1920s, their pursuits, however trivial or even amoral they might be, were informed by some artistic value. And through seeing their lives transformed into works of art they were granted a sense of identity, albeit a transient one.

The trend of 'retrospective classicism', though easier to comprehend, nonetheless had its dangers. One was that it might alienate some of Diaghilev's most prestigious collaborators: Nijinska, for instance, thought that reviving Tchaikovsky's *The Sleeping Beauty* as *The Sleeping Princess* was an absurdity and a relapse into the past.[11] If one wanted to find her counterpart in Paris after the Second World War, it might be the young Pierre Boulez who, after years of listening to his elders enthusing about how wonderful the meat used to be 'before the war', had had enough of nostalgia and was determined that the French music after the war should, at the very least, be different.[12] So if Diaghilev wanted to keep the young artists on board, he had to allow them to give 'retrospective classicism' a new slant, should they so desire.

Scene from
Milhaud's ballet
Le train bleu (1924)

This was desirable in any case, since a second danger with the trend was that a pure revival of classicism would fail to draw conservative audiences who, if they wanted this kind of thing, might well prefer to go on patronizing the Opéra they knew and loved. Diaghilev of course believed that anything the Opéra could do, he could do better, but there was no sense in setting up competition

unnecessarily, and, as Garafola points out, the conflation of artistic categories in Paris meant that he already had more rivals than in 1914.[13]

These and other trends are perhaps best analysed by looking in a little more detail at seven of the ballets that Diaghilev brought to Paris between 1920 and 1928: Stravinsky's *Pulcinella* (1920), Prokofiev's *Chout* (1921), Stravinsky's *Les noces* (1923), Poulenc's *Les biches* (1924), Sauguet's *La chatte* and Prokofiev's *Le pas d'acier* (1927), and Stravinsky's *Apollon musagète* (1928).

Pulcinella, premiered at the Opéra on 15 May 1920, might at first sight seem to have been the epitome of retrospective classicism. Sotheby's catalogue for the sale of Diaghilev's music library in 1984 records that this contained

> about twenty items of Pergolesi's music, mostly transcriptions of chamber music and arias from various libraries, including the British Museum, the Bibliothèque Nationale and the Conservatorio di Musica, Naples. Almost all are annotated by Diaghilev...a number contain his ideas and thoughts probably for the music to *Pulcinella*.[14]

Diaghilev seems to have had in mind something along the lines of the arrangement of Scarlatti keyboard sonatas made by Vincenzo Tommasini for the ballet *Les femmes de bonne humeur*, premiered by Diaghilev in Rome in 1917. But, not for the first or last time, he had reckoned without Stravinsky's questing genius. For a start, the composer found in Pergolesi not only a popular Neapolitan element but an 'exotisme espagnol'. And as he said on the day before the premiere:

> musical 'effects' are ordinarily obtained by the juxtaposition of different degrees; a soft one succeeding a loud one produces an 'effect'. But this is the conventional and banal method.
>
> I have tried to arrive at an even dynamic in the juxtaposition of instrumental timbres which have similar sounding levels. A colour has value only by the relationship to other colours juxtaposed with it. A red has no value by itself, it acquires it only by its proximity to another red or a green....
>
> I also try to obtain verity in the disequilibrium of instruments against the grain of that which one does in what is called chamber music where the basis itself is a conventional equilibrium of different instruments.
>
> [...] These are innovations which occasionally surprise. But little by little the ear becomes used to these effects which at first shock it. All this is a musical education to be undertaken.[15]

In quoting this passage, Scott Messing makes the points that 'surprise, disequilibrium, and juxtaposition...had been the central direction in French avant-garde arts and letters throughout the war', that by 1920 Stravinsky was friendly with painters such as Picasso, Braque and Delaunay, and that this may have prompted him to conceive of the sound of *Pulcinella* in visual terms.[16] At all events Stravinsky's oft-quoted remark that Diaghilev reacted to the score by going about 'for a long time with a look that suggested The Offended Eighteenth Century'[17] indicates that for once the great impresario had been imaginatively outpaced.

Two words that crop up frequently in discussions of this ballet are 'respect' and 'irony'. The historian René Dumesnil wrote of the orchestration of *Pulcinella* as one in which 'the humour, though sometimes extending into parody, nonetheless remained respectful'.[18] This personal point of view contrasts with what has been regarded until recently as the composer's own defence of the work against its detractors: 'you "respect", but I love',[19] although Messing makes a good case for the origination of this remark with a member of the audience, who made it to Reynaldo Hahn, from whom it passed via Louis Laloy to the composer!

The notion of respect in art, on which Debussy had already had some

Tamara Karsavina as Pimpinella in Stravinsky's ballet *Pulcinella* (1920)

sharp things to say,[20] perhaps naturally suffered in the general spirit of iconoclasm that followed the war. It came under attack too from the weakening of the traditional, Renaissance view that a work of art was necessarily the product, and thence a possession, of a single talented individual. In France, many in Mallarmé's circle had been attracted by the thought that ideas might be floating around the cosmos and that 'inspiration' was a matter of tuning in to the right wavelength. Stravinsky's own comment on *Le sacre* ('I heard, and I wrote what I heard. I am the vessel through which *Le sacre* passed')[21] suggests that he too might have been receptive to this notion, even if there is no indication that he ever went to the lengths of refusing royalties on the work. But clearly, if this notion is seriously entertained, then questions of respect do not arise – the material is both legally and aesthetically in the public domain.

Ballet

141

Whether or not Stravinsky felt respect for Pergolesi, he made it clear that for him respect on its own was not enough. He wrote of 'breathing new life' into the disparate fragments gathered by Diaghilev, relying on what he called his 'close spiritual and, so to speak, sensorial affinity' with the older composer.[22] Whether or not this approach qualifies as Neoclassical (Roman Vlad and Jim Samson think that it does, Robert Craft that it does not),[23] the disjunction between the eighteenth and twentieth centuries in *Pulcinella* makes the work far more Stravinsky than Pergolesi, if only because Stravinsky's style can embrace Pergolesi's while the reverse is impossible. Stephen Walsh, in one of a number of perceptive remarks on the subject, maintains that

> most of the time, the harmonic grammar of Pergolesi has enough
> energy to sustain the classical kind of phrase structure proper to the
> original material. But just occasionally Stravinsky's way of neutralising
> the harmony tends to isolate the phrases to the point where they can
> be freely reconstructed in ways that much more closely resemble the
> cellular montages of the Russian works.[24]

For 'reconstructed' might it be possible to substitute 'deconstructed'? That is, could Stravinsky be hinting that Pergolesi's music already contained Russian and/or twentieth-century elements which he, Stravinsky, is merely drawing out or emphasizing? Countering this, though at the same time possibly combining with it, is the much-vaunted ironical stance which, instead of entering into the music and engaging with it on an equal level, comments on it from the outside and from an implicit position of superiority.

As Walsh points out, the principle of renovating old scores was far from novel, and in nineteenth-century Paris examples can be found in abundance. An article by Théophile Gautier of 7 November 1843 applauded Adolphe Adam for rejuvenating the accompaniments to arias in Grétry's *Le déserteur*, an action 'which will no doubt bring down upon him the same charges of vandalism laid against him over *Richard* [*Coeur-de-lion*, also by Grétry] by certain clapped-out fanatics who do not allow anyone to touch their idols, not even to remove the dust that covers them'.[25] In one respect Stravinsky had been bolder than Adam, in that *Pulcinella* gave the Paris audience not what they wanted, but what they could be made to want – an early example of modern marketing. It was, as he said, 'a musical education to be undertaken', though he must have had doubts about the success of the venture since he later confessed that 'I had already accustomed myself not to trust any longer in that musical demi-monde of more than doubtful competence'.[26]

But in another respect Stravinsky, and Diaghilev, were more cautious than Adam, in that Pergolesi – unlike Grétry – was not French. It would have been a more stringent test of Stravinsky's power over the Parisian public to have taken music by such hallowed masters as Couperin or Rameau and rework that with tonic/dominant chords and jarring ostinatos. As it was, audiences, with plenty of tunes to hang on to, took to the work and Diaghilev programmed it no fewer than twenty-one times during the two seasons of 1920 and those of 1924–26 and 1928. Nor was its influence long in making itself felt: Boris de Schloezer in 1923 heard Tailleferre's ballet *Le marchand d'oiseaux* as deriving from it, and Scott Messing suggests that Stravinsky admired Roland-Manuel's ballet *Isabelle et Pantalon*, produced at the Trianon-Lyrique in 1922/23, 'possibly in part because its subject so clearly recalled *Pulcinella*'.[27]

A different kind of rapprochement between Russia and the West was made by Prokofiev in his *Chout* (The Buffoon), premiered at the Gaîté-Lyrique on 17 May 1921. Rather than 'lifestyle modernism', this might be called 'rural realism'. Every character in the ballet was a comic peasant, those of the priest and his wife having been removed (either by Prokofiev or by Diaghilev – opinions differ), presumably so as not to offend the clerical authorities who had taken such a strong line over Debussy's *Le martyre de Saint Sébastien* in 1911. Jim Samson states that *Chout*, begun in 1915, was, like *Ala and Lolly*, 'composed under the influence of the Stravinsky of *The Rite of Spring*'.[28] But the grotesque folk-tale scenario contains none of *Le sacre*'s mythical, transcendental qualities, and the success of the music, which at the time was considerable, was due to quite other factors, perhaps not least a view of rural Russia designed to make Parisians feel ultra-chic.

There were some detractors who disliked the work's tone of perpetual mockery and the absence of real lyricism, but Roland-Manuel for one praised 'the inexhaustible richness of its melodic vein', on a par with that of its orchestral colour, and went on to call it 'the most important work produced by the Ballets russes since the war, with the exception of *Le rossignol*'.[29] (This pointedly excluded *Pulcinella*, a fact which sets up interesting resonances with that work's suggested influence on Roland-Manuel's own *Isabelle et Pantalon*...). René Dumesnil appreciated the humour to be found in the notes themselves, with expected cadences often avoided,[30] while André Coeuroy saw Prokofiev in *Chout* as 'throwing a bridge between Russian popular dances and Western thought by treating these ethnic themes in the manner of Mozart or Scarlatti'.[31] If true, here was an example of that cross-fertilization so much prized by Ravel in 1916 (see p. 26).

Stravinsky's explanation of his techniques in *Pulcinella* in terms of colour found some echo in Diaghilev's production of *Chout*, where the audience's attention was taken not only by the music but perhaps to an even greater degree by the stage, on which 'the action unfolded like some lurid nightmare amid the hurtling rainbows of Larionov'.[32] The ballet critic Cyril Beaumont found the colour contrasts

> so vivid and so dazzling that it was almost painful to look at the stage,
> and the position was not improved when brilliantly clad figures were set
> in movement against such a background. I would say that the effect on
> the eyes was almost as irritating as those flickering streaks of coloured
> light so characteristic of early colour films.[33]

To continue the theme of cross-fertilization, it is almost as though Diaghilev were taking his cue from Paris, 'la ville lumière', and saying: 'I'll give you light!' Certainly *Chout* in its totality bears out Garafola's contention that 'with Larionov and Gontcharova, futurism impregnated all aspects of ballet design', and that

> beginning in 1915 and continuing throughout the postwar years, design not only supplanted music as the unifying element of Diaghilev's productions, but altered the relationship of choreography to the overall plan of a work. If, before, dance had been an equal, now it became a subordinate of design, with the goal of the choreographer being to enhance the inventions of scene painter and costumer.[34]

Given this shift in emphasis, we can see that any ballet composer now might have to work harder than ever to make a mark. Indeed, only the strong survived: Stravinsky, Prokofiev and (perhaps surprisingly) Poulenc. Whereas for most music-lovers, scores like Auric's *Les matelots*, Dukelsky's *Zephyr et Flore*, Rieti's *Barabau* (all 1925) and Lambert's *Romeo and Juliet* (1926) remain unknown, Stravinsky's *Renard* (1922), *Les noces* (1923) and *Apollon musagète* (1928), Prokofiev's *Le pas d'acier* (1927) and *Le fils prodigue* (1929) and Poulenc's *Les biches* (1924) have all achieved fame in varying degrees.

Stravinsky had begun writing *Les noces* as early as 1914, but, by the time the ballet in its final four-piano form was premiered at the Gaîté-Lyrique on 13 June 1923, Paris audiences had already heard other 'Russian' works of his like *Le chant du rossignol*,

Renard and *Mavra*, while the next major Stravinsky work to cross their path, on 18 October of that year, was the undeniably Neoclassical Octet for wind instruments. *Les noces* therefore came to be seen as the last fruit of his Russian period, even if over half a century later Lynn Garafola has found it as much neo-classic as neo-primitive. But as she says, only time has shown this.[35] She also maintains that after 1923 the Ballets russes would never again 'shed its veneer of frivolity'.[36] On all fronts, *Les noces* was a big, tough, hard work: hard in its subject matter (marriage as painful sacrifice), hard in its choreography (Nijinska, said the critic Edwin Denby, gave it a 'tapping' and a 'hardness',[37] and insisted the ballet must be danced on point, so that the dancers would 'resemble the saints in Byzantine mosaics').[38] It was also hard in its sound, with every instrument in the orchestra being struck – Alexandre Tansman made the comparison with a gamelan orchestra, although there is no evidence of this medium as a specific influence.[39]

Whether one liked the music or not, its force and power were undeniable: or as Poulenc put it, 'Didn't hearing *Les noces* knock you over on your arse? I bet it did.'[40] More considered responses found deeper qualities in the work than sheer brutality. André Coeuroy called it 'the finest successful attempt so far at a synthesis of contemporary music and contemporary dance',[41] and René Dumesnil, while noting that Stravinsky was against closed-eyes listening, felt the mother's lamentations qualified on this front, and that, 'for all its dynamism, Stravinsky's music often expresses something quite other than movement'.[42] As so frequently with Stravinsky, not only does the heart lie well below the carefully crafted surface, but the work creates its own world within the space of a few bars from the opening. If sophisticated Parisians could feel superior to the lumpish peasants in *Chout*, *Les noces*, for all its particular Russianness, was a too deeply human document to be taken other than seriously. A portrait of the composer in rehearsal for the work provides supporting evidence of a peculiarly personal kind:

> soon he was angrily gesticulating, and then, thoroughly aroused,
> would take off his coat, sit down at the piano and, reproducing all the
> symphonic sonority of the work, begin singing in a kind of ecstatic,
> but terrible voice, which carried so much conviction that no one could
> have thought it comical.[43]

Stravinsky later praised Nijinska's 'conception of *Noces* in blocks and masses'[44] and was happy that 'the first staging of *Les noces*...was generally compatible with my conception of the ritualistic and non-personal'.[45] But at the time he resented Diaghilev's refusal to have the orchestra in evening dress on stage with the actors[46] – which would, presumably, have given the actors an extra edge of realism as well as contributing an extra dimension to the 'conception...in blocks and masses'.

Finally, it could possibly be taken as a sign of Diaghilev's satisfaction with the work (which he staged on all eight evenings of the 1923 season and a total of twenty-three times in 1923, 1924, 1926 and 1928 – three more performances than accorded to *Pulcinella*, premiered three years earlier) that he immediately launched out in an almost diametrically opposite direction: what in modern parlance might be described as the 'been there, done that' syndrome. In May 1924, Paris witnessed the arrival of Poulenc's *Les biches* and 'lifestyle modernism', leaning on the elegant arm of Jean Cocteau.

Where *Les noces* is hard, *Les biches* is soft: after the clanging sonorities of four pianos, gentle strings set off limpid woodwind solos; after ritual Russian rhythms, ingratiating French dances; after sex as sacrifice, sex as a game, possibly even sex for sale. According to Poulenc, Diaghilev chose Marie Laurencin as designer for her 'ambiguous blend of innocence and corruption',[47] and Vera Nemtchinova complained that in her costume for the Adagietto she was showing so much leg, she felt naked:[48] after hard reality, soft porn.

Much of what was written about the ballet around the time, by critics and fellow composers, testifies to a feeling of some confusion over its message. For many of them, *Les biches* was a work on the edge – exactly what of, they couldn't be sure, but they knew its success was a near thing. Dumesnil wrote of

> questionable games, perverse grace, an atmosphere of sport and flirtation, music which keeps its distance equally from sentimentality and humour, which often seems on the point of descending into banality but then rescues itself at the last moment.[49]

Poulenc himself then was also flirting, with the banal. If so, was it a free choice on his part?

> The great difficulty and danger for Poulenc is that his music is essentially aristocratic; it is a courtly art in fact which, by force of circumstance, finds itself obliged to address the masses.[50]

The idea that Poulenc should have been making concessions to a retarded public, in Paris of all places, is a curious one. Nor is it borne out by his letters. Writing to Paul Collaer on 10 September 1922, he said, 'I'm working hard at my ballet *Les biches*.... I'm happy because I've tapped into the vein. No more wrong notes, no more polytonality! I'm wandering around the common chord and modulation.'[51] It is quite clear from this that he is pleasing himself and no one else. At the same time, the sentence 'je rôde autour de l'accord et de la modulation' has interesting implications, especially in his use of the verb 'rôder'. This can mean simply to wander or, of a ship, to veer at anchor. But it can also mean 'to prowl around spying, usually with bad intentions'.[52] The implication here is that Poulenc is up to mischief, and this is corroborated by a letter written by him to Diaghilev in December 1923 in which the onstage sofa plays a central role:

> In a Presto section the dancers sit down, jump into the air, fall back on to the tufted upholstery and roll about on their spines while the two men straddle the back of the sofa, and then pull it about every which way (it'll have to be ultra-solid). In the middle section the music calms down and then the Star and Wilzak cuddle on stage. The Young Things [Biches] then use the sofa, which has its back to the audience, as a look-out post and pop their heads over the back and then down again – and when the game restarts, *now read carefully*, the two men abruptly swing the sofa round and you see two women lying there in a position which, thinking of Barbette, I shall describe as head to tail.[53]

Questionable games indeed: Barbette being an American female impersonator much admired by Cocteau, whose biographer Francis Steegmuller tells us that 'on the sofa, between the wire and the trapeze parts of the act, Barbette was to do a little striptease as he removed his long evening gown'.[54] One could argue that, as the music was written by this time, Poulenc could not be held responsible for what happened on stage. But his manifest approval for the goings-on suggests that they fitted in well with his conception of the work.

The ambivalent nature of *Les biches* is perhaps nowhere better displayed than in two letters to Collaer from Milhaud and one from Auric. On 8 October 1923, writing from Paris before the Monte Carlo rehearsals had begun, Milhaud confessed that

> with regard to *Les biches*, everyone here is very worried. Poupoule [Poulenc] is playing his score everywhere and people like it a little less each time they hear it. Auric and I are supporting it much less warmly. Satie has come out very much against; Marcelle Meyer and Sauguet too, thanks to the pastiches of Beethoven and Schumann and the terrible influence of Stravinsky.[55]

But when the ballet reached the stage, Milhaud's opinion underwent a sea change. 'I'm astonished by *Les biches*,' he wrote on 22 January,

> I dream about it. It is a masterpiece. The music is adorable, marvellously orchestrated, always heartfelt and full of emotion. The decor and costumes, adorable, and the choreography adorable, Nijinska's masterpiece. It is the most beautiful and successful ballet in the Diaghilev repertoire.[56]

The key to Milhaud's change of heart would seem to have lain in either the orchestration or the staging or both. If the staging, then it only goes to emphasize the truth of Garafola's contention that Diaghilev's later productions were increasingly design-led; if the orchestration, then it says much for Poulenc that he should have impressed such a discriminating ear as Milhaud's with his first extended work in the orchestral medium.

Auric too soon revised his initial distaste for the work, writing to Collaer, 'I have considerable confidence that the admirable Les biches will put certain rather idiotic interpretations of the famous "esprit nouveau" in their place.'[57] But other remarks of his testify that, even up to fifty years later, his opinions too were marked by a certain degree of confusion. While he wrote of 'an orchestra which is already personal, with its solid trumpets, its expressive trombones and its alternately tender or bantering woodwinds', he also felt that orchestration was 'not the most essential aspect of Poulenc's style'.[58] The two remarks may not be mutually exclusive, but I would argue that they show Auric grappling with the slipperiness of Poulenc's music and with its curious ability to say many different things at once. Perhaps the last word on Les biches should go to Vladimir Dukelsky who, writing thirty years later as Vernon Duke, remembered that 'the morbid prettiness of Laurencin's decor was happily underlined by Poulenc's ingratiating music, slyly frivolous or voluptuously romantic by turn'. For him it 'typified the Twenties as did no other ballet'.[59]

When Les biches reached the Paris stage, at the Théâtre des Champs-Elysées on 26 May 1924, it repeated its Monte Carlo success and Diaghilev took it round Europe for the next four seasons: although, rather surprisingly, its last Paris performance by the Ballets russes, on 5 June 1926, was only its ninth in that city. Sauguet's La chatte on the other hand, premiered in Paris on 27 May 1927 with sets and costumes by Naum Gabo and Anton Pevsner and choreography by Balanchine, had reached eighteen performances by the time Diaghilev last staged it there on 11 June 1929. It is hard to think of a convincing musical reason for this discrepancy, even though Sauguet's score is full of delightful things, such as the coolly pastoral flutes in the 'Invocation à Aphrodite', and elsewhere much sprightly writing for brass. The evidence suggests that, again, it was the decor that Diaghilev particularly liked, and perhaps especially the tension between the decor on the one hand and the music and story on the other.

The libretto by Diaghilev's assistant Boris Kochno is based on one of Aesop's fables, telling of a man who prays to Aphrodite that his much-loved cat will turn into a woman; and so it does, but without losing its appetite for mice. The man dies of grief. Faced with Sauguet's resolutely tonal music, extending as far as melancholy but really no further, critics differed, as they had over Les biches, some seeing in it 'a quality of lightheartedness and freshness, others regarding this simplicity as no more than clumsiness and ignorance'.[60] Far more startling, though, was the disjunction between the music and what was to be seen on stage. What the American journalist Janet Flanner described as 'a lovely decor of isinglass'[61] had the effect of flashing,

as [it] caught the light, [its] message of an amazing new plastic age to the incredulous and blinking public.... The shining transparent armour worn by the dancers gave [the ballet] a heroic, interplanetary quality, as if the little tragedy...was taking place in a society of godlike pioneers on a newly subjugated star.[62]

What had this got to do with Aesop? The answer has to be, very little. And even though André Levinson thought Balanchine's choreography was also irrelevant to anything else,[63] the result ('Diaghilev's incongruously potent cocktail', as Buckle calls it) worked, and even Sauguet was happy with it.[64]

If one insists on trying to analyse this success, it may come down, rather bluntly, to the superb physique of the young Serge Lifar, Diaghilev's latest Nijinsky replacement. Janet Flanner records that he 'danced with the bouncing verve of gutta-percha', although we may detect a slight edge to the compliment in that she lumped him together with the isinglass decor as one of the 'two great commodities' the ballet had in its favour.[65] Sokolova too recalled that 'there have been few ballets in which the beauty of young people's bodies in motion was shown to better effect'.[66] From this it is clear that Diaghilev was determined to escape the enervating atmosphere of traditional French Hellenism and to demonstrate by a brutal juxtaposition of aesthetic planes that, for all the fable's leaning towards whimsy, this was a real man with a real sorrow and that the story, like all of Aesop's, had a moral: don't ask for too much or you may get what you hadn't bargained for. To this limited extent, perhaps, Garafola may be a little unfair to Diaghilev in saying that after 1923 the Ballets russes 'never shed its veneer of frivolity'.[67] Ultimately, though, the most honest response to the success of its disparate elements may simply be to acknowledge that Diaghilev was a genius, and pass on.

In the last two of the ballets I shall discuss, he moved back to what we might call a Stravinskyan position, looking for ideas less in diversity than in similarity. The first of the ballets, Prokofiev's *Le pas d'acier*, premiered a few weeks after *La chatte* on 7 June 1927 with sets and costumes by Georgi Yakulov and choreography by Massine, was a kind of amalgam of 'lifestyle modernism' with the barbarity of *Chout*. It aimed to portray life in the modern Soviet Union, complete with a factory scene that gave Prokofiev a splendid opportunity for noisy *machinisme*: Arnold Whittall has described the work as representing, with the opera *L'ange de feu* and the Third Symphony, the 'extreme limit of Prokofiev's aggressive anti-romanticism'.[68] Whether or not it derived from Diaghilev's nostalgia for Russia, as his *régisseur* Grigoriev claimed,[69] we can with hindsight see the ballet as a kind of preparation for Prokofiev's acclaimed return there in 1932. With roots in Futurism and the ideas of Mossolov and Deshevov,[70] it aimed to overthrow the morbid, ambivalent chic of *Les biches* in favour of something stronger, healthier and saner (although, interestingly, Prokofiev, like Poulenc, now turned back to the common chord and to composing 'a whole group of themes uniquely on the white notes').[71]

But whereas in *La chatte* the constituent elements were pulling against each other, here everything was harnessed to giving an impression of ruthless organization and purpose. At the same time, Massine's choreography emphasized a certain clumsiness, to the extent of making the dancers have one foot bare and one booted.[72] The Soviet authorities for their part did not regard the ballet as a true picture of contemporary Russian life and dismissed it as a typical bourgeois product, a mixture of various exotic clichés, although they accepted that at least the composer was well-intentioned.[73] One could argue that, since Diaghilev and Massine had been away from Russia so long, their view of it was bound to be exotic. As for Prokofiev, we are

LIFNITZKI
PARIS

presented with the curious fact of his musical style softening as he acclimatized to the realities of Soviet life in the mid-1930s, in works like *Peter and the Wolf* and *Romeo and Juliet*, as if to confirm in retrospect that *Le pas d'acier* had indeed been stereotypical.

Finally, in this highly variegated list, a work which can have done little to assuage Diaghilev's Russian nostalgia. After the premiere of *Les noces* in 1923, Stravinsky engaged on an extended game of hide-and-seek with the musical past – Bach, Beethoven, Tchaikovsky, Verdi – and the nostalgic Diaghilev might have been forgiven for looking longingly back to those years between 1910 and 1913 when the young Igor had been writing one truly Russian ballet after another with barely a pause for breath. Then in 1927 Diaghilev found himself putting on a curiosity called *Oedipus rex*. Was this the shape of the Stravinsky to come?

Yes and no. *Apollon musagète*, premiered at the Théâtre Sarah-Bernhardt on 12 June 1928 with choreography by Balanchine and with a cast including Lifar, Nikitina and Tchernicheva, proclaimed in its title Stravinsky's continuing allegiance to Greek myth. But gone was the overtly dramatic structure of *Oedipus rex*, together with its stark contrasts of orchestral colour and deliberately ambiguous moods, as in what he called the 'mortuary tarantella' of the penultimate chorus. Gone too was the pluralism of materials which prompted him forty years later to say that to a large extent he 'put it together from whatever came to hand', including 'the Folies Bergère tune at No. 40 ("the girls enter, kicking") and the Wagnerian 7th chords at Nos 58 and 74'.[74]

Apollon proclaimed perhaps more radically than any of his works so far his search for inspiration in similarity. We may now be amused by the slightly schoolmasterly tone of his claim in the *Chroniques de ma vie* that the melodic value of strings had been devalued for some time past and that a return to this value was now 'wholly timely and even urgent'.[75] And whose fault was that, we may ask? But certainly those elements of surprise, disequilibrium and juxtaposition which had been serving music so faithfully since the beginning of the First World War were now relegated to a back seat. The work's tone is perhaps best captured by a single sentence from Stravinsky's own description of it (the italics are mine): 'et comment rendrait-on mieux le dessin *dépouillé* de la danse classique que par le *flux* de la mélodie se *déversant* dans le *chant soutenu* des cordes!' ('and how better to render the stripped-down outline of classical dance than by the flux of melody flowing through the sustained song of strings'). Significantly, Stravinsky makes no attempt to mirror the *dépouillement* of classical dance with any *dépouillement* in the music: for all its restraint in the matter of orchestral colour, *Apollon* is a work of rich textures and harmonies and often of aurally demanding counterpoint, although always within an overall tonal language. The words 'flux', 'se déversant' and 'soutenu' have all to do with a liquid smoothness, at the other extreme from the abrupt, even coarse surprises of much of Stravinsky's wind and brass writing.

The ballet was recognized as a masterpiece from its inception. For all the inconsistencies of the decor and costumes, it was close enough to a French seventeenth- or eighteenth-century treatment of the myth for audiences to feel comfortable with it, while the very fact of not, for once, being intellectually challenged by a Diaghilev production may have constituted for the Parisians the saving grace of novelty. Several critics of the time saw in the music Stravinsky's rapprochement with the nineteenth century. No longer was he commenting, ironically or otherwise, on Beethoven, Verdi or Tchaikovsky (although the first violins have their Tchaikovskyan moments), but he seemed now to have absorbed the nineteenth-century repertoire into a more neutral ambience: in short, to have become more fully Europeanized.

Two contemporary comments are worth quoting in this regard. The critic Henry Prunières thought Stravinsky's classicism was 'no longer a pose as before; one feels that he is responding to an intimate need of his heart and mind'.[76] Even if 'pose' is rather strong, we may agree that the composer seems at least to have abandoned any overt aesthetic intention other than that of giving free rein to melody, which few listeners would quarrel with. The conductor Roger Desormière in a letter to Paul Collaer also felt that the ballet belied its simple materials and that Stravinsky

generates such considerable power because the development of the materials is also based on psychological growth, the climax of which is not necessarily the outburst of a great crescendo; it can also be a great ascension that is wholly internal.[77]

On this basis there would seem to be some truth in Roman Vlad's perception of *Apollon* and *Le sacre* as 'two opposing dialectical forces',[78] even if in *Apollon*, as Desormière seems to imply, the Dionysiac force is channelled rather than repressed. Garafola claims that, until *Apollon*,

> choreographic neoclassicism had been a politically neutral phenomenon. Now, making peace with the idea of social order and religious orthodoxy, it acquired a profoundly conservative aura.... Rather than a vision of the future, neoclassicism came to define an attitude toward the past, the ordered past that had vanished with modernism.[79]

This vanishing act may have taken place in the hearts and minds of modernist devotees – we can observe in later apostles such as T. W. Adorno the equating of non-modernist elements in music with original sin – but it has to be said that for the vast majority of Parisian music-lovers in the Twenties the 'ordered past' had neither lost its appeal nor ceased to exist. Whiffs of it reached their nostrils from time to time in the works of Ravel, Roussel and Poulenc, cunningly and tastefully embellished so as not to appear drab or *démodé*, as well as more openly and plentifully in those of a host of minor composers. One might even hazard that the continuing health of the 'ordered past' in what one might call the musical undergrowth of 1920s Paris gave audiences the courage to attempt the mountains placed before them by men like Koussevitzky and Diaghilev; as has often been observed, in order to have an *avant-garde* you have to have a *garde*. Perhaps the greatest achievement of *Apollon* was to imbue retrospective classicism with a transcendence that owes nothing to veneration for the ancient Greek world, for Louis XIV or for any other external icon. As Desormière pointed out, the power of the music comes from within.

What that transcendence 'means' is debatable, as it is for example in the last act of *Pelléas*. But this does not invalidate it as an aesthetic criterion. Tentatively, one notes that Stravinsky had rejoined the Russian Orthodox Church in 1926, that the *Symphony of Psalms* was to follow in 1930, and that in Parisian society in general in the late Twenties religion, specifically Roman Catholicism, attracted a number of converts (Cocteau had returned to the faith in 1925, characteristically exclaiming after taking Communion that 'a priest gave me the same shock as Stravinsky and Picasso').[80] *Apollon* was entirely congruent with this trend towards order and ritual, both entirely understandable phenomena now that France's postwar gaiety was beginning to wear thin and after the terrifying flight from the franc in the spring of 1926, when order was restored only by the return to power of a man of prewar authority, ex-President Raymond Poincaré. Diaghilev's 1928 commissioning from Prokofiev of *Le fils prodigue* may have been Boris Kochno's idea, stemming from Diaghilev's request that the story of Prokofiev's next ballet should be familiar to everyone. But it is at least possible that the impresario had, as so often, intuited a movement in French society, or that Kochno had in turn intuited this intuition. At all events, *Apollon musagète* and *Le fils prodigue* between them buried 'lifestyle modernism' for good.

Les ballets suédois

Diaghilev's propensity for falling out with his choreographers was a large factor in the emergence of the Ballets suédois and their eventual arrival in Paris in the autumn of 1920. Between Fokine's departure from the Ballets russes in the summer of 1912 and his return in 1914, he had spent a season with the Royal Opera of Stockholm and, under his enthusiastic guidance, they had made plans for a European tour. This had to be abandoned because of the First World War, but 'the creation of the Ballets suédois in 1920 can be seen as the fruit of this long-cherished dream'.[81]

Rolf de Maré, director of the Ballets suédois, in his office at the Théâtre des Champs-Elysées

The company's founding impresario was Rolf de Maré. His motives seem to have been partly artistic and partly personal: he was genuinely devoted to the songs and dances of his native Sweden, but no less devoted to the young dancer Jean Börlin, for whom the Ballets suédois were to become a vehicle, and with whom de Maré's relationship could be pursued more peacefully in tolerant Paris than in recriminative Stockholm. Like Diaghilev, de Maré was a well-informed collector of pictures, but unlike Diaghilev he was rich, with an even richer grandmother to whom he could always turn. With the help of the Parisian impresario Jacques Hébertot, he courted the anger of the Stockholm Opera by enticing away most of

their best dancers, and then used his millions to hire the Théâtre des Champs-Elysées for five seasons between 1920 and 1925. Among the conductors he employed were D.-E. Inghelbrecht and Roger Desormière, both to be appointed to the Orchestre national in the following decade.

Two of the most often repeated criticisms of the company were firstly, that it was not Swedish, and secondly, that what it was engaged in was not ballet. Neither criticism was entirely fair. Of the two dozen ballets the company staged (every one of them, be it noted, choreographed by Börlin), five had music by Swedish or Scandinavian composers and two more were based on Swedish folk tunes. The problem was that these productions were not the ones that hit the headlines, and Kurt Atterberg, Viking Dahl and Algot Haquinius never became household names on a level with other composers for the company such as Ravel, Milhaud, Honegger and Satie.

The contention that the company did not perform ballet perhaps has more substance, but needs to be understood in the context that the Ballets suédois aimed, at least after their opening season, precisely at getting away from ballet as it had been traditionally performed. The programme book for their final season beginning in November 1924 contained such provocative statements as 'the Ballets suédois distrust all preconceptions, they live in space and not in time', '[they] do not rely on the authority of anyone, do not follow anyone. They are in love with the morrow', 'and tomorrow [they] will go still further onward'.[82]

For their first season, de Maré cautiously programmed two ballets on Swedish themes together with Debussy's *Jeux*, with decor by Bonnard, and four movements from Ravel's *Le tombeau de Couperin* newly orchestrated by the composer. But for the summer 1921 season he commissioned ballets from members of the up-and-coming Les Six, getting in ahead of Diaghilev by a clear three years.

Premiered on 6 June with music by Milhaud and based on a 'poème plastique' by Paul Claudel, *L'homme et son désir* was, in the composer's own words, a 'ballet symbolique et dramatique', and as such did not please Diaghilev or Massine when Milhaud played it through to them in the summer of 1920.[83] Perhaps they were not attracted either by the polytonal evocation of the Brazilian forest, or by the suggested interplay of poetry and dancing, or by the four vertical levels of staging demanded by Claudel's text (although this was one aspect which much impressed the twelve-year-old Olivier Messiaen). The premiere by the Ballets suédois was one of the several scandals that graced Milhaud's career, as his friend Paul Collaer later recalled:

> As the performance progressed, the audience drowned out the sound
> of the music with catcalls and guffaws reminiscent of those that greeted
> Stravinsky's *Sacre du printemps*.... It is hard to understand the strange antics
> of Paris audiences. They listen with one ear and look with one eye, while
> the other ear and eye are watching the reactions of their neighbours.
> They then leave the hall quite convinced that they have thoroughly
> understood the work just performed and are entirely competent to pass

judgment on it.... On the occasion of that first performance of *L'homme et son désir* Milhaud's friends joined in offering condolences for what they considered a misguided effort at picturesque exoticism.[84]

Emile Vuillermoz, writing in *La revue musicale* the following February, remained unimpressed by this 'petit charivari puéril', and took advantage of the sixteen extra players engaged for the percussion parts to berate de Maré for performing Debussy and Ravel scores with severely diminished string sections. History has vindicated both Claudel, de Maré and Milhaud, and *L'homme* remains one of the most moving works of the decade, in which any picturesque exoticism serves a profoundly human message.

Symbolism of a fairly obvious kind also underlay the only complete ballet commission de Maré put the way of Honegger, who by the summer of 1921 was a force to be reckoned with after the successes of his *Pastorale d'été* and especially of *Le roi David*. *Skating Rink*, on a scenario by Ricciotto Canudo, evokes the monotony of human existence by means of roller-skates, tapping into the same vein that Ravel had explored a couple of years earlier in *La valse* and was to explore again in *Boléro*, and also into 'lifestyle modernism' in its cast of 'workers, midinettes, pretty boys with an equivocal allure, and other caricature types'.[85] Honegger's score has not stood the test of time, whether through too thoroughgoing an incarnation of monotony, or because, as Honegger's biographer Harry Halbreich has suggested, 'in the balance the music held between love and action, it was almost as far removed from the Freudian intentions of the scenario as Fernand Léger's 'Apacho-Cubist' designs'. This points a salutary finger at the danger of throwing heterogeneous ingredients into the pot in the hope that somehow the magic of Paris would turn them into an assimilable whole; that Cock and Harlequin were natural companions. The critic of *Comoedia* commented, '*Skating Rink*: English title, Swedish dancers, Italian scenario, Swiss music' – and, adds Halbreich, French theatre....[86]

On the other hand, we should not imagine that de Maré accepted every score submitted to him. On 11 December 1920, Honegger had written to his parents:

> I've begun composing the music and, as I want to produce something very special and very different from what is usually done, it's giving me a lot of trouble and is taking considerable thought...it would be interesting for me in every way to be played in this theatre because this company has twenty-five million francs capital and has leased the theatre for fifteen years. One must try and take advantage of this sort of money to do things that are worthwhile. The orchestra is stunning....[87]

This work was not *Skating Rink*, but *Horace victorieux*, which de Maré turned down – no reason is known, but the score does remain one of Honegger's grittiest and most bracing. Honegger's response was not a huff, but a determination to please next time: clearly the young composers of Paris regarded de Maré's star as one worth following.

Honegger's opinion that the orchestra under Inghelbrecht was 'stunning' is a useful reminder that this aspect of the Ballets suédois seems to have escaped criticism. Such unhappiness as there was over standards was directed entirely at the dancing, which never reached the level of the Ballets russes, even where the aims of the two companies could be considered comparable. Inghelbrecht touches on two reasons for this beyond the purely technical. Börlin had studied Spanish dancing in Spain, but the result, says Inghelbrecht, was disappointing 'when put at the service of a Swedish aesthetic and Swedish corpulence'. He also recalls the early days of rehearsals with Börlin: in halting French, the dancer would explain the scenario up to the phrase 'Alors, j'entre!' (or rather, 'ch'entre!')...beyond which point his performance was thought to provide all the revelation that was required.[88] Not surprisingly, the supporting dancers came to resent this monopolistic attitude.

If de Maré was willing to explore psychological depths in *L'homme et son désir* and *Skating Rink*, he was no less interested, under Cocteau's guidance, in making room for the ludicrous and lighthearted. The phrase 'petit charivari puéril', aimed by Vuillermoz at *L'homme et son désir*, would have been better applied to *Les mariés de la tour Eiffel*. This was premiered twelve days after *L'homme*, on 18 June 1921, with text by Cocteau, decor by Irène Lagut, costumes and masks by Jean Hugo and music by five of Les Six (Durey did not contribute, partly because he found the whole enterprise too silly and partly because the other members of Les Six had put their names to a denigration of Ravel which Durey could not accept).

Milhaud and Cocteau had had a dry run for this extravaganza just over a year earlier with *Le boeuf sur le toit*, a 'Spectacle-Concert' at the Comédie des Champs-Elysées financed by comte Etienne de Beaumont, in which Milhaud had mingled together memories of Brazil – 'popular tunes, tangos, maxixes, sambas and even a Portuguese fado, transcrib[ing] them with a theme which comes between each one like a rondo'.[89] Originally Milhaud thought it might accompany a Chaplin film. Cocteau, smelling competition, promptly discarded the idea and wrote for this 'pantomime-ballet' a scenario set in America during Prohibition and involving, among others, a boxer, a barman, a bookmaker and a black dwarf. Also involved were masks and a trio of celebrated clowns, the Fratellini brothers. Cocteau engaged the financial support of the comte de Beaumont and tickets at the little Comédie des Champs-Elysées were sold at inflated prices, the Shah of Persia paying 'ten thousand francs for a stage box from which he could see nothing but from which he could be seen by everybody'.[90]

Le boeuf was premiered just a month after Henri Collet's article baptizing Les Six. Even Cocteau could not manage to incorporate the new arrivals into a theatrical production in a mere four weeks, and anyway Milhaud was too important to offend; so

LE BŒUF SUR LE TOIT

something else had to be found to exploit their new-found corporate fame. *Les mariés* in any case went a stage further than *Le boeuf* in combining poetry, painting and dancing. Cocteau was quick to see that the Ballets suédois, plentifully endowed with energetic young dancers, goodwill and de Maré's money, lacked an 'ideas man', the role Diaghilev had played in the Ballets russes since the beginning. In *Parade*, Diaghilev had suppressed Cocteau's spoken text, much to his annoyance: now Cocteau could be sure of getting his own way.

If the serious, philosophical tone of *L'homme et son désir* made its appearance perhaps a little too early in the Twenties to be properly appreciated, some of the caustic remarks in *Les mariés* were on the point of going too far in the other direction. As Milhaud's widow recalls,

> it was a manifestation, I wouldn't say of wickedness, but of the
> impertinence of Cocteau and his collaborators. And in that one must
> include his text which, for that time, was astonishing – very daring, really.
> Just two years after the end of the war, when the lion says, 'Je voudrais
> rendre le général' ('I want to give up, or bring up, the general' – whom he
> has just swallowed), the answer comes back, 'Il saura bien se rendre lui-
> même' ('He'll be quite capable of giving himself up on his own').[91]

The atmosphere of snook-cocking extends, of course, to the music. Following immediately on Milhaud's four-square, bitonal Wedding March, Poulenc's 'Speech of the General' turns out to be a polka for two cornets.

Les mariés provided excellent ammunition for those decrying the Ballets suédois as being falsely named on both counts. At the same time it achieved a mild *succès de scandale* and we should be wary of Vuillermoz's statement that 'the polite indifference which greeted the humorous "discoveries" of our pseudo-revolutionaries is a judgment without appeal';[92] Parisian critics were no exception in sometimes hearing what they wanted to hear and in being indifferent to the reactions of the general public. Honegger in particular was delighted that they singled out his 'Funeral March' for praise as being real music, since the climax is underpinned by trombones parodying the Waltz from Gounod's *Faust*.

In somewhat the same vein as *Les mariés* but also as a passing salute to the North American ambience of *Le boeuf sur le toit*, de Maré in 1923 commissioned Cole Porter to write the music for *Within the Quota*, to a scenario by Gerald Murphy. The company gave the premiere on 25 October 1923 and then took it on their American tour. Näslund describes it succinctly as

> a sprightly satire on the American myth of success, with jazz-inspired
> Cole Porter tunes and a choreography by Börlin which used modern
> dances like the shimmy and the foxtrot – again, a work which broke down
> the boundaries between genres and which was wholly anti-Romantic
> in tone.[93]

In *Le courrier musical*, Charles Tenroc described it as 'un sketch de music-hall, caricatural et frénétique' and noted that the score was orchestrated by Koechlin 'whose beard is usually less frolicsome'.[94] Although Koechlin loathed jazz and undertook the job mainly for money, Milhaud, who had recommended him for it, later remembered that 'the strange collaboration between the technician of counterpoint and fugue and the brilliant future "King of Broadway" was a wonderful success'.[95] Even if in 1923 Koechlin was still regarded rather as an advanced composer than as an academic one, similar effects of cross-fertilization and distancing were commented on in another instance by Cocteau's young friend Raymond Radiguet, noting

> how much *Les mariés de la tour Eiffel* gains from being performed by
> foreigners. The gestures on which the dance and the pantomime are
> based are so familiar to us, French performers would have run the risk
> of not emphasizing them enough. There are no more faithful mirrors
> than distorting ones.[96]

In both cases, if Milhaud and Radiguet were right, Cock and Harlequin were here to be found in happy and fruitful collaboration.

For the Ballets suédois, 1923 was the jazz year. On the same evening as *Within the Quota* they premiered Milhaud's most successful jazz score *La création du monde*. Writing to Collaer in July of that year, Milhaud was delighted by the speed and sureness with which his orchestration had progressed and by the resulting orchestral balance.[97] After the second performance on 29 October, he wrote to Collaer: 'Yesterday everything went well.... The press is vile. I'm jubilant.'[98] No doubt Milhaud's jubilation was at least partly due to the good performance under Desormière, especially as he had had to replace the original conductor during rehearsals. But could some of it have been due to the 'presse ignoble'? Madeleine Milhaud is adamant that her husband never sought scandal. And yet his recreation of Harlem jazz, employed as he later said 'sans réserve'[99] and far more dangerous-sounding than the Porter/Koechlin *Within the Quota*, could not but ruffle some critical feathers. As he wrote thirty years on,

> the critics decreed that my music was not serious and was more suited to
> dance halls and restaurants than to the theatre. Ten years later, the same
> critics were writing commentaries on the philosophy of jazz and proving
> in authoritative fashion that *La création* was my best work.[100]

Even if the Ballets suédois had achieved nothing else in its five years of life, it would have left an important mark on twentieth-century music simply through this successful act of cross-fertilization – and one, incidentally, in which Diaghilev had no interest whatever. It is altogether surprising that the company gave *La création* only 12 performances, compared with the 93 of Tailleferre's delightful but unchallenging *Marchand d'oiseaux* or the 280 of Debussy's *La boîte à joujoux*.

The last five ballets the company produced in November and December 1924 were mostly unremarkable, though the line-up of contributors to *La jarre* – the writer Pirandello, the artist Chirico and the composer Casella – shows that de Maré was not resting on his laurels. The final one of the five however more than made up for the other four. *Relâche*, with scenario and decor by Francis Picabia, music by Satie and a 'cinematographic entr'acte' by René Clair, was an archetypal Twenties 'happening' of the sort that was not to be in vogue again until the Sixties. The tone was set by its title, which means 'no performance'. In the summer months, when the theatres were closed, the spaces on the kiosks at Paris street corners advertising the programmes used to read 'Relâche', and Satie explained that 'it had always been his ambition to have a work of his running at all the Paris theatres at once, and this was his only possibility of ever achieving it, even partially'.[101] Life even imitated art. The date of the premiere was postponed from 17 November to 27 November, but on that day Börlin had a high fever and the performance had to be postponed to the 29th. At the last moment, Börlin was indisposed on that night also, leaving some of the fashionable audience wandering around the closed theatre until 11 p.m., thinking it was just another Picabia hoax.[102] After a public dress rehearsal on 4 December, the first public performance in fact did not take place until 7 December. The confusion over dates has indeed persisted until this day (as no doubt Satie and Picabia would be delighted to know), with various works of reference giving the first performance date as 27 November, 29 November and 4 December.[103] Even the 1926 piano reduction opts for 29 November.

The scenario, if such it can be called, took over the policy of inconsequentiality where *Les mariés* and *Mercure* (see p. 164) had left it; suffice to say that, after the overture, the proceedings began

> with the lowering of a movie screen on which were projected images
> of Satie and Picabia leaping in slow motion on the roof of the Théâtre
> des Champs-Elysées, admiring a huge field gun which, after some
> deliberation, they gleefully fired – not surprisingly – directly at the
> audience.[104]

The audience were further attacked by the glare of 370 car headlights, whose intensity varied with the rhythm of the music.[105]

Clearly the staging was designed to provoke, and it succeeded. The press notices were almost universally hostile. Not even René Clair's filmed *Entr'acte*, which has since become a cinema classic, and for which Satie's pre-compositional sketch laid down a template followed by later film composers, could persuade the critics that these high jinks had any artistic value. Even the members of Les Six were divided. Poulenc wrote to Collaer that he had

> wasted an evening at *Relâche*. It's the music of a dotard, better orchestrated
> than *Mercure*, thank God, but even emptier of content. I came out of the
> theatre feeling very sad. I hate to see ageing in people I admire.[106]

Poulenc exaggerates rather (*Relâche*, film included, lasts only half an hour) and in his disapproval and Auric's we may partly be seeing a response to Satie's breaking off personal relations with them the previous February. The pro-*Relâche* camp included Sauguet and Milhaud, who wrote to Collaer:

> *Relâche* is a date in the history of the theatre. The orchestration is superb.
> I shall go back for every performance with Sauguet, who has already
> heard it four times and likes it more at every hearing. The audience is
> entertained continually. It's a success. It's lively, there are a few whistles,
> a few shouts, lots of applause. It's wonderful the way old Satie has stirred
> up the crowds like a young precursor. Auric and Poupoule's [Poulenc's]
> attitude is sheer stupidity. It's distressing to see them joining forces with
> all those cretinous critics and singing in chorus with them.[107]

Critical opinion about *Relâche* and about Satie's other late ballet *Mercure* has continued to be divided. A particular cause of controversy in *Relâche* was his widespread use of bawdy songs that would have been familiar to anyone who had done military service – namely, a large number of the men in the audience.[108] Satie foresaw this difficulty and wrote in the programme book:

I depict in [*Relâche*] people who are gallivanting. In order to do that, I have made use of popular themes. These themes are naturally evocative.... The 'timid' and other 'moralists' reproach me for the use of these themes. I don't have to concern myself with the opinion of such people.[109]

This was a somewhat disingenuous pronouncement since he had described *Relâche* in a letter to Milhaud of 10 August as a 'ballet obcène' [sic]: the bawdy songs may be regarded as analogous with Nijinsky's use of the scarf a decade earlier at the end of his ballet on *L'après-midi d'un faune*, illustrating an activity all male members of the audience were familiar with, but one they preferred to disown with ladies present.

A disenchanted observer could be forgiven for writing off *Relâche* as a farrago of obscene songs, glaring lights and ludicrous stage action: Satie and Picabia took their curtain calls in a 5CV Citroën, and throughout the ballet (this was Satie's idea) a man dressed as a fireman and wearing the ribbon of the Légion d'Honneur wandered around smoking and emptying one bucket of water into another. This might lead us to suppose that Satie's score was similarly a ragbag of unconnected ideas. But as Robert Orledge has shown, the music of the ballet is built on a mirrored structure, making it 'a remarkable interlocking edifice of great subtlety'.[110] Interesting as this is to a student of Satie's compositional methods, it is no less instructive on the human and social fronts: in introducing a surreptitious order into his score, he could be said to have been undermining the Dadaist elements in the production as well as providing himself privately with a defence against those like Poulenc who denigrated it as 'nulle comme matière'.

It has often been said that *Relâche* represented the last dying twitch of Dadaism – for one thing, Breton's first *Manifeste du surréalisme* had been published earlier in the year, taking over from Dada and providing it with a positive rather than a merely negative rationale. For de Maré the question undoubtedly was: what now? He had already spent millions of francs, and Börlin's health was fragile. He realized too 'that the company had progressed as far as it could and, rather than go over old ground, he preferred to disband the Ballets suédois after a performance at Epernay on 17 March 1925'.[111] A few months later de Maré was already in pastures new: still at the Théâtre des Champs-Elysées, but now launching Josephine Baker in the *Revue nègre*.

Diaghilev, as I mentioned earlier, had no interest in jazz and pretended to have none in the Ballets suédois either. The feeling of his entourage was that he despised the technical quality of the company's dancing and certainly it seems as if his attitude to it was one of seigneurial disdain since no comment of his on the subject has come down to us. But try as he might, he could not ignore the Ballets suédois's impact on the financial front: Lynn Garafola plausibly suggests that the fall in receipts for *Chout* and *Cuadro Flamenco* from 36,462 francs at the premiere in May 1921 to 14,258 francs a few days later may have reflected competition from this quarter.[112] Although the company touched on both 'lifestyle modernism' and retrospective classicism (in *Skating Rink* and in the 1924 ballet *Le tournoi singulier*, based on a poem by the sixteenth-century writer Louise Labé), it is difficult to argue that this was indubitably in imitation of the Ballets russes. But without a doubt the influence worked the other way when it came to collaboration with Les Six: the successes of *Le boeuf sur le toit* and *Les mariés* were clear signals to Diaghilev that for once he was behind the game and that action was required. Both directly and indirectly, then, the influence of the Ballets suédois extended far beyond the single success of *La création du monde*.

Soirées de Paris

In case anyone still needs, after all these years, to be impressed anew with the scale of Diaghilev's achievements, useful material can be found in the so-called Soirées de Paris organized by the comte Etienne de Beaumont in the summer of 1924. The comte's involvement, noted above, with the performances of *Le boeuf sur le toit* in 1920 had extended merely to signing the cheques. From this he now made what he may have felt was the short step to becoming an impresario on the Diaghilev model. He was after all a man not without artistic talent, who designed jewelry for Cartier in his spare time.

Plans were laid at the end of 1923 for theatrical and ballet performances at the Théâtre Cigale in Montmartre the following
May – perhaps the crowds invading Paris for the Olympic
Games were to form part of the target audience? Certainly the
profits, if any, were to go to French war widows and Russian
refugees. Massine was to be the choreographer, Braque one of the
designers, and dancers were engaged from all over Europe. One of these
was Lydia Lopokova, the future wife of Maynard Keynes. In her delightfully idiosyncratic English, she gave her future husband a running account of the preparations,[113] making it clear that from the very start things did not run smoothly. Beaumont would only offer Lopokova less than half the fee she had been receiving in London, after which she found herself dancing in a ballet choreographed by Beaumont himself:

Lydia Lopokova as
The Princess in *L'oiseau
de feu*, Ballets russes
(1928)

> The ballet called *Vogue* our tableau about three minutes with a young man
> a young girl who is like a boy, and I the woman of the smart set. We lie on
> the beach in Lido, and the man and the boy are 'getting on' so that I must
> produce a vexed face and stand in the middle, showing a costume made
> up of miroirs (dernier cri naturally).[114]

Shortly before the opening night, Lopokova finally decided she could not go on with the role and wrote to Beaumont resigning it: 'This afternoon when I saw him "Did you receive my letter forgive me." The Count "je vous déteste". So I received his answer with a smile and now am a free woman again.'[115]

Mirrors aside, this clear imitation of *Les biches*, which Diaghilev was planning to bring to Paris that same month, gives credence to Osbert Sitwell's gossip, relayed by Lopokova, 'that Big Serge in such a rage over our season that he engage everyone with a contract forever'.[116]

The eight ballets in Beaumont's season included *Les roses*, with a score by Henri Sauguet based on a waltz of that name by the nineteenth-century light music composer Olivier Métra, *Ballet espagnol* featuring Ida Rubinstein, and *Le beau Danube* set to music by Johann Strauss. But from the musical point of view, the two most interesting ballets were Milhaud's *Salade* and Satie's setting of Picasso's 'plastic poses', *Mercure* (the orchestration of which we have already found Poulenc decrying on p. 160).

Salade enjoyed the cachet of being approved by both Poulenc and Auric. It is, as Paul Collaer, wrote, 'full of sun and good humour. Along with the original tunes are some snatches of Sardinian melodies and a song by Salvatore Rosa.... French precision is combined with Italian nonchalance.'[117] It is as if Milhaud had taken on a wager to make bitonality acceptable through the strength of the melodic material. The result is wonderfully vivid and the work was immediately much in demand. Four years later, Milhaud could inform Collaer that Berlin was planning a series of 90 performances, with a further 150 in the German provinces.[118]

At the same time, it has not so far been clear quite what he meant when he wrote, on 5 February 1924, that he was 'using tunes of the period but in an opposite way to *Pulcinella* (at least, I hope so)'.[119] That hope was not inspired, his widow assures me, by distaste for Stravinsky's treatment of eighteenth-century tunes – he admired

Pulcinella without reserve. But in an unpublished letter to Collaer, Milhaud refers to *Salade* as containing 'les airs sardes bien triturés' ('Sardinian tunes thoroughly ground to powder').[120] Not only was he freer, then, in his adaptation of tunes than Stravinsky had been, but the strings of parallel triads and sevenths certainly take us a long way from Stravinsky's more cleanly contrapuntal treatment, in which the 'gently piquant diatonic clashes...have the effect of inhibiting, but not obscuring, the conventional tonic-dominant formulae and simple harmonic sequences which are the bread and butter of the early classical style'.[121] For all that, René Chalupt in his 'Paris Letter' for *The Chesterian*, while finding *Salade* 'a fascinating score', nonetheless felt that it was indeed 'powerfully influenced by Stravinsky's *Pulcinella*'....[122]

Felia Doubrovska as The Firebird, Ballets russes (1928)

Of Satie's *Mercure*, Chalupt merely observed that it 'was not well received by his best friends', leaving us to imagine its reception at the hands of those not thus favoured. The previous year, Beaumont had secured the services of the three collaborators on *Parade*, Satie, Picasso and Massine, for a three-minute divertissement, *La statue retrouvée*, to form part of one of the series of masked balls at his residence on the rue Duroc.[123] For *Mercure* this same team was enlisted. In the words of Alan M. Gillmor:

> Whereas *Parade* hid behind a thin veil of seriousness (largely owing to Cocteau, who theorized about everything), Satie's last two ballets, *Mercure*...and *Relâche*...were conceived in a spirit of pure farce.... *Mercure*, as the composer explained..., is a divertissement, a purely decorative work devoid of plot. The sole function of the music is to provide a sonic backdrop for Picasso's plastic poses.[124]

The recent discovery of a three-page scenario by the comte, which Satie followed precisely, shows that this was not in fact true.[125] But Satie's willingness to obscure the ballet's structure indicates that he wanted it to embrace the increasing emphasis on decor already noted in the postwar productions of Diaghilev. This 'farcical romp through Greek and Roman mythology', as Gillmor goes on to call the work, could also be regarded as chiming with the frivolous view of antiquity we have already seen linking Offenbach to Ibert's *Persée et Andromède*. But Nancy Perloff may be nearer the mark in suggesting that 'the utter disparity between classical mythology and ragtime and music-hall tunes was irritating, rather than amusing',[126] now that neoclassicism was achieving a new respectability.

If Chalupt was right about the general response to *Mercure* (and Poulenc's stated opinion, reinforced by Auric's condemnation of the work's 'banal repetition of café tunes',[127] suggests that he may have been), one would have expected the ballet to die on the spot. Certainly, right from the first night on 16 June Satie's many enemies and rivals were highly active:

The most malicious gossip was making the rounds. In Paris salons, for example, the rumour circulated that in order to help her son, who was henceforth known as the 'current (ac)Count', Etienne's mother had one evening bought up all the seats in the theatre but had then forgotten to hand them out, so that they had played that evening to an empty house.[128]

But two quite differing forces cooperated to keep the ballet alive, both in the audience's memory and in the theatre. At the first performance on 15 June, a group of Surrealists led by Breton and Aragon cheered Picasso but booed Satie, and so noisily that the curtain had to be lowered in the middle of the ballet (though in fairness to Satie, it has to be recorded that there was also an anti-Picasso group who ran to the artist's box shouting 'En bas, Picasso!'). Together with *Relâche*, *Mercure* embodied Dada at the height of its influence and, as Gillmor says, 'in 1924 the line was clearly drawn between the Surrealists and the Dadaists'.[129] Generally in Paris, composers preferred a riot to smatterings of polite applause, let alone an empty house. But it says something for Satie's seriousness of purpose in writing *Relâche* that its stormy reception induced him to stay away from the second performance the following night.

Another, altogether more surprising boost for *Mercure* came from none other than Diaghilev. As Richard Buckle records, 'Most of Beaumont's spectacles had been so ineffective and amateurish as to reassure Diaghilev: but *Mercure*...was striking enough to worry him.... This time Lifar noticed that Diaghilev was "pale, agitated, nervous".'[130] On the principle that 'if you can't beat them, join them', Diaghilev in June 1927 took the unprecedented and unrepeated step of incorporating this product of others into his own ballet season for four

performances, with Picasso's sets and Massine dancing in his own revised choreography. From a programming point of view, *Mercure* had much to be said for it. Diaghilev, unlike Stravinsky, preferred diversity to similarity and *Mercure's* deadpan farce must have provided a suitably startling contrast coming after *Oedipus rex* (twice), or sandwiched between *Le pas d'acier* and *La chatte*, and finally between *L'oiseau de feu* and dances from *Prince Igor*.

But by the end of June 1924 the comte de Beaumont had lost heart in his venture. 'The Cigale (Beaumont)', wrote Satie to Rolf de Maré, 'has closed its doors.... This poor comte – who is, after all, a good man – instead of compliments has only received insults and other nice things.... That's life! Most consoling!'[131] Houses had rarely been full and reviews had been mixed, with the critic of the *Dancing Times* chastising the *corps de ballet* as 'without exception, the worst I have ever seen'.[132]

Quite simply, a full purse could not replace taste or, especially, authority. Lopokova writes of nearly coming to blows with the comte for refusing to wear 'the "cheap", tasteless flowers of her costume. Beaumont stamped his foot. "Mum [Lopokova], his stubborn adversary won the day." '[133] And her letter of 13 May reads: 'By now I am like a theatrical rat, always in the theatre, and without end we wait, there is not one controlling voice in the situation, except the comte's polite but weak falsetto.' Being a second Diaghilev was not as easy as it looked.[134]

Les ballets Ida Rubinstein

Ida Rubinstein first astonished the Parisian public as Cleopatra in the ballet of that name, presented by Diaghilev at the Théâtre du Châtelet on 2 June 1909 as the fifth and final offering of his first Paris ballet season:

> Madame Rubinstein's costume...might be described as 'suggestive' by
> a provincial newspaper. The lady is nude, under bejewelled veils....
> I know no person of taste who has not been deeply impressed by this
> extraordinary spectacle; and some have come up to me to say: 'This
> is the most beautiful thing that I have ever seen!'

So gushed that determined aesthete the comte Robert de Montesquiou.[135] At the risk of sounding provincial, one has to say that Rubinstein's personal charms, and in particular her long, thin legs, continued to play a large part in her career, even if these charms moved in due course from the sexual plane to one that was more vocal and spiritual.

More immediately, her success in *Cléopâtre* was continued the following year in *Schéhérazade* and in *Le martyre de Saint Sébastien* in 1911. Her last gift to European culture before the outbreak of war was the slinky walk copied by ladies of fashion from the leopard which she walked on a chain during her own production of another d'Annunzio play, *La pisanelle*. This first venture as an impresario cost her 250,000 francs.

But her own large fortune, allied to that of her close friend Walter Guinness, would always be sufficient to absorb such disasters and, after a war largely spent nursing French soldiers in the Hôtel Carlton (in her Bakst-designed uniform) she was ready to do battle for art once more. Between 1920 and 1929, she underwrote and performed in no fewer than twelve ballets, most of them her commissions (these are marked with an asterisk, with dates of composition in brackets followed by dates of premieres at the Opéra):

> Schmitt: *Antoine et Cléopâtre** (1920) 14/6/20
> Paray: *Artemis troublée** (1922) 1/5/22
> Roger-Ducasse: *Orphée* (1913) 13/6/27
> Honegger: *Les noces d'Amour et de Psyché** (1928) 22/11/28
> Milhaud: *La bien-aimée** (1928) 22/11/28
> Ravel: *Boléro** (1928) 22/11/28
> Borodin: *Nocturne* 27/11/28
> Rimsky-Korsakov: *La princesse Cygne* (1900) 27/11/28
> Stravinsky: *Le baiser de la fée** (1928) 27/11/28
> Sauguet: *David** (1928) 4/12/28
> Auric: *Les enchantements d'Alcine** (1929) 21/5/29
> Ravel: *La valse* (1919–20) 23/5/29

Of these, only *Boléro*, *Le baiser de la fée* and *La valse* have indubitably stood the test of time – although three out of twelve may be regarded as not that poor an outcome. It could be that Rubinstein took an undue risk of turning herself into a hostage to fortune by seeking success on four fronts, often in the same piece, as impresario, speaker, dancer and mime. In all four areas, critical opinions differed over the years. When, in the summer of 1917, she mounted a performance of the fourth act of Racine's *Phèdre* at the Paris Opéra, André Gide was in the audience. 'Those', he later wrote,

> who, like me, had the good fortune to hear the fourth act of *Phèdre*...can
> testify that she was incomparable. I do not think I have ever heard the
> alexandrines recited so well as by her. Never had Racine's lines seemed
> to me more beautiful, more breathless, richer in hidden potential.[136]

It is hard to deny that the possession of money tended to make Rubinstein self-indulgent, especially as regards the length of her productions. After the first performance of *Antoine et Cléopâtre*, one critic grumbled:

> The show dragged on and, towards 1 a.m., the orchestra followed
> the audience's example and discreetly improvised a variation on the
> *Farewell* Symphony. For it was only towards 2 a.m. that Cleopatra at

last consented to die, before an irreducible squad of intrepid somnambulists.[137]

He did admit that before this hour 'Madame Rubinstein had had the satisfaction of asserting herself as a tragic actress', but even this was denied by other critics who declared that 'Ida Rubinstein no longer has an accent – not even a French one!', and that as an actress she was 'intelligent but an apprentice, whose declamation is pitiless in its monotony and harshness', while the critic of *Le Figaro* complained: 'When will amateurs stop queening it over our theatres?'[138]

Many of the critical notices in the Paris press exude a rank smell of xenophobia, with more than the occasional whiff of anti-semitism. But Rubinstein was a hard personality to place and no critic likes to be baffled for long. In the view of Madeleine Milhaud, who met her towards the end of the decade,

> she was a very astonishing lady. Difficult to know, I must say. She didn't want to be known. There was a mystery, and I think she guarded it. She was thin and extremely tall – unreachable. As an actress, she had a very special inflection, rather precious, not quite simple, not quite natural – as *she* was, in fact.[139]

This quality of being 'not quite natural', of being *intouchable*, may have been helped by her money and the confidence it gave her. But it could not endow her with a dancing technique she had never worked to acquire. The dancer Keith Lester remembered Rubinstein as 'impressive physically, but as a dancer, I must say, a great disappointment'; while William Chappell, like Lester an erstwhile member of her troupe, explained that 'to get up on your points when you've never done it in your life – and she must have been in her forties at that time – you can't do it'.[140]

If Rubinstein could at times give the impression of being merely an inspired amateur, she nonetheless insisted on having nothing but the best materials, whether in the form of props, costumes, decor, dancers or composers. Among the latter, Honegger became her favourite, collaborating with her on six projects, from incidental music to Saint-George de Bouhélier's drama *L'impératrice aux rochers*, written in 1925 but not performed until 1927, to *Jeanne d'Arc*, written in 1935 but not performed until 1938. Such delays were frequent whenever Rubinstein was involved, and an unkind historian might again lay them, together with the frequent cancellations, at the door of her self-indulgence. Certainly they caused complaints from composers, from Jacques Rouché at the Opéra, who would suddenly be faced with the prospect of an empty theatre, and from the members of her troupe. William Chappell remembered vividly the trials of being on tour with Rubinstein:

> You never knew whether you were going to be far-flung or not move.
> A lot of places I wanted to go to, we never got to because she would take

flight at the last minute and cancel the whole thing. And then we'd be left trying to live where we'd been dumped on our very meagre pay.[141]

Her second commission offered to Honegger in 1926 was for incidental music to d'Annunzio's play *Phèdre*. We can see from the above list of her productions in the 1920s that Rubinstein had not, like Apollinaire, turned her back on myth and classical history, so that when they returned to favour in the mid-1920s she appeared to be in the vanguard of fashion. This was entirely illusory. In 1926, an admirer called Fernand Nozière wrote a short biographical sketch of her, insisting that

> she does not aim to show us the banality of our times.... She does not take the elements of her productions from everyday life.... She is very far from the realists.... Most certainly she is not a realistic actress. She does not believe that art follows in the footsteps of photography.[142]

And indeed at no time did she even hint that she might follow Diaghilev or the Ballets suédois, with their Blue Trains and Skating Rinks.

Even so, during 1926 Rubinstein was in the process of rethinking her career:

> Would she succeed better as an actress or as a dancer? Her immediate decision was to concentrate upon dance as the ideal medium. But as she worked out her ideas in the period between 1928 and 1934, the result almost inevitably had to be a synthetic one, a combination of dramatic technique and dance form – a solution that realized itself in some unique and completely modern stage works.[143]

The collapse of Beaumont's Soirées de Paris in 1924 and the disbanding of the Ballets suédois the following year had left Diaghilev in undisputed command of the Parisian ballet scene; a command Rubinstein decided to challenge in 1928 by forming her own company, Les ballets Ida Rubinstein – 'not Les ballets juifs, as Diaghilev sneeringly suggested'.[144]

Details of her 'synthetic solution' can be found in some of the seven ballets, given in November and December 1928, with which she celebrated the formation of her new company. Bronislava Nijinska was engaged as chief choreographer, Anatole Vilzak as *premier danseur* and Massine was to choreograph two of the ballets. Rehearsals began on 1 August and at once it became clear that Rubinstein was not going to be a 'hands-on' presence like Diaghilev (who remains most vividly in Madeleine Milhaud's memory standing at the back of the auditorium, gazing fixedly at the stage through opera glasses). Frederick Ashton was one of several British dancers in the *corps de ballet*:

> She did all her rehearsing privately.... When she appeared among us, we

were ordered to put on clean shirts and bottles of eau-de-cologne were provided for our use. She would walk through her parts, white-gloved and richly clad in furs, while her mystified company looked on.... We had the feeling of being in a company run by an Electress of some Palatinate for her own amusement.[145]

– which, in effect, they were. Nor was there any ambiguity in the focus of each production, which was simply and solely Rubinstein herself. Yet at the same time she was moved to experiment and to encourage others to do likewise: Honegger's incidental music for *L'impératrice aux rochers* and for *Phèdre*, for example, like his later ballets *Amphion* (1931) and *Sémiramis* (1933), made none of the concessions to popular taste that had been so plainly audible in *Le roi David*.

Alexandre Benois had long nourished the hope of mounting a ballet to music by J. S. Bach.[146] Now, in 1928, Rubinstein gave him the opportunity, entrusting the music of *Les noces d'Amour et de Psyché* to the care of Honegger – this was one of three 're-creations' of the past in her series of commissions. According to Honegger's biographer Marcel Delannoy, the composer accepted the task 'with devotion' but did not share Stravinsky's view, à propos *Pulcinella*, that 'rape is permissible as long as one begets a child. Honegger would not be a party to rape.'[147] Instead he took a line different from both Stravinsky in *Pulcinella* and Milhaud in *Salade*, retaining Bach's notes unchanged, apart from a few transpositions. The novelty lay in the orchestration. Honegger uses a full symphony orchestra including two saxophones and celesta, and characterizes many of the twenty-two Bach pieces that make up the ballet by particular instrumental groupings: the D major fugue from Book I of the 48 ('Entrée de Mars and Vulcain') is scored for trumpets, trombones, tuba and strings, while the Polonaise from the sixth French Suite (the second item in the five-movement 'Entrée de Psyché') is given to flute, clarinet, muted horn, harp and muted string quartet.

This wholehearted display of orchestral colour was matched by the extravagance of the staging. After the first night on 22 November, it was described by the critic Charles Tenroc as a kind of 'mythological court ballet where one expects to see the Sun King playing Jupiter among the nymphs and divinities of Olympus, dancing to Lully'.[148] Diaghilev, not surprisingly, was caustic about the whole enterprise, remarking of Rubinstein herself that 'her figure is thicker than before, whereas her legs have grown thinner. She is as old as the devil'[149] – in fact, forty-three. But in less prejudiced quarters Rubinstein's epiphany as Sun-Queen was greeted, if not with rapture, at least with approval, taking an honourable place among the evocations of the *grand siècle* with which 1920s Paris liked to comfort itself.

The second re-creation of the past on that opening night was of Liszt's re-creations of Schubert waltzes, *Les soirées de Vienne*: this was intended, at least partly, as a centenary homage to Schubert who, as was noted in *Le courrier musical*, 'now reigns in all the radio stations of Europe'.[150] Since Milhaud was not dealing with *echt* Schubert, he felt free to go further than Liszt, employing not only an orchestra but a Pleyela player-piano to produce virtuoso sounds beyond the scope of a conventional pianist. For whatever reasons, the production was generally agreed to have been a failure, and some of this has to be attributed to Rubinstein's insistence on getting up on her points, which had at least one unfortunate effect:

> although her partner, Vilzak, was a perfectly normal-sized man and very muscular and good-looking and everything, she was much taller than him and when she got up on point she looked like a sort of great wild spider climbing about over him.[151]

The third and last of these historical re-creations, and by some way the most famous, was Stravinsky's *Le baiser de la fée*. Much ink has been spilled over the rights and wrongs of Stravinsky's treatment of Tchaikovsky's music, which is too complex a question to be debated here. But Diaghilev's vitriolic contempt for the production ('The theatre, though full, made one think of a drawing-room in which some respectable person has just farted')[152] suggests that he may have been worried by Stravinsky's 'desertion' and by the fact that the dancing was not as bad as he would have liked it to be. The Paris correspondent of *The Times*, while complaining that the music suffered from 'a persistent dryness, Tchaikovsky's tunes being in sudden contrast to the surrounding matter', nonetheless had kind words for Rubinstein: she

> easily stood out from among the other executants. The beauty of her movements, her graceful form, and the dignity of her appearance, the whole enhanced by her seemingly great height, all these were undeniably worth coming to see.[153]

But the most famous of the ballets she commissioned for her 1928 season is, of course, *Boléro*, which concluded the opening night on 22 November. Diaghilev, again, refused to be impressed, to the extent of missing the point of the music and the production: 'she spent a quarter of an hour clumsily turning round on a table as large as the whole stage of the Monte Carlo Opera'.[154] Leaving aside the word 'clumsy', with which he was always quick to label anyone he disapproved of, we may surmise that he was upset by the new balance of elements in which music reasserted its primacy over dancing and decor. Having already dismissed *La valse* as not a ballet 'but the portrait of a ballet',[155] he could not be expected to welcome *Boléro*, likewise empty of illustratable incident except for the electric modulation a mere 13 bars before the end. With Benois's help, Rubinstein created (according to Henry Prunières) 'a picture in the manner of Goya',[156] by all accounts quite close in atmosphere to the setting in a factory which Ravel ideally wanted, and which was later to be provided for the staging of the ballet at the Opéra in 1939. From William Chappell's description, it is clear that in 1928 rhythm was the dominating factor:

71. The composer quoted in Samuel, *Prokofiev*, p. 100.
72. Recalled by Alicia Markova, in Buckle, *Diaghilev*, p. 486.
73. Samuel, *Prokofiev*, p. 103.
74. Igor Stravinsky and Robert Craft, *Dialogues and a Diary* (London, 1968), pp. 29 and 27.
75. Stravinsky, *Chroniques*, p. 147.
76. *La revue musicale*, I July 1928, p. 287.
77. Collaer, *Correspondance*, 19 February 1930, p. 274.
78. Vlad, *Stravinsky*, p. 92.
79. Garafola, *Diaghilev's Ballets Russes*, pp. 140–41.
80. Steegmuller, *Cocteau*, p. 346.
81. Erik Näslund, article in *Les ballets suédois* (Paris, 1994) p. 22; much of the information in this section is taken from this source.
82. Ibid., p. 9.
83. Darius Milhaud, *Ma vie heureuse* (Paris, 1973), p. 71.
84. Paul Collaer, *Darius Milhaud*, trans. and ed. Jane Hohfeld Galante (San Francisco, 1988), p. 64.
85. Rolf de Maré, *Les ballets suédois dans l'art contemporain* (Paris, 1931), p. 63; quoted in Garafola, *Diaghilev's Ballets Russes*, p. 111.
86. Harry Halbreich, *Arthur Honegger* (Paris, 1992), p. 573.
87. Ibid., p. 79.
88. *Mouvement contraire* (Paris, 1947), p. 130.
89. Milhaud, *Ma vie heureuse*, p. 86.
90. Ibid., p. 87.
91. Roger Nichols, *Conversations with Madeleine Milhaud* (London, 1996), p. 21.
92. Emile Vuillermoz, in *La revue musicale*, I July 1928, p. 287.
93. Näslund, in *Les ballets suédois*, p. 65.
94. Charles Tenroc, in *Le courrier musical*, 15 November 1923, p. 356.
95. Milhaud, *Ma vie heureuse*, p. 128.
96. Erik Aschengreen, *Jean Cocteau and the Dance* (Copenhagen, 1986); quoted by Näslund, in *Les ballets suédois*, pp. 42, 45.
97. See letter of 19 June 1923 to Paul Collaer, in Collaer, *Correspondance*, p. 140.
98. Ibid., p. 150, n. 3.
99. See Collaer, *Darius Milhaud*, p. 125.
100. Ibid., p. 128.
101. George Antheil, *Bad Boy of Music* (New York, 1945), p. 110.
102. Robert Orledge, *Satie the Composer* (Cambridge, 1990), p. 354, n. 41.
103. I am grateful to Robert Orledge for confirming the correct date.
104. Alan M. Gillmor, *Erik Satie* (Basingstoke, 1988), p. 250.
105. Michel Sanouillet, *Francis Picabia et '391'* (Paris, 1966), p. 170.
106. Letter to Collaer of 12 December 1924, in Collaer, *Correspondance*, p. 194.
107. Letter to Collaer of 21 December 1924, in ibid., p. 195.
108. Sanouillet, *Francis Picabia*, p. 251; also Louis Schneider, 'Music in Paris', *New York Herald* [Paris], 6 December 1924, in a review of the open dress rehearsal on 4 December.
109. Nancy Perloff, *Art and the Everyday: Popular Entertainment and the Circle of Erik Satie* (Oxford, 1991), pp. 84–85.
110. Orledge, *Satie the Composer*, pp. 177–84.
111. Näslund, in *Les ballets suédois*, p. 65.
112. Garafola, *Diaghilev's Ballets Russes*, p. 220.
113. Annabel Farjeon, 'Lydia Lopokova and Serge Diaghilev', and Lynn Garafola, 'Les soirées de Paris', in *Lydia Lopokova*, ed. Milo Keynes (London, 1983), pp. 71–83 and 97–105.
114. Ibid., p. 100.
115. Ibid.
116. Ibid., p. 80.
117. Collaer, trans. and ed. Hohfeld Galante, *Darius Milhaud*, p. 76.
118. Letter of 17 July 1928, in Collaer, *Correspondance*, p. 255.
119. Ibid., p. 165.
120. Extract in the Milhaud Archive. I am grateful to Mme Madeleine Milhaud for showing me this source.
121. Walsh, *Stravinsky*, p. 98.
122. *The Chesterian*, 6, 41 (October 1924) p. 24.

123. For details of this work, including a complete score, see Robert Orledge, *Satie the Composer* (Cambridge, 1990) pp. 226–30.

124. Gillmor, *Satie*, p. 245.

125. Robert Orledge, 'Erik Satie's Ballet *Mercure* (1924): From Mount Etna to Montmartre', in *JRMA*, 123 (1998), pp. 229–49.

126. Perloff, *Art and the Everyday*, p. 208.

127. Auric, in *Les nouvelles littéraires* (21 June 1924), p. 7.

128. Ornella Volta, *Satie Seen through his Letters*, trans. Michael Bullock (London, 1989), p. 172.

129. Gillmor, *Satie*, p. 246.

130. Buckle, *Diaghilev*, pp. 433–34.

131. Volta, *Satie Seen*, p. 172.

132. Quoted in Garafola, 'Les soirées de Paris', in Keynes (ed.), *Lydia Lopokova*, p. 105.

133. Ibid., p. 104.

134. Ibid., p. 101.

135. Comte Robert de Montesquiou, *Têtes d'expression* (Paris, 1912), pp. 215, 226, quoted in Michael de Cossart, *Ida Rubinstein* (Liverpool, 1987), p. 18, to which I am indebted for some of what follows.

136. André Gide, *Ainsi soit-il ou les jeux sont faits* (Paris, 1952), p. 22.

137. P. Saegel, 'Antoine et Cléopâtre', in *Le ménestrel*, 18 June 1920.

138. Undated cuttings in *Antoine et Cléopâtre*, Paris Opéra, dossier d'oeuvre.

139. Madeleine Milhaud, in conversation with the author.

140. William Chappell, in conversation with the author. I am grateful to Jann Parry for sending me a tape of her interview with Keith Lester, and also Lester's article, 'Rubinstein revisited', in *Journal of the Society for Dance Research*, 1983, pp. 20–31.

141. William Chappell, in conversation with the author.

142. Fernand Nozière, *Ida Rubinstein*, (Paris, 1926), pp. 7–8.

143. De Cossart, *Ida Rubinstein*, p. 108.

144. Ibid., p. 125.

145. 'Miss Rubinstein', *The Times*, 21 October 1960.

146. Alexandre Benois, *Reminiscences of the Russian Ballet* (London, 1941), p. 352.

147. Marcel Delannoy, *Honegger* (Paris, 1953), p. 126.

148. Charles Tenroc, 'Les ballets de Mme Ida Rubinstein', in *Le courrier musical*, 25 December 1928, p. 744.

149. Serge Lifar, *Histoire du Ballet Russe depuis les origines jusqu'à nos jours* (Paris, 1950), p. 238.

150. 1 December 1928.

151. Willam Chappell, in conversation with the author.

152. Lifar, *Histoire du Ballet Russe*, p. 240.

153. 'A Paris Ballet Season', *The Times*, 7 December 1928.

154. Lifar, *Histoire du Ballet Russe*, pp. 238–39.

155. Francis Poulenc, *Moi et mes amis* (Geneva, 1963), p. 179.

156. Henry Prunières, 'Les ballets d'Ida Rubinstein à l'Opéra', in *La revue musicale*, January 1929, p. 244.

157. William Chappell, in conversation with the author.

7. The Establishment: the teaching institutions, the churches, the salons, the press

The teaching institutions

IF IT IS TRUE THAT THE HEALTH of a nation's musical culture is related to the musical education of its children, then the liveliness of French music in the postwar period represents some kind of serendipitous miracle. It was a fact widely acknowledged and deplored in the 1920s that primary and secondary musical education in France was dire. The singer Doda Conrad, born in 1905, remembered how as a young boy in Switzerland he had lived for his school music lessons. In France after the war, even where there were any music lessons to be had, his enthusiasm waned.[1]

There was, as always, no shortage of good intentions or of advice, good and otherwise. A ministerial *arrêté* of 18 August 1920 decreed that in Ecoles Primaires Supérieures (for 11 to 13-year-olds) there should be one compulsory hour of musical instruction and one optional per week. While d'Indy was loudly insisting that musical education should be compulsory throughout a child's school career, Florent Schmitt took a slightly softer line, agreeing that this was the ideal, but only

> on condition that music is presented as something attractive and not
> as lessons in *solfège*, dictation, scales, `passing the thumb', position of
> the hands, exercise books and other official horrors. The best way
> of learning music is to start by loving it.[2]

However, a ministerial decree of two years later was still insisting on a strong reading and writing component, even for seven-year-olds, although from the age of thirteen the compulsory music element had been increased from one to two hours. But as always, the whole edifice rested or fell on the quality of the teachers, and in 1929 Maurice Chevais could still complain that primary school teachers were sometimes able to obtain a 'brevet élémentaire', entitling them to teach music, just by answering theoretical questions and without being able to sing or play a note.[3]

The shortfall in state musical education was partially made good by the many private teachers in the capital: in 1923 and again in 1927, the *Annuaire des artistes* listed three thousand piano teachers in the capital and, even more suprisingly, five hundred teachers of the double bass, most of them not offering cello as well. But, if we are to believe Alfred Cortot, the majority of these were disappointed and embittered individuals, having failed to gain a first prize at the Conservatoire or elsewhere.[4] They had also been particularly hard hit by inflation. In 1921, unionized light industrial workers were demanding a 400 per cent pay rise. Music teachers, with no industrial muscle, who had been earning 15 francs an hour before the war, could not now start charging 75 francs. Many were therefore driven out of teaching and into playing for the cinema or in dance bands.[5]

At the other end of the social, economic and artistic scale from this depressed body sat the gods of the Académie des Beaux-Arts in the Institut. The Académie, like the British Order of Merit, is limited to forty members, of whom six represent music. At the beginning of 1921, the six were (with dates of appointment), Camille Saint-Saëns (1881), Emile Paladilhe (1892), Théodore Dubois (1894), Gabriel Fauré (1909), Gustave Charpentier (1912) and Henri Rabaud (1918). The secretary was Charles-Marie Widor, the only musician since Halévy in the 1860s to have been thought worthy of the task. Their ages ranged from 47 (Rabaud), through 60 (Charpentier), 75 (Fauré), 76 (Paladilhe), 82 (Dubois), up to 85 (Saint-Saëns). The imperviousness of the more elderly members to the friskier musical delights of the early Twenties is a matter of record (Saint-Saëns's predilection for dining at the Magic City night club,[6] and indeed for dressing up on other occasions as an Egyptian dancing girl, did not entail his acceptance of jazz or bitonality in 'serious' music).

Henri Rabaud,
director of the Paris
Conservatoire
1920–1941

Although the honour of being a member of the Institut was very great, not much was (and possibly is) required beyond attending meetings between three and five o'clock on Saturday afternoons, electing new members when someone died and, before the prize in question was abolished in 1968, voting to select a winner of the competitions for the Prix de Rome. The great gulf fixed between these venerable persons and the musical schoolchild could be bridged only be attendance at one of the Parisian schools of music. Five of these demand consideration. Although the Conservatoire national de musique et de déclamation is by some way the oldest of them, I shall deal with them in a non-chronological order, the logic of which should nonetheless become apparent, starting necessarily at a point some time before 1917.

Ecole Niedermeyer

> In 1853 the Swiss composer Louis Niedermeyer persuaded Napoleon III to recognize the small boarding-school he had just founded, under the official title 'School of Classical and Religious Music' [Ecole de musique classique et religieuse]. It became better known under its later name, the Niedermeyer School. Its aim was to train organists and choirmasters who could then be employed by the bishops of each diocese. Gabriel Fauré was admitted in 1854, at the age of nine....[7]

The Ecole Niedermeyer was still active in the 1920s, as were a number of its former pupils. Fauré apart, it had a strange tendency, for a religiously inclined foundation, to produce composers of stage music of the lighter kind, among them Edmond Audran and Edmond Missa and, of those still alive after the First World War, Alexandre Georges, Claude Terrasse and André Messager. Ex-pupils who followed the founder's intentions more nearly included Fauré, Henri Busser and the organists Léon Boëllmann (who died young), Albert Périlhou (organist at St-Séverin for thirty years until 1919), and Eugène Gigout (from 1911 until his death in 1925, organ professor at the Conservatoire and for over sixty years organist at St-Augustin).

Perhaps the most notable feature of the school's teaching in the nineteenth century was its emphasis on the choral masters of the sixteenth: 'three times a week all the students came together...to sing Josquin, Palestrina, Bach and Victoria, usually unaccompanied. The secular repertoire was sung only on student walks.'[8] This early, practical exposure to the modal and contrapuntal thinking of these great masters left an indelible mark on the music written by the school's pupils. In Fauré's, for example, as Robert Orledge points out, while 'passages of any length purely in the Gregorian modes are rare...modal cadences, however, are common, and this was one of Fauré's main means of avoiding the obvious'. And the influence lasted to the end of the composer's life: Orledge goes on to quote the final cadence, in the transposed Phrygian mode, of the song 'Danseuse' from the song-cycle *Mirages* of 1919.[9]

But for the most part the influence of the Ecole Niedermeyer on the music of the Twenties was indirect, through the example of alumni who flourished before the First World War. Its capacity to exert direct influence had been usurped some years earlier by a rival institution.

Schola Cantorum

Holy Week of 1892 in the church of St-Gervais in the centre of Paris was celebrated with a feast of music by composers including those favoured in the Ecole Niedermeyer: Josquin, Palestrina, Bach, Victoria, as well as Lassus and Lotti. On the Wednesday, the nave was full.[10] The prime mover of the event was a pupil of César Franck, Charles Bordes, and Vincent d'Indy helped with the rehearsals.

That same year, a State Commission sat to draw up proposals for reorganizing the Conservatoire. D'Indy, who was a member of the Commission, was unhappy with the general report and submitted one of his own, which was effectively rejected on grounds of expense and its impact on the student workload. From these two enterprises was born the idea of the Schola Cantorum, which, under the guidance of d'Indy, Bordes and the organist Alexandre Guilmant, opened its doors on 6 October 1894.

D'Indy's battle cry was 'Art is not a métier.' For the next thirty-five years he waged war on what he regarded as the Conservatoire's narrow concern with virtuosity and the operatic stage (both singly and in conjunction), considering these to be hostile to the true purpose of music, which was a religious one, as his teacher Franck had powerfully demonstrated. Following Niedermeyer, d'Indy began the Schola's course, preserved for posterity in the four volumes of his seven-year *Cours de composition musicale*, with the study of plainsong. From here the course progressed chronologically, with all exercises related to particular compositional styles, and with particular and unusual attention being paid to composers such as Lully and Rameau – who elsewhere were widely venerated and as widely ignored.

D'Indy was nothing if not practical, which helped give him a reputation for dogmatism. Edgard Varèse studied at the Schola for two years from 1904 and, when asked nearly sixty years later whether he would allow one of his works to be played in a Schola retrospective concert, wrote:

> From the Schola I retain happy memories of my teacher, Albert Roussel, who later became a friend, and of Charles Bordes who introduced me to the music of Léonin, Pérotin and those who came after them. But as for that 'sub-Franck', as Willy called him, he left such a nasty taste in my mouth that I'm determined to have nothing to do either with his bigoted teaching, or with his music, and still less with his hypocritical person.[11]

Some allowance no doubt has to be made for the diametrically opposed characters of the two men. But an extract from one of d'Indy's many expositions of principle leaves us in no doubt whatever of his aims. He accepts that musicians have to have a technique. But

> when that has been achieved, when one is capable of managing the most dizzily virtuosic of concertos without a mistake, of sailing through the most complicated vocalises, of putting together accurately the strictest counterpoint and even of producing a correct fugue, one should beware of thinking that this is where education ends and that by surmounting all these difficulties, often at great cost, one has become a consummate artist; the truth is precisely the contrary and, if one stops at a point which is merely, in reality, a halfway house, one risks, nine times out of ten, remaining all one's life a 'demi-savant', and consequently a mediocrity.[12]

That broadside, delivered in 1900, still brings with it a whiff of cordite. In the Twenties d'Indy, by now in his seventies, was slightly softened in some respects by his happy second marriage, but in 1927 his defence of the Schola's aims was as combative as ever:

> Today the forecasters continue to ramble on, at rather greater length than before, now that they are reinforced by the ranks of *snobs*, who – in order to appear up-to-date – take the crumbling green cheese of ignorant improvisers to be a moon lighting up the world. All the while, gently, without haste, the Schola has never ceased to climb the fruitful slopes of the mountain of art.[13]

From the vantage point of the 1950s, one old pupil, Guy de Lioncourt, still felt that French music following 1918 was not up to the standard of that following 1871, and asked the typically *scholiste* question of whether perhaps defeat released more energy than victory, through the need for reconstruction. Clearly he had still not accepted Les Six, thirty years on.

From his testimony, it seems that little changed at the Schola after the First World War, except that a teachers' association was formed in 1918, 'with the idea of promoting an exchange of views between colleagues'.[14] What success this had in influencing d'Indy's benevolent tyranny, we are not told. But there can be no doubt that the Schola played an important role in the music world of the time. Student numbers reached an all-time high in the years 1920–25, and were still at six hundred in 1929, taught in eighty classes. The programme of the Schola concerts in the Salle Gaveau during the 1928/29 season is also impressive, and contained music still hard to hear elsewhere in the city: Monteverdi's *Orfeo* and *L'incoronazione*, Gluck's *Orphée* (in the Paris tenor version), Bach's B minor Mass together with both Passions and some cantatas, and Weber's *Euryanthe* and *Der Freischütz*. Added to these were the Schola's publications of music which, says d'Indy, 'continue to be as recommended by Pope Pius X in his famous *motu proprio* of 1904 [1903], and which his current successor Pius XI has confirmed in his recent, forceful *Constitution apostolique*'.[15] No doubt more pleasing to d'Indy than any of these was the special Apostolic Blessing received from the Pontiff in 1929, 'congratulating us on our work for Gregorian Chant and religious music'.[16]

But, as with the Ecole Niedermeyer, the production of widely recognized composers by the Schola almost entirely dried up with the prewar generation of Roussel, Magnard, de Séverac, Nin and Jongen (and Satie!). Of the pupils who studied there in the Twenties, the most prominent name was that of the now forgotten Marcel Mihalovici, who arrived in Paris in 1919 after studying in Bucharest with Enesco. Few people in 1900 would have believed that, a quarter of a century later, the prestige and quality of the Paris Conservatoire was to rise to new heights, becoming, in one oft-quoted phrase, 'the school that Frenchmen criticize the most and the one most Frenchmen try to get into'.[17] It has frequently been assumed that it did so in the teeth of opposition from d'Indy and the Schola. The facts are less straightforward.

Paris Conservatoire (Conservatoire national de musique et de déclamation)

> The organization and above all the make-up of the Conservatoire promise to bring together two advantages which, up to now, have been regarded as incompatible: the conservation of what is most pure and beautiful in the art as currently before us, and the means to make good what is lacking. One has grounds for hoping that the tyranny of routines will be banished, as well as the licentiousness of innovations. The respect due to the works of the masters who deserve it will be maintained, without refusing a welcome to bold flights of genius and to the fruits of true invention [aux heureuses créations].[18]

Those precepts, voiced shortly after the founding of the Conservatoire on 3 August 1795 (le 16 thermidor an III), were still embraced two centuries later by a recent director, Marc-Olivier Dupin.[19] But understandably the balance, especially between respect for the old and welcome for the new, has continually fluctuated during that time; it would, moreover, be too much to expect any body of professors always to be unanimous over what was or was not an 'heureuse création'.

This is not the place to describe the Conservatoire's evolution over a century and more in the hands of six directors: Bernard Sarrette (1795–1815), François Perne (1815–22), Luigi Cherubini (1822–42), Louis Auber (1842–71), Ambroise Thomas (1871–96) and Théodore Dubois (1896–1905). But a large part of the character of the Conservatoire from 1917 on must be attributed to the reforms of Fauré, who took over from Dubois in 1905 in the wake of the Ravel affair (when that composer, in his last permitted year of candidature, was refused permission by the judges even to try for the final round of the Prix de Rome). Fauré handed over to Henri Rabaud in the autumn of 1920.

Lovers of Fauré's music might assume that his directorship would have passed gently, peaceably and without disruptive incident. This was far from being the case. As one who had taught composition at the Conservatoire for nine years but who had not been educated there, Fauré was in an excellent position to see what was wrong, while feeling no sentimental attachment to the view that 'this is the way it's always been done'. He laid his plans during the summer of 1905, and the results appeared in decrees and an *arrêté* of 7 and 8 October. His determination to rule rather than be ruled is clear from one of the decrees which stipulates that the director should 'be in charge of all studies and preside over all committees, in which his voice is to be preponderant'.[20]

He acted decisively to end various doubtful practices, such as that of hopeful students taking private lessons from Conservatoire professors in advance of the entrance examinations, and drove a coach and horses through the teaching reper-toire: 'to substitute [Monteverdi's] *Orfeo* for *Robert le diable* and Bach fugues for Moscheles concertos was an act of audacity such as we cannot imagine today'.[21] Several professors resigned and Fauré acquired the nickname 'Robespierre'. He also addressed the manner of performances as well as the matter, declaring war in the operatic field on

> the corruptions which, in the name of *tradition*, are inflicted [on
> masterpieces] by the caprice or bad taste of certain performers. At the
> Conservatoire we should ignore these traditions and the prime duty
> of our professors should be to make sure that scenes from opera or *opéra
> comique* are performed not as they are sung in the theatre but, *strictly*, in
> accordance with the composer's written intentions.[22]

It has perhaps not been sufficiently recognized that these reforms owed a good deal to the ideas of d'Indy, especially as regards the expansion of the repertoire and the demotion of transcendent virtuosity. It may have been partly in gratitude, as well as out of diplomacy, that Fauré appointed d'Indy to succeed Dukas as head of the orchestral class in 1912, and of the newly created conducting class two years later. Partly, no doubt, he had it in mind to soften the general perception of a sharp split between the Conservatoire and the Schola Cantorum.

But introducing reform is one thing, keeping up the impetus another. Reynaldo Hahn made notes of a harmony exam at some point before 1914:

> Fauré reads the papers, chats with Bourgeat [the secretary], writes
> telegrams, goes out several times, walks around, listen distractedly to a
> few bars.... How should it be otherwise, when it's been decided in advance
> to award innumerable prizes, when the accepted pattern at each exam is
> to release a cloud of laureates, like carrier pigeons, so that they can go off
> to the four corners of the world and bear witness to the Conservatoire's
> superb teaching! It's a very bad policy and I'm astonished to see a great
> artist like Fauré encouraging such a dangerous tendency. Instead of the
> single first prize which was merited, we awarded four....[23]

Obviously the war had a damaging effect on the Conservatoire, as on every other teaching institution, and the situation was further exacerbated by Fauré's age (he was seventy in 1915) and by his increasing deafness, which he did his best to hide. On 26 September 1919, the administration of the Beaux-Arts renewed his tenure 'for one year', 'on the understanding that the time had come for him to leave the institution.... This decision...was notified to him with no excess of tact.'[24]

Another Robespierre was sought. The enthusiasm which the prospect of the directorship inspired can be judged by Henri Rabaud's comment in a letter of 3 June

1920: 'You ask whether I've been appointed director of the Conservatoire: no – but I'm very much afraid I shan't be able to escape it!'[25] Nor was he, and he remained in the post from 1 October 1920 until succeeded by Claude Delvincourt in 1941. When Rabaud was appointed in the summer of 1920, the critic Charles Tenroc took the opportunity to spell out what he saw as the Conservatoire's problems: there was no clear chain of command, the professors were 'badly paid, badly recruited, badly supervised' and the students 'turn up to lessons when they have time'. One consequence of all this was that 'the sonority of the woodwind and the reliability of the brass both give cause for alarm in the matter of their traditional supremacy'[26] – as far as the brass go, an alarm well justified by many gramophone recordings of the 1920s.

Rabaud had no illusions over the size of his task. An *arrêté* of 25 September incorporating his wishes stipulated, among other things, that the three chamber music classes were now obligatory for prizewinners in the areas of piano, strings and woodwind, that any student missing a class three times without a valid excuse would be dismissed, and that the director would now choose the test pieces for all examinations including the end-of-year *concours*.[27] Rabaud also instituted open concerts for the various classes, the first to be heard being Lucien Capet's chamber music class early in 1921 (Schumann's D minor piano Trio, Mozart's B flat Violin Sonata K.454, Beethoven's String Quartet op. 18 no. 4).

Charles-Marie Widor

Altogether Rabaud ran a tight ship, but like every director he could do little about the staff he inherited, especially when they were celebrities. Henri Barraud, who was later to have a distinguished career as director of music for French Radio and Television, remembered how, in one of the orchestra classes conducted by d'Indy, a posse of brass players in the *Tannhäuser* overture crept out of their places unobserved and, at the point where the opening fanfare returns, delivered it from inches behind d'Indy's back. He also remembered that Rabaud's figure appearing in the doorway would be the signal for an instant show of professional concentration.[28]

Widor was another intractable problem. He had been appointed as a professor of composition in 1896 and proved surprisingly effective in training students to win the Prix de Rome competition with cantatas cast in the traditional mould of French opera. His pupil Louis Vierne recalled that Widor 'would occasionally try to make his students write symphonic music, but most of his time was taken up with the cookery of the Cantata'. Vierne wondered indeed why Widor should have wanted to become a composition professor: 'did he think he would have as positive an influence as that which he had acquired in the organ class by the personality of his teaching, and enlarge the horizons of young composers...? I do not know whether the future left him that illusion.'[29] Whether it did or not, by the end of the war Widor was in his mid-seventies and, until his retirement in 1927, was 'content to coast along, frequently arriving late after gossiping with [Isidor] Philipp in the adjoining class, engaging the students in conversation, or singling out Yvonne Lefébure to play the piano'.[30] No teacher can be held responsible for the quality of the composing talent that comes his way, so too much should probably not be made of the fact that, despite sharing the Prix de Rome honours during these years with the other composition professor Paul Vidal (five first prizes to Vidal, four to Widor), Widor's students were an unremarkable collection, whereas Vidal's included Ibert, the conductor-to-be Louis Fourestier and the prolific composer Henri Tomasi.

But Widor's successor, Paul Dukas, like Rabaud seven years before, had no illusions as to what he was inheriting:

> So much valuable opinion represented the job to me as being *necessary*. I ended up by agreeing and I hope I shall not be unequal to the task before me, which looks formidable. The state of musical disarray is profound and too many people are determined to cultivate it – as they do the high cost of living – for it to be conquered just by lofty ideals. The ancient words no longer mean anything and people couldn't give a damn about reputation! Or if there is ambition, it's along the lines of M. Citroën rather than *père* Franck! I shall very gently try to deindustrialize music. For the moment I think that's the most urgent job before me.[31]

Given that three of Dukas's pupils in the late 1920s and early 1930s were Maurice Duruflé, Jean Langlais and Olivier Messiaen, we may say that the deindustrialization programme was a success. Certainly it is hard to see what these three could usefully have learnt from Widor, for all that he shared their organist's orientation.

Questions about the value of the Prix de Rome and the four years' paid composing time it brought with it continued to be asked in much the same way as they had been since Berlioz's day. The critic and teacher Max d'Ollone, the winner in 1897, believed that the stay in Rome could be useful to composers provided they were not married (the rule of bachelorhood had been relaxed in the case of those who had got married during the war, like Ibert), and that

> they look around them and gain an understanding of a host of things that are new to them and nothing to do with the music with which they are

saturated, and that it should be for them above all a complete break with Paris, with its appalling musical atmosphere, its baleful press, its little coteries and its manifold snobberies.[32]

Like Debussy over forty years earlier, Elsa Barraine, who won the Grand Prix in 1929, found escaping the hothouse Parisian atmosphere easier said than done. Shortly after her arrival at the Villa Medici in January 1930 she wrote back to her teacher Paul Dukas:

> it's not a happy scene between these young artists, who behave rather like concierges: the general conversation is all gossip and stories going back to Berlioz's time. Everyone stares at one another, the women size each other up and spy on each other mistrustfully, in short no one can stand anyone else. It's charming...a rats' nest...terrible heat...total isolation....[33]

The titles of the texts which candidates had to set to qualify for this life of the spirit give a flavour of what the authorities were after: *Le poète et la fée* (1919; Ibert won the second prize), *Hermione* (1921), *Béatrix* (1923), *Les amants de Vérone* (1924), *La mort d'Adonis* (1925; Louis Fourestier won the Grand Prix), *Coriolan* (1927), *Heraklès à Delphes* (1928). If elsewhere ancient myth and legend were either in disrepute or being radically reinterpreted by Cocteau, they flourished still in the groves of the Académie des Beaux-Arts.

The situation Rabaud took over in 1920 was happier on the technical and instrumental fronts. Gedalge, the teacher of Ravel, Milhaud and many others, was still professor of counterpoint and fugue, Gigout of organ, Philippe Gaubert of flute, Emile Engel of singing, while Capet, Chevillard and Tournemire ran the three chamber music classes.

Of the five piano professors, the most illustrious were Isidore Philipp, Alfred Cortot, and Marguerite Long – one of Fauré's last appointments, made reluctantly by him and hardly less reluctantly by the board of the Beaux-Arts in the face of her implacable determination: as Fauré's ex-pupil Roger-Ducasse put it, 'if she knew that the bastard son of her chemist was a friend of the bastard son of the chemist of the bastard son of the under-secretary of the Beaux-Arts, she'd go and play him *Le tombeau de Couperin* – and she'd win through'.[34]

The list of pianists who emerged from the Conservatoire in these years is distinguished, and includes Vlado Perlemuter, Jacques Février, Nikita Magaloff, Jean Françaix, Jeanne-Marie Darré, Jacqueline Blancard, Monique Haas and Beveridge Webster. For all d'Indy's diatribes against virtuosity, it was not only to learn virtuosity that you went to the Conservatoire, as we are told by a journalist reporting on the 1920 *Prix d'honneur de piano*. On the morning of 10 July, five first prizewinners from the previous year presented themselves to play Dukas's *Variations sur un thème de Rameau*. Among the four young ladies was Jeanne-Marie Darré, whose sparkling scales and

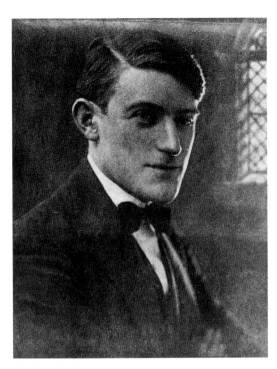

arpeggios had won her a prize the previous year at the age of thirteen; the boy was the sixteen-year-old Perlemuter. Mlle Darré, it was thought by the audience, should have won the *Prix d'honneur* outright. But the jury (including Fauré, Vidal, Chevillard, Gigout and the composer) awarded the prize to Perlemuter, 'a pupil of Monsieur Cortot and, we are assured, the most faithful interpreter of the ideas of the composer, who was on the jury'. To which the reporter adds the evocative words 'premier tumulte' – the 'deuxième tumulte' being provoked shortly afterwards by the *Prix d'honneur* for the violinists.[35]

Although Rabaud was all for open access, tumults were more than he could accept, and in the course of the decade the general public were refused entry to the performing *concours*: by 1925 the regulations stated firmly that

Vlado Perlemuter around the time of his Prix d'honneur

in order to preserve their academic character, they will take place in the presence only of the committee with overall care of the teaching, of professors at the establishment, of critics and of theatre directors in Paris or the provinces who express in good time their desire to attend.[36]

But even this did not quell the partisanship. On one occasion in the mid-1920s Artur Rubinstein was recommended by Cortot to serve with him on the piano jury – Cortot had left the Conservatoire staff by then, so they were the two external members. The test piece was the Chopin F minor Ballade, and after the performances Rabaud put in a strong plea for a fourth-year student who had already won a second prize three years earlier, and who was making his last possible attempt. The Conservatoire rules, according to Rubinstein, stated that any candidate who had won a second prize could in subsequent years win only a first prize or nothing. Rabaud pleaded that the man had a family to support and the lack of a first prize would condemn him to a life of penury. Cortot stood firm and the prize went to a fifteen-year-old. 'Out in the street,' wrote Rubinstein, 'a small crowd was waiting for us. They were the families of the losers. When they saw us, they began to scream: "Murderers! Assassins!"'[37]

It may seem curious now that a nation so uninterested in promoting music in its primary and secondary schools should have monitored the Conservatoire *concours* with such passion. Obviously money had something to do with it and, despite strictures from Hahn, Cortot and others that too many first prizes were awarded, any *premier prix* from this institution could command a safe, if not a luxurious living in one of the provincial conservatoires.

Finally, Rabaud's organizing hand can be seen in Article 91 of the *règlement* quoted above, which offered a *Diplôme d'études musicales supérieures*, on the director's recommendation, to a student who had obtained three *premiers prix*, but not just any three: one had to be in fugue, harmony, piano accompaniment (including score-reading and improvisation) or organ and one, interestingly, in the history of music. Fauré had been the first to insist that students attended the history classes, first of Bourgault-Ducoudray and then of Maurice Emmanuel, but it was left to Rabaud to take the further step of making the history class examinable. One of the first recipients of the diploma was Olivier Messiaen, following his first prizes in fugue (1926), piano accompaniment (1927), organ and music history 1929). This diploma may be said to have been a further acknowledgment of the validity of d'Indy's reforming zeal of thirty years before, especially as a *premier prix* in piano, with its connotations of virtuosity, was not accepted as a component.

Marcel Dupré, Messiaen's organ teacher, at the organ of the Conservatoire on which he played Bach's complete organ works in 1920

Ecole normale de musique de Paris

In 1919 Auguste Mangeot, the director of the magazine *Le monde musical*, suggested to Alfred Cortot that there was room for another school of music which did not insist on the Conservatoire's limits of thirty for age and only two foreign students per class. Indeed the prospectus reads, for those in the know, as a carefully worded indictment of Conservatoire policy:

The Ecole normale de musique receives pupils of all nationalities, without age limit and without entrance examination.... Through a choice of teachers representing diverse aesthetic positions, the Ecole's teaching is, in its eclecticism, as liberal and universal as possible. This teaching is respectful of the personality of each pupil, allows foreigners to retain their national character and provides them with the means of developing it and expressing it freely.[38]

Mangeot may have laid emphasis on the importance of turning out good teachers of music and, like d'Indy, on the musical limitations of naked virtuosity, but his enlistment of Cortot (who obtained three years' leave from the Conservatoire) was without a doubt the keystone of the enterprise. When Cortot asked, it was hard to say no. In 1921 the teaching staff of the Ecole included Wanda Landowska, Isidore Philipp, Marguerite Long, Reynaldo Hahn, Marcel Dupré, Jacques Thibaud and Pablo Casals, and in the years 1925–28 courses in interpretation were given by

Ysaÿe, Enesco, Dupré, Claire Croiza and Ninon Vallin, as well as by Thibaud and Cortot himself. Mangeot's 'liberalism' extended beyond this impressive range of teachers to embrace the syllabus too. While he made the final performing *concours* longer and even more difficult than those of the Conservatoire, instrumentalists were obliged to supplement their specialist classes with others, including composition, history of music, chamber music, *solfège*, sight-reading and harmonic analysis, with the aim of developing what Mangeot called their 'technique intellectuelle'.

A further distinction between the Ecole normale and the Conservatoire *concours* was that the Ecole normale would issue not a *premier prix* but a series of diplomas, thus avoiding the parade of disgruntled also-rans that we have already observed fomenting such discord at the Conservatoire. Courses lasted six years and at the beginning of them students would choose whether they were aiming to be concert artists or teachers. They would then take an examination at the end of each of the last three years: leading, for teachers, to a *brevet* (certificate), a *diplôme* and a *licence d'enseignement*, and for performers to a *brevet* and a *diplôme d'exécution*, and finally to a *licence de concert*, for which they had to play from memory for at least an hour.

Some of the prestigious teachers engaged by Mangeot were also employed by the Conservatoire, but they still undertook to find the time not only to teach at the Ecole, but to give six 'cours d'interprétation' (master classes) open both to the Ecole's pupils and to anyone who had gained a diploma in any conservatoire in France or abroad. In practice the general public also flocked to them and the Conservatoire authorities must have wondered why, over the last century or so, they hadn't had the same idea.

In 1928 Cortot gave no fewer than ten classes between 16 June and 2 July in the Salle Chopin under the overall heading 'Les formes pianistiques', with the telling rider 'et les raisons poétiques de leur développement'. Clearly he was not going to limit himself to piecemeal remarks on individual works but was going to address the 'technique intellectuelle' of both players and audience. The repertoire for these classes ran historically from J. S. Bach to Ravel, divided into 'oeuvres de forme libre' and 'oeuvres d'essence rythmique'. Bach figured only in the second category.

Despite its slightly daunting manifesto, the Ecole normale flourished, moving in 1927 to its present larger premises on the boulevard Malesherbes to which the Salle Cortot was added in 1929. The Ecole was later to welcome Honegger and Dutilleux on to its staff.[39] Cortot also promoted its values in the United States through the Normal School of Music in New York as well as through The Alfred Cortot School of Music, housed in Steinway Building on West 57th Street. A letter of 19 November 1926 from his lieutenant Berthe Bert tells Robert Brussel at the French equivalent of the British Council that, in the Steinway Building, 'everyone has been extremely helpful. This being so, I beg to ask whether the decoration for Monsieur Steinway is in train?' Brussel assures her it has already been granted.[40]

Ecole des hautes études musicales de Fontainebleau

> One day at the end of the First World War, General Pershing sent the
> great conductor Walter Damrosch to Paris, to investigate the state
> of music in the American army. Damrosch organized a concert; the
> programme included the [Third] Symphony by Saint-Saëns, and he
> asked me to play the organ part.[41]

Nadia Boulanger's involvement with the school at Fontainebleau, first as teacher and later as director, is undoubtedly the school's most celebrated feature. But the general director of studies was none other than Charles-Marie Widor, in the intervals between his organ playing at St-Sulpice, his Conservatoire composition class and his post as secretary to the Institut. The staff included other familiar names such as Isidore Philipp, Marcel Dupré, Lucien Capet and Robert Casadesus.

General Pershing's need had been for bandsmen and, with the help of French instrumental teachers,

> professional pianists and violinists were rapidly converted into
> clarinettists and cornet players.... After the War and the return of the
> US Army, a strong desire was expressed that these musical links should
> continue. Requests for lessons in the summer vacations were made, which
> led to the establishment of a special summer school for Americans, with
> Widor as the first Director-General (1921–23). This was held in the Louis
> XV wing of the Palais de Fontainebleau. The opening took place on 26
> June 1921, presided over by Widor, Damrosch and the Minister of Public
> Instruction, Léon Bérard.[42]

Since the Conservatoire year ended on 25 June, that was the starting date for the three-month summer school, giving MM. Philipp, Dupré, Capet and company no respite. In the early 1930s, Widor looked back with some pride on what had been achieved (even though this was too early for him to recognize the stature of one of the school's very first pupils, Aaron Copland). Two hundred American students a year, paying $100 a month, had been taught by the cream of the French musical profession and, at the Monday evening concerts, had mingled with a 'très élégant public'. Although in 1926 the institution was *reconnu d'utilité publique* ('recognized as socially useful'), according to Widor it never received any financial support from the French state. (Even if this claim is debatable, it may not be too cynical to observe that 1926 marked the low point of the franc's fortunes in the decade; on 21 July it sank to 50 against the dollar. Artistic questions aside, an annual influx of 60,000 dollars – 3 million francs in 1926 – could reasonably have been considered 'socially useful'). He could also say that in that time there had not been a single cause for disciplinary action. The women students slept in the palace, the men in the town.[43]

Less easy to calculate is the effect on Paris music-making of the general goodwill engendered by the Fontainebleau exercise and of the interchange between American and French musicians. The tone of the Fontainebleau school, answering the question of one young American musician as to whether there might be 'a quiet spot near Paris, a kind of retreat where we could be absorbed in the cult of Art, and follow our own ideals',[44] is well captured in a letter Copland wrote home on 27 September 1921. The publisher Jacques Durand had come backstage after a performance of Copland's song *The Cat and the Mouse*, saying he wanted to publish it:

> Let me try to calmly explain to you what this means. In the first place
> Durand & Son is the biggest music publishing firm in Paris, which means
> the world. To finally see my music printed means more to me than any
> debut in Carnegie Hall ever could.... Don't expect me to make any
> fortunes out of my compositions. Composing is not a business, but a
> luxury, which you are so good as to allow me to afford....[45]

I can't think that d'Indy, while agreeing about the business angle, would have approved the idea of 'music as luxury'.... But clearly the school set as high a priority on enjoyment as on artistic idealism and, for the less spiritually inclined, member-ship of the school also brought free admittance to the Fontainebleau golf club (entrance fee: 1,000 francs). In any case, Copland soon decided it was not Fontainebleau he needed, but Boulanger.

The churches

In religion, as in other matters, Paris was generous in catering for its minorities. In 1921 it contained ten Lutheran churches, eleven Reformed, five Free, four syna-gogues, and one Orthodox church which, by 1923, with the influx of Russians and others, had been supplemented by three more. But the religious establishment was naturally embodied in the great Roman Catholic churches, from the cathedral of Notre-Dame downwards.

On the surface, the tenor of life in these fine buildings was calm and even, and probably most parishioners were quite unaware of the stresses that lay beneath the surface. These were mainly of two sorts, personal and liturgical. While the post of *tit-ulaire* at one of the great Paris churches was no money spinner on its own, the *gloire* attached to it was very considerable. This meant, as we shall see, that organists tended to hold on to their jobs for as long as they could still climb the stairs up to the organ loft, which in turn meant that, when vacancies did occur, they were canvassed and fought for with some vigour. In the major Parisian churches, only two vacancies (St-Philippe du Roule, 1922; St-Augustin, 1925) occurred between Henri Dallier's appointment to the Madeleine in 1905 and Messiaen's to La Trinité in 1931.

The oldest incumbent was Eugène Gigout who, at the age of only nineteen, had been appointed to St-Augustin in 1863, remaining there until his death in 1925. He was the dedicatee of the second of Franck's chorales and played for his funeral, and this devotion to the *pater seraphicus* brought him into (mostly covert) conflict with non-Franckists like Ambroise Thomas and Widor. The succession to Guilmant as organ professor of the Conservatoire in 1911 provoked a momentary surfacing of the subterranean stresses referred to above. As Andrew Thomson records, when Guilmant died,

> Widor had set his heart on [his pupil] Vierne to succeed him.... Fauré,
> however, wished to nominate Gigout who had been his fellow student at
> the Ecole Niedermeyer. According to Vierne, Widor brought the issue to
> a head by undiplomatically attacking Fauré in front of mutual friends: the
> Director, on hearing of this, took offence and enlisted Saint-Saëns's help
> in persuading the reluctant Gigout to stand, as an act of retaliation.[46]

Understandably, given his age, Gigout had done most of his composing by the beginning of the 1920s, but his orientation is clear from volumes such as his *Cent pièces brèves dans la tonalité du plain-chant* of 1889 and his *Album grégorien* of six years later. He was no musical revolutionary and by all accounts not a forceful teacher – when his students improvised fugues he would allow them to drop the countersubject after the exposition (his successor Dupré soon put a stop to that), and Maurice Duruflé called him 'a fine man, but that is all'.[47] But it seems he was no diehard either. In 1915 Durand asked Fauré to revise the whole of Bach's organ music and, since Gigout helped out unofficially, it is probably fair of Jean-Michel Nectoux to assume that they both agreed the text of the preface in which Fauré

> takes sides in the current dispute about how to play old organ music. He
> does not see that he ought to 'deprive himself of the advantages possessed
> by modern organs, thanks to a long series of technical improvements' and
> suggests to the player that he should 'bring these works alive again,
> instead of emphasizing what is dated about them'. He finishes by saying
> 'the main problem with masterpieces is that they are surrounded by
> excessive respect and this ends up by making them boring'.[48]

Widor, a year younger than Gigout, was appointed to St-Sulpice at the ripe old age of twenty-four in 1869 (according to him, a one-year probationary period running from 1 January 1870 was never confirmed, so he remained as acting organist for sixty-three years).[49] The five-manual Cavaillé-Coll in St-Sulpice is the largest organ in Paris, with five manuals, 118 stops (including a 'bird' stop) and 6,588 pipes, and on it the Toccata from Widor's Fifth Symphony of 1887 gains in stupefaction what it lacks in subtlety. In Widor's time there were 'two separate blowing appara- tuses, one requiring five men to pump, on a level with the main part of the organ, and another, some twenty-five feet higher, demanding two men to operate'.[50] At the console, which he compared with the Roman Colosseum or a chemist's shop, Widor soon became an attraction for fashionable Paris, and he appears at some point in the 1880s to have been reprimanded for encouraging society ladies to make the perilous journey up the organ stairs. But by the 1920s Widor was beyond the jurisdiction of any curé and F. B. Stiven reported that he was,

> of all the musicians of Paris,...the most sought after by the aristocracy, particularly the older families of the nobility. It is not infrequently that one can have pointed out to him in the organ loft of Saint-Sulpice a Count, a Marquis, or a Baroness.[51]

And yet Widor was no mere empty-headed socialite. The critic Paul Landormy remembered his *Fantaisie* on Christmas carols as 'a masterpiece of musical imagination and registration, a perpetual surprise, an enchantment',[52] and in 1928 Widor expressed trenchant views about composers claiming royalties on sacred music:

> The Christian who composes a religious motet aspires only to sing the glory of God. Prayer cannot be a source of revenue. Does one pay royalties on a sermon? [...] In Parliament, has anybody had the idea of demanding royalties on speeches? It would, after all, bring in a tidy sum.[53]

Widor resigned his post in 1933 at the age of eighty-eight, the strength having gone out of his hands, arms and legs, and Marcel Dupré took over from him. But both Tournemire, appointed to Ste-Clotilde in 1898, and Vierne, appointed to Notre-Dame in 1900, continued until their deaths in 1939 and 1937 respectively.

The last two of Tournemire's eight Organ Symphonies date from the 1920s, but his composing energies in these years were mainly directed towards *L'orgue mystique*, a set of pieces for every Sunday of the year, each office including a Prelude, an Offertory, an Elevation, a Communion and a Finale. As Duruflé remembered,

> Tournemire never played from a prepared score at Sunday Mass; the book of Gregorian chant was always on the music rack, open at the liturgical office of the day. He improvised the entire Low Mass, pausing for the gospel and the sermon. That meant a full half-hour of music....It was not a concert, but a genuine musical commentary on the liturgy.[54]

Tournemire was a mercurial character, and threw Duruflé out when the latter could not replace him one day at Ste-Clotilde owing to a previous engagement. Vierne was calmer and more methodical, and the proof of his excellence as a teacher was that between 1894 and 1930 thirty of his students won a *premier prix* at the Conservatoire. Vierne, recalled Duruflé,

knew how to make the organ sing admirably. His touch was perfect, and his phrasing was unique to him. His slender, strong fingers, his flawless posture and the economy of his movements bestowed upon him an extraordinary sense of ease and an uncommon naturalness.... Vierne the composer and Vierne the improviser were the same person. Just as in his symphonies, the 'writing' of his improvisations was very carefully done.... From his master Widor he had learned this pure style, a classical approach.... Yet, as a pupil also of Franck, Vierne added a melodic richness, an expressiveness and a harmonic warmth which placed him more in the line of the last romantics. An aesthetic of this type was admirably fitting to Notre-Dame.[55]

At La Trinité Charles Quef had, like Vierne, been in post since 1900, when he took over from Guilmant, but he seems to have left no great mark on the organ scene. Frederic Stiven found him to be

> a very amiable, courteous gentleman with a very un-Frenchman-like eye for business [sic]. I had been in Paris scarcely a week before I received a card from him, announcing his terms for lessons, and the subjects which he taught. I found out afterwards that he obtained the names and addresses of all people who rented pedal-pianos of a certain delightfully naive little Frenchman on Boulevard Péreire. Quite different from most of the French organists, Monsieur Quef is interested in the English and German schools of organ playing, and it was he who played the only Mendelssohn which we heard in Paris.[56]

A similarly low profile was kept by Henri Dallier who, graduating from Franck's class in 1878, had spent twenty-six years at St-Eustache, before succeeding Fauré at the Madeleine in 1905 at the age of fifty-six. He had a high reputation though as an improviser, in a field where improvisation was *de rigueur*, as did his successor at St-Eustache, Joseph Bonnet. Bonnet, like Duruflé after him, was a pupil of both Tournemire and Vierne and was appointed to St-Eustache even before winning his *premier prix* in Guilmant's class in 1906. Bonnet was much more *en vue*, touring widely in Europe and North America. Stiven found him to be, at the age of thirty-nine, 'a charming young man', an accolade borne out by a letter Bonnet wrote in 1917 to Cortot while on an American tour:

Charles Tournemire
at the organ of
Ste-Clotilde

> This mystic, young people is thirsty for the Ideal, for Music and Beauty, and the artist who allowed himself to play unworthy music to them would be as culpable as someone corrupting the pure soul of a child.[57]

Bonnet's idealism is further exemplified by his willingness to add to the exiguous finances of St-Eustache by playing a programme of organ numbers actually during the eleven o'clock mass, 'stopping in the middle of the programme for the sermon. One paid three cents for a chair, and three cents for a program, and as there was generally a large audience, a goodly sum of money was gained in this way.'[58]

This kind of thing could always be justified to some extent on the grounds of alleviating poverty. But in general there were strong moves in the French Roman Catholic Church after the war to take seriously the injunctions of Pope Pius X in his celebrated *Motu proprio* of 22 November 1903. Research into Gregorian chant continued apace (congresses in Tourcoing in 1919, in Toulouse in 1920, and an assembly of 'scholae grégoriennes' in Paris in 1921) and in 1923 the

Cardinal Archbishop of Paris founded an *Institut grégorien* in the city, promoting the ideas of Solesmes.

Together with the promulgation of Gregorian chant went the disappearance, slow but sure, of curious transcriptions of Gounod's 'Ave maria', not to mention an 'Agnus Dei' derived from the entr'acte in Bizet's *L'arlésienne*, a 'Regina caeli' based on a theme from *Les pêcheurs de perles*, and that old standby, the 'Méditation' from Massenet's *Thaïs*. Careful reading of the *Motu proprio* also revealed that Pope Pius had in no way turned his back on modern music. Paragraph 5 of the document specifically states that

> the Church has always recognized and encouraged progress in the arts,
> by admitting to the liturgy everything good and beautiful that talented
> artists have been able to discover over the centuries, provided always that
> the rules of the liturgy were observed. As a result, the most modern music
> is admitted into the Church, since it too offers compositions which, by
> their merit, their seriousness and their gravity, are in no way unworthy
> of functioning as part of the liturgy.[59]

Tensions inevitably sprang up between this prescription on the one hand, supported by researchers like Dom André Mocquereau and by composers imbued with the music of Debussy and Ravel and keen to take advantage of the harmonic and colouristic possibilities of Cavaillé-Coll's organs, and on the other hand the feelings of the great majority of curés and parishioners who preferred the music they had grown up with. Some forty years earlier, after the first performance in the Madeleine of Fauré's *Requiem*,

> the vicar called Fauré into the sacristy and questioned him as follows:
> 'What was that Mass for the dead you've just conducted?'
> 'It was a Requiem of my own composition.'
> 'Monsieur Fauré, we don't need all these novelties; the Madeleine's
> repertoire is quite rich enough, just content yourself with that.'[60]

There is no reason to think the situation had changed in the meanwhile. Modern tendencies certainly did exist in the organ music of the time: witness, for instance, the organ sections of Dupré's *Les vêpres de la vierge*, in which plainsong recitation alternates with some highly dissonant passages, derived from Dupré's improvisations on the organ of Notre-Dame on the Feast of the Assumption in 1919, all in all a signal advertisement for the universality of the Church; or the Scherzo of Vierne's Sixth Symphony of 1930, in which tonality is at times a distant mirage.

It is generally held that the appointment of the 22-year-old Olivier Messiaen as *titulaire* of La Trinité in 1931 was a brave one. But even he, with an outstanding Conservatoire career behind him, had to steer a course between progressives and conservatives. His letter to the curé in advance of his appointment is instructive:

> In music one always has to seek what is new, but reserve that for chamber
> and orchestral works in which fantasy is admissible. As far as the organ is
> concerned, and in particular the church organ, the liturgy is the primary
> factor. The pattern of this, and the instrument itself, are not suitable for
> modern music, and one must not disturb the piety of the faithful with
> wildly anarchic chords. Furthermore, do not imagine that I am incapable
> of writing anything but dissonances. If they are not suitable for religious
> music, nor are they suitable for Conservatoire competitions, and if I have
> gained prizes it is because, thanks to my teachers, I possess a solid
> grounding in harmony, and in the technique of composition and organ
> playing.... I can therefore safely explore new avenues, but I can also be
> sensible and classical....[61]

Indeed, works like *Apparition de l'église éternelle* (1928), *L'ascension* (1933) and *La nativité du Seigneur* (1935) are built logically on foundations laid by Tournemire, Vierne and Messiaen's teacher Dupré. Only with *Les corps glorieux* (1939), and notably in the opening section of 'Combat de la Mort et de la Vie', did Messiaen really test the piety of the average parishioner with what the latter might well have felt were 'accords trop anarchistes'.

The salons

> One of the most pretentious and unavoidable women, with an air of
> ecstasy intended to conceal advanced deafness, was Mme Aurel, who
> cluttered up the literary scene for fifty years. The meetings in her salon
> brought together the most unlikely people, and evenings began and
> ended with the adoration of the hostess.... Of the postwar hostesses,
> Mme Alfred Mortier was certainly the vainest and most overweening.[62]

The war did not put an end to the salons, though fierce inflation forced some *salonnières* (or rather their husbands) to draw in their horns. Meanwhile magazines like *La revue musicale* and publishers like Durand continued to promote their wares through salon performances or through concerts given before select audiences (songs commissioned by *La revue musicale* for their Ronsard number of May 1924, including contributions from Ravel, Honegger, Dukas and Honegger, were sung at a *Revue musicale* concert in the Théâtre du Vieux-Colombier on 15 May of that year; Enesco and Ravel gave the first performance of the latter's Second Violin Sonata at the Concerts Durand in the Salle Erard on 30 May 1927 – a work that Enesco had memorized after playing it through just once with the composer).

Most *salonnières* were content just to play hostess to the important names of the day without thinking beyond that. A letter from Enesco to the pianist Eugène Wagner gives the flavour of such occasions:

As well as the evening of the 19th, would you be free on the afternoon of Friday 21st at five o'clock, at the house of the Vicomtesse Fleury, 2 avenue Emile Deschanel, for a private concert, and for that would you accept 400 francs? We can invent a programme at the last minute, to suit ourselves.[63]

Among this class must also be numbered Jeanne Dubost, remembered by Madeleine Milhaud as

a charming, elegant, whimsical woman who liked to surround herself with artists and writers. We would meet at her place every Wednesday afternoon. Music was often played. We were entertained by Obouhov, by Horowitz, just arrived from Russia, and above all by a Red Indian chief who sang at the top of his voice and jumped all over the place! To thank our hostess for her hospitality, a few composers such as Ravel, Schmitt, Roussel, Milhaud and some others composed a little work which was performed, to her great surprise, in her salon. Jacques Rouché, the director of the Paris Opera, was present at this friendly event and proposed making a spectacle from these pieces called *L'éventail de Jeanne*.[64]

The salon performance was on 16 June 1927 and one at the Opéra, in which the young Tamara Toumanova made her début, on 4 March 1929. As for the Red Indian chief, it later turned out that Mme Dubost's credulity had been imposed on: he had been born in the United Kingdom.

A higher class of *salonnière* cared what music was played at her gatherings. Such was Mme Paul Clemenceau, born Sophie Szeps, daughter of the friend of Archduke Francis-Ferdinand. Among the musicians attending her salon on Sunday afternoons in the avenue d'Eylau were Ravel, Milhaud, Schmitt, and artists with German/Austrian affiliations, including Marya Freund, Germaine Lubin and the Rosé Quartet. The first French performance of Schoenberg's Wind Quintet was given there.

Finally, the highest class of *salonnière* consisted of two ladies, one who was herself a fine musician, and one who, as well as being that, went to the trouble and expense of commissioning new music: Mme René de Saint-Marceaux and the princesse Edmond de Polignac.

The salon of Marguerite de Saint-Marceaux, known to her friends as Meg, dated back to 1875 when she was married to her first husband, the painter Eugène Baugnies. But its heyday lasted from 1892, when she married the sculptor René de Saint-Marceaux, until the First World War. Gounod, Massenet, Debussy, Albéniz, Messager, d'Indy, Fauré, Cortot and Maggie Teyte were all regular attenders at Meg's Friday nights, drawn by her charm and her insistence on informality: 'she didn't force anyone to listen to the music,' wrote Colette, 'but put a stop to the slightest whispering. Anyone could turn up at any time provided the men wore their ordinary jackets and the women were in day clothes.'[65] Meg herself admitted that she wouldn't have been able to attract half the interesting people she did if she'd made them change their shirts. Although she was herself a fine singer and pianist – she worked on *La damoiselle élue* with Debussy, while her sightreading abilities amazed even Albéniz – she had every intention nonetheless of retaining her place in polite, bourgeois society and Thursday nights were dedicated to this end, when evening dress was mandatory and no music was performed.

Meg's fortune was one of those hardest hit by postwar devaluations, but if the decade or so until her death in 1930 saw a diminution in her salon's activity, her

> Fridays gained in distinction what they lost in social brilliance....
> Composers were more welcome than ever. On 7 February 1917 Roussel
> came to play his still unpublished opera *Padmâvatî* in front of Messager,
> who was being reluctant to put it on at the Opéra, and on 3 February
> 1920 Falla played his *Sombrero de tres picos* which was being produced by
> Diaghilev and his *Nuits dans les jardins d'Espagne*. On 14 January 1921 Ravel
> played *La valse* on two pianos with Jacques Février and accompanied
> Claire Croiza in *Shéhérazade*, and on 18 March 1927 he played *Ma mère l'oye*
> with Marguerite Long. That same evening, the young Poulenc, probably
> introduced by his teacher Ricardo Viñes, played *Napoli* and risked singing
> his *Chansons gaillardes*.

Meg was not an uncritical hostess. Years earlier she had dismissed Massenet's *Thaïs* as 'Parsifal with white sauce'; now she noted in her diary that 'Poulenc plays the piano well. His compositions are not without talent, but he's no genius. I'm afraid he thinks he is. It's the serious failing of all this young group.'[66] But perhaps the most intriguing facet of the above quotation is the picture of Messager, glass of *cerisette* in hand, being leant on by Meg and others to produce *Padmâvatî* at the Opéra. She may never have wielded any power in the Parisian musical world, but after forty years as a high-profile *salonnière* she certainly wielded influence.

The same could be said of the princesse de Polignac. Born Winnaretta (Winnie) Singer of the American sewing-machine family, she married prince Edmond de Polignac in 1893, a liaison which the prince himself called 'the marriage of the dollar with the sou'.[67] It seems probable that Meg's salon was a model for Winnie's, even though the latter was considered more 'serious' and did not function on any set day of the week. The music room in the de Polignac *hôtel particulier* on the avenue Henri Martin was large enough to hold a full-scale concert rendition of Rameau's *Dardanus* in 1895 (the first recorded performance of the work since 1784), the expense of which gave rise to some envious comment. But mostly Winnie favoured chamber music, such as the first three volumes of Albéniz's *Iberia*, given their first public performance *chez elle* by Blanche Selva on 2 January 1908.[68] Five months later, Winnie's salon was the scene of the first moves towards Diaghilev's 1909 season of Russian opera and ballet and the setting up of the Ballets russes.

Her first efforts at musical patronage were in some degree provoked by the war. She realized that France was turning away from large musical ensembles

not only because of increasing economic problems...[but] because of their all-too-Germanic character. Also, as a fervent admirer of baroque music, Winnaretta thought it would be a profitable exercise to study its musical structures afresh. So she decided to try this out by asking various composers to write short orchestral works which could be played by small groups of around twenty musicians. She hoped that, once the war was over, she would be able to have the works she had commissioned played in her music room.[69]

The first three compositions she was responsible for handsomely repaid her faith: Stravinsky's *Renard*, Satie's *Socrate* and Falla's *El retablo de maese Pedro*. No doubt encouraged by their success, over the next twenty years she became more ambitious as to size, commissioning Tailleferre's Piano Concerto (1923), Milhaud's opera *Les malheurs d'Orphée* (1925), Igor Markevich's Partita for piano and orchestra (1930), and in the 1930s no fewer than eight works by Tailleferre, Sauguet, Nabokov, Weill, Françaix and Poulenc, including the latter's Concerto for two pianos (1932) and Organ Concerto (1938).

In addition, she came financially to the rescue of *Mavra* and thereafter specialized in *avant-premières* of Stravinsky's works. *Les noces*, the Concerto for piano and wind and *Oedipus rex* were all given in the avenue Henri Martin before being unleashed on the general public: the first two triumphantly; *Oedipus rex*, with Stravinsky and Prokofiev playing the orchestral parts on two pianos, in a glacial silence.

Like all rich people, Winnie was wary of those who might take advantage of her. Artur Rubinstein called her 'the stingiest woman I have ever met in my whole life' and resented the fact that she expected him to play for her at a lower rate than he would command elsewhere.[70] At the same time he noted that she never sold tickets to her guests, which suggests that some other hostesses did.

Stravinsky, on the other hand, was more than glad of the 3,000 francs he received for *Renard*; and when he began to feel guilty that he had asked only 300 francs for the French translator C. F. Ramuz and tried to negotiate an increase to 1,000 francs, she was willing at least to part with 500.[71] For *Oedipus rex* she paid Stravinsky $1,500 for three performances, and Diaghilev's committee a further 20,000 francs: hence the composer's assurance that 'it is with the most passionate joy that I would seat myself at the piano to perform *Oedipus* with the soloists and the chorus for an advance premiere at your house'.[72] The glacial silence which greeted that performance has long since been filled with the world's applause and Winnie's faith in the work vindicated. Since the same pattern repeated itself with Poulenc's Organ Concerto over a decade later, we may fairly say that she remained ahead of her time.

The princesse de Polignac playing the Cavaillé-Coll organ made for her in 1892, photographed by Jacques-Emile Blanche

The press

In 1933 M.-D. Calvocoressi, a critic and friend of Ravel now working in London, looked back to his years as a musical reporter in Paris and mused on the differences between the practices in the two capitals:

> One, which naturally I had realized long before the war, was on the attitude of the daily Press towards music. It had always been a source of amazement to me that even at a period when interest in music was

progressing by leaps and bounds throughout the country, so little space should be devoted to it in French dailies.... But there was a more special reason for their attitude towards musical events other than those which it was customary, and compulsory, for them to notice – they viewed them exclusively as potential sources of advertisements –not merely legitimate advertisements announcing the particulars, but 'communiqués' or 'blurbs' proclaiming how wonderful the events promised to be, and, after they had taken place, how wonderful they had been, these after-the-event 'communiqués' appearing as substitutes for *bona-fide* critical notices.... I had always been amazed at the uncritical attitude of French critics in matters of interpretation – especially of instrumental music. Ninety-nine times out of a hundred, they content themselves with declaring that it was uniformly excellent. 'L'exécution fut de tous points parfaite' is as current a formula in their concert-notices as the detective's 'This is a bad business' in English murder yarns.[73]

The specialist music magazines operated on a somewhat higher level, though even here the historian has to beware of publicity masquerading as unbiased report. A more potent danger with them was rather the sheer amount of verbiage that was generated, bringing to mind Berlioz's comment that 'the French have a mania for arguing about music without having the first idea about it, or any feeling for it. It was like this in the last century, is so now and will be again.'[74]

The scope of the present book allows only the briefest account of the specialist journals. Perhaps the most important as well as the most obvious point is that the quality of criticism varied enormously. At the lower end of the scale was the usual collection of failed composers and performers, anxious to get their own back. At the higher end, most of the major French composers wrote criticism from time to time. Fauré contributed to *Le Figaro* from 1903 to 1921, Ravel to various journals from 1909 to 1933 (though only three articles in the 1920s), and there were regular contributions from Milhaud, Honegger, Koechlin, Roland-Manuel, Hahn, Bruneau and Dukas.

In 1917 there were twenty-nine music journals in circulation, ranging from the sumptuously produced *Le théâtre* and *Comoedia illustré* to the more reticent religious pamphlets such as *Caecilia*, *La petite maîtrise*, *La revue de Sainte-Cécile* and *La tribune musicale*. Among the most widely read were *Le courrier musical*, *Le ménestrel*, restarted in 1919, and *La revue musicale*, founded in 1920.

Charles Tenroc (in reality Charles Cornet), the editor of *Le courrier musical*, managed to be both authoritative and amusing – here, from 1 January 1920, is part of his review of Debussy's *La damoiselle élue* being given in a staged version at the Théâtre Lyrique du Vaudeville:

There is a greeny grey decor in which the blessed damozel comes to rest on top of some upright artichoke stems – a position which appears to tire the pectorals of Mme Croiza, who stretches herself and gathers her garments round her. The rigid Mlle Dubost copies the posture of the byzantine armchair in order to comment on the oscillatory discomforts of the pivoting damozel. In the pit, beneath the artichokes, Monsieur Polacco cultivates the harmonies of a Debussy who 'seeks' and 'finds'. Recommended for those of a quiet, dreamy disposition.

We do not need to read too carefully between the lines to gather that Monsieur Tenroc felt *La damoiselle* should be allowed to remain as a concert work, *sans artichauds*. The validity of Tenroc's strictures was, incidentally, corroborated in a letter from Debussy's widow to the impresario P.-B. Gheusi asking him to sort out the lighting on the Damoiselle herself 'so as not to black out her hands and forearms completely and not to give such unfortunate emphasis to...her stomach...'.[75]

By and large, all three magazines seem remarkably free of the sound of grinding axes. The teaching at the Conservatoire, the dangerous popularity of jazz, dancing and sport, the impossibly high rate of tax on concert receipts, the positive discrimination in favour of artists with names ending in -ski and -ov: these are much the topics one would have expected to find debated. A perennial cause of complaint was the low level of state involvement in music. In the issue of *Le courrier musical* of 1 December 1922, Louis Vuillemin, a regular columnist, penned a heartfelt plea for more active, considered participation. As it was, music seemed to come some way after painting and literature; senior politicians were to be seen at salon openings but rarely at concerts. He then commented that 'the result of all this is that a real musical life is developing on the edge of French social life'. Today we may read that comment as undermining his own position, but obviously that was not how Vuillemin saw it – for him, presumably, the more people involved with music, the more would read his articles. The powers-that-be were regularly the target of sarcasm, either for ignoring music or for funding it parsimoniously: 'there is some surprise', wrote a journalist in the number of 1 July 1924, 'on learning that a city of over three million people is taxed at the crazy rate of 14,100 francs each year to support the development of music. The town hall must be careful, this sort of extravagance could easily lead to bankruptcy.'

Contributors to *Le courrier musical* included literary men such as Camille Mauclair and André Schaeffner, and also composers such as Roussel, Messager, Schmitt, and Milhaud, who used its columns to lambast the French for their habit of performing gobbets of Wagner in the concert hall. The standard of writing was generally high and, while some of it was guilty of the over-generosity condemned by Calvocoressi, occasionally you find small gems of equivocation: in that same number of 1 December 1922, readers were told that 'those who have already heard Mme d'Alheim can imagine how she sang and interpreted this attractive programme'. And every now and then a critic was downright rude: Tenroc dismissed Honegger's *Skating Rink* as being 'as ugly, pointless and uncouth as possible' (15 May 1923) and Ravel's *L'enfant et les sortilèges* as an example of 'talent squandered on a ladylike product' (15 February 1926), while Jean Wiéner felt it was 'detestable' for a Prix de Rome winner to try and curry favour by writing a stylized foxtrot – 'that can only work to the detriment of a cause they think they are defending with all their might' (15 March 1929).

No doubt to the readers of the time *Le courrier musical* and *Le ménestrel* each had a distinctive tone. But the mix of fact and opinion now appears much the same in both, except that *Le ménestrel* always has to be read in the knowledge that it was the organ of the music publisher Heugel. Reynaldo Hahn, Gaston Carraud and Emile Vuillermoz were among its contributors, and the magazine was no doubt delighted to print d'Indy's reply to a questionnaire about film music, to the effect that 'since the cinema has, to my way of thinking, nothing to do with art, and since it has always seemed to me to have had a depressing effect on the populace, I can have no opinion on the music that should accompany it'.[76] Some contributors wrote for both papers. Milhaud wrote for *Le courrier musical* from 1920 to 1924, but in June 1926 *Le ménestrel* printed his article 'La vie musicale en U.R.S.S.', in which he commented on the analytical spirit that reigned in Moscow, tempered with an interest in the political views of young French composers. In the second half of the decade Milhaud also wrote for *Musique et théâtre* and for *Europe nouvelle*.[77]

Le courrier musical and *Le ménestrel* were both weeklies. *La revue musicale*, being a monthly and edited by one of the more thoughtful Parisian critics, Henry Prunières, tended towards a wider range of subjects and a more philosophical and historically grounded approach. This brief discussion of the musical press can conveniently conclude with a look at a few of the topics *La revue musicale* considered between 1920 and the end of the decade.

Among its most valuable numbers were the *numéros spéciaux* on individual composers, including Fauré (October 1922), Stravinsky (December 1923), Ravel (April 1925), Beethoven (April 1927) and Roussel (April/May 1929). The pattern for these was set by the magazine's second issue, the Debussy number of December 1920, which contained not only fourteen articles on the composer and his works, including Cortot on the piano music and Falla on Debussy's Spanish vein, but a musical supplement of ten pieces in his memory, among them the first movement of Ravel's Sonata for violin and cello and the concluding chorale of Stravinsky's Symphonies of Wind Instruments.

The Debussy number was acknowledged as a triumph and the magazine prospered from then on: whereas in that number it was billed as a 'Revue mensuelle internationale d'art musical ancien et moderne' (covering most of the angles), it soon graduated to being 'La plus importante revue française d'art musical et moderne', gaining in importance what it lost in internationalism. Not that it was by any means parochial. On the back cover of the issue of 1 January 1922, for instance, forthcoming articles are advertised on forty-one subjects of which only eighteen are specifically French. Other offerings include an article on Cyril Scott, three on Spanish music including Falla on Albéniz, two on Russian music, and single articles on Ernest Bloch, Joseph Jongen, Sibelius, the young Czech school, as well as Théodore Reinach on ancient Greek music and Charles van den Borren on the instrumental music of Lassus.

Finally, the October 1924 number will usefully serve as an example of what the magazine had to offer in the second half of the period under discussion, especially as the back cover carried an announcement of three changes in emphasis for the new subscription period beginning in November. There will be a greater number of reproductions of original documents (the December issue carries a reproduction of the 1708 autograph of Handel's aria 'Fingo di non amare'); the paragraphs on 'Vie musicale en France et à l'étranger, which are generally considered to be the liveliest element in our publication, will from here on constitute a half and not a third of each number'; but the regular musical supplement will now become irregular, given the shortage of really worthwhile pieces – not perhaps the greatest compliment to Daniel Lazarus, the second-act prelude to whose opera L'illustre magicien formed the supplement to the October number itself. But then that work did not reach a Paris stage until 1937.

The five main articles cover a good deal of ground. The first, on Smetana, notes that 'a ghostly hand always halts The Bartered Bride on the steps of the Opéra-Comique. And yet this work has everything a director could ask for, especially as it has been famous right from the premiere.' The author, Etienne Fournol, would therefore seem to deserve some credit for the ultimate removal of the ghostly hand in 1928. After articles on Gérard de Nerval as a music critic and on the resemblances between music and real life (in which we find the names of Leibniz, Sainte-Beuve, Pascal, Schopenhauer and Kant), Ivan Wischnegradsky contributes four pages on quarter-tones. Aloïs Haba's String Quartet in quarter-tones had been given at one of Jean Wiéner's concerts in the spring of 1922, but Wischnegradsky, as politely as he can, indicates that not only were the audience given an imperfect idea of the whole since only the first two movements were played, but rehearsal time was insufficient and the players had nobody to guide them (i.e. 'I wasn't asked'). In short, quarter-tone music has yet to be given a fair trial.

Cover of the special Stravinsky number of *La revue musicale*

In the last article, Jean Chantavoine writes a memorial tribute to Busoni who had died at the end of July. His conclusion, that Busoni was greater as a pianist than as a composer or thinker, can hardly be argued about by those who never heard him play. But Chantavoine makes two remarks *en passant* that reveal the latent chauvinism in much French critical writing. He notes firstly that 'the velvety but slightly confused sound of German pianos brought out less clearly the infinitely varied clarity of his playing, and for his final London concerts Busoni chose a French piano'. More insidiously, he blames Busoni's failure as a composer, and even his final poor health, on his divided Italo-German parentage and on his cosmopolitan lifestyle. In this context, Liszt is identified as 'un maître dangereux'. It is hard not to read into this an implicit boast that of course we Frenchmen, born and living our lives in France, understand the value of a national tradition and our superiority rests on its support.

The highly valued section on music in France and abroad contains reports from Germany, Belgium, Denmark, Spain, Great Britain (the first Robert Mayer children's concert, Bruno Walter conducting *Der Ring* with Lotte Lehmann and Frida Leider, a surprisingly good *Pelléas* in English under Goossens), Greece, Poland and Switzerland. It is headed by Prunières's less than ecstatic report on the third ISCM Festival in Salzburg: thumbs up for Hindemith, Weill, Wellesz, and Stravinsky, whose Octet, in the 'somewhat somnolent atmosphere', had the effect of an exploding bomb; thumbs down for Krenek's interminable String Quartet op. 24, for songs by Othmar Schoeck, and especially for the international jury who turned down the recommendations of the French section, substituting for them Milhaud's *Catalogue de fleurs* and Poulenc's Sonata for clarinet and bassoon – works which 'give no idea of their composers' talents and struck Salzburg as being jokes in doubtful taste'. A poor performance of Satie's *Socrate* was also not appreciated either by the audience or by Prunières.

For an annual subscription of 50 francs, in 1924 the cost of around 2 kg of butter or twelve cheap seats at the Bouffes-Parisiens, the French reader of *La revue musicale* was well served. Further satisfaction was no doubt given by the weekly *réunions* every Tuesday between five and seven o'clock at 35–37 rue Madame, which were 'not concerts, even though sometimes one can hear excellent music and fine players, but private gatherings, intended to encourage contact between composers and artists of every country and the Parisian musical world': a sign that, for all the capital's cosmopolitanism, it had still not entirely lost its intimate, village atmosphere.

Notes

1. Doda Conrad, in conversation with the author.
2. Bulletin de l'Association amicale des Professeurs chargés de l'Enseignement de la Musique (APM), December 1920.
3. Lavignac et La Laurencie, *Encyclopédie de la musique* (Paris, 1925), II, p. 3673.
4. Alfred Cortot, in *Le courrier musical*, July 1920.
5. Albert Berthelin, in *Le courrier musical*, 15 January 1921.
6. Brian Rees, *Camille Saint-Saëns: A Life* (London, 1999), p. 409.
7. Jean-Michel Nectoux, *Gabriel Fauré: A Musical Life*, trans. Roger Nichols (Cambridge, 1991), p. 6.
8. Ibid., p. 7.
9. Robert Orledge, *Gabriel Fauré* (London, 1979), pp. 237–38.
10. Andrew Thomson, *Vincent d'Indy and his World* (Oxford, 1996), p. 81.
11. Odile Vivier, *Varèse* (Paris, 1973), pp. 13–14.
12. Vincent d'Indy, 'Une école d'art répondant aux besoins modernes', in *La tribune de Saint-Gervais*, November 1900, no. 11, pp. 304–5.
13. Vincent d'Indy, *La Schola Cantorum, son histoire depuis sa fondation jusqu'en 1925* (Paris, 1927), p. 1.
14. Guy de Lioncourt, *Un témoignage sur la musique et sur la vie au XXe siècle* (Paris, 1956), pp. 106–7.
15. Vincent d'Indy, 'Schola Cantorum', in Lavignac, *Encyclopédie* (Paris, 1925), p. 3625.
16. De Lioncourt, *Un témoignage*, p. 108.
17. Henri Rabaud, preface to *Le Conservatoire national de musique et de déclamation* (Paris, 1930), p. 1.
18. *Journal de Paris*, 27 October 1796 (le 6 brumaire an V); quoted in Laetitia Chassain-Dolliou, *Le Conservatoire de Paris ou les voies de la création* (Paris, 1995), inside cover.
19. Marc-Olivier Dupin, in conversation with the author.
20. Quoted in Jean-Michel Nectoux, 'Gabriel Fauré au Conservatoire de Paris: une philosophie pour l'enseignement', *Le Conservatoire de Paris, 1795-1995*, ed. Anne Bongrain and Yves Gérard (Paris, 1996), p. 219.
21. Ibid., p. 225.
22. Note dated summer of 1906, ibid., p. 224.
23. Reynaldo Hahn, *Journal d'un musicien* (Paris, 1933), p. 255.
24. Jean-Michel Nectoux, trans. Nichols, *Gabriel Fauré*, p. 424.
25. Letter to H. Piller, BnF, LA Rabaud 143.
26. Charles Tenroc, in *Le courrier musical*, July 1920, p. 214.
27. Ibid., 1 November 1920.
28. Henri Barraud, in conversation with the author.
29. Louis Vierne, *Mes souvenirs* (Paris, 1939), p. 51; quoted in Andrew Thomson, *Widor* (Oxford, 1987), pp. 55–56.
30. Ibid., p. 87.
31. Letter to Guy Ropartz of 13 November 1927 in Paul Dukas, *Correspondance*, ed. Georges Favre (Paris, 1971), p. 162.
32. *Les grands prix de Rome de musique*, conférence du 16 mai 1929, ed. Henri Rebois (Paris, 1929), pp. 81–82.
33. Letter of 15 January 1930, Lettres à Paul Dukas, BnF W. 48.
34. Jean-Michel Nectoux, 'Gabriel Fauré au Conservatoire de Paris', p. 233.
35. *Le courrier musical*, 16 July 1920.
36. Léon Bérard, *Règlement du Conservatoire national...* (Paris, n.d. [c.1925]), Article 88.
37. Artur Rubinstein, *My Many Years* (London, 1980), p. 243.
38. *Annuaire des artistes*, 1921–22.
39. Bernard Gavoty, *Alfred Cortot* (Paris, 1977), pp. 132–37; Lavignac, *Encyclopédie*, pp. 3626–27
40. BnF, LA Bert 12.
41. Bruno Monsaingeon, *Mademoiselle: Conversations with Nadia Boulanger* (Manchester, 1985), p. 28.
42. Andrew Thomson, *Widor* (Oxford, 1987), p. 82.
43. Charles-Marie Widor, 'Les écoles d'art américaines', Beaux Arts, Chronique des Arts et de la Curiosité, n.d.
44. *French High School of Musical Studies* (Melun, 1921), p. 3.
45. Aaron Copland and Vivian Perlis, *Copland*, I, *1900–1942* (London, 1984), p. 51.
46. Thomson, *Widor*, p. 62.
47. George Baker, 'An Interview with Maurice Duruflé', in *The American Organist*, November 1980, p. 57.

48. Nectoux, trans. Nichols, *Gabriel Fauré*, p. 43.

49. Thomson, *Widor*, p. 17.

50. Frederic B. Stiven, *In the Organ Lofts of Paris* (Boston, 1923), p. 55.

51. Ibid., p. 54.

52. Thomson, *Widor*, p. 20.

53. Widor in *Le gaulois*, reported in *Le courrier musical*, 15 November 1928.

54. Maurice Duruflé, 'My recollections of Tournemire and Vierne', trans. Ralph Kneeream, in *The American Organist*, November 1980, p. 54.

55. Ibid., pp. 56–57.

56. Stiven, *Organ Lofts*, pp. 63–64.

57. Letter from New York, 11 March 1917, BnF, LA Bonnet 1.

58. Stiven, *Organ Lofts*, p. 16.

59. *'Motu proprio' sur la Musique sacrée* (Liège, 1928).

60. Nectoux, trans. Nichols, *Gabriel Fauré*, p. 116.

61. Letter of 8 August 1931, in *Portraits d'Olivier Messiaen*, ed. Catherine Massip (Paris, 1996), p. 11.

62. R.-L. Doyon, *Mémoire d'homme* (Paris, 1952), p. 51.

63. *Scrisori/George Enescu*, ed. Viorel Cosma (Bucharest, 1974), p. 304.

64. Roger Nichols, *Conversations with Madeleine Milhaud* (London, 1996), pp. 81–82.

65. Jean-Michel Nectoux, 'Musique et beaux-arts: le salon de Marguerite de Saint-Marceaux', in *Une famille d'artistes en 1900, les Saint-Marceaux* (Paris, 1992), pp. 62–90. I am indebted to this article for most of the information in these paragraphs.

66. Ibid., p. 89–90.

67. Michael de Cossart, *Une américaine à Paris* (Paris, 1979), p. 49.

68. Ibid., p. 103.

69. Ibid., p. 131.

70. Rubinstein, *My Many Years*, pp. 134, 282.

71. Letter of 5 October 1916, in *Stravinsky, Selected Correspondence*, III, ed. Robert Craft (London, 1985), p. 29, n. 11.

72. Letter of 23 March 1927, in ibid., I (London, 1982), p. 105, n. 48.

73. M.-D. Calvocoressi, *Musicians Gallery* (London, 1933), pp. 303–4, 306.

74. Letter to his father of 20 September 1838, in *Selected Letters of Berlioz*, ed. Hugh Macdonald, trans. Roger Nichols (London, 1995), p. 155.

75. Letter of ?21 December 1919, in the collection of Robert Orledge. I am grateful to Professor Orledge for sending me a copy of the text.

76. Vincent d'Indy, in *Le ménestrel*, 16 January 1920.

77. *Darius Milhaud. Notes sur la musique*, ed. Jeremy Drake (Paris, 1982), pp. 28, 221–22.

8. Composers old and new

THE BIRTH DATES of the nine composers considered below span a period of over fifty years, from 1845 to 1899. For this reason among many others, the postwar spirit, however one interprets it, affected them in differing ways and to differing degrees, but none of them could remain wholly immune and uninvolved; and some of them, of course, made important contributions to proclaiming that spirit. The only major French composer who did remain immune was Saint-Saëns, and for that reason he is not included in this overview. His spiritual residence in a bygone age can be confirmed not only by his music and writings, but by his refusal to have *Le carnaval des animaux* performed in his lifetime – a work which a Milhaud or a Poulenc would surely have promoted proudly and not least because, as Saint-Saëns feared, it might provoke the derision of the Germans.

Any deep investigation into the technical means employed by these composers in fashioning their own 'Twenties Style' lies outside the scope of this book. But some insight at least can be gained from looking at the extent to which they relied on ostinato patterns and from asking whether they used such patterns primarily to supply a deficiency brought about by the weakening of tonal forces. It may also be interesting to speculate on the connotations the ostinato brought with it or came to possess, notably that of the impersonal machine and of the 'ronron habituel' of daily life.

Gabriel Fauré (1845–1924)

In May 1917, while *le tout Paris* was intently gossiping about *Parade*, Fauré was quietly putting the finishing touches to his Second Violin Sonata. It was given its first performance the following November by Lucien Capet and Alfred Cortot, and next day Dukas wrote to the composer:

> Cher ami, I wasn't able to see you yesterday to say how much I liked your sonata and how happy I was to hear it. Here at last is music which puts music back in its place, which isn't Javanese or Russian or Polynesian, and in which the reasons of reason enter into the reasons of the heart without preventing it from overflowing, from winning us over with its emotion and charm.[1]

We can only guess what exotic manifestations Dukas had in mind, although the previous three programmes of the SMI are likely contenders, containing as they did

Fred Barlow's *Poèmes chinois* and Roland-Manuel's *Le harem du vice-roi* (21 April), Louis Aubert's *Six poèmes arabes* (8 May), and Paul Martineau's *Deux mélodies hébraïques* and Maurice Delage's *Chant tamoul: Ragamalika* (18 May). In any case, Fauré had never really been tempted by exotica and, as Dukas implies, his attachment to reason ruled out any reliance on ear-catching fripperies.

This, together with his almost wholly sober, unjokey textures, might seem to rule out any influence either way of the postwar Zeitgeist. Whatever the truth of this, I would suggest that perhaps there was a parallelism between Fauré's late music and some of the music of the young, even if it had been attained by a different route. The clean spareness of, for example, the first 16 bars of Fauré's Thirteenth Barcarolle, published in 1921, is not unlike that of Satie's Nocturnes, written two years earlier, while the opening of the Thirteenth Nocturne, finished on the last day of 1921, lays bare Fauré's essentially contrapuntal thinking in a way that prefigures the imminent *retour à Bach*. Vlado Perlemuter remembers an evening with Fauré in Annecy in the early 1920s when, after supper, the composer moved slowly to the piano and, as everyone was settling down to listen to a Nocturne or a Barcarolle, began to play Bach's C minor organ Passacaglia.[2]

Honegger too came to Annecy, recommended by Fauré for what amounted to a study grant from his friends the Maillots, and a love of Bach was one of the most vital things the two composers had in common. But Honegger's initial reservations over Fauré's music are illuminating:

> I must admit that I myself took a rather long time to penetrate the mystery and subtlety of his language. Like many other people, I regarded his admirable discretion as a lack of strength and the elegant ease of some of his melodic lines as smacking of facility, while his harmonic ambiguity assorted ill with that Beethovenian intransigence that formed the basis of my musical attitudes.[3]

The five elements of Honegger's description ('mystère...subtile', 'discrétion', 'nonchalance', 'ambiguïté') represent points of both concord and discord with prevailing postwar attitudes. Mystery was certainly a non-starter, at least for those who, like Cocteau, chose to keep their head out of their hands. Subtlety and ambiguity were allowable, but few if any young composers possessed a technique capable of matching Fauré in this domain: who but Fauré could manage so finely the balancing act between harmonic subtlety and stark incomprehensibility in the central section of the Thirteenth Barcarolle (bars 49–71)? Discretion and ease, however, were the trademarks of a generation that wished to emulate earlier Fauré, at least in escaping from Wagner, and for this purpose he was an invaluable model. Milhaud in 1923 commented on 'that extraordinary sobriety and nakedness which we admire so much in the Second Piano Quintet, in the Second Cello Sonata and above all in the String Quartet, which is perhaps his most attractive work'.[4]

Milhaud goes on to praise the energy and sureness with which Fauré in old age 'pursues to the end those ideas which suit him' ('qui lui sont propres'). Here, as elsewhere in his writings, Milhaud is insisting on the value of a French tradition, of which Fauré is a preeminent upholder. At the same time Fauré does pursue his ideas to the end, often making it hard for the performer to grasp the shape of paragraphs whose multiplicity of meanings renders any one interpretation incomplete. This makes Fauré's music 'open' in a very modern sesne that derives from Mallarmé.

Fauré the man was similarly open to new music – he admired *Le roi David* and a score of Milhaud's *La brebis égarée* found a place in his library – but he maintained a persona that was above the combat. To some extent this was the result of deafness, but beneath the suave exterior he, like Poulenc, was *un inquiet*, a worrier. This sense of a composer undeterredly searching for some indefinable goal, so deeply immanent in much of Fauré's best music, must have been a beacon for those young men like Honegger and Milhaud who, as innately serious artists, felt the danger of being turned from their true path by success and by exposure to publicity of a kind Fauré never enjoyed until he was in his seventies. The metaphor of travelling runs through the texts of both Fauré's last two song-cycles: *Mirages*, written in 1919, and *L'horizon chimérique*, written for the baritone Charles Panzéra and first performed by him and his wife in May 1922. The third song of the second cycle, 'Diane, Séléné...', addressed to the moon and one of the most sheerly beautiful he ever wrote, ends with the words 'mon coeur, toujours las et toujours agité,/ Aspire vers la paix de ta nocturne flamme' ('my heart, ever weary and ever restless, aspires towards the

Fauré's funeral at the Madeleine on 8 November 1924 (Nadia Boulanger is delivering an oration from the podium)

peace of your nocturnal flame'), and the final song builds bar by bar to its heartfelt cry, 'car j'ai de grands départs inassouvis en moi' ('for I feel within me an unassuaged longing for great departures'). Against this, we read the reality of the aged Fauré's existence in a letter to his wife of 11 August 1922: 'despite my nomadic nature, I am beginning to realize that I have passed the age when long journeys seemed a simple matter'.[5]

For the young composers, Fauré's internal restlessness, his determination to deepen his technique, his astonishing range of resource from the modal/simple to the chromatic/complex, and not least his refusal to be seduced either by Impressionism or by the fashions of the day, were all examples which they ignored at their peril. Ostinato, for instance, held little attraction for him, other than that embodied in the continuous pulse he had always favoured, perhaps because his command of tonality and modulation was so complete that no further props were needed to hold his music together. Nor does anything in the music of his last years suggest an awareness that he was living in a machine age: his writing for the piano (an instrument present in the vast majority of his works) is rarely percussive, stemming rather from Schumann.

Milhaud, in concluding his homage, commented on the pieces Fauré's pupils had written for the special number of *La revue musicale* devoted to their teacher in 1922, and expressed surprise at how quickly they had dated; but 'the youthfulness, freshness and absolute novelty [of Fauré's own music] consoled us, because we realized that here were works and a man over whom time had no dominion'.[6]

Vincent d'Indy (1851–1931)

Like Fauré, d'Indy must have appeared to most of the postwar generation as an impregnable fortress of musical rectitude, to which were added qualities of moral worth and devotion to public service that had not always sat easily on his elder *confrère*. But d'Indy was about to surprise the musical world in a number of ways.

Everything in his character, training and experience disposed him to look askance at the activities of the avant-garde:

> All the *young* at the Conservatoire strain to imitate the great masters and enclose strings of minor seconds in casings of fifths – it's not very pretty. Following on from all that there are artistic pustules like 'Dadaism' which has just sprung up in opposition to Cubism, now decidedly old hat – I went to the Dada meeting...and returned without needing to be locked up in an asylum, which says something for my intellectual resistance![7]

Georges Auric, newly enlisted in Les Six, was also targeted by d'Indy, who called his *Foxtrot* 'the most foolish effort I have seen since the works of Th[éodore]. Dubois!'[8] But d'Indy was not indiscriminate in his condemnations. Of his one-time pupil he wrote, in the same letter to Sérieyx: 'Only Erik Satie remains sensible and confines himself to doing what he *feels able to do*; he seems now like a venerable ancestor, and really there were in his *Socrate* some truly poetic things, full of musical feeling.' The linear *facture* of *Socrate* may have played a part in gaining d'Indy's approval, but the work's atmosphere is so far from anything in d'Indy's own output that the widespread view of him as an intransigent bigot has to be revised. Unfortunately no record survives of his views on *Parade*.

Two further surprises would seem to have been linked, even if the evidence is necessarily circumstantial. D'Indy's first wife, Isabelle, had died in 1905 and his daughter Berthe in 1913. Grief and emotional isolation seem to have exacerbated his combative tendencies until, in the autumn of 1920, he married Caroline Janson, thirty-six years younger than himself, whom he had met during the war – curiously, but innocently, in a brasserie in Montparnasse. Before his marriage he was already tiring of the family home in the Ardèche and was spending more time on the Côte d'Azur. Now

> he had a villa built at Agay..., near the sea and surrounded by maritime pine-trees and red coloured rocks of porphyry. There, together with his new wife, he spent his periods of vacation, composing and frequently bathing in the transparent waters of the little creek nearby.[9]

The impact on his music is plain to hear. After the three serious operas of the years 1889–1915 (*Fervaal*, *L'étranger*, *La légende de Saint-Christophe*), he now embarked on an operetta ('yes, you read that correctly: an operetta')[10] called *Le rêve de Cinyras*. Less obviously signalled, a new spirit of joy and loving acceptance also blows through the two orchestral works *Poème des rivages* (1919–21) and *Diptyque méditerranéen* (1925–26), and through the series of six chamber works that occupied him between 1924 and the end of his life. Five of these six received their first performances at the SNM:

Piano Quintet op. 81 (1924)	2 May 1925
Cello Sonata op. 84 (1924–25) 2nd perf	13 March 1926
Suite in four movements op. 91 (1927)	17 May 1930

String Sextet op. 92 (1927)	26 January 1929
String Quartet no. 3 op. 96 (1928–29)	12 April 1930
Piano Trio op. 98 (1929)	11 January 1930

The choice of this prestigious venue might lead one to suppose that these works are merely delayed progeny from the stable that produced so many runners in the 1870s and 1880s. But after the debacle of the non-union of the SNM and the SMI, d'Indy could hardly have made a habit of taking his premieres elsewhere. Scrutiny of the works themselves reveals firstly that the Piano Quintet broke a silence on the chamber music front of nearly twenty years – the fact that the previous seven chamber works, ending with the Violin Sonata of 1903–4, coincided closely with his first marriage suggests that he may have regarded the medium as in some sense domestic. The second revelation is that these later works are radically different in structure and tone from the earlier ones.

To some extent the change is in the melodies. Léon Vallas reported that d'Indy as a teacher was severe on what he called 'la mélodasse', the charming, undemanding tunes of a Chaminade, or even a Massenet.[11] He was always finding his pupils' melodies too long, perhaps because in his own work he found inventing them difficult, preferring short phrases which he would then subject to contrapuntal elaboration.[12] But in these late chamber works he allows the tunes to blossom: the end of the Sextet, in particular, contains some of the most lyrical and sensuous music he ever wrote.

But more than that, he seems happier now to let the music flow unimpeded by 'clever' counterpoint or 'learned' modulations. The last four of the works listed above all begin with a movement entitled 'Entrée en sonate' and a courtly, ceremonial feeling frequently prefaces or absorbs the outbursts of passion. He also uses folk-songs, in the fleet second movement of the Sextet and in the last movement of the Piano Trio. In his hands the freshness is unimpaired, even if twenty years later Poulenc was to have sharp words for his imitators, comparing in a radio talk Debussy's handling of 'Nous n'irons plus au bois' in 'Rondes de printemps' with the 'painful digressions on popular tunes of various sub-d'Indyste finales'.[13]

As far as the spirit goes, it is impossible to distinguish between the effects of the *esprit nouveau* and of d'Indy's second marriage, although the likelihood is that the latter was the more influential. On the technical front d'Indy had nothing to learn from Les Six and, like Fauré, had no need of ostinatos to keep things moving. There is a brief passage of ostinato at the start of the last movement of the Third String Quartet, and he also uses it to depict the little train chugging past Falconara on the Adriatic coast in 'Horizons verts', the third movement of *Poème des rivages* where, he wrote to Ropartz: 'The scherzo itself is the train.'[14] Otherwise the only sop to postwar internationalism seems to come in his *Sept chants de terroir* op. 73, for piano duet, first performed at the SNM in February 1919, the fourth of which is called 'Yonkina (matelots japonais)'.

The only possible influence on late d'Indy might be that of Fauré: the Third String Quartet offers the same measured, contemplative, unhysterical kind of argument, with few discontinuities or dramatic surprises. As for the influence of late d'Indy on others, it has probably been non-existent – which says more about this century's penchant for the febrile than about the innate quality of these accessible and often moving works. In 1921 his pupil Erik Satie took his tongue out of his cheek to answer a newspaper questionnaire asking 'Who is the greatest French composer?' He unhesitatingly chose d'Indy: 'his age, his musical "surface", his authority as a teacher and the *comprehensive sweep of his ideas* mark him out as being the true leader of the contemporary school of French music. For me, he has been its leader for *many years*.'[15]

Erik Satie (1866–1925)

In the last two decades of his life, Satie had the slightly unusual experience of being 'discovered' three times. On 16 January 1911, at the sixth concert of the SMI, Ravel played the Second Sarabande and the Third Gymnopédie, preceded by his own transcription of the prelude to Act I of *Le fils des étoiles*. This was really the beginning of Satie's emergence from a twilight existence, first as a café and cabaret pianist and then as an outsider with strong Socialist tendencies. Satie wrote to his brother that Ravel 'assures me – every time I meet him – that he owes me a great deal. If he says so [Moi, je veux bien].' The signs are that Satie was not, for the moment, certain where this new-found interest of Ravel's was leading. 'However, as he began to realize little by little that he was being used for purposes that were quite alien to him and, above all that, musically speaking, he had nothing in common with him, Satie set about detaching himself from Ravel.'[16]

The agency of the second discovery is less clear-cut. Misia Sert claims she introduced Satie to Diaghilev in the summer of 1914, when Satie played him the *Morceaux en forme de poire*. More reliably, we know that Valentine Gross had introduced the two men to each other in the autumn of 1915, and that she then took Cocteau along to the Ravel/Satie concert at the Salle Huyghens on 18 April 1916. A week later Satie wrote to her: 'I hope the admirable Cocteau won't use any of my old works. Let's do something new, right?'[17] The 'something new' turned out to be *Parade*, after which Satie was a celebrity whether he liked it or not.

The third discovery of Satie was made by Cocteau alone. As early as February 1915 Cocteau had published a 'Réponse à de jeunes musiciens'. As Ornella Volta says,

> In fact, it is unlikely that the young composers to whom he was 'replying'
> had asked him any questions whatever, given that it was hard in 1915 to
> identify in his entourage this imagined entity of 'young composers', for
> the simple reason that they didn't exist. Or not yet; because it took only
> two years for them to materialize, grouped indeed around Satie, who was

called from then on 'le bon Maître'. The fact of this 'Maître' pronouncing that 'Satieism could not exist' constituted indeed simply another bonus, since it left the road clear, if not for a 'school', at least for a movement under Cocteau's direction.[18]

Cocteau's 1918 pamphlet *Le coq et l'arlequin*, in dismissing Wagner and Debussy's 'Russian pedals', promoted Satie's 'petite route classique' as the path to the future. But Cocteau was wise enough to begin his pro-Satie paragraphs with a near disclaimer: 'the cult of Satie is difficult, because one of Satie's charms is precisely how little he offers as a basis for deification,'[19] to which one might reply that deification, being an essentially nineteenth-century, Romantic kind of enterprise, was not something in which someone of Cocteau's beliefs should be engaged anyway. The title 'le bon Maître' was awarded by the young composers forming, first, Les Nouveaux Jeunes in 1917 and then Les Six in 1919, with no small touch of irony. Satie was certainly a 'good' person, and as determined on following his own path as Fauré was, but there was very little that he could teach Conservatoire-trained composers like Milhaud, Honegger or Tailleferre on the purely technical front. His 'maîtrise' lay in his astonishingly individual and independent view of the world and of his own duties as a composer. Like Fauré, he served the young as a fine moral example.

Like Fauré too, he left us no unambiguous evidence of being influenced by the postwar *esprit nouveau*, rather of having made his own distinctive contribution to it. Unlike Fauré, though, he did not subscribe to the nineteenth-century notion of a 'body of works': one cannot imagine Satie writing sets of thirteen Nocturnes and Bar-carolles over a period of forty-six years. Instead he exhibits what may be a typically twentieth-century attitude of 'been there, done that'. His works after *Parade* display a concern with solving ever new problems: in *Sonatine bureaucratique*, how to update Clementi (at least two years before *Pulcinella*); in *Musique d'ameublement*, how to write music that will not be listened to; in *Socrate*, how to express moral excellence within a tightly controlled harmonic and textural environment; in the *Nocturnes* how to re-interpret the Field/Chopin *datum*; and in the final ballets, *Mercure* and *Relâche* respectively, how to avoid 'stylization or any rapport with things artistic',[20] and how to disguise a carefully wrought structure as an essay in anarchy.

Of the many lessons Satie had to teach his contemporaries and successors, perhaps three stand out. Firstly, that seriousness is not the same as solemnity. For all its jokiness, *Parade* is a deeply serious commentary on the human condition, and even the wilder lunacy of *Relâche* is moralistic in its sending-up of crass officialdom. Secondly, that less can be more, and that certainly too much is always less. Historians have made much of the so-called *style dépouillé*, a style stripped to essentials. The problem for many French composers in the 1920s was that they had been brought up in the decorative tradition of Impressionism, so that when their style was stripped down there was nothing left worth listening to. Satie on the other hand had been practising economy for thirty years, from the days of the *Sarabandes* and *Gymnopédies*, so that, when the combination of scarce resources and anti-German feeling made leaner textures fashionable, he could simply continue doing what he had been doing. It is worth making this point if only because Cocteau tended to give the impression that simplicity was something he himself had invented.

The third lesson, marching with the second, was that the relationship between words and music is inevitably slippery and ambiguous. Cocteau was probably right on all counts when he wrote that the bizarre titles Satie gave some of his piano pieces, 'apart from protecting his music from persons in thrall to the "sublime" and authorizing the laughter of those who do not understand his music's value, are explicable in terms of Debussy's abuse of precious titles'.[21] But the relationship between the music and the passing verbal comments Satie makes on it is less easily explained.

A single brief example will show something of the complex issues involved. In the first of the *Avant-dernières pensées* (Penultimate Thoughts) of 1915, entitled 'Idylle', we find a tempo indication, *Modéré, je vous prie* (*Moderato*, please); an indication of performing style under the bass line, *La basse liée, n'est-ce pas?* (The bass *legato*, surely?); and beneath the right-hand tune a text beginning 'Que vois-je? Le Ruisseau est tout mouillé' ('What do I see? The Stream is all wet'). Both

Satie, drawn by Francis Picabia, with words about and music for his ballet *Relâche*

tempo and performing indications are couched in the language of the piano teacher. How does this marry with the title of 'Idylle'? Surely idylls are by nature spontaneous and effortless? As to the text under the right-hand tune, 'Que vois-je?' is pure, nineteenth-century operatic hackwork, delivered at the point where the hero or heroine sees something unexpected which is going to spark off the plot for the ensuing acts (even as late as 1933, the heroine in the Gide/Stravinsky ballet *Perséphone* can declaim 'Où suis-je?'). Finally, the banality of 'Le Ruisseau est tout mouillé' is explained, as Cocteau says, by the water fixation of Debussy and his followers. We may then note that the piece is dedicated to Debussy; and that in that same year of

1915 Debussy was writing his *Etudes* for piano, beginning with the teacherly 'Pour les cinq doigts', marked as being 'in the tradition of Czerny' and to be played 'sagement' – 'sensibly', 'in a well-behaved manner', itself a decidedly Satiean instruction. We note also that the summer of 1915 was the very time when Debussy was turning back to the eighteenth century with his Cello Sonata. Within the first fifteen seconds or so, the thoughtful pianist is brought to consider the relationships between practising and the final, poetic result, between banal words and unbanal tune, between Satie and Debussy, and between styles generally known as Impressiomism and Neoclassicism. Are there further in-jokes here which the two of them pursued over Sunday lunch and games of backgammon, and which we shall now never uncover? Or does this mark the beginning of the final split between them over *Parade*?

Maybe not all Satie's verbal instructions would be as fruitful as these ones, although Steven Moore Whiting has produced much telling evidence on this front, demonstrating Satie's reliance on verbal/musical techniques he had learnt from cabaret practitioners like Vincent Hyspa.[22] But the inescapable lesson is that performing and listening involve not just technique or technical knowledge, but a high degree of intelligence and receptivity. The 'warm bath' approach is no more appropriate than the 'head in hands' one. The tidy appearance that Satie presented to the world was matched, according to Poulenc, by his treatment of the piano:

> Whereas so many composers, even well-known ones, too often tend
> to think of the piano as a makeshift instrument which can cope with
> anything, Satie in his meticulous way knew exactly what suited it. The
> novel directness of his writing, a bold reaction against the other-worldly
> atmosphere of Debussy and Ravel, shows up as an influence as late as
> 1944, in Stravinsky's Sonata for two pianos.
>
> Satie stated that it was forbidden under pain of major excommunication
> to read out the stories and funny remarks with which he decorated his
> music, either before or during performances. ('They are the pianist's
> reward,' he sometimes used to say).[23]

– and the pianist's responsibility.

More than any other composer of the 1920s Satie provoked quarrels and defections, and since then there has never been anything like an agreed line on his stature. Understandably, a composer like Boulez, convinced of the need for musical language to progress, has no time for him: 'Satie's best joke: the "maître of Arcueil". As a title, excellent; as long as it's not followed by music.'[24] But I feel it is hard to deny that by the questions Satie asked about music, and about music and words, and by the way in which he actually set words in a work like *Socrate*, he goaded a few listeners at least into a thoughtfulness that prepared them for *Le marteau sans maître* to come. No less important were his multifaceted, omnipresent ostinatos, which he injected into the lifeblood of French music, and through which he often seemed to be presenting simultaneously the *ronron habituel* of daily life and the extraordinary fight one had to put up against it in order to come up with anything original.

Albert Roussel (1869–1937)

> Music is the most closed and inaccessible of the arts. It is true to say of
> the composer, even more than of the poet, that he is completely isolated
> in the world, alone, with his more or less incomprehensible language.
> Apart from two or three attractive works which one might write for the
> public...all the rest...everything that a composer might be tempted to
> write in an attempt to express himself, in the present state of music and
> the masses, will always be destined to have a very few listeners.[25]

From this profession of faith by Roussel, clearly born of his studies at the Schola Cantorum, we can readily understand how his postwar composing life might be strewn with difficulties, surrounded, as he would be, by younger composers like Poulenc and Auric who were deliberately writing music that was easy on the ear. At the outbreak of war he had joined the army as an artillery lieutenant and was then moved to the transport section, carrying troops to the Somme and Verdun. As with Ravel, whose war service followed a similar pattern, Roussel's experiences seem to have made the caressing sonorities of Impressionism irrelevant (see also the letter quoted on p. 31). While he might have felt free to ignore Cocteau's request to build him 'music he could live in like a house', there is no question but that his postwar music took on a harder, less ingratiating tone.

A further problem, as we have seen, was that *Padmâvatî*, although basically completed in 1918, did not reach the stage until 1923, so that Parisian audiences might well have found Roussel's apparent line of development confusing. The two orchestral works he wrote between 1918 and 1923 show him moving resolutely away from aural titillation. *Pour une fête de printemps* began life as the Scherzo of the Second Symphony. Roussel then felt it had grown beyond what the Symphony could accommodate, and developed it further into a symphonic poem. As such, it could be taken as belonging to the French tradition established by Saint-Saëns and d'Indy. Roussel wrote to Koechlin during rehearsals in 1921:

> Pierné [the conductor] assures me that this spring festival does not take
> place in France, but in one of the Asiatic countries, and that he sees it
> as an exotic dance; he's even suggesting I should add a subtitle to explain
> this to the audience. I must admit to you, I didn't think I'd written exotic
> music. What's your view?[26]

We do not know Koechlin's view, but Roussel's is plain enough: he was impatient to find Pierné, a trained musician, judging the work in the light of its exotic predecessors such as *Evocations*, and being reluctant to accept it as pure music. The only remotely Asiatic element is the occasional chromatic melisma on the oboe. Otherwise Roussel produces a mixture of ostinato rhythms, outbursts on brass and searching themes on strings that proclaims its authorship unmistakably. Typical too is his reluctance to write comfortable harmonies with a predictable outcome. The opening paragraph, for instance, is at once static (in that oboe, clarinet and flute repeat the first phrase) and dynamic (in that the underlying harmony is too acerbic to act as a neutral background and posits impending movement of some kind).

Such tensions and ambiguities within the musical material maybe explain why Roussel's music has always existed just outside the twentieth-century mainstream. The epithet often used is 'bracing' – an implicit reference, perhaps, to his naval background. Like late Fauré, Roussel often seems to be on a quest for some indefinable,

unreachable ideal, and he is even less willing than Fauré to abandon himself to the moment. There is also a frequent residue of melancholy. In *Pour une fête*, for example, although the music rises to several powerful climaxes, the ending is disconsolate – a spring fair cut short by rain.

Roussel at his most intransigent is to be heard in the Second Symphony, completed in the autumn of 1921 and first performed at the Concerts Pasdeloup on 4 March 1922, conducted by Rhené-Baton. Emile Vuillermoz, usually sympathetic to the composer, wrote of the symphony's sound: 'The orchestration is dull, gloomy and uniformly grey, with attempts at curiousness which break out occasionally but come to nothing. This style speaks of research...but never gets as far as discovery. The mixtures of timbres are without interest and constitute no enrichment to modern orchestration.'[27] Whether bringing 'enrichment to modern orchestration' is the prime task of any composer remains arguable; Roussel, one suspects, was more inclined to view orchestration as a means than as an end. From his remarks over *Pour une fête*, it would be reasonable to suppose that the 'end' of the Second Symphony was a purely abstract one. But the truth is less straightforward. A few days after the first performance, Roussel wrote to Koechlin:

> I think it would have been helpful for me to have indicated in the programme the extra-musical idea which was the motive force behind my symphony. I would have preferred it to have been understood without the help of any commentary. But in our epoch of symphonic poems and detailed explanations, listeners have got into the habit of allowing themselves to be guided by a scenario and no longer make the effort to discover for themselves the meaning of the music they hear.[28]

Whether or not Roland-Manuel was right to hear the symphony as a disguised autobiography is unknown, as is the composer's reaction to his claim that the work was governed by the axiom: 'all sounds are capable of being superimposed on each other'.[29] It is at least possible though that Roussel had intimated to Roland-Manuel such an autobiographical basis, and certainly the works that followed suggest that the composer had in some sense cleared the air with the Second Symphony and was now prepared to engage with the Zeitgeist of the Twenties, if on his own terms. As he

Roussel at his work table

admitted, the symphony was 'a rather hermetic work', and from here on he began to espouse 'a manner that was more economical (*dépouillée*), purer and more schematic...a clearer style'.[30]

The *Sérénade* for flute, violin, viola, cello and harp of 1925 represents one of the first and most beguiling fruits of this new orientation. The contrast with the symphony of four years earlier, in grammar, syntax and in the emphasis on light, bright instrumental colours, could hardly be more extreme and could almost be heard as an apology. But one result of the newly alleviated textures is to throw into greater relief Roussel's tendency to rely on 'motoric' rhythmic patterns, which Henri Dutilleux for one has admitted to finding one of the less attractive features of Roussel's writing.[31] Roussel, if less inventive in his management of ostinatos than Stravinsky, at least remained unapologetic about them and the moments in the *Sérénade* where an ostinato is gradually transmogrified into a melody have a charm of their own.

The two outer movements of the Suite in F for orchestra, completed in August 1926, show Roussel first establishing and then undermining regular successions of 2- and 4-bar phrases. In the 'Gigue' he also introduces deliberate vulgarities that suggest he was aware of works like Poulenc's *Cocardes*,[32] and the interplay between these aesthetic and rhythmic irregularities and the basically regular phrase structure is among the most entertaining things in all Roussel's oeuvre, all the more arresting because it comes after the heartfelt *legato* of the 'Sarabande'. In 1933, Messiaen told José Bruyr that 'the whole of French music, it seems to me, is polarized today between Albert Roussel, the Roussel of the Suite in F and the symphonies, and early Stravinsky'.[33]

The Suite of 1926 not only provides fascinating testimony of a meeting of minds between a Schola-trained composer in his mid-fifties and the *esprit nouveau*, it also demonstrates a dichotomy within Roussel himself. In 1934, Roussel was asked by a concert organizer to which composer he was particularly indebted. He was totally at a loss to answer and, rather charmingly, wrote to his friend Arthur Hoérée to ask in effect: 'Who am I?' Hoérée answered the question in his book on the composer: 'The art of Roussel presents two opposing tendencies: meditative seriousness and juvenile élan.' The first, he felt, derived from Wagner and Franck, possibly mediated through d'Indy; the second from the French school of 1860–80 (Berlioz, Lalo, Bizet, Saint-Saëns, Chabrier).[34]

While one may put forward the theory that the *esprit nouveau* helped Roussel develop his juvenile side, it must remain only a theory. The meditative Roussel persisted, through the 'Pastorale' of the *Petite suite* of 1929 into the last two symphonies and the ballet *Bacchus et Ariane*, and even the juvenile side of him was often free of any echo of *esprit nouveau*, as in the curious 6/8 + 4/8 of the 'Aubade' from the *Petite suite*. Although a jazz influence occasionally obtrudes, and his song 'Jazz dans la nuit' makes specific reference to it, he felt jazz was not likely to have an effect on musical forms and that 'listening to long stretches of jazz ends up by being monotonous and irritating'.[35]

More original and interesting were his forays into unusual modes, in *Padmâvatî* and in the song 'Réponse d'une épouse sage' ('reply of a sensible wife') on a text translated from the Chinese. In 1928 he wrote to Maurice Emmanuel, whose own Fourth Sonatina for piano of 1923 is based on Hindu modes: 'I firmly believe, as you do, that the use of these scales can bring new means of expression to music as well as enriching it in a very special way.'[36] Messiaen was soon to prove him right.

Maurice Ravel (1875–1937)

On the face of it, the First World War had a more profound effect on Ravel than on any other French composer, to the extent that the prewar and postwar Ravels can even appear as two quite distinct people. Pierre Boulez is not alone in feeling that,

> after the war, the second period [of Ravel] is, for me, much less attractive, although very attractive from outside. He tends to be too much self-restrictive, he doesn't want to go out of himself. After the Trio you don't find the same deep feeling as before, but more a kind of stylistic game, which is absolutely extraordinary. Only in the second song of *Don Quichotte à Dulcinée* does he go back to something very genuine.[37]

The reasons for the change are not hard to find. After serving as a lorry driver in the French army for eighteen months from March 1915, Ravel was operated on for a hernia in September 1916 and invalided out. Then, the following January, his mother died. These traumas would possibly have been enough on their own (some close friends thought he never really recovered from his mother's death), but Ravel was also in mourning for a French civilization which he felt had been irreversibly uprooted by the war.

It has become customary to describe his piano suite *Le tombeau de Couperin* as a 'war piece', on the strength of the dedications at the head of each of the six pieces to

young soldiers killed in the conflict. Strict chronology, however, tells us that Ravel began it in July 1914 (the date is on the autograph), some weeks before war broke out. The work's reliance on conventional forms, including three classical French dances, speaks of a reaction to the instability of early twentieth-century society, such as Mahler and Schoenberg had expressed in very different language that looked forward rather than back.

A similar confusion surrounds *La valse*. After its first performance in Paris in December 1920, some critics, as Ravel noted,

> saw a tragic allusion — end of the Second Empire, state of Vienna after the war etc.... Tragic, yes it can be that, like any expression – pleasure, happiness – which is pushed to extremes. You should see in it only what comes from the music: a mounting volume of sound, which in stage performance will be complemented by lighting and movement.[38]

In any case the project, under the provisional title *Wien*, had been in Ravel's mind since 1906. So in fact both *La valse* and *Le tombeau* came under the heading of 'unfinished business' and cannot strictly be included among Ravel's responses to the postwar scene.

The first of his truly postwar works to be completed was the Sonata for violin and cello, first performed at an SMI concert on 6 April 1922, in a programme almost entirely of first performances, including that of Milhaud's Fifth String Quartet. One could argue that even here Ravel was looking backwards, in that the first movement had already been published two years earlier as a homage to Debussy. But the spare austerity of much of the writing indicates a 'new' Ravel, even if one still animated by the contrapuntal interests expressed more seductively in the Trio.

A mediocre performance of this sonata can be a painful experience – and we may bear in mind Ravel's reply to a performer's complaint over how difficult it is to play: 'Good! Then I shan't be assassinated by amateurs!'[39] But even a superior performance can leave one sympathizing with Boulez to some extent, in his qualification of Ravel's postwar music as 'very attractive from *outside*' (my italics) and in his judgment that it is 'too much self-restricted', lacking in 'deep feeling' and 'more a kind of stylistic game'. But any notion that the sonata was a mere *jeu d'esprit* thrown off with a quick flourish is quashed by the evidence of Ravel's letters: 'it's the result of nearly a year and a half's slogging.... In that time Milhaud would have managed to produce four symphonies, five quartets and several dramatic settings of Paul Claudel.'[40]

In taking such trouble over his own new-found *style dépouillé* Ravel may indeed have had the efforts of his contemporaries in mind, and the reference to Milhaud may say more in this respect than he intended. But I submit that it is unhelpful, if entirely natural, to view his postwar works through the lens of his prewar ones. With the greatest respect to Boulez, it could be that these later works demand a different kind of listening which we shall find possible only as we progress through the twenty-first century. It is surely unimaginable that the composer of *Daphnis et Chloé* should bare his textures, and his heart, and have nothing to say to us.

If we ignore *Tzigane*, which was never intended to contain a great deal beneath its dazzling surface, the remaining four major works Ravel wrote in the 1920s all touch on the widely felt contemporary problem of how to integrate ostinatos into the discourse. This is not the place for a lengthy analysis of his opera *L'enfant et les sortilèges*, but it may be of interest to look briefly at ways in which the work marries the *style dépouillé* with a warm emotionality that, happily, audiences have been quick to respond to ever since its premiere in 1925. No intelligent musician at the time was without a view on the opera, and it would not be too much to say that it was one of the most important aesthetic touchstones of the decade.

The most obvious thing to say about *L'enfant* is that it is unashamedly a 'number opera', written as though Wagner had never existed. In the theatre, certainly, this sectionalism is to some extent disguised both by the strong storyline and by Ravel's finely crafted links between one number and the next. But one of the many pleasures this masterpiece affords comes from the various dosages of the lyrical and the rhythmic, of warm and cold, that Ravel offers us.

At figure 50, as the shepherd and shepherdess with their sheep and goats descend from the wallpaper, Ravel introduces a 2-bar ostinato on a high drum, setting up what he calls 'une musique naïve'. Needless to say, this 'naïveté' turns out to be 'fausse'. Apart from harmonic colourings of consecutive major sevenths and bitonal contributions from the clarinets, Ravel continuously subverts the predictable comfort of the ostinato with the irregular phrase-lengths of the tunes. He describes the members of the pastoral cortège as 'un peu ridicules, et très touchants'; his rhythmic subversion makes them seem also irresolute and magically removed from the real world (in which ostinatos 'obstinately' bend matter to their will).

The demented chanting of L'Arithmétique (The Number Man) moves from rhythmic subversion to orthodoxy. From fig. 75 phrase lengths fluctuate constantly (3 bars, 4, 6, 3, 4, etc.), culminating in phrases where both L'Arithmétique and the chorus are interrupted in mid-word. But the climax is engineered through 76 bars entirely in 4-bar phrases, leading us to the end of the scene. The machine, with its subconscious connotations of the recent war, has taken over; and the Child is left exclaiming 'Oh! ma tête!'

Finally, Ravel indulges in the extraordinary paradox of a *fugato* to close the opera and set the seal on the Child's discovery of love. This perfectly complements and corrects the Arithmetic scene, which falls almost exactly halfway through the opera. There, audible rhythm obliterates feeling. Here, audible process is harnessed to engender and sustain feeling. Not even in the 'Passacaille' in the Trio had a traditional technique been employed to such profound effect.

If *L'enfant* marked Ravel's final acceptance of his mother's death (and it is a large 'if'), the vacuum left by her departure from his life was always going to be hard to fill. Works like the Second Violin Sonata and *Boléro* obviously qualify as partaking of the 'stylistic games' Boulez referred to and, in the case of *Boléro* at least, deep feeling was explicitly admitted by Ravel to be wholly absent. The one work of the decade in which the lyrical and the rhythmic notably interact once more is the *Chansons madécasses*.

Ravel would no doubt have set his face in general against political interpretations of his music, as he did over *La valse*. The epigraph to the *Valses nobles et sentimentales* ('le plaisir délicieux et toujours nouveau d'une occupation inutile' – 'the delightful and ever novel pleasure of a pointless occupation') is a sufficient statement of his attitude to the composer's task. But it really is hard to credit that he could write the central song of the *Chansons madécasses*, in which the white invaders of Madagascar stand accused of treachery and murder, and take no thought whatever of France's imperial adventures, past and present, particularly since we know of his lifelong left-wing sentiments. The ostinato machine, which in the first song was humanized to convey the lover's heartbeat, here depicts the invaders' relentless will to power; bitonality, employed as a piquant adornment in the pastoral dance of *L'enfant*, now speaks of a violation of harmonic and social norms, and gives rise to a higher level of dissonance than in any other of his works.

In the gentle final song, an ostinato makes a brief, languid appearance, shorn of any threat. The song ends with the throwaway line 'Allez, et préparez le repas!', unaccompanied. Peace is apparently restored. But the listener is nonetheless faced with the distasteful possibility that this casual domination by the white master has been made possible only by the preceding show of brutality.

Throughout the 1920s Ravel continued the technical researches to which he had always been committed. Time will tell whether Boulez's strictures on an overall dearth of sentiment hold good or not, but it seems clear to me that Ravel was experimenting not only with musical language, but with types of feeling appropriate to a decade following a war in which 'the ceremony of innocence' had been well and truly drowned. And in this search a part was no doubt played by his own experiences at the front – about which he, like so many men who saw its horrors, was reluctant to speak in the language of words.

Igor Stravinsky (1882–1971)

In 1920 Stravinsky decided to leave Switzerland, where he had spent the war years among those whom Diaghilev was to call sourly 'your Alpine colleagues', and moved to France, 'where, at that moment, the pulse of world activity was throbbing'.[41] He and his family reached their new country in June, five months after the baptism of Les Six.

Paris had not heard a major work by him since the premiere of *Le rossignol* at the Opéra in May 1914. Six years later both Paris and Stravinsky were greatly changed. Les Six were the new vanguard, and Stravinsky, if he was to reclaim the primacy he had held before the war, needed to find a path that was both perceptibly different from theirs and also congruent with his own development. It is not surprising then to find, in his music as well as in his writings, elements of almost aggressive self-promotion and self-explanation. The success of *Pulcinella* the month before his move obviously did his cause no harm, but there was no getting away from the fact that the ballet's basic musical material was not his own. An *echt* Stravinsky masterpiece was called for.

Stephen Walsh has noted that the early Twenties were 'a period of uncharacteristic indecisiveness about sonority on Stravinsky's part',[42] and it is tempting to imagine that this might have been part of a more general insecurity about his role in the new order of things, prompting the aggression noted above. But the realization, what the French call the *mise en oeuvre*, of his first masterpiece completed on French soil, the Symphonies of Wind Instruments, is so telling and accurate, so archetypally 'windy', that one is startled to find that the first sketches for it of 1919 included strings.

The work makes clear straight away that the opposition of lyrical and rhythmic is not valid here: much of the melodic material is itself close to ostinato patterning, without ever succumbing to static regularity – something that Stravinsky may well have taken from *Parade*. Lyricism and rhythm fertilize each other (to use a slightly awkward metaphor), and in any case the sections are mostly too short for any ostinato to gain a hold. But at the same time, the work's cumulative power is undeniable. Walsh argues persuasively that the 2:3 ratio between the three tempi employed is mirrored in 'a phrase-grouping based on the alternation of twos and threes', and that it is from this pattern of common relationships that the work 'derives its unusual feeling of calm order and architectural repose'.[43] In rather the same vein, Robert Siohan speaks of the chorale, which ends the work and which, as we have seen, was published separately in 1920 as a memorial tribute to Debussy,[44] as 'framing the other elements...like an alley of funerary cypresses'. He finds in it also 'a kind of vehement combat in which hard blocks of sound clash in a breathless rhythm, in a manner close to that found in the "Danse sacrale"'.[45] Not the least of Stravinsky's achievements was to have given the impression of vehemence within a controlled, ritual structure, but even a genius of his radical instincts could not manage to make a complete and instantaneous break with his past. Walsh very reasonably describes the Symphonies as 'the culminating moment of Stravinsky's Russian period'.[46]

But after his farewell to Russia, what then? In *Mavra* Stravinsky concocted a synthesis of Russian and Western elements, and one that left most of his French audience unimpressed and even hostile, Ravel including it among the 'nombreux exercices de style arides' that preceded *Oedipus rex* and the *Symphony of Psalms*.[47] Altogether more successful was his Octet for wind instruments, first performed under Koussevitzky's direction at the Opéra in October 1923.

Stravinsky's much republished article, 'Some Ideas about my Octuor'[48] contains a good deal that is impenetrable and some things that are plainly untrue: among the latter, the Symphonies make nonsense of the claim that 'Form, in my music, derives from counterpoint', while the briefest look at the score of the Octet will demonstrate that Stravinsky has not, in fact, 'excluded all nuances between the *forte* and the *piano*', and has even committed a fair, if not lavish, sprinkling of crescendos and diminuendos. The aggressive, polemical, high-handed tone (to some extent abetted by clumsy translation from, I would suggest, a French original) and the over-repetition of the essentially simple idea that 'interpretation deforms', together give the inescapable message that, *selon* Stravinsky, modern composers and performers have got music wrong and that he alone is following the path of righteousness. The mismatch between this rather forbidding document and the delightful wit of the Octet itself could hardly be more complete.

There is no call here to bring on the sledgehammer of analysis; enough to quote two of Walsh's points, that this work 'goes farther than *Mavra* in restoring cadential tonality, periodic rhythm and traditional forms', but that 'many of his melodic lines...move by step or sequence: that is, in a clearly hierarchical way, which *apes* [my italics] the grammar of tonality'. Not for the first or last time, Stravinsky's dissembling is astonishingly skilful, a high-wire balancing act which circus-lovers like Les Six could not but admire, but with which they would compete at their peril. As a final comment on the work, Scott Messing observes:

> Stravinsky only invoked Bach's name with any frequency after critical response to the Octet and the Concerto for piano and winds had established the connection as a cliché. Both Roland-Manuel and [Nadia] Boulanger introduced Bach in their reviews of the Octet in October and November 1923. In January 1924, the composer told an interviewer for *Le matin*: 'I consider [Bach] the imperishable model for us all.'[49]

– which is not to suggest for a moment that Stravinsky was telling lies; merely that, like Les Six, he was quick to capitalize on any publicity that did not actually conflict with his beliefs.

Having revitalized the craft of writing for wind instruments, in which the French had always reckoned to have particular expertise, Stravinsky now turned to another field the French had recently made their own, that of piano writing. The fumes of 'Impressionism' and exoticism still lingered over Parisian concert halls: witness instrumental pieces like 'Enchantement matinal', 'Air magique de Tsin' and 'Kakémonos: quatre pièces japonaises', all first performed at Société nationale concerts in the first half of 1926. Predictably, Stravinsky saw the banishment of such fumes as a necessary task, and with the Concerto for piano and winds and the Piano Sonata of 1924 and 1925 he followed up the constructivist ideas propounded in his article on the Octet, based on the premise that music is about nothing but itself. These two works represent the furthest Stravinsky was to go with 'in your face', wrong-note composition. With his point made – 'Follow this if you dare!' – he then relaxed somewhat in the writing of the Serenade in A, 'in imitation of eighteenth-century examples of *Nachtmusik*'.[50]

The description 'in A' is slightly misleading, as has often been pointed out. 'On A' or 'between As' might be nearer the mark, since the first and last sounds of each movement include that pitch. Commentators have understandably noted the final As in the first three movements which are depressed silently and activated by the surrounding material, as in Schoenberg's Piano Piece op. 11 no 1; while the final A of the fourth movement carries one of only two pedal indications in the work. The almost arbitrary placing of these endings, in what Walsh calls 'a kind of textural dissolution',[51] may be related to Stravinsky's almost certain desire to fit each movement on to one side of a 78 disc[52] – a reappearance of Stravinsky the schoolmaster, deciding suddenly that enough is enough and everyone should get back into line and stand still. The fact that the syntax of the Serenade is deeply personal to the composer (as is the texture: who else could write so many thirds and sixths without conjuring up the spirit of Brahms?) means that he wields the necessary authority to bring matters so abruptly to a halt.

The third movement, 'Rondoletto', makes a nod in the direction of Bach's Two-part Inventions which 'were somewhere in the back of my mind' during the last movements of the Octet and the Piano Sonata, while occasional flattened sevenths (bars 9, 11, 12) and cross accents (bar 15) hint delicately at jazz, but no more than that. The most noticeable feature of the Serenade is a new serenity that looks forward to *Apollon musagète*. By 1925, it seems, Stravinsky had to some extent put striving behind him. A year later he rejoined the Russian Orthodox Church.

During the remainder of the decade Stravinsky wrote three major works in which the past, or his perception of it, had a role to play. In *Oedipus rex* he grappled with Greek myth and the Latin language, and with fateful, machinist ostinato; in *Apollon musagète* he again explored Greek myth through what he had called the 'sobriety' of string instruments,[53] composing a work hailed by Diaghilev as 'a product of true artistic maturity' and condemned by Messiaen as one 'in which Lully has left a number of wrong bass lines';[54] and in *Le baiser de la fée* he paid homage to Tchaikovsky, choosing and extending a number of that composer's songs and piano pieces so that, in the words of one critic, 'Tchaikovsky's faults – his banalities and vulgarities and routine procedures – are composed *out* of the music, and Stravinsky's virtues are composed *into* it'.[55]

All three works end with a kind of apotheosis, as had the Symphonies of Wind Instruments and even the Octet, and as the *Symphony of Psalms* was to do at the start of the next decade. Hearing any of these works for the first time, one would not, I think, have any reason to expect these placatory codas. And yet, in retrospect, they do much to explain or at least to give a context to the often rather busy textures and tempi that precede them. Often, too, they contain some of Stravinsky's best and most memorable music. It is as though the piece has been a search for an essence which the composer, through alchemical practices, finally offers us in distilled form; or, as the word 'apotheosis' suggests, as though everything has been directed towards some ultimate state of grace. Only rarely (Fauré at the end of his Thirteenth Nocturne, Ravel at the end of *L'enfant et les sortilèges*) did Stravinsky's French colleagues reach these heights, or depths. So almost inevitably Stravinsky, contrary as ever, chose to close the decade with a work for piano and orchestra which had no pretensions at all to spirituality, nor to grace, except in its manifestation as gracefulness, and which gave apotheosis the widest possible berth.

Although he saw fit to validate the title *Capriccio* by a reference to the seventeenth-century theorist and composer Michael Praetorius, and admitted that when composing this piece he often had Weber in his thoughts, rarely during the Twenties had he been so thoroughly himself. Compositional dexterity is hidden behind the digital, and in the last movement (written first) Stravinsky puts on a show of harmonic naivety, almost of incompetence: over a third of the movement is based on tonic or subdominant arpeggios or (from figure 86) on a teasing tonic+dominant combination. The final paragraph induces not serenity, but a vibrant sense of well-being and happy laughter.

If Stravinsky began the Twenties on his mettle, by the end of decade he had proved it many times over. Manuel Rosenthal confirms that every new Stravinsky work at this time was seized on by the young for the ground it was bound to break.[56] Nor was it only the large stage works that claimed their attention: the opening chords of the Serenade in A reappear thirty-five years later at the start of Poulenc's *Gloria*. More than anything perhaps, Stravinsky's lesson for the young was one of Protean renewal, even if they were in general better advised to read his scores than his articles. A composer's previous work was not a sofa, but a springboard. And, by making surprising leaps off it sideways, it was possible to see both where you had been and where you were going and, at best, maintain a valid connection between the two.

Arthur Honegger (1892–1955)

It has long been established, not least by Honegger himself, that while he was 'in' Les Six, he was only ever 'of' them for the occasional moment. With hindsight, the elements of his output during the Twenties seem puzzlingly disparate – which did not prevent him becoming by some way the most successful and talked-of composer in the group by the middle of the decade.

This success was due in large measure to three orchestral works written between August 1920 and December 1923: *Pastorale d'été*, *Le roi David* and *Pacific 231*, each of them incorporating a current concern of French society. But even before the summer of 1920, Honegger was showing that he did not intend to toe any party line, whether laid down by Cocteau or anyone else. In October 1919 he began his *Sept pièces brèves* for piano. He completed nos. 3, 5, 6 and 7 in January 1920, the month in which Les Six were officially born, and one cannot imagine that either Cocteau or Satie took pleasure in any of them – except possibly the last, where Honegger pays homage to Stravinsky's *Ragtime*, published in Paris in 1919, with a hammered left-hand ostinato, high, dissonant right-hand chords and regular, wild 'breaks' disrupting the melodic and rhythmic flow. In no. 3 a chromatic line unfolds over thickly dissonant, almost Schoenbergian harmonies and, even more shocking, no. 5 recalls the Spanish fragrances of Debussy and Ravel.

Honegger's first real success came in February 1921, but a letter of that month to his parents shows that, for a composer still in his twenties, he was already being played remarkably often:

> I've finished my score of *Horace* [*victorieux*] and I'm now starting work
> on *Le Roi David*.... I'm also hard at work on rehearsals for the Loïe Fuller
> rehearsals at the Champs-Élysées. She's dancing to three pieces from
> [*Les dits du*] *Jeux du monde* and the orchestra's playing *Le chant de Nigamon*.

Next week I'm getting the Ballets suédois to listen to *Horace* to see what sort of deal I might get out of them. My Violin Sonata is being played at the SMI, my Viola Sonata in Brussels, and the one for two violins in Rome in March. The competition for the Prix Verley took place last night at the Salle Gaveau. The *Pastorale* I wrote last summer was a huge success. I won the prize with 374 votes out of a total of 700.[57]

Honegger's only failure in all this was not getting the Ballets suédois interested in *Horace victorieux*. Since it remains one of his toughest works, this is no more surprising than the popular acclaim for the *Pastorale d'été*. Parisians, caught up as we have seen in a city of increasing noise and activity, liked to be reassured that the peace of the French countryside remained undefiled, especially by means of a short work for strings and five solo wind instruments, with decidedly modal inclinations and the good grace to stretch the opening pedal E over the first 33 bars. One knew where one was. It is indeed a charming work, but reconciling it in any way with the harshnesses of *Horace victorieux* is not easy.

Honegger and train

The problem (if problem it is) was posed yet again by the oratorio *Le roi David*. As Halbreich says, it 'is remarkably close to the oratorios of the eighteenth century in its musical constituents'; he also claims that the replacement of recitatives with spoken dialogue, by speeding up the action, 'enabled the genre to find new life as a musical form, and to keep pace with the psychological tempo of our century'.[58] Where *Pastorale d'été* presented a conventional vision of country life, *Le roi David* makes moves, through the dialogue and through occasional dissonance, towards bringing

the conventional oratorio into the modern world; at the same time, the unequivocal D major of the Alleluia and of the final chorale seemed to some, notably Milhaud and Poulenc, a cheap solution – the latter described the whole work as 'a bad Prix de Rome cantata, it's falsely grandiose, it's idiotic'.[59] Yet audiences in Paris, who had heard the work piecemeal for some three years before its first complete performance in the city on 14 March 1924, loved it, and Honegger was even nick-named 'Le roi Arthur'. Again, as Milhaud noted, 'people know where they are and call the work sublime'.[60]

The challenge, then, still lay before Honegger of writing a popular work that would make no concessions to accepted ideas: of the pastoral, the religious, or any other ready-made musical subject. He met it head-on with the first of his three *Mou-vements symphoniques*, entitled *Pacific 231*. Of course trains in 1923 were not exactly new: already in 1884 the French were making 211 million railway journeys,[61] and six years later Zola had personalized the locomotive 'La Lison' in *La bête humaine*. But the challenge of representing a locomotive in music had yet to be met, and there was therefore no conventional wisdom about how it should be done.

But was this in fact Honegger's aim? His various pronouncements, after Kousse-vitzky had given *Pacific* its first performance at the Opéra on 8 May 1924, speak of some confusion in his mind. On the one hand, 'I have always been passionately fond of locomotives. For me they are living beings and I love them as others love women or horses'; and he described the scenario of *Pacific* in Zolaesque terms as 'the tranquil breathing of the machine in repose, the effort of getting up steam, then the gradual picking up of speed, culminating in the lyrical, engrossing vision of a train weighing 300 tons hurtling through the night at 75 miles an hour.' On the other hand he insisted, despite his use of words such as 'lyrique' and 'pathétique', that the work was a 'musical construction...based on objective contemplation', and that

> in *Pacific* I was after an extremely abstract and wholly ideal notion: that of
> giving the impression of a mathematical acceleration of rhythm while the
> speed itself decreased. From the musical point of view, I composed a kind
> of large chorale variation, shot through in the first part with *alla breve*
> counterpoint and conjuring up the style of Johann Sebastian Bach.[62]

Honegger was understandably annoyed by those critics who wrote of *Pacific* as though it were merely a collage of train noises, and this may have been one reason prompting him to take a more constructivist stance. But there could be another reason. When starting *Le roi David* early in 1921, Honegger had asked Stravinsky for advice about the scoring. Now, *Pacific* received its first performance only four months after the publication of Stravinsky's article about his Octet, in which he consigned narrative and descriptive music to outer darkness. Honegger's appeal to J. S. Bach suggests that he was well aware of the critical currents of the time, as he was, in Marcel Delannoy's estimation, of the popular ones:

Like *Le roi David*, *Pacific* was lucky enough to arrive at an opportune moment. In 1924 people still believed in Happiness through Technology.... But today [1953], even if nuclear physics offers composers new themes, they are not themes of confidence and joy such as Honegger employed in 1924![63]

During the remainder of the Twenties, Honegger continued to mix the consonant with the dissonant and the descriptive with the abstract. He met the rest of Les Six on their own ground with delightful, wholly tonal works like the Concertino for piano and orchestra of 1924, and in 1928 composed a second *Movement Symphonique* called *Rugby*, in which the underlying D major tonality is only gradually arrived at through passages of uncompromising dissonance. The pattern of apparent anarchy resting on a basis of rules is obviously appropriate. The resulting tension is an important feature of this, one of Honegger's most energetic and stirring orchestral works. But the composer's schizophrenia had not abated:

It would be wrong to consider my piece as programme music. It simply tries to describe in musical language the game's attacks and counterattacks, and the rhythm and colour of a match at the Stade de Colombes.[64]

But is that not tantamount to a programme, even if of the most general kind? Halbreich even posits a final score, the first theme winning by 4–3 over the second!

In both *Pacific* and *Rugby*, Honegger turned his back on myth and evocations of rustic bliss to create his own kind of 'lifestyle modernism'. That he could find something 'lyrical' in *Pacific* suggests that here we need a new definition of the term. In both pieces the machinery bears the affective message. 'Locomotives vibrate with harmonies, they sing,' he wrote after a journey on the footplate from King's Cross to Hitchin in 1927; 'it's a symbol of the mammoth struggle of mankind, who is ever battling against forces greater than himself and triumphing over them.'[65]

But there were those who regarded both these orchestral pieces as the end of a rather short road. Honegger chose *Rugby* as his contribution to the tenth anniversary celebrations of Les Six at the end of 1929, rather than *Pastorale d'été* or *Pacific* or the Piano Concertino. Three years later Paul Collaer, enthused by a performance of the *Symphony of Psalms*, wrote:

As for 'utility', 'fashion' or 'dating' in this music, works like this stand far above such nonsense! Adaptation to the times, musical Darwinism, we can leave all that to *Pacific* and *Rugby*.[66]

It should however be mentioned that *Rugby* both celebrates and surpasses the time in which it was written. French rugby expanded hugely after the First World War, and by 1930 there were no fewer than 800 clubs. Honegger wrote *Rugby* in August and September 1928, a year after France's first victory over England, so perhaps pride in his adopted country was also a motive. But his remarks about the game's rhythm and colour need to be read in the context of a less poetical reality: that French rugby of the time, powered (like much French operatic singing) from the south-west, was extremely rough, with men not infrequently killed; and that in the early 1930s France was expelled from the Five Nations Championship for this reason. Honegger's symphonic movement therefore inescapably includes violence among its ingredients.

The single work of the Twenties into which Honegger put the most of himself - and his personal favourite – was the musical tragedy *Antigone*, with a libretto by Cocteau based on Sophocles. But, as Halbreich says,

> the absence of easily recognizable melodic outlines, closed forms,
> repetitions, cadence points, or tonal moments where one can catch
> one's breath, together with the abjuration of lyricism and a wild speed
> of utterance that leads to an exceptional density of information – all
> these elements make *Antigone* the most arduous and least accessible
> of Honegger's works.

Halbreich goes on to call the work 'the ultimate supernova of opera' because its 45-minute duration 'contains enough musical material for three hours'.[67] Whether this constitutes good theatre is a question few can answer since opera houses have in general fought shy of it since its premiere at La Monnaie on 28 December 1927. Nor has it ever been recorded on CD, while the one LP made of it gives little idea of anything other than its grittiness. The reading panel of the Opéra-Comique, to which Honegger submitted the work in March 1927, rejected it in horror, preferring Samuel-Rousseau's *Le bon roi Dagobert* and, less timidly, Milhaud's *Le pauvre matelot*.

The one aspect of *Antigone* which Honegger himself drew attention to is the declamation of Cocteau's text. *Pelléas*, in his view, had been a dangerous model for French opera, and he set his face against the 'imperturbable syllabics by which the sub-Debussystes had effectively dragged opera down to its death'. The cliché that you could never understand the words in opera was the fault, not of singers, but of composers:

> I was determined at all costs to get away from this lazy prosody. I
> therefore tried to find the right stress, especially on initial consonants....
> The important thing in the word is not the vowel but the consonant. This
> plays the role of a locomotive, dragging the complete word behind it....
> My personal rule is to respect the shape of the word so as to give it its full
> power. To take an example from *Antigone*: at one juncture Creon violently
> interrupts the chorus with the words 'Assez de sottises, vieillesse!'

(Enough nonsense, you geriatrics!).... In conformity with the dramatic situation and Creon's fury, I set these words 'Assez de <u>sottises</u>, <u>vieillesse!</u>'[68]

By the end of the decade, Honegger's popularity had begun to wane. *Antigone* had not been heard in Paris, while the First Symphony and the oratorio *Cris du monde*, Honegger's first major offerings of the 1930s, were received in the capital with coldness and outright hostility respectively. In *Cris du monde* Honegger played the prophet, warning of the dangers of pollution both material and spiritual, and the work found no echoes in the hearts of 'the frivolous Parisians, already unconsciously making the bed they would have to lie on in 1940'.[69]

Honegger was to work his way back into popular affection by the end of the 1930s, notably with his oratorio *Jeanne d'Arc*, but his gradual fall from grace after around 1926 says something about the confusion in the minds of Paris audiences about what they wanted from contemporary music: clearly no ugly truths about the real world, although violence and power remained as potent attractions as they had been in *Le sacre du printemps*. In particular, there was a question mark over their commitment to the kind of renewal and experimentation in musical language which composers like Honegger and Milhaud felt to be necessary and inevitable. Here the ostinato, omnipresent in both *Pacific* and *Rugby*, acted both as a lifeline through the waves of dissonance and as a symbol of undeviating strength and violence, while listeners no doubt differed in their ability to hear the lyricism or the colour which Honegger himself felt he had put into these pieces.

Neither did there seem to be any way round the fact that, for all the pseudo-intellectualizing found in the musical press, Parisian audiences in general continued to hear music through the mediation of pictures and literature. If Honegger chose not to give a 'programmatic' title to his third *Mouvement symphonique*, he should know what to expect; and when you did provide a title, there would almost inevitably be one critic at least who, like Pierre Lalo after the premiere of Debussy's *La mer* in 1905, would think he had concluded the argument once and for all by stating that he 'does not hear, does not see, does not smell the sea'.[70]

It is possible, finally, to argue that Honegger compounded his problems simply by showing every now and then that he could write in a wholly accessible, traditional vein, as in his operetta *Les aventures du roi Pausole* which ran for some four hundred performances from the end of 1930. The complaint is familiar from responses to Picasso: if he can draw so well, why put both eyes on the same side?

Darius Milhaud (1892–1974)

At the end of December 1916, Paul Claudel was appointed French Minister in Brazil, and as his secretary he took with him the 24-year-old Milhaud. By that time Milhaud had had his first two string quartets performed in Paris as well as several sets of songs, and in May 1914 Robert Schmitz had conducted his *Première suite symphonique*, but Milhaud had as yet made no very great impact on a musical scene still dominated by Debussy and Ravel.

The two years that he was away from France were those in which a new music in the capital was born. His cousin Madeleine, who was to become his wife in 1925, remembers that on his return to Paris in January 1919 he too 'had changed, and he also gave me the impression that he was not adapted to the youthful excitement of that postwar period, that he was not at ease with it'.[71] But then, as Milhaud himself admitted, even before going to Brazil

> I was a rather serious young man and I was a little disturbed by the
> publication of the *Préludes* by Debussy in which there are several pieces
> like 'Minstrels', like 'General Lavine, excentric', 'Mr Pickwick Esq.', which
> shocked me a little bit because I didn't understand why he gave this sort
> of consecration to the atmosphere of the music-hall.[72]

In the revised 1973 edition of his autobiography, Milhaud plays down this feeling of being out of joint with the times, merely remarking that the artistic life of 1919 Paris was vigorous enough to drag him away from his memories of Brazil.[73] In fact, each culture had a contribution to make to the mix that was Milhaud.

The Brazilian influence can readily be heard in the rhythms, both boisterous and languorous, of the ballet *Le boeuf sur le toit* and of the delightful *Saudades do Brazil* for piano. It reaches more profoundly into the sonorous essence of *L'homme et son désir* (see p. 154), which was itself an amalgam of two influences: the atmosphere of the Brazilian forest, and the dancing of Nijinsky, who came to Rio with the Ballets russes in August 1917. From all that we know of Nijinsky's dancing, it is hardly surprising that both Milhaud and Claudel were transported with the idea of Nijinsky as forest animal. Unfortunately the dancer's mental illness prevented any collaboration, but *L'homme et son désir* carries still the imprint of his magic presence, and positive reactions to the ballet have always tended towards the poetical, as in Paul Collaer's description of the music as 'a vast, mysterious shimmer, like the continuous twinkling of starlight, combined with sounds that rise upward from the earth toward the enormous dome of the firmament'.[74]

This numinous side of the Brazilian influence, and especially the evocative use of percussion, accords with a side of Milhaud already found in *Les choéphores*, completed before he left for Brazil although not premiered until June 1919. The other aspect of this influence, the snappily rhythmical, coloured-postcard side, was one to which, if we believe his future wife, he turned less out of inner necessity than out of curiosity to see what he could make of it in a Paris now demanding music that was 'robust, clearer and more precise, while remaining human and sensitive'.[75]

Between these two poles, which could roughly be categorized as the 'otherworldly' and the 'worldly', Milhaud swung to and fro throughout the Twenties, but in doing so he would not infrequently bring to one pole elements from the other, like

Honegger in *Pacific 231*. Outright high spirits are to be found in *Le boeuf sur le toit*, Milhaud's two contributions to *Les mariés de la tour Eiffel*, the *Trois rag-caprices*, *Salade* and *Le train bleu*, and profound seriousness in *L'homme et son désir* and the operas *Le pauvre matelot* and *Christophe Colomb* (not forgetting the polytonally complex Fifth String Quartet). Among the works of mixed complexion, pride of place must go to his two settings of a catalogue and an imitation catalogue, *Machines agricoles* (composed 1919, first performed 1920) and *Catalogue de fleurs* (composed 1920, first performed in voice/piano version 1922), the twelve *Saudades do Brazil* (composed and first performed 1920), and above all the ballet *La création du monde* (composed and premiered 1923), arguably his finest masterpiece.

Shortly before the war Milhaud had been to an exhibition of agricultural machinery:

> He thought they were beautiful – sort of insects – and he brought back
> all the catalogues and put them in a drawer. And then, a few years later,
> he took them out and he realized that they were written in a very
> charming way, like little prose poems, and he decided to write songs
> on those words. But they were not at all satirical or anything of that
> type: they were like *pastorales*.[76]

One is tempted to say 'paradoxical pastorales', because part of the joy of these pieces lies in the deliberate mismatch between the generally dense textures (even though the instrumental ensemble contains only seven instruments: flute, clarinet, bassoon, violin, viola, cello and double bass) and a gentle, regular pulse, especially in the triplets of the fourth song. Possibly Milhaud enjoyed the ironies of employing these amiable triplets to describe a machine imposingly named 'la déchaumeuse–semeuse–enfouisseuse' (the plower–sower–burier) and then dedicating the result to the most 'imposing' of his colleagues in Les Six, Arthur Honegger…. But, as Madeleine Milhaud says, there is no hint of satire in the music, Milhaud seeing through the imposing name to the object itself; not that this prevented critics from citing it as proof of his 'accentuated taste for leg-pulling and eccentricity'.[77]

If agricultural machinery implied dense textures, flowers called for that 'dépouillement' which has often been commented on as a prime characteristic of the music of Les Six. Again, in Milhaud's settings of Lucien Daudet's poems, inspired by a seedsman's catalogue, satire is wholly absent, unless we read it into his use of a fugal texture for 'Les crocus' which, we are told, 'are forced in clumps' and 'make a very fine effect'. The emphasis throughout is on line, and even the final chords of the cycle, with rising fifths disappearing into an infinity of anticipated pleasure ('prices can be had by post'), are a verticalization of the many intervals of the fifth previously heard in both voice and accompaniment. Here the deliberate restraint and the uniform movement of the seven songs finally blossom into something as near ecstasy as the no-head-in-hands policy would allow. It is one of those endings that alters our memory of the score, prompting us to reinterpret in retrospect what may initially have seemed like cool detachment as that 'emotion without epilepsy' which Debussy felt to be a feature of truly French music.

This emphasis on linear writing in Milhaud's music dates from around 1917. Before then, as Jeremy Drake observes with reference to *Les choéphores* (1915) and to a large extent to *Les euménides* (1917–22),

> for once melody is almost entirely subordinated to harmony, which is
> also the decisive element for the organisation of form. We find here, as
> in *Agamemnon*, the structural employment of a pre-ordained succession
> of multiple chords, organised in the form of strophe and antistrophe.[78]

Together with a new primacy of melody went a move in around 1922 from polytonality to bitonality. Clearly Milhaud had in *Les euménides* to match the dense, hieratic style of its predecessors in the Aeschylus trilogy but, once he had reached the *ne plus ultra* of polytonal writing in the Fifth String Quartet of 1920, he opted in general for lighter, clearer textures until he again embraced a heroic subject in *Christophe Colomb* in 1928. As for Milhaud's intellectual defence of bitonality with reference to a canon by J. S. Bach,[79] critical opinions have differed over its persuasiveness, and it is hard not to have some sympathy with Norman Demuth when he claims that this example 'does not go far enough, since Bach deliberately avoids the danger points. The twentieth century, however, cultivates those snags which Bach by-passed and turns what in Bach would have been a vice into a virtue.'[80]

The mixed complexion of the twelve *Saudades* for piano, written in Copenhagen and Aix and orchestrated by Milhaud in 1920–21 for a Loie Fuller dance evening, derives in part from the tug between the repetitive simplicity of the ostinato rhythms and the feeling of mild danger engendered by the relative complexity of the bitonal 'snags' between tune and accompaniment. The phrase lengths also tend to be of 4 bars with the occasional shortening to 3 or 2; but, most importantly, the thrust to the cadence is always audible so that even where we feel the 'pain' of the bitonality, we know it will soon be over. We may also note how close the rhythms of these *Saudades* come to the 'Habanera' from *Carmen*, reinforcing the point that the exotic, in the hands of a good composer, is not necessarily a cue for critical disdain.

The mixed complexion of the *Saudades* is hard to analyse and is perhaps easiest to hear if compared with the more consistent extraversion of *Le boeuf sur le toit*, inspired by the antics of Charlie Chaplin and showing, according to Milhaud's close friend Paul Collaer, 'the same kind of frenzy that goes nowhere'.[81] Technically this is untrue, since the rondo theme in its fifteen hearings goes through all twelve major keys before ending back in C major where it began. But emotionally Collaer is surely right: *Le boeuf* is no more than a diversion, a 'passe-temps'; whereas many of the *Saudades*, in briefly and economically creating their own small emotional worlds, are curiously moving.

The ambivalence of Milhaud's ballet *La création du monde* can be measured to some extent by the reactions of the critics who, in Milhaud's words quoted earlier, 'decreed that my music was not serious and was more suitable for dance-halls and restaurants than for a theatre. Ten years later, the same critics were writing about the philosophy of jazz and producing learned proofs that *La création* was my best work.'[82] It is worth mentioning too that at least one of those critics in 1923 was careful to prepare the ground for demolition of the score by stating that writing it 'took Milhaud more than a week, including a day's rest'.[83]

In 1922 Milhaud had gone to the USA and had been taken by the singer Yvonne George to hear 'real' jazz in Harlem. On his return to Paris he joined forces with Blaise Cendrars to write a work for the Ballets suédois based on African folklore, and his widow remembers the two of them and the designer Fernand Léger 'wearing raincoats with their collars up like gangsters and with their hats on the sides of their heads, going to those little halls where the Martiniquais are, near the Bastille – dangerous little places'.[84] The impact on Milhaud of black music is clear from his much-reprinted article 'L'évolution du jazz-band et la musique des nègres d'Amérique du Nord'.[85] Although his jazz experiences in Paris at the hands of Jean Wiéner and the saxophonist Vance Lowry, and in London and New York with Billy Arnold and Paul Whiteman, had played their part, in the final paragraph of his article he comes close to Debussy once again in effectively warning against the undue civilizing of this primitive music:

> With the blacks, we escape the purely 'fashionable' musical character
> which we find too unrelievedly in American jazz. With them, the dance
> retains a character that is African and savage; the insistence and intensity
> of the rhythms and tunes turn it into something tragic and desperate....
> This music is far from the elegant Broadway dances we hear at Claridges

in Paris! In it we touch the very source of this music, the profoundly
human aspect it is capable of possessing and which overwhelms you
as completely as any other universally recognized musical masterpiece
you care to mention!

Although the orchestration of black music intrigued Milhaud, its rhythm was for
him the single most important element. Even after he had outgrown jazz in the late
1920s, he could still in 1934 advocate playing it as an excellent means of inculcating
a rhythmic sense where this was lacking.[86] But it is clear that the ostinato background
of jazz never held for him any dehumanized, machinist connotations: in the first
paragraph of his article he refers to this regularity as being 'as vital as the circulation
of the blood, as the beating of the heart or the pulse'. It is this ineluctable humanity,
this understated but engulfing pity for mankind, born possibly of a Jew's 'sympathy
for another persecuted race',[87] which absorbs all the syncopated acrobatics and
makes of *La création du monde* one of the most important and enduring works of
the decade. As Poulenc said thirty years later, it is an example of 'beauty without
wrinkles, without period mannerisms'.[88]

Francis Poulenc (1899–1963)

When Poulenc's *Rapsodie nègre* was given its first performance at the Théâtre du Vieux-
Colombier on 11 December 1917, it was the first piece of his that Paris audiences
had heard. Although he wrote it in the spring of that year – that is, before the premiere of *Parade* in May – those hearing it would undoubtedly have done so to some
extent in the light of the Satie ballet; and indeed of Satie's humorous piano pieces, as
did Paul Vidal on the famous occasion when Poulenc took the score of the *Rapsodie* to
him and was thrown out on his ear.[89]

In the kind letter Satie sent Poulenc after this débâcle,[90] he warned him of the
dangers of 'mixing schools', a process that was bound to lead to an explosion. The
warning was all the more weighty because this scholastic mixture was exactly what
Satie himself had been practising for years, though with a more experienced hand.
Interestingly, Poulenc was to follow Satie's path quite closely: where Satie had grown
up with *café-concert*, cabaret and music hall before going to d'Indy for technical
instruction, so Poulenc imbibed the music of Christiné, Scotto and the style of
Chevalier, before taking lessons with Koechlin between 1921 and 1925.

But in 1917 Poulenc had what, in retrospect, looks like the advantages of being
untrained by any teacher of prewar tendencies (such as Vidal) and of having no
baggage of prewar compositions to live down; in which respect he was alone among
Les Six. He was therefore well placed to write that new postwar music, of which
Roussel had written in 1916 that it would be based on 'a new conception of life'.

The exotic played a very small part in Poulenc's make-up. At fifteen he wrote a *Pro-
cessional pour la crémation d'un mandarin*, which he destroyed; the *Rapsodie nègre* purported

to draw on an exotic source but is in fact constructed on combinations of modal scales and relentless ostinatos; and his 1918 'hispano-italian' setting of Cocteau's *chanson* 'Toréador' is, by his own admission, an example of that mixing of schools which Satie warned him against, and in which he obeyed Cocteau's instruction to write it well so that it sounded cheap ('il faut la faire *bien* mais *moche*').[91] His first and almost only serious use of the exotic was to come in 1932 with the gamelan sonorities of the Concerto for two pianos, inspired by those he heard at the Paris Colonial Exhibition the previous year.

Instead, Poulenc searched for a new style mostly within the confines of what he saw as being truly French, that is, Parisian. This could be resumed under three parallel headings: popular culture, as outlined above, Chabrier, and Satie – to which we have to add the foreign influence of Stravinsky. It is not always easy to separate the tangled threads of these four sources but, to generalize grossly, where the popular influence is felt mostly in Poulenc's tunes, Chabrier's is felt in the overall *allure* and atmosphere, Stravinsky's in the clear. spiky textures, and Satie's in the fruitful use of ostinato and blocks of material. This last influence, which the reader can perhaps

find most readily in the *Trois mouvements perpétuels* of 1918, persisted throughout Poulenc's life. To put the matter negatively, he rarely found his feet in development sections and wisely tended to avoid them - maybe this was one reason why he could never love the music of Fauré, who excelled in this area.

Analysing pieces like the *Mouvements perpétuels* is a thankless task, since the music gives the impression that 'anyone could have written this'. But they didn't. Once one has noted Poulenc's determination to tread on anything that might smack of development, one is left with the memorable tunes, the perfect keyboard spacing of the textures, the *ronron* of the ostinatos and, most curious of all, the little tag that often does duty for a final cadence – what Keith Daniel calls 'a flippant tail'[92] – which was to be a characteristic of his music up to *Le bal masqué* of 1932 and occasionally beyond. The emotive force of these tags is hard to analyse, too. Are they Poulenc's way of disclaiming Wagnerian, or Fauréan, seriousness? Or do they say, 'I didn't mean quite what you may have thought'? Perhaps the best way of understanding them is to replace them with a conventional cadence and judge what is lost – always something, but never the same thing.

Despite Satie's warning about the danger of 'mixing schools', much of Poulenc's best music of the 1920s is of mixed complexion. Cocteau wrote in *Le coq et l'arlequin* about 'the music-hall, the circus, American Negro bands, all that stimulates an artist in the same way that life does...[but] these spectacles are not art. They excite like machines, animals, landscapes, danger.'[93] In other words, the composer has to supply the 'artifying' process. In Poulenc's case, this generally involved little alteration to rhythm (never the field of his greatest invention), some to melody and more to harmony. And in this, credit must be given, as Poulenc always did, to the teaching of Koechlin.

From the detailed account of their lessons given by Robert Orledge,[94] we learn that Koechlin was quick to recognize his pupil's individuality and to encourage it, with a minimum of pedantic restraints. 'Technique', he wrote, 'opens the doors to the imagination.' Koechlin was, like all the best teachers, adept at understanding what Poulenc was trying to do and then helping him achieve it; and it is instructive that, when Poulenc in 1929 looked back over their lessons, he should recall 'the *too much movement* or the *not enough*' with which Koechlin sought to remedy his rhythmic deficiencies. But the harsh sevenths and ninths of Poulenc's harmony were either allowed to stand or were redistributed in more telling fashion.

The effectiveness of Koechlin's teaching can be judged by Poulenc's successful mixing of elements in *Les biches*, in which Koechlin praised the '"melodic vein", relaxed, natural' and the 'charming harmonies', almost as if he had been programmed by Jean Cocteau! But there are the odd darker moments in the score (not entirely surprising in a work that is effectively about emptiness), as well as varying bar-lengths which are not to be found in Chevalier's songs. Did these rhythmic dislocations come perhaps from Stravinsky? Poulenc made no secret of his idolization of the

Russian composer's postwar manner, and this seems to have been one of the few bones of contention between him and Koechlin. Sauguet, in telling Poulenc how he had not been as impressed by the first performance of Stravinsky's Octet as he had expected, explained: 'it is true that I was sitting next to Koechlin, which moderated and reduced my admiration.'[95] As Orledge points out, Stravinsky's well-known description of the Octet as 'a musical composition based on objective elements which are sufficient in themselves' found no favour with a composer whose approach was 'subjective and essentially Romantic'.[96] Where Poulenc stood on this question is anybody's guess. He was a far stronger writer of melodies than Stravinsky, and this strength would always tend to carry his works through without his needing to concoct elaborate aesthetic programmes. Certainly, in the occasional work where his melodic gifts are either set aside or simply fail (the piano *Promenades* of 1921 or the cantata *Sécheresses*), nothing is able to compensate for their absence.

Les biches made Poulenc's reputation, but arguably he reached equal heights of imagination and control in the Trio of 1926 for piano, oboe and bassoon. After a call to attention on the piano in which we can detect the acidic harmonies of his chorale exercises for Koechlin, the tunes flow in extraordinary abundance. Sequential writing straight out of the French operettas of Christiné and Scotto alternates with pseudo-eighteenth-century classicism, complete with 'wrong' notes and Stravinskyan asymmetrical phrases. And yet the whole thing is an entity. Not only that, but it is unmistakably 'emotional' in the sense in which the word has been understood for the last hundred years – this in spite of Stravinsky giving Poulenc advice that turned the first movement into 'tout autre chose'.[97] In the central slow movement, a disposition towards spirituality is barely disguised beneath its frivolous surface: one brief woodwind phrase was to return thirty years later in the *Gloria*, set to the words 'pater omnipotens', while the piano at one point decorates the texture with a brief snatch of Messiaen's second mode of limited transposition. The 'naughty' style of the earlier chamber sonatas is now absorbed into a less self-conscious act, no longer taunting 'see what I can do with just a couple of clarinets', but exploring new emotional territory.

During the last three years of the decade, following the composition of the Trio, Poulenc was not hugely productive. Some of his time, it is true, was taken up with the house he had bought in the Touraine, and some with works like the *Marches militaires* which would never see the light of day, but there are glimpses in his correspondence of the depressions that would increasingly haunt him in middle age. 'January is such a bad month,' he wrote to a friend in November 1928, asking him to come and stay; and in the summer of 1930, after the death of his great friend Raymonde Linossier, 'In my life I have known pleasure but never, alas, happiness. I no longer expect it.'[98]

Whether or not as the result of a growing sense of his responsibility to the Muse – and certainly for the moment he turned his back utterly on Satiean jokes – the two major works he wrote in the years 1927–29 were 'two indispensable steps in my evolution'.[99] The American scholar Keith Daniel gives them a slightly different slant, calling them 'two of Poulenc's most difficult, unusual works; each is unique in his oeuvre'.[100]

In June 1923 Poulenc had been present at the princesse de Polignac's when Falla's *El retablo de maese Pedro* was given with an orchestra conducted by Vladimir Golschmann and with Wanda Landowska playing the harpsichord. Poulenc immediately promised (or was commanded – the story varies) to write a concerto for her, but did not finish it until 1928. Some of that time was spent absorbing the technical possibilities of an instrument he had never used before, and some of it with Landowska, '[clarifying] the writing, either by simplifying chords or by deleting notes'.[101] But as Daniel says, the *Concert champêtre* is a difficult and unusual work from the aesthetic point of view. Can Landowska really have been in earnest when she wrote to the composer: 'Do you know why I adore it? Because it makes me totally <u>carefree and happy</u>!' (her underlining).[102]

The critic Paul Bertrand felt that the work 'wraps itself in an autumnal chill' ('un frisson automnal') which he went on to qualify with two paradoxical epithets 'ardent et apaisé' – 'passionate and appeased'[103] – and reluctant though one may be to challenge an artist of Landowska's standing, it is hard to square her judgment with Poulenc's music, where abrupt changes, hysterical accelerandos and moments of heartrending pathos interrupt and darken the carefree happiness of the tunes themselves. In the words of Wilfrid Mellers, 'the final antiphony [of the first movement] between soloist and orchestra...is unexpectedly grim'; in the slow movement 'the coda is at once romantically emotive and classically heroic. Nor does the finale dispel ambiguity.' Mellers speaks of the work's 'mingle of merriment and melancholy' and, though he finds himself 'invigorated' by this, others may well remain 'bewildered',[104] as the energy of the finale, initially doffing its cap to Handel's 'Harmonious Blacksmith', evaporates in a cheerless, dispirited D minor. Just as the ironic 'tails' elsewhere question what has gone before, so this conclusion seems to ask of the preceding high jinks, 'is this truly our life?'

The second of these two key works, the *Aubade* written for the vicomte and vicomtesse de Noailles to be performed at their Paris home on 18 June 1929, is 'a ballet about women, about feminine solitude'.[105] When Balanchine and Lifar later took it upon themselves to change the story, Poulenc defended his own view:

> At a period of my life when I was feeling very sad, I found that dawn was the time when my anguish reached its height, for it meant that one had to live through another horrible day. I wanted to give a detached rendering of this impression, so I chose Diana as my symbolic heroine.[106]

In a recent article, Denis Waleckx has put forward an illuminating proposition:

> As early as 1924 and 1929, with *Les biches* and *Aubade* respectively, Poulenc was already composing ballets for women, just as very much

later *Dialogues des carmélites* was essentially an opera for women. A further dimension was the theme of sexual ambiguity, already hinted at in *Les biches* and later omnipresent in *Les mamelles de Tirésias* in which the male and female leads reverse their roles. It is perhaps worth considering that the composer, by systematically identifying with his female characters, may have been exploring his own share of femininity.[107]

It may also be that Poulenc, through this exploration of the feminine and through his acceptance of his melancholy, depressive side, was providing a fuller and more honest musical portrait of Paris in the postwar years than that usually associated with *les années folles*. If the 'up' side of this society has understandably been given more prominence, we should not forget that, as in the 'naughty Nineties', those who were not carried along by the swell could find themselves adrift in it and drowning. For artistic spirits, peace could be every bit as hard as war. There were suicides, including Jean Börlin, Yvonne George and Bizet's son René, and drink and drugs were rife, with Satie prey to the former and Cocteau and Auric to the latter. On the other hand, all the composers considered in this chapter so far produced music that spoke of control, and in this sense Poulenc was an exception.

What I have called the 'mixed complexion' of his best works (and *Aubade* is certainly one) consists not only of a blend of the popular and the academic, but also of the frivolous and the despairing, and of the masculine and the feminine principles, the 'animus' and 'anima' identified by Jung. We can hear these last two contrasted in the slow movements of both the *Concert champêtre* and the Concerto for two pianos at the points where Poulenc's spare, goal-orientated, Neoclassical style suddenly softens into something richer and stranger.

It is also worth mentioning that in writing *Aubade* for the Noailles, Poulenc had an absolutely free hand as to orchestral forces and genre, as well as knowing that no artistic compromise was expected by such enlightened and intelligent patrons. His declared intention was 'to touch them'[108] rather than to entertain by wit or impress by virtuosity. It seems that in order to do this he was now moved to delve more deeply than ever before into his own psyche, producing a work that disorientates the listener through its ambiguous tone, and the feeling that at any moment naked terror may expose itself.

Finally it is indisputable that, of all the composers of Les Six, Poulenc was the one who developed most surprisingly throughout his life. For years this growth was disregarded by those who preferred to hear only his lighter side. Norman Demuth spoke for many when he wrote in 1952 that

> Poulenc has proved himself the essence of elegance and polish in a number of works which are rather higher than salon music, but approach it very nearly – and in this regard they have their value – and he may be said to illustrate one aspect of the French *goût* in its purest form.[109]

Since *Aubade* was very little played after the Second World War and *Dialogues des carmélites* was still to come, Demuth may readily be forgiven. But in 1954 Poulenc, then at work on the opera, could say of the depression he was currently suffering, 'No doubt this climate of anguish is necessary for my ladies.'[110] *Aubade* was the harbinger of this climate, and a crucial demonstration of how Cocteau's tenets of lightness, clarity and tunefulness could be harnessed to the portrayal of deep and disturbing emotions. With it Poulenc, and perhaps also the French music of the Twenties, came of age.

Notes

1. Letter of 11 November 1917, in Gabriel Fauré, *Correspondance*, ed. Jean-Michel Nectoux (Paris, 1980), p. 296.
2. Vlado Perlemuter, in conversation with the author.
3. Jean-Michel Nectoux, *Gabriel Fauré: A Musical Life*, trans. Roger Nichols (Cambridge, 1991), p. 435 (article of 20 March 1943).
4. Darius Milhaud, *Etudes* (Paris, 1927), p. 38.
5. *Lettres intimes* ed. Philippe Fauré-Fremiet (Paris, 1951), p. 282.
6. Milhaud, *Etudes*, p. 39.
7. Letter of 11 April 1920, in Vincent d'Indy, Henri Duparc, Albert Roussel, *Lettres à Auguste Sérieyx*, ed. M.-L. Sérieyx (Lausanne, 1961), p. 26.
8. Letter to Guy Ropartz, 20 September 1920, in Andrew Thomson, *Vincent d'Indy and his World* (Oxford, 1996), p. 196n.
9. Ibid., p. 200.
10. Letter of 10 July 1922, in d'Indy, *Lettres à Auguste Sérieyx*, p. 29.
11. Léon Vallas, *V. d'Indy*, II (Paris, 1950), p. 127.
12. Serge Gut and Danièle Pistone, *La musique de chambre en France de 1870 à 1918* (Paris, 1978), p. 110, n. 2.
13. Francis Poulenc, *A bâtons rompus*, ed. Lucie Kayas (Arles, 1999), p. 119.
14. Letter to Ropartz, 20 September 1920. I am grateful to Andrew Thomson for providing this text.
15. *La liberté*, 31 December 1921. I am grateful to Dr Deirdre Donnellon and Professor Robert Orledge for providing this text.
16. Ornella Volta, trans. Michael Bullock, *Satie Seen through his Letters* (London, 1989), pp. 88–89.
17. Ibid., pp. 107, 109.
18. Ornella Volta, *Satie/Cocteau, les malentendus d'une entente* (Paris, 1993), p. 46.
19. Jean Cocteau, *Le coq et l'arlequin* (Paris, 1979), p. 56.
20. *Paris-Journal*, 30 May 1924, 2; quoted in Robert Orledge, *Satie the Composer* (Cambridge, 1990), p. 232.
21. Cocteau, *Le coq*, p. 56.
22. Steven Moore Whiting, *Satie the Bohemian* (Oxford, 1999).
23. Francis Poulenc, 'La musique de piano d'Erik Satie', in *La revue musicale*, 214, June 1952, pp. 24–25.
24. Ibid., 'Chien flasque', p. 154.
25. Letter of Albert Roussel to his wife, 3 January 1916, in Marc Pincherle, *Albert Roussel* (Geneva, 1957), p. 121.
26. Letter of 12 October 1921, in *Albert Roussel. Lettres et écrits*, ed. Nicole Labelle (Paris, 1987), pp. 88–89.
27. Emile Vuillermoz, in *Excelsior*, 6 March 1922; repr. in Labelle (ed.), *Albert Roussel*, p. 304.
28. Letter of 15 March 1922, in ibid., p. 94.
29. See review in *La revue musicale*, April 1922, pp. 71–72; repr. almost complete, in Labelle (ed.), *Albert Roussel*, p. 304.
30. 'Un entretien avec Albert Roussel', *Le guide du concert*, 12 October 1928; repr. in Labelle (ed.), *Albert Roussel*, p. 210.
31. Henri Dutilleux, in conversation with the author.

32. See his article 'Young French Composers', in *The Chesterian*, I/2, October 1919, pp. 33–37. In this article, published three months before the official birth of Les Six, the composers considered are Auric, Durey, Honegger, Roland-Manuel, Milhaud, Poulenc and Tailleferre, with the briefest of mentions for Pierre Menu and Henri Cliquet.

33. José Bruyr, *L'écran des musiciens*, 2nd series (Paris, 1933), p. 128.

34. Arthur Hoérée, *Albert Roussel* (Paris, 1938), p. 111.

35. André Coeuroy and André Schaeffner, *Le jazz* (Paris, 1926), p. 120.

36. Letter of 7 February 1928, in Labelle (ed.), *Albert Roussel*, p. 140.

37. Pierre Boulez, in conversation with the author.

38. Letter to Maurice Emmanuel, 14 October 1922, in *Catalogue de l'Exposition Ravel* (Paris, Bibliothèque nationale, 1975), no. 323.

39. Hélène Jourdan-Morhange, *Ravel et nous* (Geneva, 1945), p. 180

40. Letter to M.-D. Calvocoressi, 24 March 1922, BnF, LA Ravel 99.

41. Igor Stravinsky, *Chroniques de ma vie* (Paris, 1962), p. 95.

42. Stephen Walsh, *The Music of Stravinsky* (Oxford, 1993), p. 123.

43. Ibid., p. 103.

44. In *La revue musicale*, December 1920.

45. Robert Siohan, *Stravinsky* (Paris, 1965), p. 99.

46. Walsh, *Stravinsky*, p. 108.

47. 'Une visite chez Maurice Ravel', in *Maurice Ravel. Lettres, écrits, entretiens*, ed. Arbie Orenstein (Paris, 1989), p. 362. Interview dated March 1931.

48. *The Arts*, January 1924; repr. in Eric Walter White, *Stravinsky: The Composer and his Works* (London, 1966; 2nd edn 1979), pp. 574–77.

49. Messing, *Neoclassicism*, pp. 134–35.

50. Stravinsky, *Chroniques*, p. 133.

51. Ibid., p. 132.

52. Ibid., p. 133.

53. Ibid., p. 146.

54. José Bruyr, *L'écran des musiciens*, 2nd series (Paris, 1933), p. 128.

55. Lawrence Morton, 'Stravinsky and Tchaikovsky: Le Baiser de la Fée', in *Stravinsky: A New Appraisal of his Work* (New York, 1963); quoted in White, *Stravinsky*, p. 351.

56. Manuel Rosenthal, in conversation with the author.

57. Letter of 18 February in Harry Halbreich, *Honegger*, trans. Roger Nichols (Portland, 1999), pp. 73–74.

58. Ibid. p. 398

59. Letter to Paul Collaer, 28 July 1921, in *Paul Collaer, Correspondance avec des amis musiciens*, ed. Robert Wangermée (Liège, 1996), p. 84.

60. Letter to Paul Collaer, 24 October 1921, in ibid., p. 91.

61. Theodore Zeldin, *France 1848–1945*, III, *Intellect and Pride* (Oxford, 1980), p. 99.

62. Statements, all undated, in Halbreich, trans. Nichols, *Honegger*, pp. 350–51.

63. Marcel Delannoy, *Honegger* (Paris, 1953), p. 94.

64. *Chantecler*, 2 April 1927; repr. in Halbreich, trans. Nichols, *Honegger*, p. 111.

65. Undated, in Halbreich, trans. Nichols, *Honegger*, p. 354.

66. Letter to Jean Binet, 15 December 1932, in Collaer, *Correspondance*, p. 322.

67. Halbreich, trans Nichols, *Honegger*, p. 456–57.

68. Arthur Honegger, *Je suis compositeur* (Paris, 1957), pp. 112–13.

69. Halbreich, trans. Nichols, *Honegger*, p. 124.

70. *Le temps*, 16 October 1905.

71. Roger Nichols, *Conversations with Madeleine Milhaud* (London, 1996), p. 16.

72. BBC Archives, LP 24202 (October 1957).

73. Darius Milhaud, *Ma vie heureuse* (Paris, 1973), p. 81.

74. Paul Collaer, *Darius Milhaud*, trans. and ed. Jane Hohfeld Galante (San Francisco, 1988), p. 64.

75. Milhaud, *Ma vie heureuse*, p. 81.

76. Madeleine Milhaud, in conversation with the author.

77. Milhaud, *Ma vie heureuse*, p. 105.

78. *Darius Milhaud. Notes sur la musique*, ed. Jeremy Drake (Paris, 1982) p. 32.

79. Darius Milhaud, 'Polytonalité et atonalité', in *La revue musicale*, 1 February 1923; repr. in Drake (ed.), *Darius Milhaud*, pp. 173–88; Eng. trans. in *Pro Musica Quarterly* (New York), October 1924.

80. Norman Demuth, *Musical Trends in the Twentieth Century* (London, 1952), pp. 75–76.

81. Collaer, *Darius Milhaud*, p. 68.

82. Milhaud, *Ma vie heureuse*, p. 128.

83. *Le courrier musical*, 15 October 1923, unnamed contributor.

84. Nichols, *Conversations with Madeleine Milhaud*, pp. 51–52.

85. Milhaud, *Le courrier musical*, 1 May 1923; repr. in Drake (ed.), *Darius Milhaud*, pp. 99–105; minus the first paragraph, in *Etudes* (Paris, 1927), pp. 51–59; Eng. trans., as *Living Age*, October 1924.

86. Milhaud, *Le jour*, 15 June 1934, quoted in Drake (ed.), *Darius Milhaud*, p. 31, n. 3.

87. Drake (ed.), *Darius Milhaud*.

88. Francis Poulenc, *Entretiens avec Claude Rostand* (Paris, 1954), p. 44.

89. Letter to Ricardo Viñes, 26 September 1917, Francis Poulenc, *Correspondance 1910–1963*, ed. Myriam Chimènes (Paris, 1994), p. 55; Poulenc, *Moi et mes amis* (Paris, 1963), p. 48.

90. Poulenc, *Moi et mes amis*, p. 49.

91. Letter to Poulenc, 15 October 1918, in Chimènes (ed.), *Correspondance*, p. 72.

92. 'Poulenc's choral works with orchestra', in *Francis Poulenc, Music, Art and Literature*, ed. Sidney Buckland and Myriam Chimènes (Aldershot, 1999), p. 61.

93. Jean Cocteau, *Le coq et l'arlequin* (Paris, 1978), p. 63.

94. 'Poulenc and Koechlin: 58 lessons and a friendship', in Buckland and Chimènes (eds), *Francis Poulenc*, pp. 9–47.

95. Letter of 20 November 1923, in Chimènes (ed.), *Correspondance*, p. 214.

96. 'Poulenc and Koechlin', in Buckland and Chimènes (eds), *Poulenc*, p. 36.

97. Letter to Stravinsky, April 1926, in Chimènes (ed.), *Correspondance*, p. 267, n. 1.

98. Letters to Maurice Lecanu, in Chimènes (ed.), *Correspondance*, p. 295; to Alice Ardoin, in ibid., pp. 325–26.

99. Letter to Paul Collaer, 1 October 1932, in ibid., p. 376.

100. Keith Daniel, *Francis Poulenc: His Artistic Development and Musical Style* (Ann Arbor, 1982), p. 97.

101. Lucien Chevaillier, 'Un entretien avec...Francis Poulenc', in *Le guide du concert*, 26 April 1929.

102. Undated letter, quoted in Henri Hell, *Francis Poulenc* (Paris, 1958; 2nd edn 1978), p. 89, n. 1.

103. *Le ménestrel*, 3 May 1929, quoted in Daniel, *Francis Poulenc*, p. 140, and p. 333, n. 9.

104. Wilfrid Mellers, *Francis Poulenc* (Oxford, 1993), pp. 24–25.

105. Poulenc, *Entretiens* (Paris, 1954), p. 81.

106. 'Francis Poulenc on his ballets', *Ballet* 2, no. 4 (September 1946), p. 58 (trans. Keith Daniel).

107. Denis Waleckx, '"A musical confession": Poulenc, Cocteau and *La voix humaine*', in Buckland and Chimènes (eds), *Francis Poulenc*, p. 321.

108. Poulenc, *Entretiens*, p. 141.

109. Demuth, *Musical Trends*, p. 72.

110. Letter to Henri Hell, 14 February 1954, in Chimènes (ed.), *Correspondance*, p. 785; *Francis Poulenc, 'Echo and Source': Selected Correspondence*, trans. and ed. Sidney Buckland (London, 1991), p. 216.

9. Paris, the past and elsewhere

IN THE LATE 1920s Ravel dictated to his friend and pupil Roland-Manuel what was later published as an 'autobiographical sketch'.[1] Some sixty years after that, the American scholar Arbie Orenstein unearthed a previously unpublished addendum to this sketch in which Ravel commented on the title of his piano pieces called *Miroirs*, ending with a quotation from Brutus in Shakespeare's *Julius Caesar*:

> ...the eye sees not itself
> But by reflection, by some other things.
> (Act I Scene 2)[2]

In trying to draw together the Burckhardtian, thematic threads of the previous chapters, I shall, initially at least, opt for a Shakespearian/Ravelian approach, 'seeing' this period of music in Paris not 'by itself' but by two 'reflections': a historical one, from the music of the past; and a geographical one, from the music of other early twentieth-century cultures.

The syllabus of the Conservatoire in the 1920s was still heavily weighted towards the nineteenth century, despite Fauré's reforms. Earlier music was better served, as we have seen, at the Schola Cantorum and the Ecole Niedermeyer, but for many of the Paris music-going public life began with J. S. Bach, went on to Mozart and thence to Beethoven and his successors. In the issue of *Le ménestrel* of 6 February 1920, Pierre Bernard congratulates the conductor Vladimir Golschmann on including six-teenth-, seventeenth- and eighteenth-century works in his concerts, 'a gap that this column has already often deplored in the programming by the major orchestras'. Dominique Sordet notes that Golschmann, who was only twenty-six at the time of this concert, did not always manage to enthuse the older hands under his direction, but that he fought hard for both new and old music. Together with the latest works by Schoenberg, Tansman and Milhaud, he espoused what Sordet calls 'les chefs d'oeuvres les plus aimables, les plus infailliblement charmants, ordonnés et jolis de Mozart, de Mendelssohn et de Schubert'; and, Sordet continues, 'la délicate, la classique *Symphonie en Sol* de Mozart est une des oeuvres dans l'interprétation desquelles il a toujours eu la coquetterie d'obtenir le succès personnel le plus vif, le plus mérité' (his interpretation of Mozart's delicate, classical Symphony in G minor is one of those in which his stylishness has always produced a very marked and well-deserved success)[3] – I have here given a charitable translation of 'coquetterie', but the overtones of its English counterpart cannot have been wholly absent.

Clearly Ravel was in a minority when he enthused to Gaby Casadesus, 'If you look at the Mozart quartets, they are much more interesting than the Beethoven. And the concertos...you have only five concertos by Beethoven, but look how many you have by Mozart!'[4]

This generally patronizing attitude to anything pre-1850 that was not Bach, Beethoven or Berlioz can be found everywhere in the musical press of the 1920s. Henri Expert made pioneering editions of Renaissance choral music and of Rameau, and the harpsichord music of Couperin, Rameau and Scarlatti was well suited to the digital dexterity typical of French pianists – the later recordings of this repertoire by Marcelle Meyer (1897–1958) and Robert Casadesus (1899–1972) are among the high points of French pianism. Other members of the Casadesus family were at the centre of the Société des instruments anciens which operated in parallel with the Société de musique d'autrefois, founded in 1925 by Geneviève Thibault (otherwise the comtesse Hubert de Chambure), with Lionel de la Laurencie, Georges le Cerf and Eugénie Droz; Thibault also collected instruments and published, beginning with an article on Dufay when she was only twenty-two.[5] Meanwhile, at St Leu-la-Forêt the queen of harpsichordists, Wanda Landowska, held court, mixing Bach, Rameau and Scarlatti with Poulenc and Falla.

But all this was appreciated only by an elite. To its 'délicate' Mozart G minor Symphony Le ménestrel later added the 'exquis' D minor Piano Concerto[6] (one hopes for Ravel's sake that he never read this). Nor did Haydn fare any better: the Oxford Symphony, conducted a fortnight earlier by Inghelbrecht at the Concerts Pasdeloup, was found to display an 'allure un peu vieillote'[7] and likewise the quartet op 54 no. 2 was dismissed as 'à vrai dire un peu désuet' ('truth to tell, rather old-hat').[8]

A Société J. S. Bach had been founded in 1904 by Gustave Bret, who had been Widor's assistant at St-Sulpice from 1898 to 1903 and who conducted the society's concerts until 1939. Four 'grands concerts spirituels' given in the Eglise de l'Etoile in November and December 1928 contained three cantatas, the 'Wedge' organ prelude, and the First Brandenburg Concerto, and ended with a performance of the Christmas Oratorio. The remaining music was by Vivaldi, Handel, Pergolesi, Fauré and Franck. It is possible that considerations of style were not uppermost, since the tenor solo in Cantata 65 was sung by José de Trévi, fresh from his success as Don José in the first recording of Carmen.

For those who found Bach rather austere and intimidating, real music began with Beethoven. The complex and fascinating history of Beethoven's music and reputation in France has been traced in detail by Leo Schrade,[9] and no more than the briefest outline can be given here. When the first two symphonies were heard in Paris in 1811, the critic Cambini wrote that 'after penetrating the soul with a sweet melancholy he soon tears it by a mass of barbaric chords. He seems to harbour doves and crocodiles at the same time.'[10] Berlioz developed the natural metaphor by speaking of Beethoven as an eagle, but at the same time as a poetical composer (for him, the highest praise). As the nineteenth century progressed, Beethoven and his music came to embrace a moral dimension: he was the composer of the infinite, his was the genius that was possible only through pain, and the 'Ode to Joy' was 'the Marseillaise of humanity'.[11]

The high point of Beethoven's reputation in France was marked, and to a large extent produced, by Romain Rolland's 1903 biography *La vie de Beethoven* – Henry Prunières called it 'the breviary of a whole generation'. Words such as 'battle', 'energy' and 'will' abound, suggesting perhaps that these qualities were felt to be lacking in contemporary French music. Raymond Bouyer's *Le secret de Beethoven* (1905) developed the theme, treating the composer effectively as a god, 'a magnificent harbour of safety', and in 1906 a complete series of the piano sonatas was performed for the first time in Paris by Edouard Risler. D'Indy, as a good Catholic, naturally refused to endorse the composer-as-god in his *Beethoven* (1911), and emphasized that the *Missa solemnis* is truly Catholic in character.[12] But, in Schrade's words,

> the World War inflicted sudden and complete ruin upon the image of Beethoven in France.... After [it] scholarship and historical research filled the gap opened by the loss of the Beethoven religion. Research is wont to rob myth and legend of their enchantment with such thoroughness as to undo any hallowing of a deity and to reduce to pitiful illusion what has once been a sacred creed. History thus brought Beethoven down to earth and removed his image from its holy shrine.[13]

Such French writing as there was on Beethoven after the war tended to be highly specialized, with the exception of an expanded reprint in 1926 of André de Hevesy's *Petites amies de Beethoven* of 1914. The special Beethoven number of *La revue musicale* (1 April 1927), marking the centenary of the composer's death, included articles on Berlioz as promoter of Beethoven, on the history of the Violin Concerto and on the earliest Beethoven performances on Brussels, and a rather belated review of the 1923 publication of three of the *Conversation Books*. Possibly the most interesting article was by Charles Koechlin, significantly entitled 'Le "Retour à Beethoven"' (referring both to the contemporary and ubiquitous 'Retour à Bach' and to the fact that there had indeed been an 'abandon de Beethoven'). Koechlin makes detailed pleas for intelligence in matters of speed, phrasing and dynamics before coming to the conclusion that 'his works (like Mozart's) are perhaps the hardest to conduct, because one has constantly to divine the thought behind the notes'.[14]

The Beethoven myth survived, however, as an embodiment of the European ideal, and specifically of the League of Nations in which 'all men shall become brothers'. The centenary of the composer's death in 1927 found in Paris something less than wholehearted enthusiasm, though there were naturally a number of celebrations in addition to the regular Sunday concerts, where Beethoven continued to appear. On 22 March (the President of the Republic was otherwise engaged on the 26th, Beethoven's birthday) the Heiligenstadt Testament was read out as part of a concert,

and in June there was 'a second day of Beethovenian glorifica-
tion in the form of a festival of international reconciliation'. But
the fund proposed by the impresario Arthur Dandelot for a
Beethoven monument progressed only slowly: by April 1928, of
the 100,000 francs required only 39,728 had come in, with 12,000 of
that from the state. The target had still not been reached a year later.[15] As
Romain Rolland remarked in 1927, 'Beethoven is no longer the fashion in the musical
circles of Paris';[16] while for some he had never been the fashion. When Manuel
Rosenthal asked Ravel why he was refusing to contribute, Ravel said, 'Let them first
of all put up a monument to Mozart, then we'll see.'[17] The Beethoven monument was
never built and the composer now has to be content with a little rue Beethoven in
the 16th arrondissement, leading on to the very much larger avenue du Président
Kennedy.

The German music written in the thirty years or so after Beethoven's death never
achieved parallel status. Georges Auric remembered d'Indy describing all Schubert's
symphonies as 'incomplètes' (and not just the *Unfinished*) and Schumann's as 'mal con-
struites'.[18] Schubert's piano sonatas were thought to be too long and rambling, and
only a small selection of his songs were heard regularly. Schumann was considered to
be almost solely a piano composer. The Cortot master classes of 1928, mentioned
above, offered smaller pieces like Schumann's *Novelettes*, *Intermezzo* op. 4, *Humoresque*
and *Arabesque*, and Schubert's *Moments musicaux*, *Ländler* and the sixth of the *Soirées de
Vienne* arrangements by Liszt, although in the 1920s Cortot's recordings included

two versions of Schumann's *Carnaval* and one of the *Etudes symphoniques*. Mendelssohn was polite and charming, Brahms deadly dull. But then of course came Wagner....

Wagner's reputation in Paris seems not to have suffered the decline of Beethoven's. As pointed out earlier, Milhaud's famous cry 'A bas Wagner!' was aimed, not at the composer, but at the habit of playing concert extracts. In any case, the French now had other German composers to aim at: Bruckner and his 'adagios where the grass grows between the notes', and Mahler, one of those whose 'elephantine dreams go no further with their heavy artillery than Couperin did with three notes.'[19] As for Richard Strauss,

> nothing is further removed from French art than that of Strauss....
> A Frenchman, for whom the ultimate artistic rule is the subordination
> of the individual elements to the overall picture, the dependence of the
> detail on the directing idea, will never fully appreciate the art of Strauss,
> concerned only to enjoy juxtaposed sensations whose diversity is their
> guarantee of value.[20]

And at this point the past meets the present, the historical view the geographical one. Certainly Paris in the Twenties was well placed to observe itself, Brutus-like, 'by some other things', since these had never been in such abundant supply in the city where, as Stravinsky said, 'at that moment, the pulse of world activity was throbbing.'[21]

Paris has always been selective in her enthusiasms and the field of 1920s music gave Parisians no cause to change the habit. The presence of so many émigrés from Russia and Central Europe might lead us to think that there was a danger of French music being swamped. Maybe the French agreed. Maybe that is why they held on to the traditional notions of Frenchness (such as Coeuroy's above) with such unyielding tenacity, in accordance with the motto on the city's arms, 'Fluctuat nec mergitur' ('It oscillates, but is not submerged'). A comparison can be made with the ordinary Parisian who, while being charming and friendly, will take his time inviting new acquaintances *chez lui*: so Paris likewise was happy for foreigners to play their music in the city (as Ravel said, one tended to learn things that way) so long as the 'domicile' of Frenchness was not invaded.

What follows is a clockwise tour of European visitors, interrupted by a brief excursion to the Americas. One of the higher-profile groups of émigrés in the latter half of the Twenties was that of the so-called Ecole de Paris, consisting of four composers from Central Europe, all of whom were in Paris by 1924: the Pole Alexandre Tansman, the Hungarian Tibor Harsányi, the Rumanian Marcel Mihalovici and the Swiss Conrad Beck. Between them, in the five years from 1924, they wrote five symphonies, three operas, two piano concertos, a ballet, and quantities of songs and chamber music. But, Tansman apart, the group is now forgotten and cannot be said to have had an influence on French music even in the Twenties. Other natives of Central Europe were Georges Enesco, who had additional talents as violinist and conductor to draw on and had in any case studied at the Paris Conservatoire from 1895, and Bohuslav Martinů, who lived in Paris from 1923 to 1940. Martinů's studies with Roussel led him from his early Impressionistic style to one that was sharper and more Classical.

The Greek composer Dimitri Levidis had been in Paris since 1910. His music was performed regularly during the Twenties, and his interest in new sounds was evinced by works like the *Divertissement* for cor anglais, harps, celesta, percussion and strings (1925) and the *Poème symphonique* for ondes Martenot and orchestra (1928). His compatriot Petro Petridis had studied with Roussel and Albert Wolff before the war, but stayed only briefly after it, returning to Athens in 1922. No Italian composers of any note lived in Paris during this period – Rouché's battles over Malipiero's *Sette canzoni* cannot have done much to encourage them. Meanwhile Puccini's operas continued to thrive, *Tosca* reaching its five-hundredth performance at the Opéra-Comique on 16 June 1926.

Manuel de Falla had lived in Paris from 1907 to 1914 and he maintained his links with the city during the Twenties. He was made Chevalier de la Légion d'Honneur in 1928 and in 1934 succeeded Elgar as a foreign member of the Institut, on Dukas's recommendation. Paris heard four of his best works during this decade: *El sombrero de tres picos* (Ballets russes, 23 January 1920), *El amor brujo* (Concerts Colonne, 28 January 1923), *El retablo de maese Pedro* (Polignac salon, 25 June 1923), Harpsichord Concerto (Salle Pleyel, 14 May 1927). The historian René Dumesnil devotes over two pages of unstinting praise to these, an indication of Falla's standing in Parisian eyes, and writes of *El retablo de maese Pedro* that its 'vigour and concision and its perfect accommodation to its subject, without attempts at archaism and by the most modern of means, transport us far away in time and space'.[22] His fellow Spaniard Federico Mompou studied in Paris from 1911 to 1913, and returned to live there between 1921 and 1941. During the Twenties he wrote many of the piano pieces for which he is best known, including *Fêtes lointaines* (1920), Three Variations and *Charmes* (1921), and the first five of his Preludes (1928). His use of repetitive phrases suggests the influence of Satie, although there is no evidence that the two ever met.

Paris was clearly all the happier to accept Falla and works by other Spanish composers because of its own past musical links with Spain, forged by Bizet, Chabrier, Debussy and Ravel. But British music was a different matter, and its nineteenth-century manifestations remained absolutely unknown territory for most French music-lovers, and indeed critics. In the spring of 1924, the Philharmonic String Quartet from London, aided by Auguste Mangeot and John Barbirolli, played Eugene Goossens's Sextet, and the younger English school was also represented in 1927 by a far from eulogistic article on Arthur Bliss, in which French readers must have been further mystified by reference to a London concert venue called 'Wigniore Hale'.[23] Bliss had already given the first performance of his Piano Quintet at the Salle Gaveau in 1920, with Goossens as second violin – a not wholly happy occasion, as Bliss recorded later, because the date had to be changed at the last moment:

Our agent in Paris was completely bouleversé: he had with great difficulty, he said, packed the Salle Gaveau with those who *should* be there, and not one of these would think of turning up again at a later date.... When the changed date of our concert at last came and I went on the platform of the Salle Gaveau to play, I thought at first on looking round that the hall was completely empty: then I observed a dozen or so at the back, who at once shifted to the front for a more cheerful effect, led, I was most grateful to see, by Darius Milhaud.

The excitement of being in Paris soon wiped this fiasco from my mind, and I greatly enjoyed being part of the stir that the young hornets, Honegger, Poulenc, Auric as well as Milhaud were causing. Edwin Evans, the music critic, had given me a letter to Maurice Delage, the composer of the *Poèmes hindous*...[who] led me to the piano, and asked for fifteen or sixteen bars of my own music, not more, he emphasised, so that he could appraise my musical personality. A light touch on my shoulder stopped me, and my personality was not again referred to.[24]

Nor is Bliss referred to in the index to Dumesnil's 1946 history of the period, along with Goossens, Walton, Vaughan Williams and Elgar. Diaghilev's protégé Vladimir Dukelsky presumably represented mainstream Paris opinion when, writing in 1955 as Vernon Duke, he declared that 'of the younger men, Arthur Bliss and Eugene Goossens were the only ones with any spunk at all', and that in 1925

English music was in a sad state.... The great men of English music were such purely local figures as Elgar (whose *Dream of Gerontius* was dismissed by George Moore...as 'holy water in a German beer-barrel') and Diaghilev's *bête noire*, Delius.[25]

Duke continues with a typically vivid account of an audition given by Diaghilev to William Walton and Constant Lambert, the latter with his ballet *Adam and Eve*:

Willie played first – he was no pianist, and got an icy reception from Sergei Pavlovitch, who then told me what he thought of *Portsmouth Point* in Russian, and it wasn't much. Lambert, a self-assured and efficient performer, went on next, gave an excellent account of his skimpy piece and – miracle of miracles – was rewarded by a beatific smile by the listener.

'Are you English?' he queried. 'Yes, I am, why?' countered Lambert. 'That's most surprising. I don't like English music, yet I like your little ballet. I'm going to produce it, but not with that silly title,' Diaghilev went on. He took a big red pencil, crossed out 'Adam and Eve' and wrote 'Romeo and Juliet' over it. Constant burst into uncontrollable tears.[26]

Lambert's *Romeo and Juliet* was premiered at the Théâtre Sarah-Bernhardt on 18 May 1926, danced by Karsavina, choreographed by Nijinska and with decor by Miró, and given a total of seven performances in Paris, the last on 10 June 1927. The only other English composer Diaghilev showed an interest in was Lord Berners. His *Le triomphe de Neptune*, to a scenario by Sacheverell Sitwell and with choreography by Balanchine, was also given its Paris premiere at the Théâtre Sarah-Bernhardt on 27 May 1927, but was taken off after only three performances. Sitwell remembered that 'it wasn't an enormous success' but that it contained 'a kind of tipsy rendering of the "Last Rose of Summer" at one moment, which was interestingly done and a very good finale'.[27] The other English stage work performed in Paris during the decade was also by Berners, his one-act opera *Le carrosse du Saint Sacrement*, based on the Mérimée story already used by Offenbach. This had been put on by Marguerite Bériza at the Théâtre des Champs-Elysées on three consecutive nights (24–26 April 1924), together with Stravinsky's *Histoire du soldat* and Sauguet's *Le plumet du colonel*.

Of Elgar and Vaughan Williams, possibly in the eye of history two of the finest English composers of the century from 1860, little was heard or said, and much of that unsatisfactory. On 25 April 1919 the elitist Société musicale indépendante put on a programme of contemporary English chamber music under the patronage of the British Ambassador, Lord Derby, including *On Wenlock Edge* and works by Holbrooke, Goossens, Cyril Scott, Lord Berners, Bax, Ireland amd Bantock. The first Paris performance of Vaughan Williams's *London* Symphony under Monteux in June 1921 provoked no strong response, but the knives were out for Elgar. On 26 October 1919 Landon Ronald conducted the First Symphony at the Concerts Lamoureux, and Florent Schmitt drew on his capacious reserves of invective.[28] When Elgar himself conducted the London Symphony Orchestra in the Second Symphony on 14 June 1924, Pierre Leroi was slightly less damning, noting that while it was 'rather roughly made [d'une facture un peu fruste] and at times bombastic [emphatique], its particular virtues are a ready invention [une inspiration facile] and a wealth of feeling [une générosité sentimentale copieuse]'.[29] It is necessary for readers to have the original French in front of them on occasions like this in order to be able to crack the critical code: 'fruste' can also mean 'rough', 'old-fashioned' or, of coinage, 'worn' or 'defaced'; 'emphatique' can also mean 'affected', 'stiff' or 'high-falutin"; 'facile' can also mean something nearer to English 'facile', in this case music which does not engage the higher reaches of the intellect; as for 'une générosité sentimentale copieuse', the extended length of the phrase itself leaves the reader with the impression that this music is simply *too much*, on the lines of Bruckner and Mahler. Descriptions like these, deploying what Mrs Malaprop called 'a nice derangement of epitaphs',[30] are common in the French critical literature, and have the virtue of permitting endorsement from a wide range of viewpoints. They also posit puzzlement in the mind of the critic. Altogether the French were happier with productions like Cocteau's 1924 *Roméo et Juliette*, after Shakespeare, which was enlivened with incidental music by Roger Desormière, after English popular tunes.[31]

Music from the Americas fell on more fruitful ground. Milhaud's *Saudades do Brazil* fitted comfortably into the French penchant for the exotic (that is, the melodically simple, harmonically colourful, rhythmically repetitive) and paved the way for the truly South American music of Villa-Lobos, who was active in Paris between 1923 and his final return to Brazil in 1930. He came bearing Brazilian government money directed towards promoting the music of South American composers in general. Apart from several chamber concerts, his first high-profile appearance early in 1924 was as conductor of works by Nepomuceno (Brazil), Soro (Chile), Ponce and Carillo (Mexico), and Pedrell (Uruguay) at a 'réception solennelle du Comité d'Honneur de la Maison de l'Amérique Latine et l'Académie Internationale des Beaux Arts par la Municipalité de Paris'.[32] He followed this up with a concert on 30 May, in which Artur Rubinstein took part, including the first performance of his *Nonetto*. The *Revue musicale* touched on the music's 'metric diversity and complexity' and concluded that 'one cannot escape being impressed and fascinated by this fiery force and abundance.'[33] Villa-Lobos then returned to Brazil, but in January 1927 he came back to Paris, and from then until May 1930 his music raised more than its share of shouting and fisticuffs. He was determined that, if it was exoticism Paris wanted, then exoticism it should have. Parisian readers were informed that the Brazilian soul

Nadia Boulanger and
Walter Damrosch

> is often savage, rough, loud, disconnected. It liberates itself rather by
> shouting, noise, than by the kind of music with which we are familiar.
> Nobody should therefore be surprised that Villa-Lobos expresses himself
> in his characteristic works in a noisy manner, as shown in the astonishing
> *Nonetto* or the *Chôros no 10*, where the essential nucleus of the orchestra
> is the percussion, further enriched by a great number of additional
> instruments which produce an Indian effect.[34]

Brazilians back home were less happy about this composer 'who makes us look ridiculous in Paris. He pretends that xylophones and rattles, as well as other instruments purely used for the carnival, are native instruments.'[35] Whatever the rights and wrongs of provenance, the results impressed the young Messiaen who later described Villa-Lobos as 'a very great orchestrator'.[36] Beyond that, Paul Griffiths has pointed out that 'the fast movements of Messiaen's early works for orchestra, up to and even including the *Turangalîla-symphonie*, taste the same frenzy and vividness.'[37]

The North American composers active in Paris during this period were essentially of three kinds. First, there were the pupils of Nadia Boulanger, most notably Aaron Copland (who studied with her from 1921 to 1924), Virgil Thomson (1921–22), Walter Piston (1924–26) and Roy Harris (1926–29). Their presence went virtually unnoticed on the concert scene. Two exceptions were the last four pieces played

at the Société musicale indépendante on 7 December 1922, collectively entitled 'Ecole américaine' and billing music by Marion Bauer, Alexander Steinert, Charles Griffes and Emerson Whithorne, and a whole concert on 5 May 1926 which was an all-American programme under the patronage of the US ambassador, Myron T. Herrick, and Walter Damrosch. Among the soloists were the pianist Marcel Ciampi and the violinist Samuel Dushkin, and the programme included first performances of Piston's Piano Sonata, Copland's *Nocturne* for violin and piano and Thomson's *Sonate d'église* for clarinet, viola, trumpet, horn and trombone. Elsewhere the occasional American work, mostly by Copland, appeared outside the US ghetto, but overall Virgil Thomson felt that what endeared Nadia Boulanger most to Americans

> was her conviction that American music was about to 'take off', just as Russian music had done eighty years before. Here she differed with the other French musicians, who, though friendly enough toward Americans (we were popular then), lacked faith in us as artists.[38]

The second kind of American composers were nearer in essence to their South American colleagues, tapping into the city's taste for the exotic. Henry Cowell and Edgard Varèse were the chief proponents. The 1 April 1926 number of *Le courrier musical* reminded readers that a Cowell concert had been a sensation at the Salle Érard some time back, and that for his concert the following month Cowell would be leaving the piano stool and playing directly on the strings of the instrument; the article was accompanied by a picture of the artist with his Amerindian 'thunderstick'.

Varèse caused an even greater stir, in both positive and negative senses. The first work of his to be heard in Paris after the war was *Octandre*, on 2 June 1927, conducted by Vladimir Golschmann, but according to one critic, this 'mediocre execution betrayed its author considerably',[39] so perhaps the two concerts in the spring of 1929 were the city's first opportunity to form a true impression of the composer's worth. On 23 April Marius-François Gaillard conducted *Intégrales* for small orchestra and percussion. Varèse's biographer Fernand Ouellette observes that 'on the whole the criticisms were much more lucid than those expressed in New York'. Paul le Flem wrote of 'this sober, powerful style, a sort of purging of means which disdains facile skills', Pierre Wolff of its 'pulsating vigour...a great and truly new work', and the critic of *Le monde musical* found that Varèse 'knows what he wants, where he is going, and he gets there. No sensibility, no lyricism; this is toughened metal, screaming as it is contorted by the forces of fire and rhythm. Is it a precursor of the music of the future?'[40]

But if those responses to *Intégrales* conjure up a vision of Paris seduced by a show of virility, those to *Amériques* a few weeks later on 30 May cry 'Rape!'. The talk was of 'the moanings of the siren [in fact, an ondes Martenot] (that) spread their swelling menace' and of 'laboratory experiments (that) kill music rather than revivify it: but also, from the poet Robert Desnos, of 'an arduous, virile ascent...we held our breath as we followed this male endeavour'. By the end, 'half of the audience was howling its indignation'.[41] Then came the fighting, which left Tristan Tzara needing four stitches. The evening was a success.

The third kind of North American composer consisted of one man: George Gershwin. He made brief visits to Paris in 1925 and 1926, and then a more extended one between 25 March and early June 1928. He began serious work on developing the sketches of *An American in Paris* and, on 31 March, attended the Paris premiere of *Rhapsody in Blue* at a Pasdeloup concert conducted by Rhené-Baton. Although the conductor felt he had to apologize for the orchestra's performance, saying they were unfamiliar with the piece, Gershwin and the rest of the audience enjoyed it, and 'there was real spontaneous applause all over the house and lots of cheers and bravos.'[42] If jazz in general was no longer *le dernier cri* in 1928, Paris knew a genius when it heard one. Gershwin also played at various soirées and, from various shops along the avenue de la Grande Armée, made a collection of taxi horns which were to find their way into the opening of *An American in Paris*, as 'the traffic sound of the place de la Concorde during the rush-hour'. The premiere of this work took place at Carnegie Hall on 13 December 1928, but had not reached Paris by the end of the summer of 1929.[43]

For all the scandal, Varèse's *Amériques* was nonetheless a 'safe' work in that a great gulf was fixed between its shattering dissonances and the traditional French virtues of clarity, brevity and grace. Varèse may have been born in the 10th arrondissement, but he now represented North America with its naivety and violence – Villa-Lobos minus the Iberian inflections and with the volume turned up even further. The French *patrimoine* was not under attack, even if the audience was. The position of contemporary German music, though, was more ambiguous, reflecting tensions on the military and political fronts. French troops occupied the Ruhr in January 1923, withdrawing only in July 1925, and in 1928 the decision was taken to build the Maginot Line. This distrust, combined with the sort of antipathy we have observed in the writings of André Coeuroy to the perceived gigantism of German music, meant that the works of Alban Berg made little headway: as already noted, Walter Straram's performance of the Chamber Concerto at the Salle Pleyel in February 1928 caused a near-riot, although his rendition of Webern's Five Pieces op. 10 on 21 March 1929 made little stir. Even the SMI, with all its pride in being up-to-date, programmed Berg only once between 1917 and 1929; and even then his Four Pieces for clarinet and piano op. 5 of 1913 were last-minute replacements for Bartók's Second String Quartet. Otherwise over the same period the SMI presented only Wellesz's *Chants sacrés* (7 May 1924), Hindemith's String Quartet op. 10 and Viola Sonata op. 11 (4 December 1924; 13 January 1926), and an all-Schoenberg concert in the composer's presence (15 December 1927), linking up with the one of his orchestral works conducted by him at the Concerts Colonne (8 December). The SMI programme consisted of the Suite op. 29, Five Pieces for piano op. 23 (played by Eduard Steuermann), Four Songs op. 6 and *Pierrot lunaire* with Marya Freund. In all, rather a meagre haul in 106 concerts – and no Webern....

At the same time, audiences were beginning their acquaintance with the so-called lighter side of German music: Krenek's opera *Jonny spielt auf* reached the Théâtre des Champs-Elysées on 21 June 1928 in a French translation (*Jonny mène la danse*), conducted by Inghelbrecht. But Weill's *Die Dreigroschenoper*, premiered in Berlin on 31 August 1928, was not given in Paris until October 1930, again in French (*L'opéra de quat' sous*), at the Théâtre Montparnasse. Dumesnil noted rather sourly that

> Mack's Lament and Polly's Song were hummed in a society which, ten
> or twenty years earlier, would have blushed at Weill's music, even without
> the crudity of the words. The French translation placed the accented
> syllables of the German on mute ones, thus accidentally emphasizing
> the vulgar tone of the Pirate's Moll.[44]

The privileged position of Schoenberg no doubt reflected to some extent his reputation as the head of the new school of German music. But the alert reader will also have noticed throughout this chapter how the Parisians paid more attention to those composers who took the trouble to be physically present in their city. For a composer to be seen, heard, interviewed, talked to, and hence talked about, was crucially important if his music was not to disappear into the limbo of competing foreign products. Was this another reason why Scandivanian music was practically unheard in Paris at this time? Sibelius's Third Symphony at the Salle Gaveau in May 1920 and Nielsen's Third at the Concerts Philharmoniques in April 1927 were rare exceptions.

This round trip of Europe and the Americas ends with a group of composers who were very definitely present in Paris, even if it is very hard to collect them under any single rubric of style or artistic aim. Russian music had been extremely popular in the city in the 1890s and over the turn of the century – the Apaches, the in-group to which Ravel belonged, used the opening rhythm of Borodin's Second Symphony as their private knock – and this rapport had been crystallized in the Franco-Russian Alliance of 1895. It may have waned immediately before the war, but the influx of Russians fleeing the Revolution brought with it a number of lively talents who did not intend to be ignored. On this front the SMI was by some way the most generous patron. After programming Balakirev and Mussorgsky songs and Borodin's Second String Quartet in 1919, presumably as a gesture of friendship as well as for artistic reasons, the society found room to promote Nicolas Obouhov (who studied with Ravel when he was not designing a new system of notation); Nicolas Tcherepnin (who left Russia in 1921 and directed the Conservatoire de musique russe in Paris from 1925 to 1929); and, even more keenly, his son Alexander who became a piano

pupil of Isidor Philipp; Vladimir Dukelsky, who wrote the ballet *Zephyr et Flore* for Diaghilev in 1925 and emigrated to the United States in 1929, where he was transmogrified into Vernon Duke; Nicolas Nabokov, who studied at the Sorbonne from 1923 and whose ballet-oratorio *Ode* was produced by the Ballets russes in 1928; and Igor Markevich, 'le petit Igor', Diaghilev's last discovery. And then there were the two big names: Serge Prokofiev and Igor Stravinsky, 'le grand Igor'.

Prokofiev installed himself in Paris in October 1923 and the city heard plenty of his music during the Twenties: the *Scythian Suite* in April 1921, *Chout* in May 1921, the Third Piano Concerto in May 1922, the First Piano Concerto in February 1923, the First Violin Concerto in October 1923, the Fifth Piano Sonata in March 1924, the Second Symphony in June 1925, *Le pas d'acier* in June 1927, the

Classical Symphony in February 1928, the second act of *L'ange de feu* in June 1928, the Third Symphony and *Le fils prodigue* in May 1929. With the exception of the Second Symphony, every work was met with a chorus of praise. Without wishing to denigrate Prokofiev's extraordinary talents, both as composer and pianist, one may nonetheless postulate that his music, too, was 'safe': 'people got into the habit of opposing Prokofiev to Stravinsky; they saw the first as a specifically Russian composer, the second as one who was more cosmopolitan.'[45]

And there lay the Stravinsky problem. As the composer of *Petrushka* and *Le sacre*, he had exercised his genius on matters far from the concerns of the French; now, not only had he come in June 1920 to live in France, but he seemed determined to challenge the French on their own artistic ground. Whatever one's views about 'Neoclassicism' (and since the term can mean more or less what anyone wants it to mean, it will not be discussed further here),[46] one cannot fail to register that works like *Pulcinella* (1919–20), the Octet (1922–23), the Serenade in A (1925), *Apollon musagète* (1927–28) and *Capriccio* (1928–29) by and large meet all the traditional French criteria of grace, lightness, clarity and elegance. Even *Oedipus rex* (1926–27), which plumbs greater depths, never for a moment hints at Mahlerian elephantiasis or Elgarian 'emphase'. Stravinsky's music, then, was *not* safe – and, as we have read above, young composers like Manuel Rosenthal looked to the next Stravinsky work as the beacon that would guide them towards the future.

The Parisian Establishment's revenge, when it came, was cruel, swift and irrefutable. On the death of Paul Dukas on 17 May 1935, a place (*fauteuil*) in the Institut became free; Stravinsky was persuaded by Gabriel Pierné to stand. He duly sent in a *curriculum vitae* and a list of compositions, and embarked on the necessary visits to members of the Institut including, in the words of Robert Craft, 'such musicians as Widor and Henri Rabaud, to whom, under other circumstances, Stravinsky would not have extended his hand'. Five ballots were held on 25 January 1936; 'Schmitt was elected on the last ballot with twenty-eight votes to Stravinsky's four.'[47] Doda Conrad was present that night at a reception held to honour the supposed future Academician, and remembered how, when the terrible news filtered back, the party melted like the summer snow.[48]

Stravinsky with lyre

Musical Paris may indeed have been 'where the pulse of world activity was throbbing', but it was quite prepared to reject any foreign body that threatened its autonomy. It is a mark of Stravinsky's genius that it was enough to provoke to action a society which in general absorbed foreigners, white and black, rich and poor, entrepreneurs and artists, because its 'yearning for ritual and participation in a collective identity made it susceptible to any new fad that promised spiritual stimulation'.[49] The blindest eye could see that Stravinsky was no 'new fad'. He therefore stands as a signal exception to the rule of Parisian tolerance that marked the Twenties, a tolerance born both of the French people's general sense of artistic and intellectual superiority ('Perhaps nothing is properly understood in Europe until the French have explained it')[50] and, in the particular case of music, of the extraordinary flowering of the art since the Franco-Prussian War – perhaps especially in the twenty-five years between the first performance of *Prélude à l'après-midi d'un faune* in 1894 to that of *Le tombeau de Couperin* in 1919. Also France, almost alone of continental European countries, had emerged from the war with her political institutions intact.

In the light of this social and political confidence, the emergence of three identifiable groups of French composers also takes on a socio-political colour. Satie had a hand in all of them. On 6 June 1917, a few weeks after the premiere of *Parade*, Auric,

Durey and Honegger organized a homage to Satie in the Salle Huyghens, and this was followed by concerts at the Théâtre du Vieux-Colombier. Satie dubbed these three young musicians and himself the Nouveaux Jeunes (he was fifty-two at the time) and to this nucleus Tailleferre and Poulenc were added, plus Milhaud and Koechlin (aged fifty-one) in 1918. In November 1918 Satie resigned from the group to pursue an independent course, while Koechlin had been prevented by circumstances from taking advantage of Satie's offer to link himself with a group that would have 'no subscriptions; no statutes; no committee: simply, *Ourselves*. No presidency; no treasury: nothing, but Ourselves.' But the project fell through and had to be reborn under the banner of Les Six.

The six young composers, Georges Auric, Louis Durey, Arthur Honegger, Darius Milhaud, Francis Poulenc and Germaine Tailleferre, were catapulted into the limelight by an article of Henri Collet in *Comoedia* of 16 January 1920 entitled 'Un livre de Rimsky et un livre de Cocteau, les Cinq russes, les Six français et Erik Satie', comparing Cocteau's *Le coq et l'arlequin* with the writings of Rimsky-Korsakov, and drawing parallels between the French group and the Russian 'Mighty Handful' (Rimsky, Mussorgsky, Borodin, Balakirev and Cui). However, plans had been laid in advance: the group was already formed in 1919 and they all met Collet at Milhaud's flat on 8 January 1920, where the critic was favoured with a proof copy of the forthcoming set of piano pieces, the *Album des Six*.

Whether Les Six was ever a group in any aesthetic sense has been debated since their formation. Honegger always claimed they were just a group of friends, and in 1921 Satie divided the group into two halves,

> Auric, Poulenc and Milhaud, who were representative of the 'new
> spirit' and showed 'modern sensibility…spontaneity, fantasy and audacity';
> and second, Durey, Honegger and Tailleferre, who were 'pure *impressionists*
> and more conventional in their use of 'tried and tested formulae',[51]

and by 1924 he reckoned the Six had been reduced to one: Milhaud.

The third group was the Ecole d'Arcueil, named after the suburb where Satie lived, and

> organized by Milhaud and Satie around Henri Sauguet (newly arrived
> from Bordeaux), by the addition of Henri Cliquet-Pleyel, Satie's favourite
> conductor Roger Desormière, Baron Jacques Bénoist-Méchin (who soon
> left), and Maxime-Benjamin Jacob. All but Bénoist-Méchin were pupils of
> Charles Koechlin. Milhaud's role in organizing both Les Six and the Ecole
> d'Arcueil as viable groups seems to have been greater than Satie's.[52]

Of these three groups, the one to survive was Les Six. Obviously the sheer talent of its more prominent members had much to do with this, but it is worth pondering

briefly the historical, and hence the social and political resonances of the comparison with the Russian Five. Just as the Five had shaken off the earlier Italian influence on Russian music, so now the Six shook off the German. Both groups espoused a certain technical roughness, partly to demonstrate that they were not in thrall to an academic past, partly for the opportunities this roughness gave for individuality of expression. The tension between this roughness (heard, for example, even in Poulenc, in his piano pieces *Promenades*) and the traditional suavity, clarity, etc., of French music, brought both scandal and notoriety in the short term. In the longer term, it led to many examples of fruitful cross-fertilization, bringing with them a number of more or less concealed political messages: that France was tough; that she still held to many of her traditional characteristics; that she was nonetheless flexible and accommodating; and that her *élan vital* was undiminished after four years of appalling slaughter. Finally, one must not discount the fact that the snappy title, Les Six, goes one beyond Les Cinq.

Four of Les Six, c. 1920: (l. to r.) Auric, Milhaud, Honegger and Poulenc

The emergence of Les Six also testified to a rise in the importance in Paris of musical marketing. As the traditional engines such as the salons and the state opera houses lost some of their impetus, so the notion of *sauve qui peut* gradually took hold. This was abetted by the arrival of the radio and, far more importantly, of electrical recording in 1925.[53] Stravinsky typically saw the value of the record as a marketing tool, and each of the four movements of his Serenade was designed to fit on to one side of a 10-inch disc. The improvement in the quality of recorded sound over that of the old acoustic system also meant that the player-piano gradually lost its place as a focus of home entertainment.

In the world at large, newspaper publicity and handouts continued as ever but, if we are to believe Inghelbrecht, with a new emphasis on 'personality', as in the brochures advertising a pianist

> carefully guarding the deliberate disorder of his hair, his fixedly
> distant – or empty – gaze, his head bowed beneath the burden of
> genius, and determinedly cultivating a Beethovenian aspect with
> childishly pouting lip.[54]

As in later decades, this emphasis on marketing was often laid at the door of the Americans; and, as in later decades, the Parisians' attitude towards their transatlantic friends was often confused. The presence of American money underpinning Parisian activities in many fields could not be denied. But one does not have to wait until the Thirties to find remarks such as that of the conductor Gustave Doret: 'I spent Christmas Day with dear Paderewski. And on Sunday we were alone at table, without ghastly bourgeois and beautiful, stupid American women.'[55] But, came the crash in 1929, and 'the chauvinistic French suddenly resented the absence of American tourists with their easily spent money'.

Paris in the Twenties, like any flourishing society, was energized by a number of antitheses. As a conclusion to this book, I should like to examine twelve of these, some already touched on, some new, and see to what extent they were implicated in the city's musical life.

Paris/France

Ever since the Revolution, France has been dominated by Paris. Even quite recent attempts at decentralization have not always succeeded: promotion of the Lyons Conservatoire has simply meant that teachers from Paris get on the TGV, turning the institution into an outpost of its Parisian counterpart. The Parisian view of the provinces, *la France profonde*, has always been a mixture of affection and contempt, seasoned with incredulity. The provincial view of Paris has always been of a place where style rules over content, where tradition is routinely subverted, where impatience undermines staying power, and where human values are crushed under the wheels of the impersonal state machine. At the same time, it is the dream of every ambitious provincial to make a name in Paris, just as it is the dream of many successful Parisians to get away from it all and live a peaceful existence in the provinces. In the words of Sanche de Gramont, Paris 'is the glory and misfortune of France, the circle of selfishness, the magnet that draws the iron filings, the grated heart that beats at the expense of the rest of the organism. It is the antidote to the complexity of the French nation and its lack of geographical definition.'[57]

Musical Paris in the Twenties spent no little part of its time writing, playing, recording and listening to *pastorales*. It was nice to be reminded that the provinces were still there, even if you didn't want to work in them. For all the respect accorded the directors of provincial conservatoires, such as Ropartz (Strasburg), Paul Ladmirault (Nantes) and Georges Witkowsky (Lyons), they were not really in the swim, and they paid the same price as those composers, already mentioned, who chose not to come to Paris in person. The *pastorale*, then, was a kind of homoeopathic pill, a small injection of rurality to enable you to continue living in Paris without guilt. Of the major French composers of the Twenties, only Milhaud truly drew strength from his rural roots, claiming, in the oft-quoted opening sentence of his autobiography, 'Je suis un Français de Provence et de religion israélite.'[58] For most of the others, *la province* was no more than just another branch of the exotic.

Native/foreign

It remains to add only three riders to what has already been said. French certainty of the value of its own composers did sometimes lead to something approaching paranoia, even in normally equable people, when they felt these composers were not being appreciated by the world outside. Thus Paul Dukas, one of the most rational and intelligent of men, could write to a friend in 1925:

> I pretty much agree with you about the latent *bochisme* of the SIMC
> [ISCM]. For some time now I've smelt intrigue beneath their activities,
> and the policy of playing only the weirdest and most fatuous French
> works so as to show the remainder in a good light....[59]

But in general, as I have said, the cultural *mélange* of Paris was felt to be a good thing, and French culture strong enough to hold its own. 'It seems reasonable to expect,' wrote the American critic Edward Burlingame Hill in 1924,

> that when French composers of the present and the immediate future have
> profitably absorbed what foreign influence has to teach, they will once
> more return to a more exclusive dependence upon the living traditions of
> their illustrious past.[60]

In a broader perspective still, French culture could be regarded both as unique and as forming part of a larger European culture. H.-R. Lenormand, writing in 1949, quoted his own article in *Comoedia* of 13 January 1919, going beyond the confines of music:

> Whether one likes it or not, a European mentality has been created: from
> one end of the continent to the other, a kind of emotional agreement has
> been reached over certain forms of thought. The good European spoken

of by Nietzsche has finally come into existence. For him it is the names of Strindberg, Chekhov, Shaw, and Claudel that dominate our time.[61]

Whether in fact the average Parisian music-lover of the Twenties was an avid reader of Strindberg and Shaw must remain doubtful. I would guess too that the order of allegiance would have been possibly Parisian, then French, with European a long way behind. But if one looks further to the three major French composers of the middle and later twentieth century and beyond (to Messiaen, Dutilleux and Boulez), then Lenormand's European perspective seems decidedly apt.

Old/new

Again, little more remains to be said on this score. One quotation, again from André Coeuroy, perhaps sums it all up: 'the banjo and black arms are replacing the harp and white arms'.[62]

Male/female

French women, still disenfranchised throughout the decade and beyond, were allowed to play stringed instruments, the harp, and the piano, and of course to sing and dance. Their power in the musical field was no greater than before the war, but their influence was just as great. Misia Sert, Coco Chanel, the princesse de Polignac, Lili and Nadia Boulanger, Germaine Tailleferre, Ida Rubinstein, Josephine Baker, Wanda Landowska and Mistinguett all made huge contributions of one sort and another to the musical life of the period. But by common consent they were *extra-ordinary*. The opera houses, the major concert-giving bodies and the teaching institutions were all run by men.

Brain/heart

In the spring of 1920, Arthur Bliss visited Paris and recorded this impression in the magazine of the Royal College of Music:

> Every concert hall develops its own peculiar personality. The Queen's Hall, I feel, radiates a happy holiday humour, is out to enjoy itself, overlooks mistakes, and applauds with indiscriminate relish; the Salle Gaveau, on the other hand, wears an air of brilliant snobbery, anxious not so much for its musical traditions, as that the society it has invited shall not demean themselves by any excess of enthusiasm.[63]

Gustav Holst confirmed this English view a decade later in a letter to Adrian Boult about his *Hammersmith Prelude*:

the Scherzo should be as quick as possible, as long as it sounds easy and good-tempered and not brilliant, hard or efficient. In short, it must sound like London and not Paris.[64]

This dominance of brain over heart is described in so many words by the historian Armand Lanoux:

> Paris in 1925 was intelligent but did not have much heart. It is the worst reproach one can level against it, together with indifference to social matters. Very well, but why these excesses of homosexuality…sex parties, alcoholism, drugs, or to put it bluntly, Sodom and Gomorrha? Paris in 1925 had a frantic sense of liberty, and if it did not really know *how far it could go too far*, in Cocteau's phrase, it had the virtue of not tolerating any limitation.[65]

Sentiment, yes; sentimentality, no.

Decency/scandal

One of the most useful things about shocking works like Milhaud's *Protée*, Satie's *Mercure* and *Relâche*, Schoenberg's Five Orchestral Pieces or Varèse's *Amériques*, was that they forced their way through the inbred decorum noted by Bliss, and through the concern that one should be *à la page* in one's enthusiasms. When everyone else was shouting, it was safe to shout. And with these major scandals, it seemed to matter less which side one was on, since the very nature of the works was provocative and their meaning ambiguous: in the same sense that Tzara's stitches after the *Amériques* premiere were badges of honour, so to have sat through the performance unmoved would have been the mark of an irredeemable bourgeois. The fact that the vast majority of Parisian concerts passed off peacefully serves only to underline the strength of the decorous crust overlying them, placed there for safety's sake by a society that well knew its own emotions to be both deep and volatile.

Art/money

The relationship between these two in the musical world of the Twenties was probably as ambivalent as at any other time and place. D'Indy might inveigh against music as a *métier*, but his high ideals could hardly survive in the market. Jacques Rouché, Ida Rubinstein and the *salonnières* all set examples of private money devoted to public good, but for the average orchestral musician or piano teacher it was a hard life. In the early 1890s Fauré had spent much of his life during the summer in trains, going from one pupil to another, and admitted he felt 'the need, just for ten days or so, to have a break from it all, to see other parts

Ida Rubinstein

of the country than the Gare Saint-Lazare...'.[66] Possibly the trains in the 1920s were a shade faster than they had been thirty years before, but the stresses of travel were no less and, as we have seen, the sharp rise in the cost of living had left teachers behind.

Whereas d'Indy upheld the standing of the 'artist', it is interesting to find his one-time pupil Erik Satie saying: 'We no longer need to call ourselves "artists", a glossy appellation we can leave to hairdressers and chiropodists.'[67] No doubt this was Satie the socialist speaking – not a side of him with which d'Indy would have had much sympathy, I suspect. The Opéra strikes at the start of the decade, and the grumbles of players and Conservatoire teachers throughout it, all tended to imply that someone, somewhere, was making money out of them. But maybe this was no more than the feeling of not being appreciated to which musicians seem to be particularly prone. Probably the greatest contribution made by impresarios like Diaghilev and Ida Rubinstein was, for a moment, to lift music-making out of the mundane world of money: Rubinstein by her own wealth, Diaghilev by astute appropriation of the wealth of others. But few musical ventures could ignore the bottom line. Piero Coppola, working for the Gramophone Company, had as an administrator a man who had been a razor manufacturer and who delivered himself of the plain warning: 'I don't give a toss for your music, I'm running this business on commercial lines and there are storms ahead, my friend, you can be sure of that.'[68]

Society/self

The composer and conductor Manuel Rosenthal remembers the Paris of the Twenties as being a village in which you were isolated only if you wished to be. Otherwise ideas were bandied about along a wide network of friends, both musicians and others. As an example of that Paris network, one can cite those in the audience for the premiere of Apollinaire's *Les mamelles de Tirésias* on 25 June 1917: Matisse, Picasso, Braque, Derain, Modigliani, Dufy, Léger, Cocteau, Eluard, Aragon, Breton, Satie, Auric, Poulenc, Diaghilev, Massine....[69] How you saw yourself in relation to society obviously depended largely on what you meant by 'society'. The Paris of government and big business had, as we have seen, no great interest in music. Inghelbrecht records that 'the Hungarian composer Tibor Harsányi, many years before his death, was refused the French naturalization he was asking for with this note on his file: profession of no social value (profession socialement inutile)'.[70] There were virtues too, of course, in keeping away from the unmusical herd and cultivating one's garden. But one commentator has taken a more positive view of the artist's place in the Parisian life of that time, even if he disagrees to some extent with Rosenthal's recollection of Paris as a cooperative village:

> it was in essence the final flowering of the Romantic conception of the
> artist and one can say, without being paradoxical, that in 1925 we were
> coming to the end of the nineteenth century.... In what respect does a
> Cocteau differ from the Romantic artist as conceived by Baudelaire? [...]
> The society of the Twenties had a taste for the unusual, and the artist was
> naturally led to single himself out and to consider that his message was
> valuable only to the extent that it owed as little as possible to others. I
> think that when, later on, the first half of this century comes to be judged,
> it will be seen to contain a very great transition, namely the passage from
> the singular to the plural, to the realization of a collective sense and to an
> interest, sometimes even an exaggerated one, in what is called collectivity,
> the emergence of the socialist artist....[71]

Similarity/diversity

The impulse towards cultivating similarity is described clearly by Stravinsky in his *Poetics of Music*:

> Contrast is everywhere. One has only to take note of it. Similarity
> is hidden; it must be sought out, and it is found only after the most
> exhaustive efforts. When variety tempts me, I am uneasy about the
> facile solutions it offers me. Similarity, on the other hand, poses more
> difficult problems but also offers results that are more solid and hence
> more valuable to me.[72]

This description contains a number of ideas that coincide with the French way of thinking. Most obviously, the idea that things hidden are, in some way, essentially superior to things lying about on the surface where everyone can see them. The innate French feeling of superiority ties in here with their natural propensity for understatement, for symbols, and for wit. But the idea has a sound psychological basis too, in that the harder listeners work, the more they are likely to make the music they are listening to 'their own', in the same way that imagined scenery on a Shakespearean stage can be more powerful than the most expensive combinations of hardboard, paint and lighting. This in turn ties in with the essentially élitist conception of French art – in the Twenties, a coterie of composers, performers, critics and enlightened *mélomanes* made up the court. Those whose faces didn't fit for whatever reason (one thinks of Koechlin and Durey, both of whom boldly asserted their Leftist political views) were excluded with little ceremony.

French also is the idea that a composer has to work hard if his art is to be worth anything. This owes its being, not to Puritanism, but to a long tradition of superlative craftsmanship in the fine arts. D'Indy, in saying 'l'art n'est pas un métier', was not decrying competence in craftsmanship, merely pointing out that *métier* is but a means to a spiritual end. In all this, as Coeuroy indicated in a passage already quoted, for a Frenchman, 'the ultimate artistic rule is the subordination of the individual elements to the overall picture, the dependence of the detail on the directing idea.'[73] That is, diversity must always be governed by similarity. The field of painting offers a point of comparison, in that every great painting, however diverse its elements, will have an appreciable overall 'tonality'. Needless to add, Stravinsky's embrace of similarity was another reason why his presence in Paris was regarded as dangerous for native French composers. With hindsight, we can see that the three French composers mentioned earlier (Messiaen, Dutilleux and Boulez) were unaffected by Stravinsky's Neoclassical phase, indeed largely antipathetic to it, while they have learnt much more from the earlier, Russia-inspired works. Certainly, Messiaen's conception of 'similarity' (for example, in the last movement of *Et exspecto*) is Berliozian rather than Stravinskyan – and, to that extent, un-French!

Small/large

The range of textures and time-scales in the music played during this period was enormous. At one end lie Stravinsky's Pieces for solo clarinet and Honegger's *Danse de la chèvre* for solo flute, at the other *Amériques*, and Antheil's *Ballet mécanique*, requiring sixteen electric pianos, eight xylophones, four drums, two electric motors with special rumbling capacity (à ronflement spécial), a siren, two discs, one of zinc and one of steel, and two complete octaves of electric bells. Few Parisian listeners were naive enough to confuse size with quality, although there was obviously some truth in the equation: volume + dissonance = scandal.

Two letters from Ansermet to Stravinsky shed interesting light on what audiences and impresarios wanted, or were prepared to accept:

> I was saying that you had written some pieces for solo clarinet, and
> Massine opened his eyes wide in amazement. But Diaghilev immediately
> said: 'Good, there's a lot of interest in the clarinet in Paris!' [...] I gave
> a general idea of the tendency of your most recent works, and then
> Diaghilev said: 'But why these small orchestras all the time? The victory
> is won; there's no need to fight against Mahler, I'd like to get back to
> large-scale things now.' Always this slightly naive interest in 'effect' for
> the sake of the 'effect' on Mme [Misia] Edwards and the three or four
> people who matter.[74]

A couple of months later Ansermet reported a conversation with Rouché about *Les noces*:

> [Rouché] said to me, with a typically Parisian smile: 'I offer Diaghilev 100
> players, and he tells me that for *Les noces* he needs only four, but that they
> won't come from the orchestra. It's rather complicated, can you explain?'[75]

In any contest between sheer noise and 'nouvelles sensations', the latter was always likely to be more attractive; which was why Diaghilev was prepared to accept the four pianists for *Les noces*, even though it meant 'getting one from Honolulu, one from Budapest and the others from God knows where'.

Truth/beauty

> 'Beauty is truth, truth beauty' – that is all
> Ye know on earth, and all ye need to know.[76]

Not everyone in Paris would have agreed with Keats's famous definition. Thirty years earlier, Gounod in his memoirs had stated that the public and the composer are in a reciprocal relationship, each required to contribute to the artistic education of the other: the public, through being for the composer the criterion and the sanction of the True; the composer, through initiating the public into the elements and conditions of the Beautiful.[77]

For Gounod, then, Truth and Beauty were quite separate entities. In positing the composers as the guardian of Beauty, Gounod was surely saying nothing new. More interesting is his suggestion that the public is the keeper of the Truth, that their instincts for what is true and honest are acute. Later in the same paragraph he refers to the 'incessante mobilité' of their opinions, so he is obviously not suggesting that Truth is constant. Rather there is a Truth which is valid for a given audience at a given time, but which is then discarded – he might have added, in Paris faster than elsewhere. Gounod's view received some kind of support from an unlikely source, Francis Picabia, who claimed that: 'Life has nothing to do with what the grammarians call Beauty.... Art is, and can only be, the expression of contemporary life.'[78] The fit between the two propositions is not perfect, since it supposes an equality between Truth and Life, but I submit that the two points of view are close nonetheless.

It was the composer's task to try and reach an accommodation between this imposed yet evanescent Truth/Life compound and what he or she believed to be Beauty. In using the word 'initier', Gounod presents the composer as a teacher (a role Stravinsky liked to assume, as we have seen) or as a priest (perhaps d'Indy best fulfilled this role). The composer knows important things which the public doesn't and the need to initiate them springs from the fact that these things are, as with similarity, hidden from immediate view. Like the young Doda Conrad at the first concert performance of *Le sacre*, the public needs to be shown the difference between what is 'beau' and what is merely 'joli'. Of course, the 'joli' may also be 'beau' – Debussy admitted to his publisher while writing his *Etudes* that 'a little charm never spoilt anything'[79] – or the 'beau' may lie on a level below the 'joli'. The composer's hardest job was to convince the public that works entirely devoid of the 'joli' could also be 'beau': in the Twenties this often involved recourse to talk about 'real life' and machines. Finally, there was a widespread feeling among the cognoscenti that the new age needed new music to go with it, and that any backsliding, as with *Le roi David*, was to impugn one's role as educator and priest, and to sacrifice the 'beau' to the facile attractions of the 'joli'. It was one of the many marks of Stravinsky's genius that he was continually rewriting the rules of this game. We could possibly, in 1928, have regarded *Apollon musagète* as a case of backsliding – of Constant Lambert's 'time travelling'.[80] Now we see more clearly that it was in fact one of many dangerous attempts by Stravinsky to break that reciprocal relationship of which Gounod spoke. Stravinsky felt he did not need to be 'artistically educated' by the public; and this supreme self-confidence of his leads us on to the final pair of antitheses.

Anarchy/tyranny

In 1954 Poulenc made the claim, echoing Debussy's above, that 'it is because French composers hide the plans of their constructions out of a desire for elegance, that Central Europe reproaches us for our lack of form.'[81] And not only Central Europe. The notion that French music of the period 1890–1930 is just a bundle of random Impressionist sensations dies hard and is regularly reinforced by Monet and Renoir paintings on CD covers. The truth is that, in the best works at least, concern for strong construction is paramount, whether in Milhaud's *La création du monde*, in Poulenc's *Les biches* or in Ravel's *L'enfant et les sortilèges*. Ravel's well-known put-down of the pianist Paul Wittgenstein when he introduced changes into the Left-hand Concerto ('Performers must not be slaves.' 'Performers ARE slaves!')[82] is but one example of the firm impress of tyranny on the Parisian musical life of the time.

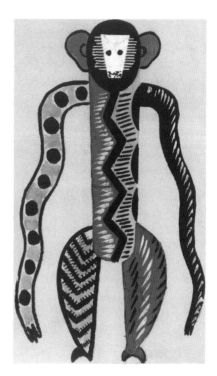

Léger's design for a monkey in Milhaud's ballet *La création du monde* (1923)

Henri Rabaud at the Conservatoire, Diaghilev in the Ballets russes, Jacques Rouché at the Opéra, Ida Rubinstein and Serge Koussevitzky in their own enterprises, Nadia Boulanger in her composition classes, Igor Stravinsky in his compositions – all, in their varying ways, were tyrants. When, in 1924, the Cartel des Gauches effectively collapsed, 'The Chamber turned again to the one strong man and elder statesman it possessed, Poincaré...'.[83] The effects of weak leadership could be seen both in the comte de Beaumont's travails over the *Soirées de Paris* and in the chronic difficulties of the Opéra-Comique. Understandably, the benefits of tyranny have been considered rather warily in the aftermath of Fascism, nor is the world at the time of writing (2001) free of its more repulsive manifestations. It may though be salutary, if close to being politically incorrect, to quote on this subject a French writer of 1965:

Various Frenchmen and friends of France tend to think that régimes that are authoritarian, paternalistic, based on the notion of moral order, monarchist, Catholic, imperial, dictatorial, established for the purpose of recovery, renewal, union, revival, national unity, to cope with a crisis, through a resurgence of effort, and which punctuate French history since 1789, are accidents along a pure democratic and revolutionary path. And yet the exact opposite is true: these régimes are the norm in France, and the exceptions are the governments inspired by popular sentiment: in all, several months in 1848, a total of four years scattered here and there throughout the Third Republic, and two or three months after the Liberation.[84]

The ultimate paradox is that it was precisely this framework of order, of tyranny if you will, that was strong enough to contain the anarchy, the Sodom and Gomorrah referred to earlier by Armand Lanoux. I leave the last words to Darius Milhaud who, through his mediation between more-than-competent technique and wild experiment, between common sense and crazy humour, and between personal fulfilment and wider social responsibility, comes perhaps closer than any other single composer to incorporating the values of this extraordinary time and place:

> I am always very angry when I hear now people speaking of the Twenties and referring to them as the 'silly Twenties', or when I read about the 'silly Twenties', because I think it has been the most marvellous period that I have been through. I think at this time everything was possible, we could try everything we wanted, it was a period of experiment, of liberty in expression in the widest sense of this word. We had a lot of possibility that we enjoyed very much.[85]

Notes

1. Roland-Manuel, 'Une esquisse autobiographique de Maurice Ravel', in *La revue musicale*, December 1938, p. 20.
2. *Maurice Ravel. Lettres, écrits, entretiens*, ed. Arbie Orenstein (Paris, 1989); Eng. trans. A. Orenstein (New York 1990), p. 35, n. 17.
3. Dominique Sordet, *Douze chefs d'orchestre* (Paris, 1924), p. 86.
4. Roger Nichols, *Ravel Remembered* (London, 1987), p. 110.
5. Geneviève Thibault, 'Quelques chansons de Dufay', in *Revue de musicologie*, v (1924), p. 97.
6. *Le ménestrel*, 26 January 1923.
7. Ibid., 12 January 1923.
8. *Le courrier musical*, 15 April 1924.
9. Leo Schrade, *Beethoven in France* (Yale, 1942; repr. New York, 1978).
10. Ibid., p. 3.
11. Ibid., pp. 83, 129, 136.
12. Ibid., pp. 152ff., 200.
13. Ibid., pp. 203–4.
14. Charles Koechlin, 'Le "retour à Beethoven"', in *La revue musicale*, 1 April 1927, p. 130.
15. *Le courrier musical*, 15 April 1928, 15 April 1929.
16. Schrade, *Beethoven in France*, p. 170
17. *Ravel. Souvenirs de Manuel Rosenthal, recueillis par Marcel Marnat* (Paris, 1995), p. 7.
18. Georges Auric, in conversation with the author.
19. André Coeuroy, *Panorama de la musique contemporaine* (Paris, 1930), p. 79.
20. Ibid., p. 88.
21. Igor Stravinsky, *Chroniques de ma vie* (Paris, 1962), p. 95.
22. René Dumesnil, *La musique en France entre les deux guerres, 1919–1939* (Geneva, 1946), pp. 45–48.
23. H. E. Wortham, 'Arthur Bliss', in *La revue musicale*, 1 May 1927, pp. 135–42.
24. Arthur Bliss, *As I Remember* (London, 1970), p. 56.
25. Vernon Duke, *Passport to Paris* (Boston, 1955), p. 160.
26. Ibid., p. 173.
27. Cited in John Drummond, *Speaking of Diaghilev* (London, 1997), p. 276.
28. Florent Schmitt, in *Le courrier musical*, 15 November 1919.
29. Pierre Leroi, in ibid., 1 July 1924.
30. Richard Brinsley Sheridan, *The Rivals*, Act III, scene 3.
31. *Jean Cocteau, magicien du spectacle*: catalogue de l'exposition au Musée Borely et au Musée Provençal du Cinéma, Marseille, November 1983 – February 1984, p. 50.
32. Lisa Peppercorn, *Villa-Lobos* (London, 1989), p. 50.
33. Ibid., p. 52.
34. Ibid., p. 77.
35. Ibid.
36. Olivier Messiaen, *Music and Color: Conversations with Claude Samuel* (Portland, 1994), p. 194.
37. Paul Griffiths, *Olivier Messiaen and the Music of Time* (London, 1985), p. 24.
38. Virgil Thomson, *Virgil Thomson* (London, 1967), p. 54.
39. Louise Varèse, *Varèse: A Looking-glass Diary* (London, 1975), p. 264.
40. Cited in Fernand Ouellette, *Edgard Varèse: A Musical Biography* (London, 1973), pp. 98–99.
41. Ibid., p. 100.
42. E. Jablonski and L. Stewart, *The Gershwin Years* (New York, 1973), p. 132.
43. R. Kimball and A. Simon, *The Gershwins* (New York, 1973), p. 95.
44. Dumesnil, *La musique en France*, p. 44.
45. Ibid., p. 36.
46. For a full discussion, see Scott Messing, *Neoclassicism in Music: From the Genesis of the Concept through the Schoenberg/Stravinsky Polemic* (Rochester, 2nd edn 1996).
47. Stravinsky, *Selected Correspondence*, II, ed. and with commentaries by Robert Craft (London, 1984), Appendix J, 'Stravinsky and the Institut de France', pp. 482–87.
48. Doda Conrad, in conversation with the author.
49. Petrine Archer-Straw, *Negrophilia, Avant-garde Paris and Black Culture in the 1920s* (London, 2000), p. 78.
50. Joseph de Maistre, *Trois fragments sur la France*, in *Oeuvres inédites du comte de Maistre* (1870), pp. 7–9, quoted in Theodore Zeldin, *France 1848–1945*, III, *Intellect and Pride* (Oxford, 1980), p. 18.

51. Robert Orledge, *Satie the Composer* (Cambridge, 1990), pp. 249–50; also Erik Satie, *Ecrits*, ed. Ornella Volta (Paris, 1977), pp. 87–91.

52. Orledge, *Satie the Composer*, p. 365, n. 18.

53. The range of the Grafonola Columbia model of gramophone was extended from just over three octaves (b–e'''') in 1920, to just over five octaves (A'–b'''') in 1927; see *Le courrier musical*, 15 April 1927 (Numéro consacré à la musique mécanique).

54. D.-E. Inghelbrecht, *Diabolus in musica* (Paris, 1933), p. 14.

55. BnF, LA Doret 6, 3 January 1936.

56. Artur Rubinstein, *My Many Years* (London, 1980), p. 295.

57. Sanche de Gramont, *The French: Portrait of a People* (New York, 1969), pp. 44–45.

58. Darius Milhaud, *Ma vie heureuse* (Paris, 1973), p. 9.

59. Letter to Pereyra of 15 June 1925, *Correspondance de Paul Dukas*, ed. Georges Favre (Paris, 1971), p. 156.

60. Edward Burlingame Hill, *Modern French Music* (London, 1924), p. 384.

61. H.-R. Lenormand, *Les confessions d'un auteur dramatique*, I (Paris, 1949), p. 311.

62. Coeuroy, *Panorama*, p. 153.

63. Bliss, *As I Remember*, p. 57.

64. Lewis Foreman, *From Parry to Britten: British Music in Letters 1900–1945* (London, 1987), p. 151.

65. Armand Lanoux, *Paris 1925* (Paris, 1957), pp. 106–7.

66. Jean-Michel Nectoux, *Gabriel Fauré: A Musical Life*, trans. Roger Nichols (Cambridge, 1991), p. 224.

67. Quoted in Lanoux, *Paris 1925*, p. 83.

68. Piero Coppola, *Dix-sept ans de musique à Paris, 1922–1939* (Lausanne, 1944; 2nd edn Paris, 1982), p. 58.

69. Francis Poulenc, *Entretiens avec Claude Rostand* (Paris, 1954), p. 144.

70. D.-E. Inghelbrecht, *Le chef d'orchestre parle au public* (Paris, 1957), pp. 122–23.

71. Igor Markevich, *Point d'orgue* (Paris, 1959), pp. 41–42.

72. *Poetics of Music*, trans. Arthur Knodel and Ingolf Dahl (Cambridge, Mass., 1942; 2nd edn, 1974), pp. 32–33.

73. Coeuroy, *Panorama*, p. 88.

74. Letter of 4 May 1919, *Correspondance Ansermet–Stravinsky*, ed. Claude Tappolet (Geneva, 1990), p. 88.

75. Letter of 18 July 1919, in ibid., pp. 134–35.

76. John Keats, *Ode on a Grecian Urn*.

77. Charles Gounod, *Mémoires d'un artiste* (Paris, 1896; 2nd edn 1991), p. 138.

78. *Dadas on Art*, ed. Lucy R. Lippard (New Jersey, 1971), p. 167.

79. Letter to Jacques Durand of 28 August 1915, in *Debussy Letters*, selected and ed. François Lesure and Roger Nichols (London, 1987), p. 300.

80. Constant Lambert, *Music Ho!* (London 1934; pub. 1948), pp. 47–54.

81. Poulenc, *Entretiens avec Claude Rostand*, p. 131.

82. Marguerite Long, *At the Piano with Ravel*, trans. Olive Senior-Ellis (London, 1973), p. 59.

83. Alfred Cobban, *A History of Modern France*, III, 1871–1962 (London, 1965), p. 134.

84. Jean-François Revel, *En France* (Paris, 1965), p. 42; quoted with trans. in Philip Thody and Howard Evans, *Faux Amis and Key Words* (London, 1985), pp. 74–75.

85. Talk on BBC Third Programme, 4 February 1962, recorded on LP 27314.

Select bibliography

Composers and artists: autobiographies, biographies, monographs and their own writings

Antheil, George
Bad Boy of Music (New York, 1945)

Aubert, Louis
Vuillemin, Louis, *Louis Aubert, son oeuvre* (Paris, 1921)
Landowski, Marcel and Morançon, Guy, *Louis Aubert, musicien français* (Paris, 1967)

Auric, Georges
Quand j'étais là (Paris, 1979)

Baker, Josephine
Baker, Josephine and Bouillon, Jo, *Josephine*, trans. Mariana Fitzpatrick (New York, 1977)
Haney, Lynn, *Naked at the Feast* (London, 1981; repr. 1986)

Bliss, Arthur
As I Remember (London, 1970)

Cocteau, Jean
Le coq et l'arlequin (Paris, 1918; repr. 1978)
Le rappel à l'ordre (Paris, 1926)
Brown, Frederick, *An Impersonation of Angels: A Biography of Jean Cocteau* (New York, 1968)
Steegmuller, Francis, *Cocteau: A Biography* (London, 1970)

Copland, Aaron
Copland, Aaron and Perlis, Vivian, *Copland, Volume I, 1900–1942* (London, 1984)

Diaghilev, Serge
Lifar, Serge, *Histoire du Ballet Russe depuis les origines jusqu'à nos jours* (Paris, 1950)
Kochno, Boris, *Diaghilev and the Ballets Russes*, trans. Adrienne Foulke (New York, 1970)
Buckle, Richard, *Diaghilev* (London, 2nd edn 1984)
Garafola, Lynn, *Diaghilev's Ballets Russes* (Oxford, 1989)
Drummond, John, *Speaking of Diaghilev* (London, 1997)

Dukas, Paul
Les écrits de Paul Dukas sur la musique (Paris, 1948)
Correspondance, ed. Georges Favre (Paris, 1971)

Dupré, Marcel
Marcel Dupré raconte (Paris, 1972)
Murray, Michael, *Marcel Dupré: The Work of a Master Organist* (Boston, 1985)

Durey, Louis
Frédéric Robert, *Louis Durey, l'aîné des Six* (Paris, 1968)

Enesco, Georges
Les souvenirs de Georges Enesco (Paris, 1955)
Scrisori/George Enescu, ed. Viorel Cosma (Bucharest, 1974)

Fauré, Gabriel
Lettres intimes, ed. Philippe Fauré-Fremiet (Paris, 1951)
Correspondance, ed. Jean-Michel Nectoux (Paris, 1980)
Nectoux, Jean-Michel, *Gabriel Fauré: les voix du clair-obscur* (Paris, 1990); trans. Roger Nichols, as *Gabriel Fauré: A Musical Life* (Cambridge, 1991)

Gershwin, George
Jablonski, E. and Stewart, L., *The Gershwin Years* (New York, 1973)
R. Kimball and A. Simon, *The Gershwins* (New York, 1973)

Hahn, Reynaldo
Journal d'un musicien (Paris, 1933)
Thèmes variés (Paris, 1945)
Gavoty, Bernard, *Reynaldo Hahn* (Paris, 1976)

Honegger, Arthur
Incantation aux fossiles (Lausanne, 1948)
Je suis compositeur (Paris, 1951)
Delannoy, Marcel, *Honegger* (Paris, 1953)
Halbreich, Harry, *Arthur Honegger* (Paris, 1992; Eng. trans. Roger Nichols, Portland, 1996)

d'Indy, Vincent
Thomson, Andrew, *Vincent d'Indy and his World* (Oxford, 1996)

Inghelbrecht, D.-E.
Diabolus in musica (Paris, 1933)
Mouvement contraire (Paris, 1947)
Le chef d'orchestre et son équipe (Paris, 1947); trans. G. Prerauer and S. Martin Kirk, as *The Conductor's World* (London/New York, 1953)

Koechlin, Charles
Orledge, Robert, *Charles Koechlin (1867–1950): His Life and Works* (Luxemburg, 1989; 2nd edn 1995)

Malipiero, Gian Francesco
Gian Francesco Malipiero: il carteggio con Guido M. Gatti 1914–1972, ed. Cecilia Palandri (Florence, 1997)

Markevich, Igor
Point d'orgue. Entretiens avec Claude Rostand (Paris, 1963)
Etre et avoir été (Paris, 1980)

Martinů, Bohuslav
Large, Brian, *Martinů* (London, 1975)

Milhaud, Darius
Etudes (Paris, 1927)
Correspondance Claudel/Milhaud, 1912–53, Cahiers Paul Claudel, III (Paris, 1961)
Entretiens avec Claude Rostand (Paris, 1963)
Ma vie heureuse (Paris, 1973), p. 46
Darius Milhaud. Notes sur la musique, ed. Jeremy Drake (Paris, 1982)
Collaer, Paul, *Darius Milhaud* (Geneva, 1982); trans. and ed. Jane Hohfeld Galante (San Francisco, 1988)

Poulenc, Francis
Entretiens avec Claude Rostand (Paris, 1954)
Hell, Henri, *Francis Poulenc* (Paris, 1958; 2nd edn 1978); trans. Edward Lockspeiser (London, 1959)
Moi et mes amis (Paris, 1963); trans. James Harding (London, 1978)
Daniel, Keith, *Francis Poulenc: His Artistic Development and Musical Style* (Ann Arbor, 1988)
Francis Poulenc: 'Echo and Source', Selected Correspondence 1915–1963, trans. and ed. Sidney Buckland (London, 1991)
Correspondance 1910–1963, ed. Myriam Chimènes (Paris, 1994)
Francis Poulenc, Music, Art and Literature, ed. Sidney Buckland and Myriam Chimènes (Aldershot, 1999)
A bâtons rompus. Ecrits radiophoniques (Arles, 1999)

Prokofiev, Serge
Samuel, Claude, *Prokofiev* (Paris, 1960)
Moisson-Franckhauser, Suzanne, *Serge Prokofiev et les courants esthétiques de son temps* (Paris, 1974)

Rabaud, Henri
d'Ollone, Max, *Henri Rabaud, sa vie, son oeuvre* (Paris, n.d.)

Ravel, Maurice
'Esquisse autobiographique', *La revue musicale*, numéro spécial, December 1938, p. 21
Jourdan-Morhange, Hélène, *Ravel et nous* (Geneva, 1945)
Ravel au miroir de ses lettres, ed. René Chalupt (Paris, 1956)

Orenstein, Arbie, *Ravel, Man and Musician* (New York, 1975)
Marnat, Marcel, *Maurice Ravel* (Paris, 1986)
Nichols, Roger, *Ravel Remembered* (London, 1987)
Maurice Ravel. Lettres, écrits, entretiens, ed. Arbie Orenstein (Paris, 1989; Eng. trans. Columbia, 1990)
L'enfant et les sortilèges/L'heure espagnole, L'avant-scène no. 127 (Paris, 1990)
Ravel, Souvenirs de Manuel Rosenthal, recueillis par Marcel Marnat (Paris, 1995)
The Cambridge Companion to Ravel, ed. Deborah Mawer (Cambridge, 2000)

Roussel, Albert
Vuillemin, Louis, *Albert Roussel et son oeuvre* (Paris, 1924)
Hoérée, Arthur, *Albert Roussel* (Paris, 1938)
Bernard, Robert, *Albert Roussel, sa vie, son oeuvre* (Paris, 1948)
Pincherle, Marc, *Albert Roussel* (Geneva, 1957)
Surchamp, Dom Angelico, *Albert Roussel, l'homme et son oeuvre* (Paris, 1967)
Albert Roussel, Zodiaque 80, April 1969, Paris
Lettres et écrits, ed. Nicole Labelle (Paris, 1987); see also d'Indy, Duparc, Roussel, *Lettres à Auguste Sérieyx* (Lausanne, 1963)

Rubinstein, Ida
Cossart, Michael de, *Ida Rubinstein* (Liverpool, 1987)

Satie, Erik
Erik Satie, son temps et ses amis, ed. Rollo Myers, *La revue musicale*, numéro spécial, 214 (1952)
Ecrits, ed. Ornella Volta (Paris, 1977)
Gillmor, Alan M., *Erik Satie* (Basingstoke, 1988)
Volta, Ornella, *Satie Seen through his Letters*, trans. Michael Bullock (London, 1989)
Orledge, Robert, *Satie the Composer* (Cambridge, 1990)
Volta, Ornella, *Satie/Cocteau, les malentendus d'une entente* (Paris, 1993)
Orledge, Robert, *Satie Remembered* (London, 1995)
Whiting, Steven Moore, *Satie the Bohemian* (Oxford, 1999)

Schmitt, Florent
Ferroud, Pierre-Octave, *Autour de Florent Schmitt* (Paris, 1927)

Stravinsky, Igor
Chroniques de ma vie (Paris, 1935; repr. 1962)
Poétique musicale (Cambridge, Mass., 1942); trans. Arthur Knodel and Ingolf Dahl, as Poetics of Music (Cambridge, 1974)
Lederman, Minna, ed., Stravinsky in the Theatre (London, 1951)
Expositions and Developments (London, 1962)

Stravinsky in Conversation with Robert Craft (London, 1962)
White, Eric Walter, Stravinsky (London, 1966)
Stravinsky, Igor and Craft, Robert, Dialogues and a Diary (London, 1968)
Vlad, Roman, Stravinsky (Oxford, 1971)
Selected Correspondence, ed. and with commentaries by Robert Craft, 3 vols (London, 1982, 1984, 1985)

Correspondance Ansermet-Stravinsky, ed. Claude Tappolet, I (Geneva, 1990)
Walsh, Stephen, The Music of Stravinsky (London, 1988; 2nd edn, 1993)

Thomson, Virgil
Virgil Thomson (London, 1967)

Varèse, Edgard
Ouellette, Fernand, Edgard Varèse, A Musical Biography (London, 1973)

Vivier, Odile, Varèse (Paris, 1973)
Varèse, Louise, Varèse, A Looking-glass Diary (London, 1975)

Villa-Lobos, Heitor
Peppercorn, Lisa, Villa-Lobos (London, 1989)

Books of general interest

Ansermet, Ernest, Ecrits sur la musique (Neuchâtel, 1971)
Archer-Straw, Petrine, Negrophilia: Avant-Garde Paris and Black Culture in the 1920s (London, 2000)
Astruc, Gabriel, Le pavillon des fantômes (Paris, 1929)

Baedeker's Paris and its Environs (Leipzig and London, 1924)
Benois, Alexandre, Reminiscences of the Russian Ballet (London, 1941)
Bernard, Philippe, La fin d'un monde 1914–1929 (Paris, 1975)
Berteaux, E., En ce temps-là (Paris, 1946)
Bertrand, Paul, Le monde de la musique (Geneva, 1947)
Bizet, René, L'époque du music-hall (Paris, 1926)
Blanche, Jacques-Emile, La pêche aux souvenirs (Paris, 1949)
Bongrain, Anne and Gérard, Yves (eds), Le Conservatoire de Paris, 1795–1995 (Paris, 1996)
Bost, Pierre, Le cirque et le music-hall (Paris, 1931)
Brody, Elaine, Paris, The Musical Kaleidoscope, 1870–1925 (London, 1988)
Bruyr, José, L'écran des musiciens, 2 vols (Paris, 1930; 1933)

Calvocoressi, M.-D., Musical Criticism (Oxford, 1923)
—— Musicians Gallery (London, 1933)
Caradec, François and Weill, Alain, Le café concert (Paris, 1980)
Carré, Albert, Souvenirs de théâtre (Paris, 1950)
Casanova, Nicole, Isolde 39 – Germaine Lubin (Paris, 1974)
Chassain-Dolliou, Laetitia, Le Conservatoire de Paris (Paris, 1995)
Chevalier, Maurice, I Remember it Well (New York, 1970)
Clouzot, Marie-Rose, Souvenirs à deux voix (Toulouse, 1969)
Cobban, Alfred, A History of Modern France, III, 1871–1962 (London, 1965; repr. 1975)

Coeuroy, André, La musique française moderne (Paris, 1924)
—— Panorama de la musique contemporaine (Paris, 1928; 2nd edn 1930)
—— Association artistique des concerts Colonne (Paris, 1929)
—— Panorama de la radio (Paris, 1930)
—— La musique et le peuple en France (Paris, 1941)
—— and Schaeffner, André, Le jazz (Paris, 1926)
—— and Clarence, G., Le phonographe (Paris, 4th edn 1929)
Collaer, Paul, La musique moderne (Brussels, 1955)
—— Correspondance avec des amis musiciens, ed. Robert Wangermée (Liège, 1996)
Le Conservatoire national de musique et de déclamation, preface by Henri Rabaud (Paris, 1930)
Cooper, Martin, French Music: From the Death of Berlioz to the Death of Fauré (Oxford, 1951)
Coppola, Piero, Dix-sept ans de musique à Paris (Lausanne, 1944; repr. Geneva and Paris, 1982)
Crespelle, J.-P., La folle époque (Paris, 1968)

Damase, Jacques, Les folies du music-hall (London, 1970)
Demuth, Norman, Musical Trends in the Twentieth Century (London, 1952)
Dolin, Anton, Autobiography (London, 1960)
Doret, Gustave, Temps et contretemps (Fribourg, 1942)
Doyon, R.-L., Mémoire d'homme (Paris, 1952)
Duchesneau, Michel, L'avant-garde musicale à Paris de 1871 à 1939 (Liège, 1997)
Duke, Vernon (Dukelsky, Vladimir), Passport to Paris (Boston, 1955)
Dumesnil, René, La musique contemporaine en France (Paris, 1930)
—— La musique en France entre les deux guerres, 1919–1939 (Geneva, 1946)
—— L'envers de la musique (Paris, 1948)

—— La danse à l'Opéra de Paris depuis 1900 (Paris, 1952)
Dunoyer, Cecilia, Marguerite Long, A Life in French Music, 1874–1966 (Bloomington, 1993)
Dupêchez, Charles, Histoire de l'Opéra de Paris, 1875–1980 (Paris, 1984)
Duverney, Anne-Marie and d'Horrer, Olivier, Mémoire de la chanson française depuis 1900 (Neuilly, 1979)

Flanner, Janet, ed. Irving Drutman, Paris was Yesterday, 1925–1939 (New York, 1972)
Fragny, Robert de, Ninon Vallin, princesse du chant (Lyon, 1963)
Fréjaville, Gustave, Au music-hall (Paris, 1923)

Galerne, Maurice, L'Ecole Niedermeyer (Paris, 1928)
Gardiner, James, Gaby Deslys: A Fatal Attraction (London, 1986)
Garnier, Charles, Le théâtre (Paris, 1871; repr. Arles, 1990)
Gavoty, Bernard, Alfred Cortot (Paris, 1977)
—— and Hauert, R., Wanda Landowska (Geneva, 1957)
Gheusi, P.-B., L'Opéra-Comique pendant la guerre (Paris, n.d.)
Gourret, Jean, Histoire de l'Opéra-Comique (Paris, 1978)
Guilleminault, Gilbert, Le roman vrai des années folles: 1918–1930 (Paris, 1975)

Harding, James, The Ox on the Roof (London, 1972)
—— Folies de Paris (London, 1979)
Hill, E. Burlingame, Modern French Music (London, 1924)
Hugo, Jean, Avant d'oublier, 1918–1931 (Paris, 1976)
Hurard-Viltard, Eveline, Le groupe des Six ou le matin d'un jour de fête (Paris, 1988)

d'Indy, Vincent, La Schola Cantorum, son histoire depuis sa fondation jusqu'en 1925 (Paris, 1927)

Jean-Aubry, Georges, French Music of To-day (London, 1919)
Joll, James, Europe since 1870: An International History (London, 1973; repr. 1978)
Jourdan-Morhange, Hélène, Mes amis musiciens (Paris, 1955)

Kahane, Martine, 1909–1929, Les Ballets Russes à l'Opéra (Paris, 1992)
Keynes, Milo (ed.), Lydia Lopokova (London, 1983)
Knapp, Bettina and Chipman, Myra, That was Yvette (London, 1966)
Kessler, Count Harry, The Diaries of a Cosmopolitan (London, 1971)

Lalo, Pierre, La musique retrouvée 1902–1927 (Paris, 1928)
Lambert, Constant, Music Ho! (London, 1934; repr. 1948)
Landormy, Paul, La musique française après Debussy (Paris, 1943)
Lanoux, Armand, Paris 1925 (Paris, 1957)
Lenormand, H.-R., Les confessions d'un auteur dramatique (Paris, 1949; 2nd edn, 1953)
Léon-Martin, Louis, Le music-hall et ses figures (Paris, 1928)
Lioncourt, Guy de, Un témoignage sur la musique et sur la vie au XXe siècle (Paris, 1956)
Lourié, Arthur, Sergei Koussevitzky and his Epoch (New York, 1931)

Marnold, Jean, Le cas Wagner (Paris, 1920)
Mayer, D. and Souvtchinsky P. (eds), Roger Desormière et son temps (Monaco, 1966)
Mead, Christopher Curtis, Charles Garnier's Paris Opéra (New York, 1991)
Merlin, Olivier, L'Opéra de Paris (Fribourg, 1975)
Messing, Scott, Neoclassicism in Music (Rochester University Press, 1988; repr. 1996)
Meylan, Pierre, Les écrivains et la musique (Lausanne, 1952)
Middleton, W. L., The French Political System (New York, 1933)

Monsaingeon, Bruno, *Mademoiselle: Conversations with Nadia Boulanger* (Manchester, 1985)
Mulet, Henri, *Les tendances néfastes et antireligieuses de l'orgue moderne* (Paris, 1922)
Myers, Rollo, *Modern French Music* (Oxford, 1971)

Nabokov, Nicolas, *Old Friends and New Music* (London, 1951)
Näslund, Erik, *Les Ballets Suédois 1920–1925* (Paris, 1994)
Nichols, Roger, *Conversations with Madeleine Milhaud* (London, 1996)

Oulmont, Charles, *Noces d'or avec mon passé,* (Paris, 1964)

Parès, Philippe, *33 tours en arrière* (Paris, 1978)
Patureau, Frédérique, *Le Palais Garnier dans la société parisienne, 1875–1914* (Liège, 1991)
Perl, Jed, *Paris without End* (San Francisco, 1988)
Perloff, Nancy, *Art and the Everyday: Popular Entertainment and the Circle of Erik Satie* (Oxford, 1991)

Perrin, Olivier (ed.), *Théâtres des Champs-Elysées* (Paris, 1963)
Poincaré, Raymond, *How France is Governed* (London, 1913)

Raynor, Henry, *Music and Society since 1815* (London, 1976)
Rearick, Charles, *The French in Love and War* (New Haven, 1997)
Rebois, Henri, *La musique française contemporaine*, conférence faite à la Villa Médicis le 19 mai 1928 (Rome, 1929)
Rohozinski, L. (ed.), *Cinquante ans de musique française, 1874–1925,* 2 vols (Paris, 1925)
Roubaud, Louis, *Music-hall* (Paris, 1924)
Rouché, Jacques, *L'art théâtral moderne* (Paris, 1924)
Roy, Jean, *Le Groupe des Six* (Paris, 1994)
Rubinstein, Artur, *My Many Years* (London, 1980)

Sachs, Maurice, *Au temps du boeuf sur le toit* (Paris, 1939)
—— *La décade de l'illusion* (Paris, 1950)
Samazeuilh, Gustave, *Musiciens de mon temps* (Paris, 1947)

Samson, Jim, *Music in Transition* (London, 1977)
Sanouillet, Michel, *Dada à Paris* (Paris, 1965)
Sauvy, Alfred, *Histoire économique de la France entre les deux guerres* (Paris, 1972)
Schrade, Leo, *Beethoven in France* (Yale, 1942; repr. New York, 1978)
Segond, André, *Georges Thill ou l'âge d'or à l'Opéra* (Lyon, 1980)
Séré, Octave, *Musiciens français d'aujourd'hui* (Paris, 1921)
Sert, Misia, *Two or Three Muses,* trans. Moura Budberg (London, 1953)
Shattuck, Roger, *The Banquet Years* (London, 1959)
Shead, Richard, *Music in the 1920s* (London, 1976)
Silver, Kenneth, *Esprit de corps* (Princeton, 1989)
Simeone, Nigel, *Paris: A Musical Gazetteer* (Yale University Press, 2000)
Sordet, Dominique, *Douze chefs d'orchestre* (Paris, 1924)
Spalding, Albert, *Rise to Follow* (New York, 1943)
Spycket, Jérôme, *Clara Haskil* (Lausanne/Paris, 1975)

Stiven, Frederic B., *In the Organ Lofts of Paris* (Boston, 1923)

Whittall, Arnold, *Music since the First World War* (London, 1977; repr. 1988)
Wiéner, Jean, *Allegro appassionato* (Paris, 1978)
Willett, John, *The New Sobriety: Art and Politics in the Weimar Period, 1917–1933* (London, 1978)
Wolff, Stéphane, *Un demi-siècle d'Opéra-Comique (1900–1950)* (Paris, 1953)
—— *L'Opéra au Palais Garnier* (Paris, 1962)

Zeldin, T, *France 1848–1945,* vol I, *Ambition and Love* (Oxford, 1973; repr. 1988); vol III, *Intellect and Pride* (Oxford, 1977; repr. 1980); vol IV, *Taste and Corruption* (Oxford, 1977; repr. 1980)

Articles

Aplin, John, 'Aldous Huxley and Music in the 1920s', *Music and Letters*, LXIV/1–2, 1983, 25–36
Apollinaire, Guillaume, '"Parade" et L'Esprit Nouveau', *Excelsior*, 11 May 1917, 5
—— 'L'esprit nouveau et les poètes', *Mercure de France*, 1 December 1918
Auric, Georges, 'L'Enfant et les sortilèges', *Les nouvelles littéraires*, 11 April 1925
—— 'La leçon d'Erik Satie', *La revue musicale*, 6, August 1925, 98–99
—— 'A propos du "Gendarme incompris"', *Cahiers Jean Cocteau II,* Paris, 1969, 39

Bancroft, David, 'Stravinsky and the NRF (1920–29)', *Music and Letters*, LV/3, 1974, 261–71
Barrell, E.A., 'A decade of 'The Six'', *Etude*, 47, December 1929, 883, 944
Bathori, Jane, 'Les musiciens que j'ai connus', trans. Felix Aprahamian, *Journal of the British Institute of Recorded Sound*, 15, 1964, 238–45
Bellas, Jacqueline, 'Francis Poulenc ou le "son de voix de Guillaume"', *La revue des lettres modernes*, III, nos 104–7, 1964, 130–48

Benjamin, George, 'Last dance', *Musical Times*, 135, July 1994, 432–35

Casella, Alfredo, 'Tone problems of today', *Musical Quarterly*, X, October 1924, 159–71
Cocteau, Jean, 'Les Biches. Les Fâcheux. Notes de Monte-Carlo', *Nouvelle revue française*, 126, March 1924, 275–78
Coeuroy, André, 'Further aspects of Contemporary Music', *Musical Quarterly*, XV, 1920, 547–73
Collaer, Paul, 'Il gruppo dei Sei', *L'approdo musicale*, 19/20, Rome, 1965
Collet, Henri, 'Un livre de Rimsky et un livre de Cocteau les cinq russes, les six français et Erik Satie', *Comoedia*, 16 and 23 January 1920
Copland, Aaron, 'The lyricism of Milhaud', *Modern Music*, 6, January–February 1929, 14–19

Durey, Louis, 'Francis Poulenc', *The Chesterian*, XXV, 1922, 1–4
Duruflé, Maurice, 'My recollections of Tournemire and Vierne', trans. Ralph Kneeream, *The American Organist*, XIV/11, November 1980, 54–60

Evans, Edwin, 'Albert Roussel', *The Chesterian*, VII/51, December 1925, 73–78

Ferroud, Pierre-Octave, 'La musique de chambre d'Albert Roussel', *La revue musicale*, April 1929, 52–64

Gillmor, Alan M., 'Erik Satie and the Concept of the Avant-Garde', *Musical Quarterly*, LXIX, 1983, 104–19

d'Indy, Vincent, 'Une école d'art répondant aux besoins modernes', *La tribune de Saint-Gervais*, XI, November 1900, 304–5

Jean-Aubry, Georges, 'The End of a Legend', *The Chesterian*, 6, 1924–25, 191–93

Koechlin, Charles, 'Les tendances de la musique moderne française', *Encyclopédie de la musique et dictionnaire du Conservatoire*, II/1, 1925, 56–145

Nectoux, Jean-Michel, 'Maurice Ravel et sa bibliothèque musicale', *Fontes Artis Musicae*, 24, 1977, 199–206

Pirro, André, 'L'enseignement de la musique aux universités françaises', *Acta musicologica*, II/2, April 1930, 45–56

Revue internationale de musique française, 29, 'Les années vingt', June 1989
Roland-Manuel, 'Ravel and the New French School', *Modern Music*, II/1, January 1925, 17–23
Roussel, Albert, 'Young French Composers', *The Chesterian*, I/2, October 1919, 33–37

Schloezer, Boris de, 'Le Festival français de Monte-Carlo', *La revue musicale*, V/4, February 1924, 161–67
Schmitt, Florent, 'Padmâvatî, opéra-ballet en deux actes de M. Roussel', *La revue de France*, 1923, 373–86

Wilkins, Nigel, 'Erik Satie's letters to Milhaud and others', *Musical Quarterly*, 66, July 1980, 404–28

List of photographs

Page 8. Boulevard St-Germain
18. Saint-Saëns listening out for Wagner
26. Celebrating the Armistice
29. Apollinaire
37. Picasso and the *Parade* drop-curtain
42. Messager at work
45. Conservatoire Concerts programme
49. Koussevitzky
54. Albert Wolff
55. The Conservatoire Orchestra
59. Façade of the Opéra
62. Jacques Rouché
64. An *abonné* of the Opéra
71. Georges Thill
73. Germaine Lubin
75. Paul Franz
81. Opéra-Comique poster
84. 'Au travail!'
89. Falla
93. Autograph of *L'enfant et les sortilèges*
95. Set for Ibert's *Angélique*
98–99. Vanni-Marcoux as Don Quichotte
101. Miguel Villabella
109. Modern dance under scrutiny
112. Yvonne Printemps
115. Gaby Deslys
118. Concert Mayol (inside)
120. Yvette Guilbert
121. Concert Mayol (outside)
122. Mistinguett and Maurice Chevalier (prewar)
123. Mistinguett and Maurice Chevalier (postwar)
125. Josephine Baker

131. Cabaret l'Enfer
137. Stravinsky, Diaghilev, Cocteau and Satie
139. Scene from *Le train bleu*
141. Karsavina in *Pulcinella*
144. Scene from *Les matelots*
150. Serge Lifar as Apollo
153. Rolf de Maré
157. Design for *Le boeuf sur le toit*
163. Lydia Lopokova
165. Felia Doubrovska as The Firebird
177. Henri Rabaud
183. Charles-Marie Widor
186. Vlado Perlemuter
187. Marcel Dupré
188. Teachers at the Ecole normale de musique
194. Charles Tournemire
200. Princesse de Polignac
205. Cover of *La revue musicale*
211. Fauré's funeral
213. D'Indy
217. Satie
220. Roussel at his work table
223. Ravel at home
227. Cocteau, Picasso, Stravinsky and Olga Picasso
232. Honegger
239. Darius and Madeleine Milhaud
242. Poulenc and friends
253. Koechlin
259. Nadia Boulanger and Walter Damrosch
262. Stravinsky the performer
265. Four of Les Six
270. Ida Rubinstein
275. Character from *La création du monde*

For permission to reproduce illustrations on the following pages I am grateful to © ADAGP, Paris and DACS, London 2002 (29, 137, 157, 200, 217, 275), BBC Hulton Picture Archive (89), Bibliothèque nationale de France (18, 29, 42, 45, 49, 62, 64, 98–99, 112, 125, 137, 141, 144, 150, 186, 187, 188, 194, 211, 217, 220), Henri Dutilleux (265), Fondation Singer-Polignac (200), Giraudon (84, 120, 122, 123), Pascale Honegger (232), Yves Koechlin (253), Lebrecht Collection (139, 165, 227), Madeleine Milhaud (239), Roger-Viollet (109)

Index

Numerals in italics refer to illustrations

abonnés, Opéra, abonnés des trois soirs 19, 63–4, *64*, 66, 69, 76, 136; Opéra-Comique 83
Académie des Beaux-Arts 177, 262
Adam, Adolphe 142; *Le chalet* 79, 80, 81; *Giselle* 135
Adorno, T. W. 152
Agate, James 112–13
Albéniz, Isaac 198, 199
Albert, François 60
Alhambra 119
American music, Parisian responses to 256–60
Americans in Paris 128; composers 258–9; Ecole des hautes études musicales de Fontainebleau 190–1; patronage 266, see also Polignac, princesse Edmond de and Rubinstein, Ida; SMI concert, 'Ecole américaine' 259; troops 9, 117–18, 190
Annuaire des artistes 42, 43, 46, 47, 49, 55, 119, 176
Annunzio, Gabriele d' 29; *Phèdre* 169
Ansermet, Ernest 53, 114, 273
Ansseau, Fernand 100–101
Antheil, George, *Ballet mécanique* 273
Apaches 261–2
Apollinaire, Guillaume 28–31, *29*; *Calligrammes* 29–30; Classical culture, dismissal of 29, 31, 69; *Les mamelles de Tirésias* 246, 271; *Parade* 30, 39
Aragon, Louis 165
Archer-Straw, Petrine 124
Arnold, Billy 240; Billy Arnold Orchestra 117
Ashton, Frederick 169–70
Association des Concerts Pasdeloup *see* Concerts Pasdeloup
Astruc, Gabriel 27
atonality 24
Atterberg, Kurt 154
Auber, Louis 181; *Le domino noir* 79, 84; *Fra diavolo* 79
Auber, Louis et al. (arr.), *Taglioni chez Musette* 134
Aubert, Louis 22, 42, 43; *Six poèmes arabes* 210; (arr.), Chopin, *La nuit ensorcelée* 135
Audran, Edmond 178; *Le grand mogol* 96
Auric, Georges 39, 92–3, 132, 147, 148, 253, *265*; *Les enchantements d'Alcine* 167, 172; *Les fâcheux* 92; Foxtrot, d'Indy's condemnation of 212; *Les matelots* 144, *144*; *Philémon et Baucis*, recitative for 97
avant-garde 57, 124, 140, 152, 212
Aveline, Albert 134, 135, 136

Bach, J. S. 239, 250, 251; Brandenburg Concertos 53, 251; *Christmas Oratorio* 251;

Conservatoire, Fauré reforms 182; organ works, Fauré revision of 192; return to 170, 182, 210, 233, 251; Wedding Cantata, Paris premiere 54
Bachelet, Alfred, *Quand la cloche sonnera* 87; *Scémo* 86
Baker, Josephine 123–4, *125*, 127, 161
Balakirev, Mily Alexeivitch 262
Balanchine, Georges 37, 138; choreography: *Apollon musagète* 150; *La chatte* 148; *L'enfant et les sortilèges* 91; *Le triomphe de Neptune* 257
Balguerie, Suzanne 86, 102, 103
ballet 134–75; *see also* Ballets Ida Rubinstein; Ballets russes; Ballets suédois; Opéra; Soirées de Paris
Ballets Ida Rubinstein 166–72
Ballets russes 22, 23, 24, 27, 34, 36, 63, 73, 124, 136–53, 161–2, 199, 201, 255
Ballets suédois 153–62, 240
bals-dancing 126
Bantock, Granville 257
Barbirolli, John 255
Barlow, Fred, *Poèmes chinois* 210
Barraine, Elsa 185
Barraud, Henri 43, 183
Baton, René 43, 221
Bauer, Marion 259
Baugé, André 99
Bax, Arnold 257
Bazin, René, *Donatienne* 86
Beaumont, Cyril 143
Beaumont, Etienne de 156, 162, 164, 165–6
Beck, Conrad 254
Beecham, Thomas 24, 49, 104
Beethoven, Ludwig van, centenary celebrations 252–3; *Egmont* overture 50; estimation of 251–3; *Fidelio* 74, 76; *La revue musicale*, special issue 252; in Paris concert repertoire 50, 56, 57, 74; Symphony no.5, Koussevitzky's conducting of 50
Bellaigue, Camille 68
Benois, Alexandre 170
Bérard, Adolphe 126
Bérard, Christian *242*
Berg, Alban, Chamber Symphony 52, 261; *Wozzeck* 74, 76
Bériza, Marguerite 257
Berkeley, Lennox, Violin Sonatina 48
Berlin, Irving, 'Alexander's Ragtime Band' 113
Berlioz, Hector 27, 33; Beethoven, promotion of 251, 252; *La damnation de Faust* 66; *Symphonie fantastique* 20
Bernard, Pierre 250
Berners, Edward, Lord, *Le carrosse du Saint Sacrement* 257; *Le triomphe de Neptune* 257; *Trois petites marches funèbres* 48
Bert, Berthe 189
Bertrand, Paul 86, 245
bitonality 32, 73, 167, 177, 226, 239, 240
Bizet, Georges 33; *Carmen* 70, 79, 80, 83, 88, 90; *Carmen*, recording of 251
Blancard, Jacqueline 185

Bliss, Arthur 255–6, 268
Bloch, André, *Brocéliande* 67
Boëllmann, Léon 178
Boeuf sur le toit, Le (nightclub) 117
Boïeldieu, Adrien 134; *La dame blanche* 79, 84; *Ma tante Aurore* 96; *Le nouveau seigneur du village* 79
Boito, Arrigo, *Nerone* 98
Bondeville, Emmanuel, *Madame Bovary* 98
Bonnard, Pierre, Debussy's *Jeux*, décor 154
Bonnet, Joseph 195
Borchard, Adolphe, *Sept estampes amoureuses* 47
Bordes, Charles 178, 179
Borel-Clerc, Charles, 'Le train fatal' 126
Börlin, Jean 153, 154, 156, 159, 161, 246
Borodin, Alexander 261, 262; *Nocturne* 167
Boston Symphony Orchestra 51
Bouffes du Nord-Concert 119
Bouffes-Parisiens 107, 108
Boulanger, Nadia 190, 191, *211*, 258, 259, *259*
Boulez, Pierre 33; Berg's *Wozzeck*, Paris premiere (1963) 74; *Improvisations sur Mallarmé* 24; neoclassicism, imperviousness to 272; Nijinska, role similar to 139; on Ravel 224, 225, 226; on Satie 218
Boult, Adrian 268
Bourdin, Roger 99
Bouyer, Raymond 252
Boyer, Lucien, 'Le pyjama présidentiel' 126
Brahms, Johannes 33, 42, 50, 230, 254
Brancour, René 43
Brandejont-Offenbach, Jacques, operetta, decline of 106, 107, 110
Braque, Georges 141
Brazilian music, and Milhaud 154, 156, 237, 238, 239–40, 258
Bret, Gustave 251
Breton, André 129, 165; *Manifeste du surréalisme* 161
Bréville, Pierre de 48
Brown, Frederick 35
Bruant, Aristide 119
Bruckner, Anton 254; Symphony no.9 47
Bruneau, Alfred, *Le jardin du paradis* 67; *Messidor*, entracte 56
Brussel, Robert 189
Brussels, Théâtre de la Monnaie 72, 99, 235
Buckle, Richard 24, 149, 165
Buffet, Eugénie 127
Bull, William 47
Busoni, Ferruccio 68, 206
Busser, Henri, *La pie borgne* 85; (arr.), Auber et al., *Taglioni chez Musette* 134, 135; Debussy, *Petite suite* 134; Delibes, *Soir de fête* 135

Cabaret Aristide Bruant 119
Cabaret l'Enfer *131*
cabarets-artistiques 119–20
café-concerts ('caf-conc') 119, 129–30
Caffaret, Lucie 119
Calvocoressi, M.-D. 23, 201–2

Cambini, Giuseppe Maria 251
Canal, Marguerite, *La flûte de jade* 47
Candide (magazine) 123
Canteloube, Joseph 42; *Chants d'Auvergne* 43; *Le mas* 67
Canudo, Ricciotto, *Skating Rink*, scenario 155
Capet, Lucien 183, 185, 190, 209
Caplet, André 22, 43, 44, 48; *Epiphanie* 42; *Le masque de la mort rouge* 22
Carpenter, John Alden 138
Carré, Albert 82, 85–6, 87
Carré, Marguerite 95
Cartel des Gauches 10
Caruso, Enrico 98, 100, 101
Carvalho, Léon 78
Casadesus, Gaby 251
Casadesus, Robert 48, 190, 251
Casals, Pablo 188
Casella, Alfredo 48; *La jarre* 159; Partita 53
Casella, Mme Alfredo 23, 32
Casino de Paris 115, 119, 124
Cendrars, Blaise 240
Cerf, Georges le 251
Cernay, Germaine 99
Chabrier, Emmanuel, *Bourrée fantasque* 57; *Briséis* 62; *L'éducation manquée* 62, 97; Wagner, view of 18, 19
Chabrier revival 84
Chalupt, René 164
chamber groups 47–9
Champs-Elysées, Théâtre des 44, 51, 114, 123, 148, 154, 156, 160, 161, 231, 257, 261
chanson de Paris, La 125
Chantavoine, Jean 88, 91, 206
Chappell, William 168, 171–2
Charpentier, Gustave 25, 177; *Louise* 31, 80, 82, 107; *Louise*, film of 125
Chat noir, Le 119
Châtelet, Théâtre du 44, 55, 166
Chausson, Ernest 18, 47, 56
chauvinism, *abonnés des trois soirs* 136; Berg's *Wozzeck*, exclusion of 74; Malipiero, *Sette canzoni*, demonstrations against 72; Opéra repertoire 73–4, 136; *Parade* as work of 'sales Boches' 38; Stravinsky and Diaghilev confronting 142–3
Cherubini, Luigi 181
Chester, J. and W. 114
Chesterian, The 164
Chevalier, Maurice 108, 110, 117, 120, 125, 122, *122*, *123*, 129, 176
Chevillard, Camille 43, 62, 74, 76, 135, 185
chic brutal 32
Chirico, Giorgio de, *La jarre*, design for 159
Chopin (arr. Aubert), *La nuit ensorcelée* 135; (arr. Messager, Vidal), *Suite de danses* 134
Christiné, Henri 244; *Dédé* 108, 122; *Phi-Phi* 107–8
churches, the **191–7**
Ciampi, Marcel 259
Cigale, Théâtre 162
Cimarosa, Domenico, *Il matrimonio segreto* 96
cinema 70, 124–5

Clair, René, *Entr'acte* 160; *Relâche*, 'cinematographic entr'acte' 159
classical mythology, Apollinaire's impatience with 30; *Apollon musagète* 230; *Mercure* 160, 163–6; *Phi-Phi* 107; *La statue retrouvée* 164; Poulenc 245; Prix de Rome, set titles 185
classicism, retrospective 137, 139
Claudel, Paul 154, 155, 236
Clemenceau, Georges 108; 'Au Travail!' (1920) 84
Clemenceau, Mme Paul (née Sophie Szeps) 198
Clementi, Muzio 216
Cocteau, Jean 31, 137, 147, 210, 227, 231, 246, 247, 271; *Antigone* (libretto, after Sophocles) 235; Ballets suédois 156; *Le boeuf sur le toit*, text 156; *Le coq et l'arlequin* 9, 39, 137, 138, 243; *Le dieu bleu* 24, 35; 'lifestyle modernism' 137, 146; *Les mariés de la tour Eiffel*, text 156; *Parade*, involvement in 36–8; *Roméo et Juliette*, production of 257; Roussel and 219; Satie and 215–16; Satie's titles, explanation of 217; significance, in Paris of the 1920s 35–6; on Stravinsky 51; Stravinsky, projected collaboration on *David* 34–6; 'Toréador', Poulenc setting of 242; on Wagner 104
Coeuroy, André 143, 145, 254, 261, 268, 272
Colette 198; *L'enfant et les sortilèges*, libretto 91, 92, 94
Collaer, Paul 43, 146, 147, 151, 154–5, 159, 160, 163, 234, 237
Collet, Henri, Les Six, baptism of 156, 264
colonialism 124
Colonne, Edouard 42; *see also* Concerts Colonne
comédie musicale 113;
Comédie-Française 104
Commune 78, 81
Comoedia 72, 155, 264, 267
Concerts Colonne 42, 54, 55, 255, 261
Concerts Durand 197
Concerts Koussevitzky 50–1, 54
Concerts Lamoureux 42, 43, 54, 257
Concerts Pasdeloup 22, 43–4, 54–5, 221, 251; 'Schoenberg scandal' 44, 54, 56
Concerts Philharmoniques 261
Concerts Rouge 56
Concerts Straram 51, 54
Concerts Touche 56–7
Conrad, Doda 32, 176, 263, 274
Conservatoire 22, 177, **181–7**; Concerts 41–2, 44–5, 45, 54, 56; Fauré reforms 250; Prix de Rome 66; master classes 189, 253; professorial salaries, cf. Opéra 65; voice teaching, inadequacy of 101–2
Conservatoire de musique russe 262
Cooper, Martin 78, 81, 85
Copland, Aaron 48, 190–1, 258, 259
Coppola, Piero 271
Cortot, Alfred 50, 53, 117, 176, 185, 186, 187–9, 188, 195, 198, 204, 209, 253
Cossart, Michael de 172

Couperin, François 21, 251, 254
courrier musical, Le 50, 52, 53–4, 65, 72, 126, 158, 202–4, 259
Coward, Noël 114–15
Cowell, Henry 259–60
Craft, Robert 142, 263
Croisset, Francis de, *Ciboulette*, text 110–11
Croiza, Claire 99, 189, 199
Cubism, Cubists 28, 30, 37, 138
Curtiss, Fred 119
Czech music, reception of 90–1, 205

Dabit, Eugène 132
Dada, Dadaism 161, 165, 212
Dahl, Viking 154
Dalayrac, Nicolas-Marie, *Une heure de mariage* 96
Dallier, Henri 191, 195
Damia [Marie-Louise Damien] 127, 128–9
Damrosch, Walter 190, 259, 259
dance, in operetta 106, 109, 110
dance, popular 107, 109–10, 109; *bals-dancing* 126
Dancing Times 166
Dandelot, Arthur 253
Daniel, Keith 244–5
Darré, Jeanne-Marie 185–6
Daven, André 123
Dean, Winton 33
Debussy, Claude 19–20, 115, 198, 214; *La bôite à joujoux* 159; Cello Sonata 218; 'Ce qu'a vu le vent d'ouest' 32; chamber sonatas 21; *La damoiselle élue*, Tenroc review of 202–3; *En blanc et noir* 21, 25; *Etudes* 32, 218, 274; 'Gigues' 42; 'Golliwogg's Cake Walk' 113; 'Ibéria' 42; and 'Impressionism' 20, 22; *Jeux* 42, 154; Koussevitzky, view of 49; *Le martyre de Saint Sébastien* 29, 143; *La mer* 33, 41, 236; *Nocturnes* 50; *Noël des enfants qui n'ont plus de maisons* 21; *Pelléas et Mélisande* 19, 33, 68, 80, 82, 86, 87, 99, 235; *Le petit nègre* 113; *Petite suite* (arr. Busser) 134; *Prélude à l'après-midi d'un faune* 47, 263; *Préludes* 20, 237; *Préludes*, Grovlez orchestration of 119; 'proletarianism', contempt for 31; respect, importance of in art 141; *La revue musicale*, special issue 204; Satie 217–18; Stravinsky, Symphonies of Wind Instruments, as tribute to 228; *Suite bergamasque* 56; titles 217; Wagner, view of 18, 19, 21
'debussystes' 22, 33, 235
Defreyn, Henri 111
Degas, Edgar 28
Delage, Maurice 256; *Chant tamoul: Ragamalica*
Delannoy, Marcel 170, 233; *Le marchand des lunettes*, suite 52
Delaunay, Charles 141
Delibes, Léo, *Coppélia* 134, 135; *La cour du roi Pétaud* 96; *Lakmé* 79, 80, 94, 96; *Sylvia* 134, 135; (arr. Busser), *Soir de fête* 135
Delius, Frederick 256
Delmas, Marc, *Cyrca* 135
Delvincourt, Claude 48, 183
Demuth, Norman 239, 246
Denby, Edward 145

Deschanel, Paul 126
Deshevov, Vladimir 149
Deslys, Gaby 114–15, 115, 117
Desnos, Robert 260
Desormière, Roger 44, 50, 151–2, 154, 159; *Roméo et Juliette*, incidental music to 257
Devienne, François, *Les visitandines* 78, 79
Devriès, David 100
Diaghilev, Serge 24, 27, 35, 37, 97, 124, 134, 137, 154, 159, 162, 201, 271, 273; *Le baiser de la fée*, contempt for 171; Ballets Ida Rubinstein, contempt for 169, 170; Ballets russes 136–53; Chevalier, view of 108; competition to 153, 165; Delius as *bête noire* of 256; jazz, lack of interest in 161; Lambert's audition with 256; *Parade* 39; Satie, meeting with 215; *Sleeping Princess*, production of 135–6, 139; as Wagner lover 138
Disney, Walt, *Snow White* 94
Donizetti, Gaetano, *La favorite* 65, 66; *La fille du régiment* 79, 80, 82, 84
Doret, Gustave 266; *La tisseuse d'orties* 87
Doubrovska, Felia 165
Doucet, Clément 117
Drake, Jeremy 116, 239
Dranem [Albert Menard] 100, 110, 122
Dreyfus, Alfred 22
Dreyfus case 27, 48
drink and drugs 85, 246
Droz, Eugénie 251
Dubois, Théodore 25, 177, 181
Dubost, Jeanne (Mme René) 135, 198
Duchesnau, Michel 48
Dufay, Guillaume 251
Dufranne, Hector 87, 99–100
Dufy, Raoul 29; *Le boeuf sur le toit*, design 157
Dukas, Paul 91, 209, 263, 267; *Ariane et Barbe-bleue* 81, 82; Conservatoire, teaching at 184, 185; *La péri* 134, 135; *Variations sur un thème de Rameau* 185
Dukelsky, Vladimir (later Vernon Duke) 148, 256, 262; *Zéphyr et Flore* 144, 262
Dulac, Germaine 70
Dumesnil, René 44, 51, 114, 141, 143, 145, 146, 255, 261; Opéra-Comique, 'crisis' of 82–4
Duni, Egidio 78
Duparc, Henri 18
Dupin, Marc-Olivier 181
Dupont, Gabriel, *Antar* 67
Dupré, Marcel 187, 188, 190, 193, 197; Symphony in G minor 52; *Les vêpres de la vierge* 196
Durand (publishers) 192, 197
Durand, Jacques 32, 126, 191
Durey, Louis 272
Duruflé, Maurice 184, 189
Dushkin, Samuel 259
Dutilleux, Henri 189, 222, 268, 272

'Ecole américaine' 259
Ecole d'Arcueil 264
Ecole de Paris 254
Ecole des hautes études musicales de Fontainebleau 190–1
Ecole Niedermeyer 178, 179, 180, 192, 250

Ecole normale de musique de Paris 187–9; staff at 188
education *see* teaching institutions
Eglise de l'Etoile, 'concerts spirituels' 251
Elgar, Edward, low standing of 256, 257
émigrés 254, 262
Emmanuel, Maurice 222; *Salamine* 67
Empire music hall 120
Enesco, Georges 189, 197–8, 254–5; *Oedipe* 42
Engel, Emile 185
English music, responses to 255–7
Erlanger, Camille, *Aphrodite* 81, 82
Erté, *La marche à l'étoile*, designs 117
Evans, Edwin 256
Expert, Henri 251
Expressionism 34

Fairchild, Blair 42
Falla, Manuel de 48, 89, 199, 204, 255; *Psyché* 48; *El retablo de maese Pedro*, 87–8, 201, 245, 255; *El sombrero de tres picos* 137, 255
Farrar, Geraldine 98, 111
Fauré, Gabriel 20–21, 41, 177, 178, 192, 198, 209, **209–12**; Barcarolle no.13 210; Conservatoire, reform of 181–2, 187; *Figaro*, contributions to 202; funeral 60, 211; *L'horizon chimérique* 211; d'Indy, potential influence on 215; *Mirages* 178, 211–12; Nocturne no.13 230; *Pénélope* 81, 82, 85; Piano Quintet no.2 48; postwar Zeitgeist 210; *Requiem* 22, 196; *La revue musicale*, special issue 212; Satie's role resembling 216; SMI 48, 49; Violin Sonata no.2 209
Favart, Edmée 111
Fémina, Théâtre 117
Féraldy, Germaine 102
Février, Henri, *L'île désenchantée* 67
Février, Jacques 185, 242
Figaro, Le 168
film 107, 125; film effects in opera 69–70
Five, The 264, 265
Flanner, Janet 148–9
Flers, Robert de, *Ciboulette*, text 110–11
Foire St-Germain 80
Fokina, Vera 134
Fokine, Michel 134, 138
Folies-Bergère 119, 124, 125
Fourestier, Louis 53, 185
Fournier, Pierre 114
Françaix, Jean 185, 201
Franck, César 178, 251; Offertoire for cello and organ 56; *Variations symphoniques* 53
Franco-Prussian War 20, 78, 81, 106
Franz, Paul 66, 70, 74, 75, 76, 100–101
Fratellini brothers 156
French identity, in art 254; Fauré 211; operetta 118–19; popular song 129, 130; Poulenc 242–4
Freund, Marya 198, 261
Friant, Charles 100, 104
Fuchs, Georg 61
Fugère, Lucien 100
Fuller, Loïe 231, 239
Futurism 149

Gabo, Naum, *La chatte*, sets for 148
Gaîté-Lyrique 63, 143
Gaillard, Marius-François 260
Gall, Yvonne 102
gamelan 145, 242
Garafola, Lynn 24, 27, 135, 137, 140, 148, 149, 152, 161
Gardiner, James 115–16
Garnier, Charles 19, 59
Gatti, G. M. 72
Gaubert, Philippe 41, 43, 55, 185; *Naïla* 67
Gautier, Théophile 142
Gedalge, André 41, 185
George, Yvonne 120, 127–8, 240, 246
Georges, Alexandre 178; *Miarka* 67
Georgius [Georges Guibourg] 129–30
German music, responses to 250–4, 260–1
Gershwin, George 260
Gheusi, P.-B. 82, 94, 203
Gide, André 167; *Perséphone*, libretto 217
Gigout, Eugène 178, 185, 191–2
Gillmor, Alan M. 164, 165
Glazunov, Alexander 56
Gluck, Christoph Willibald 21; *Orphée* 80, 82
Gogry, Odette 57
Golschmann, Vladimir 245, 250, 259
Gontcharova, Natalia 144
Goossens, Eugene 255, 256, 257
Gounod, Charles-François 33, 198; aesthetics 273–4; *La colombe* 97; *Faust* 62, 65, 69; *Faust*, lifted by Yvain in operetta 110; *Faust*, parodies 127, 158; Guilbert, Yvette, singing for 119–20; *Le médecin malgré lui* 97; *Mireille* 79, 80; *Philémon et Baucis* 69, 79, 96; *Roméo et Juliette* 60, 79
Gramont, Sanche de 266
grand opéra, Wagner on 78
Gregorian chant 180, 195–6
Grétry, A.-E.-M., *Richard Coeur-de-lion* 78, 79; *Zémire et Azor* 78; (arr. Adam), *Le déserteur* 142
Grieg, Edvard 56
Griffes, Charles 259
Griffiths, Paul 258
Grigoriev, Serge 149
Gromort, Georges 52
Gross, Valentine 215
Grovlez, Gabriel 41, 48, 119; *Maimouna* 134
Guilbert, Yvette 119–20, 120, 126
Guilmant, Alexandre 179, 192, 195
Guinness, Walter 166
Guitry, Sacha 112; *Mozart*, text 86, 111

Haas, Monique 185
Habeneck, François 41
Hahn, Reynaldo 86, 141, 182, 189; *Ciboulette* 103, 110–11, 113; *Le dieu bleu* 24, 35, 110; *La fête chez Thérèse* 134; *Mozart* 111–13
Halbreich, Harry 155
Halévy, Daniel 28
Halévy, Fromental 177; *La juive* 61, 65, 66
Handel, George Frederick 56, 245, 251

Haquinius, Algot 154
Harding, James 107
Harris, Roy 258
Harsányi, Tibor 254, 271
Haydn, Joseph, attitudes to 251; symphonies, performances of 52, 56, 57, 58, 251
Hébertot, Jacques 153
Heldy, Fanny 69, 70, 74, 102
Hérold, Ferdinand, *Le pré aux clercs* 79; *Zampa* 79
Herrick, Myron T. 48
Heugel (publisher), *Le ménestrel* 204
Hevesy, André de 252
Hindemith, Paul 261; Concerto for Orchestra (op. 38) 53; String Quartet no.1 48; Viola Concerto 52
historical re-creations, Ballets Ida Rubinstein 170–1
Hofmannsthal, Hugo von 24
Holbrooke, Joseph 257
Holst, Gustav 268–9
Honegger, Arthur 168, 189, 210, 216, 231–6, 232, 264, 265; *Amphion* 170; *Antigone* 235–6; *Les aventures du roi Pausole* 108, 109–10, 236; *Cris du monde* 235; *Danse de la chèvre* 273; *Le dit des jeux du monde* 52–2; *Horace victorieux* 50, 155, 231–2; *L'impératrice aux rochers* 168, 170; *Jeanne d'Arc* 168, 236; *Mouvement symphonique* 236; *Les noces d'Amour et de Psyché* 167, 170; *Pacific 231* 52, 231, 233, 234; *Pastorale d'été* 155, 231; *Phèdre* 169, 170; Piano Concertino 52; *Le roi David* 155, 170, 231, 232–3; *Rugby* 234–5; *Sémiramis* 170; *Sept pièces brèves* for piano 231; *Skating Rink* 155–6, 161, 203; *The Tempest*, prelude 52
Horne, Marilyn 67
Horowitz, Vladimir 198
Hüe, Georges, *Siang Sin* 135
Hugo, Jean, *Les mariés de la tour Eiffel*, costume 156
Hyspa, Vincent 218

Ibert, Jacques 184; *Angélique*, set 95; *Divertissement* 69; *Escales* 43; *Persée et Andromède* 67, 69
Impressionism 20, 22–3, 229, 255; rejection, Fauré 212, Satie 216–17, 218
inflation 10, 64–5, 177, 199
Inghelbrecht, D.-E. 43, 154, 156, 251, 261, 266; *Le diable dans le beffroi* 135
Ireland, John 257
ISCM 267
Isherwood, Christopher 128

Isnardon, Jacques 101; *L'art théâtral* 104
Isola, Emile and Vincent 82

Jammes, Francis 90
Janáček, Leoš 68
Janes, Sidney, *La geisha* 95
Janson, Caroline 213
jazz 9, 54, 113–17, 177, 230, 260; Ballets suédois and 158; Harlem jazz 116, 240; 'jazz age' 123–4; Milhaud, *La création du monde* 158–9, 240–1; and operetta 107; Porter, Cole, *Within the Quota* 158–9; Roussel, 'Jazz dans la nuit' 222; Stravinsky 230; Yvain, *Paris qui jazze* 120, 130
Johnsson, Anna 135
Jongen, Joseph 41, 180
Journet, Marcel 70, 98–9
Judic 127
Julliot, Marguerite 97–8
Jusseaume and Ronsin, *Pelléas*, Opéra-Comique sets for 86

Karsavina, Tamara 111, 257
Kessler, Count Harry 24
Keynes, John Maynard 162
Kochno, Boris 108, 152; *La chatte*, libretto for 148
Koechlin, Charles 23, 25, 48, 219, 221, 252, 253, 264, 272; Poulenc, as teacher of 241, 243, 244; *Within the Quota*, orchestration 158
Korngold, Erich 103
Koussevitzky, Serge 49–51, 49, 56, 152; Concerts Koussevitzky 50–4
Kreisler, Fritz 56
Krenek, Ernst 68, 206; *Jonny mène la danse* (*Jonny spielt auf*) 261

Labé, Louise, *Le tournoi singulier* 161–2
Ladmirault, Paul 267
Laforgue, Jules, *Moralités légendaires* 69
Lagut, Irène 29; *Les mariés de la tour Eiffel*, decor 156
Lalande, Madeleine 98
Lalo, Pierre 236; *Le roi d'Ys* 80, 82
Laloy, Louis 64, 141
Lambert, Constant, 97, 274; *Adam and Eve* 256; Diaghilev, audition with 256; Romeo and Juliet 144, 257
Lamoureux, Charles *see* Concerts Lamoureux
Landormy, Paul 193
Landowska, Wanda 47, 53, 188, 245, 251
Landré, Guillaume, *Beatrice* 74
Langlais, Jean 184
Lanoux, Armand 268
Laparra, Raoul, *La habanéra* 85
Larionov, Mikhail 137, 143, 144
Laurencie, Lionel de la 251
Laurencin, Marie, designs *Les biches* 146
Lazarus, Daniel, *L'illustre magicien* 205
Lazzari, Sylvio, *Le sauteriot* 85; *La tour de feu* 67, 69
Le Flem, Paul 260
Lecocq, Charles, *La fille de Madame Angot* 95, 96, 111
Léger, Fernand 155; *La création du monde*, programme 275
Lehmann, Lili 111
Lenormand, H.-R. 267–8
Leoncavallo, Ruggero, *I pagliacci* 71, 81

Leroi, Pierre 257
Lester, Keith 168
Levidis, Dmitri 255
Levinson, André 135–6, 149
Lifar, Serge 144, 149, 150, 150
'lifestyle modernism' 137, 138, 143, 146, 149, 153, 155, 161
Ligue nationale pour la défense de la musique française 25–6
Lioncourt, Guy de 180
Liszt, Franz 43; *Les soirées de Vienne* 170, 253
Lockspeiser, Edward 20
London Symphony Orchestra 257
Long, Marguerite 185, 188, 199
Lopokova, Lydia 162, 163, 166
Lowry, Vance 240
Luart, Emma 102
Lubin, Germaine 70, 73, 76, 102, 103, 198
Lucia, Fernando de 102
Lully, Jean-Baptiste 170, 179, 230
Lyon, Gustave 52, 53

Madeleine, La 195, 211
Magaloff, Nikita 185
Maginot Line 260
Magnard, Albéric 22, 180
Mahler, Gustav 44; 'elephantine dreams' of 254; *Lieder eines fahrenden Gesellen* 44; *Das Lied von der Erde* 44
Maillart, Louis-Aimé, *Les dragons de Villars* 79, 82
Maistre, Joseph de 27
Malherbe, Henri 68, 88, 90
Malipiero, Francesco, *L'Orfeide* 72–3; *Saint-François d'Assise* 53; *Sette canzoni* 71, 72–3, 136, 255
Mallarmé, Stéphane 23, 24, 141
Mangeot, Auguste 187–9, 255
Maré, Rolf de 134, 153–4, 153
Margueritte, Victor, *La garçonne* 111
Marigny, Théâtre 111, 113
Mariotte, Antoine, *Esther* 67
Markevitch, Igor 262; Partita for piano and orchestra 201
Marnold, Georgette 117
Martineau, Paul, *Deux mélodies hébraïques* 210
Martinů, Bohuslav 255
Mascagni, Pietro, *Cavalleria rusticana* 80
Massé, Victor, *Galathée* 69, 79; *Les noces de Jeannette* 79
Massenet, Jules 198; *Le cid* 60; *Don Quichotte*, Vanni-Marcoux in title role 98, 99; *Esclarmonde* 70; *Grisélidis* 70; *Hérodiade* 66; *Le jongleur de Notre-Dame* 81, 82, 91; *Manon* 66, 70, 79, 80, 83, 94; *La navarraise* 80, 82; *Thaïs* 60, 66, 199; *Werther* 66, 70, 80, 82, 83
Massine, Leonid 154, 162, 164; choreography for: *Le chant du rossignol* 136; *Parade* 36, 37; *Le pas d'acier* 149, 150; *Mercure* 164
Masson, Louis 82, 86, 91–2, 96
master classes 189, 253
Matisse, Henri, *Le chant du rossignol*, designs 136
Mauclair, Camille 203,
Mazellier, Jules, *Graziella* 86; *Les matines d'amour* 67
Méhul, Etienne-Nicolas, *Joseph* 79
Mellers, Wilfrid 245
Mendelssohn, Felix 43, 254

285

ménestrel, Le 64–5, 126, 202, 203, 250
Mercier, René, Déshabillez-vous 110
Messager, André 41, 42, 66, 95, 178,
    198; La basoche 80, 82, 93; Béatrice
    113; Coups de roulis 113, 126; Les
    deux pigeons 135; L'enfant et les
    sortilèges, review of 92–3; Fortunio
    85, 113; Hahn, derogation of 110;
    Hahn's Mozart, rejection of 111;
    Monsieur Beaucaire 113; Mozart,
    Così, revival of 87; operettas 113;
    Passionnément 113; Pelléas, premiere
    at Opéra-Comique 82; Véronique
    95, 113; (arr., with Vidal), Chopin,
    Suite de danses 134
Messiaen, Olivier 27, 154, 184, 186,
    222, 258, 272; Apparition de l'église
    éternelle 197; L'ascension 197; Les corps
    glorieux 197; Hymne au Saint
    Sacrement 52; La Trinité,
    appointment to (1931) 196–7;
    La nativité du Seigneur 197; Offrandes
    oubliées 52
Messing, Scott 140–1, 143
Métra, Olivier 163
Metropolitan Opera, New York 87, 100
Meyer, Marcelle 251
Meyerbeer, Giacomo 134; L'africaine
    65; Les huguenots 65; Le pardon de
    Ploërmel 79; Le prophète 65; Robert le
    diable 65
Meyerhold, Vsevolod 61
Mihalovici, Marcel 180, 254
Milhaud, Darius 23, 53, 87, 132, 198,
    216, 236–41, 239, 250, 256, 264,
    265, 267; Les biches, views of 147–8;
    La bien-aimée 167; Le boeuf sur le toit
    156–8, 157, 237, 240; Brazilian
    influences 154, 156, 236, 237,
    238, 239–40, 258; La brebis égarée
    90, 211; Caramel mou 116; Catalogue
    de fleurs 238–9; Chabrier, L'éducation
    manquée, recitative for 97; Les
    choéphores, 237, 239; La création du
    monde 116, 158–9, 238, 240–1, 275;
    Les euménides 239; Fauré, comments
    on 210–11, 212; L'homme et son désir
    154–5, 156, 237, 238; jazz, appeal
    of 116, 240, 241; and Koechlin
    158; Koussevitzky concerts 50;
    Laissez-les tomber, effect of 115–16;
    Machines agricoles 238; Magnard,
    admiration for 22; Mahler 254; Les
    malheurs d'Orphée 201; Première suite
    symphonique 236–7; Protée 43;
    Ravel's La valse, criticisms of 49;
    reviews 50, 51, 203, 204; Salade
    163; Satie's Mercure, cf. Pulcinella
    163–4; Saudades do Brazil 237, 238,
    239–40, 258; Sonata for flute,
    oboe, clarinet and piano 117;
    String Quartet no.5 49, 224, 239;
    Symphonic Suite no.2 32; Le train
    bleu 92, 139, 139; Twenties,
    summing up of 276; Wagner,
    extracts overperformed 74, 254
Milhaud, Madeleine 159, 168, 169,
    198, 237, 239
Miró, Joan 257
Missa, Edmond 178
Mistinguett 113, 120, 122, 122, 123,
    123, 127
Mocquereau, Dom André 196
modernism 137; 'lifestyle modernism'
    146, 149, 153

Mogador, Théâtre 44
Mompou, Federico 255
money, Art and 269–70
Monnaie, Théâtre de la 72, 99, 235
Monsigny, Pierre Alexandre, Le
    déserteur 78, 79, 82
Montbreuse, Gaby 127
Monte Carlo, premieres 91, 148
Montesquiou, Robert de 166
Monteux, Pierre 32, 53, 257
Monteverdi, Claudio, L'incoronazione
    di Poppea 62
Montmartre, Théâtre 261
Moore, Grace 125–6
Morand, Paul 39
Moretti, Raoul, Trois jeunes filles nues 110
Morton, Jelly Roll 114
Mossolov, Alexander 149
Moulin Rouge 119
Mozart, Wolfgang Amadeus, Così fan
    tutte, revival 87; Don Giovanni 65,
    111; estimation of 250, 251; Die
    Zauberflöte 71, 72, 76, 79; operetta,
    iconic status in 111–12; Le nozze di
    Figaro 79, 80, 83; Requiem, at
    Josephine Baker's funeral 124; in
    repertoire of Paris concerts 56;
    Vienna Opera tour (1928) 76
Murphy, Gerald, Within the Quota,
    scenario 158
museum culture 83–4
music from abroad, responses to
    250–63
music hall 106, 119–26; bals-dancing,
    competition from 126; cinema,
    competition from 124–5; Concert
    Mayol 118, 121; Pierné, Impressions
    de music-hall 135, 136, 137–8
music hall, revues, chansons 106–33
Mussorgsky, Modest 262; Boris
    Godunov 33, 73; Kovanchchina 23,
    71, 72, 73; Kovanshchina,
    orchestration by Stravinsky and
    Ravel; Tableaux d'une exposition,
    Ravel orchestration
    of 51; song cycles 33
Muzio, Claudia 73

Nabokov, Nicolas 201, 262
Napoleon III 60, 178
Näslund, Erik 158
National League for the Defence of
    French Music 48
Nectoux, Jean-Michel 192
Nemtchinova, Vera 146
neoclassicism 21, 164, 216, 218, 246,
    272; 'choreographic neoclassicism'
    137, 152; Stravinsky 142, 145, 152
Neue Freie Presse 103
Neues Wiener Journal 103
Newman, Ernest 18
Nicolo (Isouard), Les rendez-vous
    bourgeois 79
Niedermeyer, Louis 178
Nielsen, Carl, Symphony no.3 261
Nietzsche, Friedrich 26
Nijinska, Bronislava 137, 138, 139,
    145, 257
Nijinsky, Vaslav 124, 136, 161, 237
Nikitina, Alice 150
Nin, Joaquín 180
Nino, Persée et Andromède, libretto 69
Notre-Dame 193–4
Nouveaux Jeunes, Les 216, 264
Nozière, Fernand 169

Obouhov, Nicolas 262
obscenity 161
Offenbach, Jacques, La belle Hélène 69;
    La chanson de Fortunio 96; Les contes
    d'Hoffmann 79, 80, 94; La créole 124;
    La fille du tambour-major 95, 96;
    Orphée aux enfers 69
Ollone, Max d' 184–5; L'arlequin 67;
    Le retour 67
Olympia 119
Olympic Games (1924) 162
ondes Martenot 255, 260
Opéra, the (Palais Garnier; Académie
    nationale de musique) 59–77, 59;
    abonnés des trois soirs 63–4, 66, 69;
    ballet 134–6; funding 61, 63–4,
    65, 66–7; house lights, lowering of
    61–2; Malipiero, Sette canzoni,
    withdrawal of 72, 132; new works
    68–9, 70–2; premieres (1928–9)
    67; Palais Garnier, construction of
    59–61; repertoire 60, 65–6, 67–8,
    70–2; singers 97–104; stage boxes,
    removal of 62–3; state subsidy 61,
    65, 66; strikes (1918–20) 64–5,
    270; touring opera companies 74;
    transfers 70–2; Wagner operas,
    performance of 18–19, 44, 60–2,
    71, 74–6
opera singers 97–104
opéra comique 78–9, 100, 106
Opéra-Comique 66, 67, 78–105,
    111; decline (1930s) 94–5;
    financing of 83; Honegger's
    Antigone, rejection of 235; librettos
    suggested by 86; new theatre,
    inauguration of 82; Opéra, merger
    with (1936) 95; Opéra, relations
    with 70–71, 72; repertoire 79,
    80–82; role, as home for intimate
    French opera 71; Salle Favart, fire
    of 1887 82; Salle Favart,
    Malherbe's criticisms of 88;
    singers 97–104; spoken dialogue,
    contract for 78; Tristan und Isolde
    76, 86
operetta 78, 100, 106–13; dance in
    106–7, 108
orchestras, conductors, chamber
    ensembles 41–58; concerts and
    recitals (1927/8) 53–4; finances
    44, 45; first performances 42, 43,
    47, 48, 49, 50–1, 52, 53, 54;
    repertoire 250–3; Prokofiev's
    criticisms of 46; salaries 55;
    schedules 45–7; unions 47, 48,
    50, 54–5; women 55–6; see also
    Concerts Colonne; Concerts
    Koussevitzky; Concerts
    Pasdeloup; Concerts Straram;
    Conservatoire Concerts;
    Concerts Rouge; Concerts
    Touche; Orchestre symphonique
    de Paris
orchestration, Honegger 170;
    Milhaud 116, 241; Parade 41–2;
    Poulenc 147–8; Roussel 221; Satie
    160, 163; Stravinsky 33, 51, 68,
    111, 114, 141, 145, 158
Orchestre symphonique de Paris
    (OSP) 51–3
orientalism 37, 135, 136, 220, 222,
    242
Original Dixieland Jazz Band 114
Orledge, Robert 161, 178, 243

ostinato 33; Fauré not attracted by
    212; Honegger 231, 236; d'Indy,
    lack of need for 214; Milhaud 239;
    Poulenc 242; Ravel 226; Roussel
    220, 222; Satie 218; Stravinsky
    143, 209, 226, 228, 230
Ouellette, Fernand 260

Paderewski, Ignacy 266
Paer, Ferdinando, Le maître de chapelle 79
Paladilhe, Emile 177
Palais Garnier see Opéra
Panzéra, Charles 99, 211
Parade 30, 35, 36, 36–9, 37, 41, 136,
    137–8, 209, 215, 228, 241, 263–4;
    La petite dactylo prefiguring 107;
    reception 38–9
Paray, Paul 43; Artémis troublée 167
Paris (1920s), map 7; provincial
    dreams of 266; visitors 254–63;
    and passim
Paris Conservatoire see Conservatoire
Paris Opéra see Opéra
Pasdeloup, Jules, see Concerts
    Pasdeloup
'Pastorale, La' (amateur orchestra) 55
patronage, and adventurous
    programming 52, 56; Americans
    266; Le boeuf sur le toit 156;
    Diaghilev 24, 27; Polignac,
    princesse Edmond de 198,
    199–201, 200; Saint-Marceaux,
    Mme René de ('Meg') 198–9;
    salons 197–201; Sandberg, Serge
    43, 44; Rubinstein, Ida 166–72;
Pavlova, Anna 124, 134
Perchicot 129
Pergolesi, G. B. 251; La serva padrona
    79, 80, 96; Stravinsky's inspiration
    from 140, 142
Périer, Jean 95, 111
Périlhou, Albert 178
Perlemuter, Vlado 185, 186, 186,
    210
Perloff, Nancy 164
Perne, François 181
Pernet, André 126
pétomane, le 117
Petridis, Petro 255
Pevsner, Anton, La chatte, costumes
    148
Philharmonic String Quartet 255
Philidor, François-André Danican,
    Le maréchal ferrant 96
Philipp, Isidor 184, 185, 188, 188,
    190, 262
Piaf, Edith 128
piano tax 126–7
Picabia, Francis 160; Relâche, scenario
    and décor 159, 217
Picasso, Pablo 35, 36, 87, 141, 163,
    164, 227; Mercure, designs 164;
    Parade, designs 36, 37, 37, 38
Picasso, Olga 227
Pierné, Gabriel 41, 43, 55, 219, 263;
    Cydalise et le chèvre-pied 135;
    Impressions de music-hall 135, 136,
    137–8
Pilcer, Harry 115
Pirandello, Luigi, La jarre, text 159
Piston, Walter 48, 258, 259
Pius X, Motu proprio (1903) 195–6
Planquette, Robert, Les cloches de
    Corneville 96
Pleyel (firm) 52

Société des auteurs 78
Société J. S. Bach 251
Société des Concerts du
    Conservatoire 41–2, 44–5
Société des instruments anciens 251
Société musicale indépendante see
    SMI
Société de musique d'autrefois 251
Société nationale de musique see SNM
Soirées de Paris 28
Sokolova, Lydia 144, 149
Sorabji, Kaikhosru Shapurji 48
Sordet, Dominique 250
Sousa, John Philip 113
Spanish music, responses to 255
Spessivtseva, Olga 134
Staats, Léo 135, 136
Stanislavsky, Konstantin 61
Steegmuller, Francis 147
Steinert, Alexander 259
Steuermann, Eduard 261
Steuermann, Emmanuel 49
Stiven, Frederic 193, 195
Straram, Walter 51–2, 54, 56, 261
Strauss, Johann, Le beau Danube 163
Strauss, Richard 43, 68, 103; Ariadne
    auf Naxos 103; as antithesis of
    French art 254; Der Rosenkavalier
    71, 72, 73–4; Elektra 32; La légende
    de Joseph 24; Salome 32, 71
Stravinsky, Igor 36, 68, 84, 87, 108,
    137, 144, 226–31, 227, 233,
    262–4, 262; Apollon musagète 51,
    97, 137, 144, 150–3, 150, 230,
    263, 274; Le baiser de la fée 167, 171,
    230; Capriccio for piano and wind
    97, 230–1, 263; Le chant du rossignol
    136, 144; Chroniques de ma vie 96,
    151; classicism 151; and Cocteau
    34–6; Concerto for piano and
    wind 51, 229; Histoire du soldat 114,
    257; jazz, use of 114; Jeu de cartes
    97; Mavra 68, 145, 201, 228;
    neoclassicism 142, 145, 152, 272;
    Les noces 36, 137, 138, 140, 144,
    145–6, 201; Octet for wind
    instruments 51, 145, 228, 229,
    230, 244, 263; Oedipus rex 150,
    166, 201, 228, 230, 263; L'oiseau
    de feu 31, 34, 138, 163, 165;
    orchestration 33, 51, 68, 111, 114,
    141, 145, 158; Paris Establishment
    and 263; Perséphone, libretto 217;
    Petrushka 20, 31–2, 38, , 262; Piano
    Sonata 229; Piano-Rag-Music 114;
    Pieces for solo clarinet 272; Poetics
    of Music 272; Pribaoutki 34;
    Ragtime 114, 231; recording,
    perceiving value of 265; Renard 36,
    68, 144, 145, 201; La revue musicale,
    special issue 205; Le rossignol 34,
    143; Russian Orthodox Church,
    return to 152, 230; Le sacre du
    printemps 31, 32–4, 117, 141, 274;
    Satie, friendship with 34; Scherzo
    fantastique, basis of ballet Les abeilles
    62; Serenade in A 97, 229–30,
    231; significance of in 1920s Paris
    31–4, 36; Symphonies of Wind
    Instruments 227–8; Symphony of
    Psalms 152, 228, 230; Three Easy
    Pieces (piano duet) 34; Trianon-
    Lyrique, recollections of 96; Trois
    poésies de la lyrique japonaise 23, 34

strikes 127, 270
style dépouillé 216–17, 224
Sur la bouche 126
Surrealism, Surrealists 129, 138, 165
Symbolism, Symbolists 24, 33, 155
syncopation 113–14
Szymanowski, Karol, Masques 48

Tailleferre, Germaine 216; Le marchand
    d'oiseaux 143, 159; Piano Concerto
    201
tango 109; 'Tango de Manon' 127
Tansman, Alexandre 145, 250, 254;
    Piano Concerto no.1 51
Tchaikovsky, Peter Ilyich, Sleeping
    Beauty 135, 139; Stravinsky,
    Le baiser de la fée 171, 230
Tcherepnin, Alexander 262
Tcherepnin, Nicolas 42, 262
Tchernicheva, Lyubov 150
teaching institutions 176–91
temps, Le 68
tenors, shortage of 102
Tenroc, Charles 87, 88, 97, 102,
    124, 158, 170, 183, 202–3,
    203–4;
Terrasse, Claude 178
Teyte, Maggie 99, 198
theatres: Bouffes-Parisiens 107;
    Casino de Paris 115; Champs-
    Elysées 44, 51, 114, 123, 148,
    154, 156, 160, 161, 231, 257, 261;
    Château d'Eau 82; Châtelet 44,
    55, 166; Cigale 162; Fémina 117;
    Foire St-Germain 80; Gaîté-
    Lyrique 63, 95; Gymnase 107;
    Italien 80; Lyrique 82; Marigny
    111, 113; Mathurins 73; Mogador
    44; Montparnasse 261; Sarah-
    Bernhardt 51, 150, 257; Trianon-
    Lyrique 95, 96–7; Variétés
    110; Vieux-Colombier 51, 197,
    241, 264
Thibaud, Jacques 188, 188
Thibault, Geneviève (comtesse
    Hubert de Chambure) 251
Thill, Georges 70, 71, 101–2, 104,
    125
Thomas, Ambroise 181, 192; Le cäid
    79; Hamlet 65; Mignon 79, 80
Thomson, Virgil 48, 258, 259
Times, The 171
Tommasini, Vincenzo (arr.), Scarlatti,
    Les femmes de bonne humeur 140
Toscanini, Arturo 52
Toulouse-Lautrec, Henri de 119, 120
tourism (1920s) 9, 132
Tournemire, Charles 52, 185, 193,
    194, 195, 197; Les dieux sont morts
    67
trade unions see unions
trains, Honegger and 232, 233
Trévi, José de 251
Trianon-Lyrique 143
Trinité, La 195, 196–7
Turina, Joaquín 48
Tzara, Tristan 260

unions 22, 44, 47, 50, 54–5, 94,
    127, 129, 177

Valéry, Paul 87
Vallas, Léon 214
Vallin, Ninon 102, 102–3, 189
Vanni-Marcoux 87, 98, 98, 99

Varèse, Edgard 259–60; Amériques 260,
    273; Intégrales 260; Schola
    Cantorum, memories of 179
Variétés, Théâtre des 110
vaudeville 106
Vaughan Williams, Ralph 257
venues: Alhambra 119; Bouffes du
    Nord-Concert 119; Casino de
    Paris 119, 124; Empire 120; Folies-
    Bergère 119, 124; Moulin Rouge
    119; Olympia 119; Salle Chopin
    189; Salle Cortot 189; Salle Erard
    197, 259; Salle Gaveau 44, 52,
    180, 255–6; Salle Huyghens 215;
    Salle Pleyel 52–3, 255, 261;
    Trocadéro 44, 53; see also theatres
Verdi, Giuseppe, Aida 60, 73; Don
    Carlos 78; Falstaff 71, 72; Jérusalem
    78; I lombardi 78; Otello 71; Rigoletto
    71, 73; La traviata 71, 72, 79, 80 Les
    vêpres siciliennes 78
Verdière, René 100–101
verismo 31, 82
Vidal, Paul, La maladetta 134, 241;
    (arr. with Messager), Chopin,
    Suite de danses 134
Vienna Opera, Paris season (1928)
    76, 97
Vienna Staatsoper, Lubin's success at
    103
Vierne, Louis 184, 192, 193–4, 195,
    197; Symphony no.6 196
Vieux-Colombier, Théâtre du 51,
    197, 241, 264
Villabella, Miguel 101, 101
Villa-Lobos, Heitor 258, 260
Viñes, Ricardo 199
Vivaldi, Antonio 251
Vix, Geneviève 102
Vlad, Roman 142, 152
Volta, Ornella 215–16
Vuillemin, Louis 126, 203
Vuillermoz, Emile 94, 155, 156, 158,
    221

Wagner, Eugène 197
Wagner, Richard, Concerts
    Lamoureux in dissemination of 43;
    Fauré on escape from 210; French
    responses to 18–19, 18, 25–6,
    26–7; Lohengrin 18, 19, 74–5, 75;
    Die Meistersinger 21, 56, 76;
    Meyerbeer and Halévy as 'effects
    without causes' 78; Paris, first
    productions of operas in 18–19;
    Parsifal 18, 19, 24, 62, 74; Opéra,
    lowering of lights for 19, 62;
    proscribed during World War I
    18–19; reinstatement (1919) 44,
    74; Rienzi 18, 19; Der Ring 19, 62;
    Siegfried 74; standing of 254;
    Tannhäuser 18; Tristan und Isolde 19,
    71, 74, 76; Die Walküre 74
'Wagnermania' 18
Waleckx, Denis 245–6
Walewski, Comte de 60
Wall Street Crash 132, 266
Walsh, Stephen 34, 142, 228, 228–9
Walter, Bruno 206
Walton, William 256
Weber, Carl Maria von 230; Der
    Freischütz 65
Webern, Anton, Five Pieces (op. 10)
    261
Webster, Beveridge 185

Weill, Kurt 68, 201; L'opéra de quat' sous
    (Die Dreigroschenoper) 261
Wellesz, Egon, Chants sacrés 261
White, Eric Walter 51, 114, 136
Whiteman, Paul 240
Whithorne, Emerson 259
Whiting, Steven Moore 218
Whittall, Arnold 149
Widor, Charles-Marie 177, 192–3,
    251; Conservatoire, teaching at
    183–4, 183; Nerto 67
Wiéner, Jean 117, 204, 240
Wiéner, Jean, and Clément Doucet,
    'Chopinata' 117; La leçon du
    Charleston 117
Willemetz, Albert, Les aventures du roi
    Pausole, libretto 108, 109–10; Cach'
    ton piano, lyrics 127; Dédé, libretto
    108; Ta bouche, libretto 109
Wischnegradsky, Ivan 205
Witkowsky, George 267
Wittgenstein, Paul 275
Wolf, Hugo, Der Feuerreiter 50
Wolff, Albert 54, 54, 255
Wolff, Pierre 260
women 9; femininity, Ciboulette
    promoting virtues of 111; the 'new
    woman' 111; in Parisian musical
    life 268; in Paris orchestras 55–6
World War I 9, 24, 28, 36, 81;
    American bandsmen training at
    Fontainebleau 190; Armistice,
    celebration of 26; Beethoven's
    image, effect on 252; composer
    casualties 21–2; Conservatoire,
    effect on 182; Opéra 61, 62–3, 83,
    135; Opéra-Comique 82, 83;
    operetta 106–7; in popular song
    122, 128; postwar music and 'new
    conception of life' 31, 241; Ravel,
    pre- and postwar styles 223–4;
    references to in L'enfant et les sortilèges
    94; Roussel, war service 219;
    sentimental stories, irrelevance in
    aftermath of 85, 128; Société
    nationale de musique (SNM) 47;
    Wagner's music proscribed during
    19; women, role of 9

Yakulov, Georgi, Le pas d'acier, designs
    149
Yeats, William Butler 81
Ysaÿe, Eugène 189
Yvain, Maurice, Cach' ton piano 127;
    La dame en décolleté 110; Là-haut 110,
    111; 'Mon homme', Mistinguett's
    performance of 120, 122; Paris qui
    jazze 120, 130; Ta bouche 109–10

Zambelli, Carlotta 134, 135, 136
Zeitgeist 20, 57, 210, 221
Zola, Emile, La bête humaine 233

Pleyela player-piano, Milhaud's use of 171
Poincaré, Raymond 152
Polignac, comte and comtesse Jean de 242
Polignac, princesse Edmond de (née Winnaretta Singer) 38, 87, 198, 199–201, 200, 255
political satire 126–7
Porter, Cole (with Charles Koechlin), *Within the Quota* 158–9
postwar music and 'new conception of life' 31, 241
Poueigh, Jean 38
Poulenc, Francis 39, 87, 132, 144, 199, 201, 214, 241–7, 242, 265, 265, 275; *Aubade* 245–6, 247; *Le bal masqué* 243; *Les biches* 92, 139, 140, 144, 146–9, 243–4, 246; Cocteau's 'Toréador', setting of 242; *Concert champêtre* 53, 245, 246; Concerto for two pianos 242; *Dialogues des carmélites* 246, 247; *Gloria* 231; Gounod, *La colombe*, recitative for 97; Honegger, views on 233; *Les mamelles de Tirésias* 246; *Les noces*, view of 241–2; *Relâche*, dislike of 160; Sonata for two clarinets 48; Trio for piano, oboe and bassoon (1926) 244; *Trois mouvements perpétuels* 243
Praetorius, Michael 230
press, the 201–6
Printemps, Yvonne 86, 112–13, 112
Prix de Rome 177, 183, 184, 185
Prokofiev, Serge 262; *Ala and Lolly* 143; *L'ange de feu* 51, 149, 262; anti-romanticism 149; *Chout* 95, 140, 143–4, 262; *Le fils prodigue* 144, 152–3, 262; Paris orchestras, criticisms of 46, 54, 58; *Le pas d'acier* 140, 144, 149–50, 262; *Peter and the Wolf* 150; Piano Concerto no.3 50; *Romeo and Juliet* 150; *Scythian Suite* 50, 262; *Sept, ils sont sept* 51
Proust, Marcel 25
Prunières, Henry 91–2, 151, 171, 204, 252
Puccini, Giacomo, *Gianni Schicchi* 87; *Madama Butterfly* 81, 83, 87; pastiche of (Christiné) 109; *Tosca* 71, 72, 80, 87, 255; *Il trittico* 87; *Turandot* 66, 71, 72, 73–4; *La bohème* 31, 80, 82
Purcell, Henry 47

Quef, Charles 193–4

Rabaud, Henri 41, 177, 177, 263; Conservatoire, direction of 182–7; *La fille de Roland* 70; *Mârouf* 70, 81, 82, 86–7; piano tax, opposition to 126
Radiguet, Raymond 158
radio 130
ragtime 114, 136, 231
Rakhmaninov, Sergey, *Isle of the Dead* 50; Piano concerto no.3 50
Rameau, Jean-Philippe 21, 22, 52, 142, 179, 251; *Dardanus*, revival 201; *Variations sur un thème de Rameau* 185; *Pygmalion* 48
Ravel, Maurice 19, 21, 26, 49, 198,

199, 223, 223–6; autobiographical sketch 250; Beethoven monument, refusal to contribute to 253; *Boléro* 155, 167, 171–2; *Chansons madécasses* 226; *Daphnis et Chloé* 22, 23, 134, 135; *Deux mélodies hébraïques* 23; Duo for violin and cello 48; *L'enfant et les sortilèges*, 67, 91–4, 93, 117, 136, 203–4, 224, 230; *Gaspard de la nuit* 20; *L'heure espagnole* 70, 92; *Histoires naturelles* 31–2; jazz, response to 117; *Ma mère l'oye* 41, 47, 62; *Miroirs*, title of 250; Mozart quartets, admiration for 251; Mussorgsky, *Tableaux d'une exposition*, orchestration of 51; Piano Trio 23; pre- and postwar styles 223–4; ragtime 136; *Rapsodie espagnole* 32; Satie, *Le fils des étoiles*, transcription of 215; *Shéhérazade* 37, 47; SMI 47, 48, 49; Sonata for violin and cello 224; *style dépouillé* 224–5; *Le tombeau de Couperin* 23, 154, 223–4, 263; *Trois poèmes de Stéphane Mallarmé* 23, 24; *Tzigane* 225; *La valse* 49, 155, 167, 172, 223–4; *Valses nobles et sentimentales* 20, 22, 23, 24, 26, 226; Violin Sonata no.2 117, 197, 225–6; and Wittgenstein, Paul 275
Ravel et al., *L'éventail de Jeanne* 135
realism 31, 38, 39
Rearick, Charles 130
recording 126, 130, 251, 265
Régnier, Henri de 26, 87
Reinach, Théodore 25
Renaissance and early music 250–1
Respighi, Ottorino, *Le astuzie femminili* 73; (arr.), Rossini, *La boutique fantasque* 136–7
retrospective classicism 137, 139, 140, 152, 161–3
Réunion des théâtres lyriques nationaux 95
revue 117–19
revue musicale, La 68, 155, 197, 202, 203, 204, 258; Beethoven issue 252; Fauré issue 212; Stravinsky issue 205
revue nègre, La 123, 161
Reyer, Ernest, *Sigurd* 60
Rhené-Baton 43, 221
Ricou, Georges 82, 86, 88, 91–2
Rieti, Vittorio, *Barabau* 144
Rimsky-Korsakov, Nikolai, *Capriccio espagnol* 57; *Flight of the Bumblebee* 50; *La princesse Cygne* 167; *Schéhérazade* 24
Risler, Edouard 252
Ritter-Ciampi, Gabrielle 87, 102
Robine, Marc 116–17, 128
Roger-Ducasse, Jean 41, 185; *Orphée* 167
Roland-Manuel 68, 143, 221, 250; *L'écran des jeunes filles* 135; *Le harem du vice-roi* 210; *Isabelle et Pantalon* 143
Rolland, Romain 26, 252, 253
Ronald, Landon 257
Ropartz, Guy 41, 85–6, 214, 267; *Le pays* 85
Rosé Quartet 198
Rosenthal, Manuel 231, 253, 263, 271
Rossini, Gioacchino, *Il barbiere di Siviglia* 79, 80, 83; *Guillaume Tell* 65; (arr. Respighi), *La boutique fantasque* 136–7
Rouché, Jacques 30, 62, 91, 168, 198,

273; ballet programming 135, 136; Malipiero, *Sette canzoni*, withdrawal of 72–3, 255; Opéra, direction of 61–76; *Réunion des théâtres lyriques nationaux* 95; Thill, excessive demands on voice of 102
Rousseau, Emile 98
Roussel, Albert 30, 179, 180, 198, 219–22, 220, 241, 255; *Bacchus et Ariane* 222; *Le festin de l'araignée* 30–1, 52, 56, 57, 58, 62; jazz ('Jazz dans la nuit') 222; *Joueurs de flûte* 48; *Padmâvatî* 30, 31, 67, 68–9, 199, 219; *Petite suite* (1929) 222; and Poulenc 222; *Pour une fête de printemps* 219, 221; *Sérénade* for flute, violin, viola, cello and harp 221; Suite (1926) 222; Symphony no.2 219, 221; World War I, effects on 31, 81
Rubinstein, Artur 185, 201, 258
Rubinstein, Ida 29, 134, 163, 166, 167–8, 269, 270, 271; Ballets Ida Rubinstein 166–72
Ruhr, French occupation of 260
Russian music, responses to 261–2
Russian Revolution, émigrés from 10, 50, 261–2

Sabata, Victor de 91
Sablon, Jean 110
Sachs, Léo, *Les burgraves* 67
St-Augustin 178, 192
Ste-Clotilde 193–4, 194
St-Eustache 195
Saint-Marceaux, Mme René de ('Meg') 198–9
Saint-Saëns, Camille 18, 20–21, 49, 177, 192; *Hélène* 70; Ligue nationale pour la défense de la musique française 25; Milhaud's 'lunatic aberrations' 43; night clubs, predilection for 177; *Ouverture de fête* 56; *Samson et Dalila* 60, 66; SNM 47; *Une nuit à Lisbonne* 57; *Vive la France* 21; words, inaudibility of in opera 103–4
St-Séverin 178
St-Sulpice 192–3, 251
Salabert, Francis 130, 132
Salle Chopin 189
Salle Cortot 189
Salle Érard 53, 197, 259
Salle Favart see Opéra-Comique
Salle Gaveau 44, 52, 120, 180, 255–6
Salle Huyghens 215
Salle Pleyel 52–3, 255, 261
salons, the 197–201
Samazeuilh, Gustave 87; *Chant d'Espagne* 48
Samson, Jim 142, 143
Sandberg, Serge 43
Sarah-Bernhardt, Théâtre 150, 257
Sarrette, Bernard 181
Satie, Erik 19, 137, 180, 215–19, 231, 270; *Avant-dernières pensées* 217; and Diaghilev 215; as exemplar to young composers 216; Gounod, *Le médecin malgré lui*, recitative for 97; *Gymnopédies* 215, 217; homage to 263–4; d'Indy 213, 215; jazz, use of 114; *Le marteau sans maître* 218; *Mercure* 160, 163–6, 216; meticulousness 218; *Morceaux en forme de poire* 215; *Musique d'ameublement* 216; 'new conception

of life' 30; *Parade* 36, 37, 114, 216, 218, see also under *Parade*; 'Le Piccadilly' 113; Ravel's role in recognition of 215; *Relâche* 159–61, 165, 216, 217; *Socrate* 201, 213, 216, 218; *Sonatine bureaucratique* 216; *La statue retrouvée* 164; 'Steamboat Ragtime' 114; and Stravinsky 34; *style dépouillé* 216–17; titles and verbal comments 217–18
Sauguet, Henri 132, 201, 244; *La chatte* 140, 148–9; *David* 197; *Le plumet du colonel* 257; *Relâche*, admiration of 160; *Les roses* 163
scandals 44, 54, 56, 269
Scarlatti, Domenico 251; (arr. Tommasini), *Les femmes de bonne humeur* 140
Schaeffner, André 114, 203
Schloezer, Boris de 143
Schmitt, Florent 42, 48, 176, 198, 263; *Antoine et Cléopâtre* 167; *Salammbô* 70; *La tragédie de Salomé* 134, 135
Schmitz, Robert 236
Schoeck, Othmar 206
Schoenberg, Arnold 250, 261; Five Orchestral Pieces 44; Four songs (op. 6) 49, 261; Piano Pieces (op. 11) 23, 229; *Pierrot lunaire* 23, 24, 49, 261; 'Schoenberg scandal' 44, 54, 56; Six Little Piano Pieces (op. 19) 20, 23; SMI concert (1927) 261; Suite (op. 29) 48, 261; Wind Quintet 198
Schonberg, Harold C. 49
Schola Cantorum 28, 178–81, 219, 250
schools, music education in 176
Schrade, Leo 251, 252
Schubert, Franz, centenary 170–1; in concert repertoire 42, 56; standing of 250, 253
Schumann, Robert 43, 253–4
Scott, Cyril 257
Scotto, Vincent 123, 244
Scribe, Eugène 86
Selva, Blanche 199
Sérieyx, Auguste 47, 48
Sert, Misia 62–3, 215
Séverac, Déodat de 180
Sibelius, Jean, Symphonies, performances of 20, 261
Silver, Charles, *La mégère apprivoisée* 67
singers 97–104
Siohan, Robert 228
Sitwell, Osbert 163
Sitwell, Sacheverell 257
Six, Les 39, 212, 214, 216, 226, 228, 231, 233, 241, 246, 264–5, 265; *Album des Six* 264; Ballets suédois, commissions for 154, 156–7; *Les mariés de la tour Eiffel* 156, 157–8, 160, 238
Slavinsky, Thadée 144
Smetana, Bedrich, *La fiancée vendue* (*The Bartered Bride*) 90–91
SMI (Société musicale indépendante) 23, 47–9, 56, 209, 214, 215, 224, 261, 262; 'École américaine' concert 259; English chamber music concert (1919) 257
SNM (Société nationale de musique) 47–8, 213, 214
social change (1920s) 9–10